D1148000

The Scottish Regiments

A Pictorial History 1633-1987

The Scottish Regiments

A Pictorial History 1633-1987

P.J.R. MILEHAM

HIPPOCRENE BOOKS INC
New York

SPELLMOUNT LTD
Tunbridge Wells, Kent

In the Spellmount Military list:

The Territorial Battalions – A pictorial history
The Yeomanry Regiments – A pictorial history
Over the Rhine – The Last Days of War in Europe
History of the Cambridge University OTC
Yeoman Service
The Fighting Troops of the Austro-Hungarian Army
Intelligence Officer in the Peninsula
The Scottish Regiments – A pictorial history
The Royal Marines – A pictorial history
The Royal Tank Regiment – A pictorial history
The Irish Regiments – A pictorial history
British Sieges of the Peninsular War
Victoria's Victories
Rorke's Drift
Napoleon's Military Machine

In the Nautical list:

Sea of Memories
Evolution of Engineering in the Royal Navy Vol 1 1827–1939

In the Aviation list:

Diary of a Bomb Aimer

First published in the UK in 1988 by
Spellmount Ltd,
12 Dene Way, Speldhurst,
Tunbridge Wells, Kent TN3 0NX
ISBN 0-946771-13-8 (UK)

First published in the USA in 1988 by
Hippocrene Books Inc,
171 Madison Avenue,
New York NY10016
ISBN 0-87052-361-9 (USA)

British Library Cataloguing in Publication Data
Mileham, P. J. R.
The Scottish Regiments: a pictorial history
1. Great Britain, *Army* – Scottish regiments – History
I. Title
355.3′1′09411 UA664

ISBN 0-946771-13-8 (UK)

Design by Words & Images, Speldhurst,
Tunbridge Wells, Kent.
Typeset by Vitaset, Paddock Wood, Kent.
Printed in Great Britain by Anchor Brendon Ltd,
Tiptree, Essex.

A section of the 6th Royal Scots Fusiliers march near Hill 113, Normandy, July 1944. IWM

Frontispiece:
Salt of the earth. A Cameron soldier, Pte J. Crosbie of Glasgow, photographed in 1945 after 25 years in the army. IWM

Title page:
Sir Colin Campbell and the Camp of the Highland Brigade, Kamara, near Balaclava 1855.
Engraving after W. Simpson, published by P. and D. Colnaghi

CONTENTS

FOREWORD

Scotland's regiments have given noble service to our nation over three full centuries. Her soldiers, while remaining near the hearts of their countrymen, have gained a fighting reputation world-wide, in the giving of it. They have helped to win Britain an Empire and, defended it courageously when it has been threatened and during its decline. They have taken their place on the battlefronts of two world wars. Pride in belonging to their regiments and in their magnificent traditions, has been their special trait. Indeed, they have helped to strengthen the British Army's regimental system, itself the envy of so many other armies.

I commend this book for its comprehensive descriptions, even though necessarily in outline, of the histories, the campaigns and the battles of the Scottish Regiments. It will prove to be a useful compendium of facts, both for military readers and for those interested in military history; the more detailed extracts help to illustrate the nature of war as a human experience. The illustrations themselves show Scottish soldiers in every type of exploit, mood and dress, and reveal faithfully what life was, and is like in the many different periods of service of the regiments of our great nation.

Norman Arthur

LIEUTENANT GENERAL
SIR NORMAN ARTHUR KCB

Colonel, The Royal Scots Dragoon Guards (Carabiniers & Greys)
General Officer Commanding Scotland, and Governor, Edinburgh Castle 1985-1988

INTRODUCTION

To a military author there are few places more rewarding than the headquarters of a regular regiment in the British army. Here records are carefully maintained, tradition nourished, honour and reputation jealously guarded. Each is a unique treasure house of oil paintings, uniforms, arms, medals, shelved albums of photographs, regimental rolls, battalion and campaign reports, letters and diaries, prints, sketches and watercolours, memoirs and memorabilia – the very stuff of which history is made. To be granted access to these riches is a rather humbling experience. There are perhaps too many reminders of the grim nature of the soldier's trade, and possibly the imagination is too vividly aroused by the glory and the pathos, the intensity and the dreariness, of the soldier's life.

The story of the regiments starts with the period at home in Scotland after the Civil War, sees the rise and fall of the Empire, and ends with brief mention of post-colonial times – NATO, Northern Ireland and the Falklands conflict. Their history is the history of the British Army, since virtually every campaign has included Scottish regiments in the order of battle. Furthermore it is worth reflecting that upwards of three million men have served in these regiments over the last two or three centuries, half of whom died or were wounded on active service.

The Scottish regiments are all highly distinctive in character: this is both a cause and a consequence of the well-deserved reputation of the Scottish soldier as a fighting man. It is therefore appropriate to comment briefly on the concept of the regiment as an institution within the British Army. Continuity of course is a valuable attribute to most institutions, and the British Army is fortunate indeed in possessing an unbroken history since the constitutional settlement of the mid-17th century. Some parts of the army, notably the cavalry and infantry, still strongly maintain regimental continuity and traditions, but the phenomenon is more often described than explained.

In war the soldiers' often desperate struggle with an unknown future is eased by companionship within a group, and identification with a continuously renewable human institution to which they belong. The most hardened of men, taking part in the most violent and dangerous of actions, feel the compulsive necessity of being bound together by moral and spiritual forces – even if they could not articulate the nature of such forces. Indeed any intuitive uplifting of human consciousness that can mitigate the awfulness of disaster, destruction, pain and death must be valuable to soldiers carrying out their legitimate duties. On a more practical level, any means, however intangible or unexplained, whereby the disintegration of a fighting force under stress can be prevented, must be worth encouraging. The 'regimental system', albeit formalised more recently and perpetuating greater inconsistencies than many people realise, has had many proponents and not a few detractors over the years, but the public at large seems as well content nowadays with the system as hitherto.

The battles and reputations of British regiments are well recorded. Regimental histories are traditionally written not only to recount particular events and personalities by use of graphic description and rich

Royal Scots Greys mounted drill, 1918. It was only during the final weeks of the war that cavalry could once again be used to good effect in the mounted role.
IWM

Kilted again for the first time since 1940, men of the 1st Seaforth Highlanders 'dress off' during a guard-mounting ceremony at Surabaya, Java, Nov 1945.
IWM

anecdote, but also to accentuate the real or assumed distinction between regiments. By promoting idiosyncracy of style and detail, the majority of regimental histories are therefore not accorded much academic weight by serious and professional historians, and are out of print within a few years of publication. There are dangers of course in relying too heavily on what regiments think of themselves!

Moreover a fair number of acknowledged campaign researchers in the past are now being faulted, and with good reason. For instance, William Siborne's account of the battle of Waterloo, written in the 1840s, is now believed to be highly inaccurate; and many well-respected historians have relied heavily on his research. Thus the famous stirrup charge of the Greys and Gordons is unlikely to have happened in the way so graphically depicted by authors and artists at a later date.

As regards the twelve Scottish regiments, there are the numerous histories, more or less based on original research and first-hand accounts, starting with the Historical Records of every regiment by Richard Cannon and his assistants in the 1830–50s. A second source is that of brigade and divisional histories of the two world wars. They admirably put the tactical events into context with the strategic background – regiments and battalions fight at the tactical level, and contribute to strategic events. A third category which should be mentioned comprises those general works written to emphasise the Scottishness of the regiments – they could be called anthropological anthologies. The more recent and praiseworthy ones are by John Laffin (1963), Michael Brander (1971) and Stephen Wood (1987). To them should be added the somewhat racy series of 'Famous Regiments' (1960s), edited by General Sir Brian Horrocks, whose Scottish titles are included in the bibliography.

The purpose of this book is to tell the story of regiments chiefly by illustration, but also with a brief resumé of the active service of their constituent battalions. I have included a few illustrative passages to indicate the nature of the fighting. The amount of historical fact almost defies such condensation, but I hope that the illustrations, which are representative of all the regiments, do duty for many unstated words by revealing how intensely personal is the story. Thus I have tried to select photographs which show the character of the 'jocks' and 'rories' and the nature of their activities both in war and peace. Of the paintings and prints, some are portraits, while the remainder are characteristic of their period, stylistic maybe, but I hope of interest nonetheless. The battle scenes represent an unambiguous artistic genre, upholding unreservedly the dictum *Dulce et decorum est pro patria mori*: whether an 'old lie' or not, it is up to the reader to decide.

My gratitude is due to a number of people, firstly to the regimental secretaries and staff of the various regimental headquarters, in particular Lt-Col A. A. Fairrie of RHQ, Queen's Own Highlanders. They all gave me much assistance and encouragement, and are exonerated from blame for any shortcomings. The illustrations belonging to particular regiments I have acknowledged as 'RHQ' in the captions. Headquarters Scotland and Headquarters the Scottish Division also gave me support.

I also thank the Scottish United Services' Museum (National Museums of Scotland) at Edinburgh Castle, the Department of Photographs at the Imperial War Museum (IWM) and in particular Mr Michael Willis, the National Army Museum (NAM), the National Gallery of Scotland and the Parker Gallery; they all allowed me to spend many hours researching the illustrations. The Victoria and Albert Museum (V&AM), Cheshire Yeomanry, Mr Matthew E. Taylor, Southampton City Museum, Astley Fine Art (of Moreton-in-Marsh) and Valentines of Dundee also kindly gave me permission to reproduce paintings or photographs in their possession. Lt-Col I. Shepherd of the Royal Highland Fusiliers, Mr Thomas Scott-Roxburgh and Mr Peter John photographed many of the illustrations from regimental collections, for which I am extremely grateful.

PJRM
August 1988

In memory of my mother
and for Alexandra, Felicity, Sally and Arabella

The battle of Drumclog of 1679 during the 'killing times', in which troops of dragoons fought Covenanters, the extremist presbyterians who ten years later formed the Cameronian Regt. The Cameronians

CHAPTER 1
THE RAISING OF THE REGIMENTS

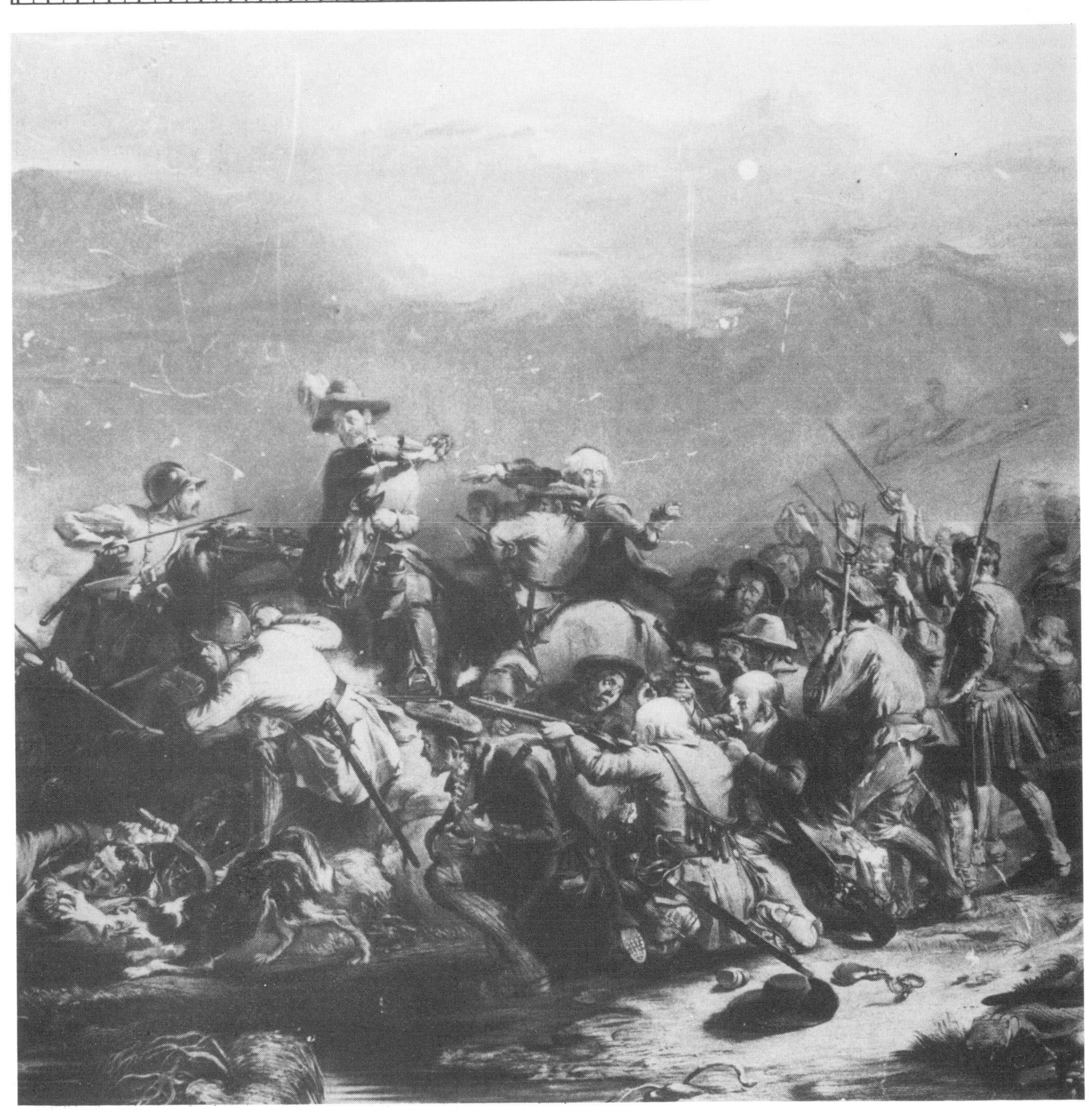

Britain is unique in modern history for the longevity of its military institutions. Whereas the Royal Navy claims unbroken descent from the time of Henry VIII, the history of the British Army, although with traceable antecedents, effectively dates from the restoration of the monarchy in 1660.

The royalist army of Charles I had disappeared with his defeat in the Civil War. The experience of the Protectorate, which relied heavily on military power for its survival, was a painful one, even in Scotland and Ireland which had not been fully subdued by Cromwell's armies. Thus the new partnership of power, entered into between Charles II and parliament, included provisions deliberately designed to limit the monarchy from maintaining too powerful a royal army with which to upset the constitutional settlement. The later attempts by Charles II and his brother James II (VII of Scotland) to regain authority ceded to parliament cost the latter monarch his throne. By then the army was an established national institution.

The 'establishment' of regiments was effectively decided by the national parliaments, since they controlled expenditure. The task of the army was to guard the monarch and thereby protect the constitution. In the early years after the restoration there was little requirement for overseas forces, so the army was kept small in size. On the English establishment there were two regiments of horse and two of foot; the Scots Regiment of Guards was the only regiment at first on the Scottish establishment. Quite apart from regular troops, it must be added that in times of expected invasion, the duty of able-bodied men to muster for the defence of their kingdom was an ancient tradition and feudal obligation. From this arrangement was to evolve the Militia, which spread to all three kingdoms, but it was always an entirely separate force from the standing army – and was to remain so until the present century. (The last time the monarch vetoed an act of Parliament was in 1707, when Queen Anne refused to allow the Scottish Militia to be assimilated to the English Militia.)

There was of course a long history of individuals and regiments from the British Isles serving foreign monarchs in continental campaigns. Commanders could indeed gain much reward for military service, whether serving their own or another monarch. To be a soldier was an honourable profession, whatever the risks and rewards.

Scottish soldiers had always been in much demand for their fighting qualities. In the early 15th century, for instance, a regiment of Scots Guards was maintained by Charles VII of France, augmented by a force of 7,000 under the Earl of Buchan, who later became Constable of France. A Scottish brigade of four regiments, together with an English brigade, were in Dutch service, while Gustavus Adolphus of Sweden employed at one time eighteen British regiments, thirteen of which were Scottish. The renowned 'Scots Brigade' (formed in 1568) remained mainly in foreign service, sometimes comprising as many as 6,000 soldiers. In 1793 it joined the British establishment with two battalions as the 94th Foot, fought in many engagements in India, including the capture of Seringapatam, served with Wellington in the Peninsula and was reduced to a cadre as late as 1818. Its British battle honours were then carried by the 2nd Bn, Connaught Rangers, until their disbandment in 1922.

For a century-and-a-half after the restoration, the system operated whereby the monarch commissioned men of proven loyalty from the ranks of the peerage and gentry to command regiments of horse and foot. The twofold purpose was to protect the royal person and his family and to constitute an army with which to pursue foreign policy. Until reforms were introduced, colonels could make a reasonable profit for maintaining their regiments, and this was viewed as an acceptable return on the considerable sums they needed to invest in their commissions and regiments. To serve their monarch successfully could bring enormous prestige and power at home, with attendant advancement in the ranks of the peerage. Although many took the risks, few gained the prizes. The system lasted until the growth of military professionalism gradually replaced it during the course of the 19th century.

A Scotch Dragoon of 1680. The firearm known as a 'dragon' is seen slung behind him. Dragoons were mounted infantry during this period.

Unrest in Scotland in the latter years of Charles

The 94th Regt (the Scots Brigade) and the 73rd, 74th and 75th Highlanders took part in the siege and capture of Seringapatam in 1799 during the Mysore War.
Parker Gallery

II's reign, and the constitutional crisis in all three kingdoms in James II's brief period on the throne, necessitated the raising of a number of new regiments in Scotland. The peculiar circumstances of the times are explained more fully in Chapter 7. In 1666 General Thomas Dalyell of the Binns formed a regiment of foot, and Sir William Lockhart, Sir George Monro and Lord James Douglas raised regiments between 1672 and 1679. The Earl of Dumbarton's Regiment, serving Louis XIV of France, was added to the English establishment in 1678 (later 1st Foot, The Royal Scots). In the same year The Earl of Mar's Regiment (later 21st Foot, The Royal Scots Fusiliers) was raised together with three troops of dragoons – regimented in 1681 with newly-raised troops as The Royal Regiment of Scots Dragoons (later Royal Scots Greys). Other mounted troops raised in Scotland had included a troop of Life Guards (1661, by the Earl of Newburgh on the English establishment from 1707), several troops of horse (1666–7, raised by Major General William Drummond), the Marquess of Douglas's, Earl of Errol's and Lord Ross's troops of horse (1674–6), and in 1678, Claverhouse's Dragoons. Under Graham of Claverhouse, later Viscount Dundee, this regiment became 'The King's Own Regiment of Horse', and remained loyal to James II.

At the time of the 'Glorious Revolution' of 1688–9 ten further regiments of foot were raised to serve William of Orange. The Earl of Leven's or the Edinburgh Regiment of Foot (later 25th Foot, The King's Own Scottish Borderers), and The Earl of Angus's Regiment (later 26th Foot, the Cameronians) were the only two which have survived; the others were raised by the Earls of Argyll, Mar and Glencairn, Viscount Kenmure, Lord Strathnaver, Lord Blantyre, Lord Bargenny and the Laird of Grant. Mounted troops raised in Scotland between 1689–91 included several independent troops of horse, Jedburgh's, Cardross's, Ker's and Cunningham's Dragoons: of these the only one to survive (despite temporary disbandment in 1714) was the last named, subsequently the 7th Queen's Own Hussars.

During King William's foreign wars commissions were issued for the raising of new regiments by Sir James Moncrieff, Lord Strathnaver, Sir William Douglas, Col Robert Mackay, John Lord Lindsay, John Lord Murray, the Earl of Mar, the Master of Strathnaver, Lord Mark Ker, and Lt-Col George MacCartney. In 1694 John Lord Carmichael (later Earl of Hyndford) raised a regiment of dragoons, and a second one in 1702. A troop of horse grenadiers also served between 1702 and 1707. Most of these regiments served on the continent or in Ireland.

The revolution had been assured by the royal army's acquiescence to the deposition of the Catholic James, and the parliamentary settlement of William and Mary as joint monarchs. By the time of the union of the two parliaments in 1707, all remaining Scottish regiments had been added to the joint establishment, thus ensuring their permanence and regimental precedence. Most regiments in the British army continued to be known by the name of their colonels for many years. There were no regimental depots to support the regiments, but depot companies were often left behind for the purpose of supplying recruits for the battalions serving overseas.

The 18th century witnessed the most determined attempt to bring the highlands of Scotland within the purview of central control. This was achieved in part by the building of three garrison fortresses at Fort George, Fort Augustus and Fort William along the Great Glen. They were joined by the new military roads – the responsibility of General George Wade, later Field Marshal and Commander-in-Chief – to the existing garrisons of Edinburgh, Stirling and Dumbarton. The Jacobite rebellions of 1715 and 1719 had necessitated such measures, and when the final rebellion took place in 1745–6, the forces of the Hanoverian monarchy were the more able finally to break the military power of the highland clans.

The highland clan system was based on the strength of family and tribal loyalty, and a feudal obligation of the clansmen to maintain the chief materially and by military service. In many parts of the highlands, even in the early 18th century, many clans still lived by the sword. The clansmen were the most determined of fighters, proudly standing by their own codes of loyalty and conduct. They were of course hated by the lowlanders, whose fear was undoubtedly enhanced by the highlanders' dress and warlike appearance. Their quality as fighters was recognised by the military authorities, and in the latter part of the 17th century companies of highlanders had been formed to serve the crown in policing parts of the highlands. In 1725 new companies were raised. They were known as 'Am Freiceadan Dubh', The Black Watch, distinct in their highland dress from the regular soldiers. In 1739 these companies were regimented as The Highland Regiment of Foot on the regular establishment.

In 1746 after the battle of Culloden the fighting strength of the clans had been estimated at 31,930 by Lord Forbes and many highland chiefs were more than enthusiastic to prove their loyalty to the crown.

The breakdown was as follows:

Argyle	3,000
Breadalbane	1,000
Lochnell and other Chieftains of the Campbells	1,000
Macleans	500
Maclachlans	200
Stewart of Appin	300
Macdougals	200
Stewart of Grandtully	300
Clan Gregor	700
Duke of Athole	3,000
Farquharsons	500
Duke of Gordon	300
Grant of Grant	850
Macintosh	800
Macphersons	400
Frasers	900
Grant of Glenmorriston	150
Chisholms	200
Duke of Perth	300
Seaforth	1,000
Cromarty, Scatwell, Gairloch and other Chieftains of the Mackenzies	1,500
Menzies	300
Munroes	300
Rosses	500
Sutherland	2,000
Mackays	800
Sinclairs	1,100
Macdonald of Slate	700
Macdonald of Clanronald	700
Macdonell of Glengary	500
Macdonell of Keppoch	300
Macdonald of Glencoe	130
Robertsons	200
Camerons	800
McKinnon	200
Macleod	700
The Duke of Montrose, Earls of Bute and Moray, Macfarlanes, Colquhouns, McNeils of Barra, McNabs, McNaughtans, Lamonts, etc, etc	5,600
	31,930

Thus once the loyalty of individual highland gentlemen could be assured, the government capitalised on this supply of willing military manpower and a number of regular regiments were raised in the highlands. Military service offered the opportunity for honourable employment, pay, and the lawful wearing of highland dress, which had been proscribed by act of parliament in 1746. Moreover the system of regimental command and personal loyalties was quite natural to the clansmen: thus the focus of their warlike instincts was in time transferred from the clan to the highland regiments, which they served with passionate pride. In turn, these regiments contributed significantly to the strength of the 'regimental system', which only in later years was given a territorial basis.

'I sought for merit wherever it could be found,' claimed William Pitt, Earl of Chatham in 1766. 'It is my boast that I was the first minister who looked for it, and found it in the mountains of the north. I called it forth, and drew into your service a hardy and intrepid race of men: men who when left by your jealousy, became prey to the artifices of your enemies, and had gone nigh to have overturned the state in the war before last (War of the Austrian Succession). These men in the last war (Seven Years' War), were brought to combat on your side; they served with fidelity, as they fought with valour, and conquered for you in every quarter of the world.'

In 1747 the regiments of horse, dragoons and foot were 'ranked' and numbered in order of precedence. They ceased to be referred to by the name of their Colonels in 1751, when the Army underwent considerable reorganisation and new regimental names were established.

The maintenance of standing armies is, however, a serious economic burden at any time, and civilian governments are obviously loath to employ more soldiers than are necessary. During the course of the 18th century there was an increasing need for the raising of new regular regiments for the King's wars. The intention in most cases was that the regiments should be disbanded after a specific term, usually three years, or at the conclusion of the war.

It should be mentioned that the distinction between regular regiments for overseas service, and Militia and fencible regiments for home defence was by no means always clear. The terms under which various regiments were formed differed in detail, according to the commission issued to the colonel. Sometimes the authorities broke faith with the soldiers by forcible drafting, disbandment far from home or use in campaigns excluded by the terms.

One Scottish regiment was raised at the time of the War of Austrian Succession (1740–8) in which Britain was involved owing to the need to defend George II's Hanoverian Kingdom. That was Loudon's Highlanders and it was raised in 1745. The regiment

Numerous regiments were raised for home defence and not placed on the regular establishment. Here a Fraser Fencible gallantly defends his post against the French at Castlebar, Co Mayo, 1798.

fought at the Battle of Preston against the Jacobites but was captured. Before disbandment in 1748, it fought bravely in Holland.

The British Army was heavily involved in three theatres during the Seven Years' War (1756–63), and a large number of regiments were raised including many in Scotland. The 31st Foot raised its second battalion in 1756 in Glasgow; it was re-numbered two years later as 70th Foot and was known as the 'Glasgow Greys' on account of its grey facings. (It lost its Scottish character finally in 1825.) In 1757 two regiments of highlanders were raised, the 77th Montgomery's disbanded in 1763) and the 78th Fraser's Highlanders (disbanded in 1767). They both served in the American colonies, and Fraser's Highlanders were present at the capture of Quebec. Many of the soldiers remained in North America on discharge.

Two years later four Scottish regiments were raised. They were the 17th Light Dragoons (raised by Lord Aberdour, disbanded in 1763), 87th Keith's Highlanders, 88th Campbell's Highlanders, and 89th Gordon's Highlanders. The 87th and 88th served in Germany and the 89th served in India. The Strathspey or Grant Highlanders were raised in 1760 together with 101st Johnston's Highlanders. Also formed were the 100th Regiment, the 105th Queen's Own Royal Regiments of Highlanders, 113th Royal Highlanders (1761), 114th Royal Highland Volunteers (1761) and the 115th Royal Scotch Lowlanders

The Duke of Wellington was always very complimentary about the quality of his Scottish soldiers. Although he never joined the regiment he was gazetted Ensign in the 73rd Highland Regt in 1787. Parker Gallery

(1761). Some of these regiments had been expanded from highland companies. All these regiments of foot were disbanded in 1763. A regiment was raised in America in 1775 from Scots who had remained after the previous war, known as the Royal Highland Emigrant Regiment, the 84th Foot. A second battalion also served, known as the Young Highland Regiment.

In 1775 the war of American Independence began, and three years later the French declared war on Britain. More regiments were needed by the crown, thus in 1775 the 71st Fraser Highlanders were formed. In 1777 the 73rd (Highland) Foot was raised by Lord McLeod – it was re-numbered in 1786 as the 71st, and subsequently became the 1st Battalion, Highland Light Infantry. In the same year seven more regiments were raised in Scotland, the 74th Argyllshire Highlanders, 76th Macdonald's Highlanders (both of which served in America), 77th Atholl Highlanders, 78th Highland Regiment, 80th Royal Edinburgh Volunteers, 81st Aberdeenshire Highlanders and the 83rd Royal Glasgow Volunteers. These regiments were all disbanded between 1783 and 1784 with the exception of the 78th, which was re-numbered 72nd in 1786 and became in time the 1st Battalion, Seaforth

Highlanders. In 1779 the 42nd (Royal Highland) Regiment raised a second battalion which became a separate regiment seven years later; it remained in service as the 73rd Highland Regiment until 1881 when once again it became the 2nd Battalion, The Black Watch.

Although the war against the French and American colonies was concluded in 1783, the requirement to police the King's colonies elsewhere continued, and more regiments were raised. Amongst these were the 74th and 75th Highland Regiments, specifically for service in India. They became eventually the 2nd Highland Light Infantry, and the 1st Gordon Highlanders.

From the outbreak of the French Revolutionary War in 1793, in addition to a very large number of part-time volunteer units – cavalry, infantry and artillery – as well as full-time 'fencible' regiments for home defence, many new regiments were required. Thus came into being in Scotland the 78th, 79th, 90th, 98th (later 91st), 100th (later 92nd), 109th (Aberdeenshire), 116th (Perthshire), 117th, 132nd and 133rd Regiments, and in 1800 the 93rd Highlanders. The histories of those which survived disbandment can be followed in later chapters. Finally in 1824 the 99th Regiment was raised in Glasgow and bore the title 'Lanarkshire' from 1832 for many years. It subsequently became the 2nd Battalion the Wiltshire Regiment.

It has been estimated that between 1795 and 1806 70,000 men enlisted and were embodied for full-time service in Scotland. Thus it is not surprising that the following order was issued from Horse Guards in 1809.

'As the population of the Highlands of Scotland is found to be insufficient to supply recruits for the whole of the Highland corps on the estabishment of His Majesty's army, and as some of these corps laying aside their distinguishing dress, which is objectionable to the natives of South Britain, would, in a great measure, tend to facilitate the completing of their establishment, as it would be an inducement to the men of the English militia to extend their services in greater numbers to those regiments:– it is in consequence most humbly submitted, for the approbation of His Majesty that His Majesty's 72nd, 73rd, 74th, 75th, 91st, and 94th regiments should discontinue, in future, to wear the dress by which His Majesty's regiments of Highlanders are distinguished, and that the above corps should no longer be considered as on that establishment.'

The raising and disbandment of these regiments serves to illustrate the precariousness of regimental continuity, which is often overlooked both by the authorities in London and the members of regiments which had the good fortune to survive over the years.

Although in the British Army the 'regiment' existed as an institution, the fighting organisation was, and still is, the battalion, comprising a varying number of companies. Until the 19th century there was a pronounced lack of conformity of organisation and numbers on the official battalion and regimental establishment.

Many regiments had two or more battalions at various times, the battalions abroad being kept up to strength with the fittest men. From 1857 the senior twenty-five regiments were established for two battalions, and from 1872 the remainder were linked in pairs for the same purpose. (The abolition of the purchase of commissions was in 1871.) In times of peace numbers declined; in emergency, recruiting was hastily conducted by the regiments. Until 1881 enlistment of an individual soldier was for life. Without regimental depots (there were very few barracks until the 19th century), regimental recruiting had been a most haphazard affair, and at times a high

Colin Campbell, Lord Clyde. This legendary soldier's career spanned from the Peninsular War to the Indian Mutiny. He commanded the Highland Brigade in the Crimea and was responsible for the relief and capture of Lucknow. Parker Gallery

proportion of those serving in highland and lowland regiments were not Scotsmen, and some regiments lost their status as such for a number of years.

In 1881 the greatest reorganisation of the British Army to date was conducted under the auspices of Hugh Childers the Secretary of State for War. Each regiment set up a permanent depot and supplied two regular battalions. Those regiments numbered from the 26th Foot onwards were linked or amalgamated in pairs of battalions, and given names or county titles, the only exception being the 60th and 79th which remained at single battalion strength. The only new Scottish regiment which incorporated both previous names in its title was the Argyll and Sutherland Highlanders. These reforms established the 'regimental system' that lasted until the 1960s.

Top right:
Members of the Highland Brigade at a Field Dressing Station after the action at Paardeburg, 1900, during the Boer War. Cheshire Yeomanry

The Highland Gathering at Lucknow, 1912. It is on record that the Seaforth Highlanders scored the highest number of points. The Black Watch

Below:
A Coy of the 2nd Scottish Rifles test their practice bridge for the record, c1900. RHQ

In this way the Scottish regular regiments assumed the names by which they are still familiarily known, and adopted common regimental uniforms with minor battalion differences, and it was normal practice to have one battalion at an overseas station and the other in the United Kingdom. As can be understood, the separate battalions retained a distinctive identity for many years and continued to be known by their former names or numbers, particularly within the regiment – such as the 'Scottish Rifles' and the '93rd', for the second battalions of the two regiments.

During the same period, the opportunity was taken to reorganise the non-regular military forces. For the first time they were linked directly with the regular army. Thus the county militias became the third or fourth battalions of the regular regiments, and the county Rifle Volunteer Corps (raised mainly in 1859–60) were affiliated also to the appropriate regular regiment. In Scotland, the volunteers were given 'volunteer battalion' numbers of named regiments, but they often retained a county title as well.

Such links proved valuable at the time of the Boer War in 1899; not only were some militia battalions embodied, but numerous volunteer service companies served with the regular battalions in the war. The Haldane reforms of 1906 to 1912, whilst significant for the employment of the Army in terms of imperial strategic planning, did not markedly affect the regimental organisation.

On mobilisation in 1914, it was decided that the battalions to be raised from the flood of volunteers would be 'new' battalions under regular Army direction, not an immediate expansion of the Territorial Force. The War Office considered that the quantity of battalions required needed a professional cadre in command in order that they could be trained quickly, and be a match for the huge conscript armies of the continent. The Territorial battalions were allowed to expand separately and to fight overseas in due course, but it was not until compulsory conscription in 1916 that the differences between regular, Territorial Force and new army battalions began effectively to diminish. The Scottish regiments raised many new or 'service' battalions in line with all British regiments, and the strength of regimental ties formed the vital cohesiveness which time and again proved invaluable in battle. The 'Special Reserve' 3rd and 4th Battalions (formerly Militia) fulfilled the depot and training roles for the whole regiment: sequentially the numbering followed with the Territorial Force battalions (usually with first and second line battalions, *sic* 1/5th, 2/5th, and sometimes even third line units); then came the several 'service' battalions, and in some instances extra reserve, provisional or Territorial Force battalions.

Many battalions thus raised were formed into Scottish formations, and fought with them throughout the war – such as the 9th, 15th Scottish, 51st Highland and 52nd Lowland Divisions, and their

A raiding party of the 11th Royal Scots prepare for a daylight raid on the Western Front. They hand in personal belongings to prevent identification. IWM

The Territorial battalions volunteered wholesale for service overseas during the First World War. The 1st Liverpool Scottish, seen here at St Eloi, May 1915, were amongst the first to be sent to France. IWM

constituent brigades. Each built up a reputation founded on the strength of regimental ties and fighting qualities.

The effect, therefore, of the First World War was to strengthen greatly the territorial basis of the regimental system, as whole villages and towns went to war in identifiable units. As can be imagined, those at home were intimately connected with the fortunes of the local regiments, particularly in suffering the news of death and injury from the front. It is certainly true to say that even to this day, most families in Scotland can identify with one or more regiments through the service of grandfathers, fathers, brothers, uncles or nephews during the two world wars.

The same system was repeated in 1939 on the outbreak of the Second World War, although the Territorial Army had been allowed to double in strength during the year preceding the war. Throughout the war the Scottish regiments remained fiercely Scottish, despite the disappearance of kilt and tartan from the battlefield. The necessity of keeping battalions up to strength meant that the proportion of Scotsmen in their ranks varied greatly, particularly in the latter stages of the war. But the strength of the regimental spirit was unaffected by the influx of non-Scotsmen who often became more Scots than the Scots. Of course many Englishmen and Irishmen had served in Scottish regiments from the earliest years of their existence.

During both wars the dominions had contributed Scottish regiments for the defence of the Empire,

South African Scottish troops near St Quintin, 23 Mar 1918, during the German spring offensive. IWM

Centre:
Jocks of the 51st Highland Division and tanks of the 1st Northamptonshire Yeomanry near s'Hertogenbosch, Holland, 29 Oct 1944. Close co-operation between infantry and armour was essential during the campaign in North-West Europe, as elsewhere, during the war. IWM

Below:
7th Cameronians double forward across the Dortmund-Ems Canal near Rheine, April 1945. IWM

many of them named directly from existing regiments of the British Army. Affiliations were very strong between the overseas and home Scottish regiments, and were a source of much pride. The history, however, of these dominion regiments is their own, but they are listed in the appendix.

With the coming of peace in 1945 the battalions were gradually reduced or returned to part-time Territorial Army service. The second battalions of all regiments, except for the Brigade of Guards, were disbanded or amalgamated with the first battalions in 1947–8. Thousands of national servicemen served with the regular and TA battalions during the 1950s.

Further reductions of the infantry took place between 1958 and 1861, and again between 1968 and 1970. The reasons were that fewer battalions were required to defend and police the dwindling number of colonies, and other defence commitments were discarded. Two amalgamations took place amongst the Scottish regiments: The Royal Scots Fusiliers joined with the Highland Light Infantry, and the Seaforth

Scots Guards recruits. WOs and NCOs of the regiments of Foot Guards have paid the minutest attention to the detail of drill, appearance and general behaviour of generations of soldiers – and officer cadets. IWM

Under the stern gaze of William Wallace, 'Guardian of Scotland', stands Pte Wallace of the 1st Black Watch at Edinburgh Castle, Oct 1986.

Highlanders with The Queen's Own Cameron Highlanders. The regular battalion of the Cameronians was disbanded and the Argyll and Sutherland Highlanders were reduced to one company. The anomalies and inconsistencies of the criteria by which all the amalgamations and disbandments over the years were chosen have never been fully and publicly documented. Suffice it to say that in the first-mentioned amalgamation 10,000 people turned out for a rally in the streets of Glasgow and one million people signed the petition to prevent the disbandment of the last-named regiment. Such was the feeling and strength of regimental identity in Scotland.

With the disappearance of all but a handful of overseas stations during the past twenty years, the regiments now mainly alternate between duty stations in the United Kingdom and West Germany. The history of military service in Northern Ireland in aid of the civil power is a subject in itself. All Scottish regiments have served a number of short or longer tours in the province. The reconciliation of feelings within the civil population could take a number of generations to achieve, and the British Army has served there for many generations in the past.

Scotland was represented in the Falklands Campaign in 1982 by the 2nd Battalion, Scots Guards. Since then a number of Scottish battalions have served in the British garrison there. Although Britain's defence commitments are now geographically diminished, the world is as dangerous as ever: thus the motto borne by a number of Scottish regiments is particularly appropriate – "Nemo me impune lacessit. No one provokes me with impunity". Britain's potential antagonists recognise this well, and long may they continue to do so.

CHAPTER 2

THE ROYAL SCOTS DRAGOON GUARDS

(Carabiniers and Greys)

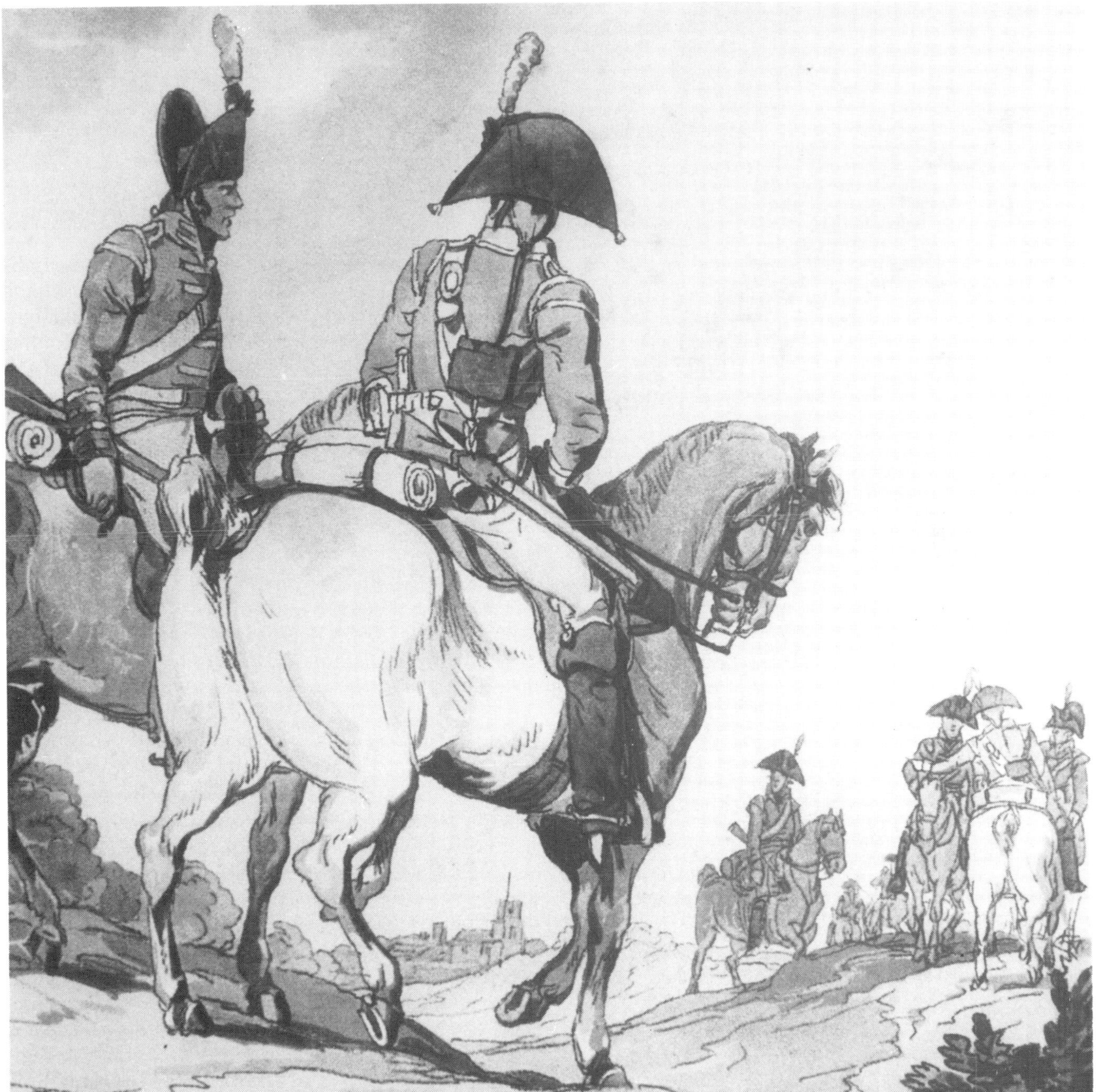

At a parade in the grounds of Holyroodhouse Palace on 2 July 1971 in the presence of Her Majesty the Queen, two regiments of cavalry were amalgamated: they were the 3rd Carabiniers (Prince of Wales's Dragoon Guards) and The Royal Scots Greys (2nd Dragoons). The Carabiniers had been formed in 1922 from two English regiments – originally raised in 1685 as the Earl of Plymouth's and the Queen Dowager's Regiments of Horse – respectively the 3rd (Prince of Wales's) Dragoon Guards and The Carabiniers (6th Dragoon Guards). Regiments of 'horse' had subsequently been re-styled 'dragoon guards' and, although the Royal Scots Greys had been formed four years earlier in 1681 as 'dragoons', they took precedence after the Carabiniers.

THE ROYAL SCOTS GREYS

1681–1913

The British Isles are not noted for the expanses of territory that can truly be called 'cavalry country', and the cavalry arm of the British Army in its early years was quite different in composition, style and equipment from the cavalry of continental armies. The term 'dragoon', derived from the firearm known as a 'dragon', was the term for a mounted infantryman. He was unencumbered by body armour, and mounted on a lighter animal than a member of a troop of 'horse'.

In 1678 three troops of dragoons were formed in Scotland, one of which was commanded by Lt-Gen Thomas Dalyell of The Binns. Their purpose was to break up the illegal gatherings and prevent armed coventicles of the Covenanters. Much of the time the troops acted independently, but occasionally together and with troops of horse. Twice in 1679 they joined with royal infantry to fight armed convenanters, at Drumclog and Bothwell Bridge. The latter was a particularly bloody affair, but in the 'killing times' nobody expected or gave quarter in an armed encounter. In the following year a strong party of dragoons and horse followed and attacked a party of Covenanters at Airds Moss, Ayrshire. There were many casualties on both sides, one of which was Richard Cameron, leader of the 'Cameronian' sect.

In 1681 three new troops of dragoons were raised owing to the deteriorating political and religious situation, and Lt-Gen Dalyell, who by now was Commander-in-Chief of Scotland, formed the six troops into a regiment known as 'The Royal Regiment of Scots Dragoons'. Detachments of the regiment were then quartered in many parts of the south and west of Scotland to enforce royal authority, and in several areas were ordered to administer the loyal oath on the inhabitants on pain of death for refusal.

On the death of Charles II in 1685, the Earl of Argyll led a revolution against James II in Scotland. A troop of the regiment fought a dismounted action against part of Argyll's army at Stonedyke Park near Dumbarton. On the same day Argyll was captured and his troops dispersed. The Royal Scots Dragoons were subsequently ordered south to assist the royal army against the Duke of Monmouth's rebellion, but they were recalled without taking an active part in suppressing it. They returned to Scotland and were used to seek out rebels in various parts of the country, putting them to the sword and destroying their property.

In the autumn of 1688 the regiment marched to London, summoned by James II to defeat the expected invasion forces of William, Prince of Orange. In November the Royal Scots Dragoons moved to Salisbury and on 10 December the royal army was informed that James had fled to France. William of Orange, preferring to allow the army to decide its own loyalties, did not look for a fight. Most of the regiments decided for the Williamite claim to the throne, and the protestant cause. Their part in the constitutional and religious conflict, however, was by no means finished.

The Royal Scots Dragoons, with some misgivings about personal loyalties, returned to Scotland. During the early part of 1689 they were employed in following the elusive Viscount Dundee, who led the highlanders against the new monarch. There was much manoeuvring and some skirmishes with the clansmen in the vicinity of the Spey and Inverness, but after the death of Dundee at Killiecrankie the rebel cause rapidly began to dissolve. In April 1690, however, a large number of clansmen re-assembled at Cromdale in Strathspey. The Royal Scots Dragoons were part of a force which surprised the highlanders in the middle of the night, and after killing 400 of them caused the remainder to flee. At Abergeldie another party of highlanders was attacked by two troops of dragoons with the same result. The rebellion was gradually contained and in 1692 an oath of allegiance to William and Mary was required of all highland chieftains, which more or less signalled the acceptance of the

Previous page:
Soldiers of the 2nd Royal North British Dragoons, from a print of 1808. RHQ

constitutional settlement.

In 1694 the regiment joined King William's army in Holland, where the war of the League of Augsburg was in progress. Twice during the year the regiment skirmished with French cavalry, and in 1695 the regiment acted as a covering force during the siege and capture of Namur. It continued to act in this role interposed between the French and allied armies until the end of the war, and in 1697 the regiment returned to Scotland. It is believed that the regiment began to be mounted on grey horses during this period, and the names 'Grey Dragoons' and 'Scots Regiment of White Horses' came into use.

In 1702 the Royal Scots Dragoons returned to Holland with General John Churchill (later Duke of Marlborough) at the start of the war of the Spanish Succession. They were employed to cover the sieges of Venlo, Ruremond and Stevenswaert, and in early 1703 were present when Marlborough besieged Bonn, Huy and Limburg.

In the following year the regiment accompanied Marlborough's march up the Rhine to the Danube, in order to attack France's allies, the Bavarians. A battle for the high ground at the Schellenberg, near Danauworth took place on 2 July, and

Gen Thomas Dalyell. The varied career of this redoubtable warrior included commanding a brigade at the battle of Worcester, escaping from the Tower of London, serving the Csar of Russia and raising the Scots Dragoons in 1681. RHQ

'At six in the evening the signal for the attack was given, and the British infantry, advancing with a firm and resolute step, assaulted the entrenchments, whilst the Royal Scots Dragoons and other cavalry moved forward to support the attack. The post was defended with great bravery, and a fierce contest had continued for some time, when the Scots Greys were ordered to dismount, form as infantry, and assault the trenches. The regiment instantly obeyed the order and, led by its gallant Colonel, Lord John Hay, advanced boldly to the attack and mixed fiercely in the conflict. At this instant the enemy gave way on every side, and the English cavalry, rushing forward, sabred numbers of the fugitives as they fled towards the Danube.'

On 13 August the regiment mounted an attack on the French in the village of Blenheim, during the battle of that name. The purpose was to neutralise the French right flank and the Scots Dragoons repeatedly fired and charged at the enemy. When the large force of defending infantry attempted to withdraw from the village, the regiment galloped around and outflanked them. The French infantry subsequently surrendered en masse as they were totally encircled by British and allied troops. The victory of Blenheim ensured that the Bavarians could no longer take an active part in the war.

Returning to Holland, the Royal Scots Dragoons spent some months covering the various manoeuvres of British troops. In July 1705 they formed part of a force which attacked the French defences at Neer-Hespen and Helixem. Having surprised the defenders, the regiment charged the enemy with other cavalry regiments, and broke the enemy lines. The French withdrew with considerable losses of dead, wounded and captured.

The following year at the battle of Ramillies the regiment was on the high ground to the right of the allied line, formed up with two other cavalry regiments. The Royal Scots Dragoons were called forward to drive off the French infantry and then attack the enemy's left. The charge of the British cavalry caused the French cavalry to retreat, and the infantry was decisively defeated: during the action the regiment forced the surrender of the 'Regiment du Roi', part of the French King's household troops, and captured its colours. After the battle the regiment proceeded to cover a number of allied sieges.

In 1707, on the Union of English and Scots Parliaments, the regiment was styled 'The Royal Regiment of North British Dragoons', but the soubriquet 'Scots Greys' was by this time well established. In 1713 the regiment was ranked as the 2nd Dragoons.

The following year the regiment played a minor part in the mainly infantry battle at Oudenarde. The Greys were used in pursuit of the withdrawing French army after the battle, and later they covered the siege of Lille. In mid-1709 they carried out the same task at Tournai, and later in the year they were in the centre of the British line at the battle of

Malplaquet. With the Royal Irish Dragoon Guards they moved through a wood and attacked a party of French cavalry, whereupon some French household cavalry squadrons attacked the Greys and a close-quarter cavalry action ensued. Joined by some squadrons of British horse, the Greys made three charges on the French who finally withdrew.

During the following three years the Scots Greys continued to cover numerous sieges and manoeuvres. In 1713 the Treaty of Utrecht was concluded, and in 1713 the regiment returned to England.

In 1715 the Royal Scots Greys were sent to Scotland, and in the autumn were involved in preventing rebels joining the Earl of Mar's force raised in support of James the old Pretender, son of James II. Skirmishes were fought at Kinross and Dunfermline. On 13 November, at Sheriffmuir, the Greys formed the right of the line of the royal army facing the rebels. The royal cavalry charged and forced the left of Mar's army to pull back. The rebels, however, defeated the left of the royal army, and the outcome of the battle was inconclusive. Mar's troops remained on the field of battle but withdrew during the night. The rebel army subsequently dispersed and the rebellion failed.

In April 1719, some 500 mainly Spanish troops landed at Kintail on the west coast, the remnants of an expedition mounted by the King of Spain in support of the Pretender. Three squadrons of the Greys, four guns and a number of infantry regiments advanced on the Spaniards who had been joined by 1,500 highlanders. In the battle of 'Glenshiel' the Greys captured and held a pass through the mountains, whereupon the remainder of the royal troops then charged and routed the enemy. The highlanders subsequently dispersed and the Spanish quickly surrendered.

For the next twenty-three years the Scots Greys were stationed in many parts of England and Scotland. Occasionally they were called upon to act in aid of the civil power to prevent civil unrest and against smugglers.

In 1742 the regiment left Britain to take part in the War of the Austrian Succession. It remained at Ghent for some months, and with the army commanded personally by George II, advanced into Germany early in 1743. At Dettingen the French blocked the British route. During the first part of the battle, the Greys were in support of the infantry, but were then ordered to charge a body of French cuirassiers.

'Before them appeared the enemy's squadrons, formidable in numbers, and bright in polished armour; – but undismayed by the opposing ranks of war, the Greys raised a loud huzza, and rushed at speed upon their steel-clad opponents, who were overthrown and pursued to the rear of their own lines. The Greys dashed, sword in hand, upon the French household cavalry; – the conflict was short; the result decisive; – a British shout arose above the din of battle, and the French horsemen galloped from the field in confusion. The Greys pursued their adversaries to the banks of the river, and captured a white standard, with which they returned in triumph to their own lines.'

A grenadier of the North British Dragoons, 1742.
NAM

This action contributed to the defeat of the French, who eventually withdrew.

The regiment remained on the continent for the next five years and in 1745 fought at Fontenoy. The allies were outnumbered in this battle and the Greys' charge failed to break the enemy lines; an orderly retirement from the battlefield followed. In 1746 the Greys were present at the action at Roucoux, and followed the successes of the allied infantry by a charge and pursuit. In the following year the same tactics were adopted at Val, but here the Greys were counter-attacked during the pursuit and lost many casualties. At the same time the allied centre broke, and the Duke of Cumberland in command had to give the order to withdraw from the battlefield. The war of manoeuvre continued for another year, when it was concluded by the Treaty of Aix-la-Chapelle.

The years between 1749–58 were spent mainly in England, and in 1758 the light troop of the regiment joined three raiding expeditions sent to France. In the first the dragoons and some infantry entered St Malo and set fire to the shipping before re-embarking. In the second the force captured Cherbourg, destroying the ships, fortress and artillery batteries. Another expedition to St Malo was unsuccessful.

The remainder of the Greys meanwhile were sent to Germany to fight in the Seven Years' War. The regiment spent much of the time on the march through various north German provinces. An attempt in 1759 to defeat the French at Bergen failed, and eventually the two armies met at Minden. The Greys supported the infantry, but were denied an opportunity to charge the enemy. Minden, however, was an undoubted victory and the Greys pursued the withdrawing enemy, harassing them for many miles.

Whereas Minden had been chiefly an infantry battle, Warburg in 1760 gave the British cavalry the opportunity to attack and rout the French cavalry. The regiment then assisted in breaking up the French infantry. In the same year, at the first of two engagements at Zierenberg, the Greys successfully destroyed an enemy force twice their size. A week later the Greys accompanied a force which carried out a successful attack by night for the capture of the town. In 1761 the regiment took part in a number of skirmishes, and in the final year of the war were at the action of Groebenstien; there the enemy army was outmanoeuvred and forced to withdraw. In July 1763 the regiment returned to England.

There followed a long period in its history when the regiment was stationed at home, mainly in England. As before, it was occasionally called upon by the authorities to prevent civil disturbance.

* * * * *

In 1793 the Duke of York led an expeditionary force to assist the Dutch, who had been invaded by the French revolutionary army. The Royal Scots Greys (still officially the Royal North British Dragoons) were used as covering troops at the sieges of Valenciennes, Dunkirk and Landrecies. Then at Tournai in May 1794, the French launched an attack on the British positions. The Greys, as part of a cavalry brigade, charged and broke the French cavalry line. After withdrawing, the enemy eventually returned with great numbers and the allied troops had to return first to Holland and subsequently to Germany. When the expedition was abandoned in 1795 the Greys returned to England, and remained at home duty for the next twenty years.

When Napoleon Bonaparte returned from exile in

RSM of the 2nd Royal North British Dragoons, 1818.
NAM

1815 and threatened the Netherlands, British troops quickly returned to the continent under the Duke of Wellington. The Greys were in the Union Brigade with the Royal Dragoons and Inniskilling Dragoons and on 15 June were ordered to cover the road at Quatre Bras. The following day the cavalry covered the withdrawal of the British troops and reached Waterloo that evening.

The brigade took up positions on 18 June behind the centre of the British line. A column of massed French infantry attacked Sir Thomas Picton's division in the afternoon and the Royal Scots and 42nd, 79th and 92nd Highlanders faced the enemy with bayonets fixed and fired volleys. Although accounts differ, the Greys attacked the leading French regiment and having forced their way through, charged at a second column. 'We saw some gallant, but over rash fellows,' stated a witness, 'without stopping to form again,

Lt-Gen Sir Alexander Clark-Kennedy, KCB, Col of the Royal Scots Greys, 1865. While serving with the Royal Dragoons at Waterloo he personally captured a French Eagle of the 105th Regt. RHQ

HIM, Tsar Nicholas II of Russia, Col-in-Chief of the Royal Scots Greys, 1894-1916. Portrait by Serov. NAM

ride on headlong at what appeared to me to be an immensely strong corps of support in perfect order.' The Royals, Inniskillings and Household Cavalry joined in the attack on this second column, the Scots Greys having suffered severe casualties by this stage. The Greys then in some disarray set about sabring enemy artillerymen. Two Eagle standards had been carried off, Sgt Ewart of the Greys capturing that of the 45th Regiment. At the end of the battle more than half the regiment had been killed or wounded, but the remainder joined in the pursuit of the French army as it left the battlefield.

In 1816 the regiment returned to the United Kingdom and remained at home duty for many years. Ireland was in a continual state of tension and the regiment spent two periods of duty there, during which it helped to maintain public order.

* * * * *

In 1854 the Scots Greys embarked for the Crimea, which they reached in September. At first the regiment was used to cover the movement of British troops and on detachment duties. In October the Russians attacked the British at Balaclava in great force and the British were obliged to withdraw. The Heavy Brigade, comprising the Greys and four other regiments, were then ordered forward to relieve the infantry defending Balaclava, which included the 93rd Highland Regiment. Two squadrons of the Scots Greys and one of the 6th Inniskilling Dragoons then charged against a large body of enemy cavalry nearly 3,000 strong. The Greys rode into the enemy

'partly between the files, dismounting some of the Russians, and partly at the angles formed by the Russian centre. After the first crash our men knocked or pulled them off their horses in every conceivable way. Of course there were some of our own men knocked off also, who were staggering about with bleeding faces.'

The squadrons were followed by the remainder of the Heavy Brigade. The fiercest hand-to-hand combat followed, and the Russians were pushed back until they broke and retreated. Later in the day the Greys were fired on as they formed up in support of the charge of the Light Brigade. There was, however, no appropriate opportunity for assisting in that dashing

This steel engraving by R. Caton Woodville c1880 bears the caption, 'The Irish Land League agitation: Scots Greys charging the mob at Limerick'. National Museums of Scotland

2
3
4
5
FINE
REAL

but almost suicidal action, although the regiment had further action against cossacks before the end of the battle.

The Scots Greys remained in the Crimea until 1856, taking part in some minor actions, while the main concentration of troops was occupied in besieging the fortress of Sevastopol.

For the next forty-four years the 2nd Dragoons (Royal Scots Greys) – as they were designated in 1877 – remained at home duty. They were stationed in a number of places, and spent many years in Ireland. Like many other regiments, both of infantry and cavalry, they were frequently involved in maintaining the peace in that troubled part of the British Isles. The only foreign action for the Greys was when a detachment of the regiment took part in the relief force sent to Khartoum in 1884, forming part of the Heavy Camel Regiment. Its most notable engagement was against the Mahdi's force at Abu Klea, where the enemy were held off by hastily formed squares.

* * * * *

In September 1899 the Royal Scots Greys were mobilised for service in the second Boer War, but they were not in action until February 1900. They quickly adapted to the new form of warfare, although their horses had to be dyed to make them less conspicuous. They formed part of the 1st Cavalry Brigade and, with the Cavalry Division, took part in the march on Kimberley during which there was a high rate of horse casualties.

The enemy were discovered to be holding the high ground on the approaches to the town and Sir John French ordered the whole division to charge in line of brigade. It was the last major cavalry charge to be performed by the British Army and was entirely successful.

The regiment's next action was at Paardeburg where they covered the infantry who had surrounded Cronje and his Boers. The British casualties were enormous compared to the Boers, but after ten days the enemy surrendered. Advancing on Bloemfontein the Greys attacked and held an important approach to the town, which contributed to its capture. By early June the regiment had helped to take both Johannesburg and Pretoria.

In the next phase of the war the regiment pursued and engaged whenever possible the Boer columns which were seriously disrupting the lines of communications. Like all mounted troops, the regiment was much affected by horse sickness and the poor conditions of living and fighting in the veldt. Nevertheless during the following months the Greys continued to take part in numerous patrols, escorts and defence duties. One such detached duty carried out by C Squadron in July 1900 involved the picquetting of Zilikat's Nek. It was attacked by a very strong force of Boers and, having eventually run out of ammunition, the squadron was forced to surrender.

The war ended in May 1902, but the Royal Scots Greys remained in South Africa until 1904. During the next ten years they served in various home stations.

The officers' 'Greys Race', 1905, was run over part of West Norfolk. Regimental races are still run to this day.
RHQ

THE ROYAL SCOTS GREYS
1914–38

The Royal Scots Greys reached France on 17 August 1914 and went into billets on 19 August near Mauberge. The horses were dyed a chemical chestnut colour in order to reduce the likelihood of the regiment being identified.The troopers were armed with both swords and rifles, and the regiment had integral machine-gun sections. For two days the Greys advanced with the British Expeditionary Force to the Mons-Condé Canal. On 23 August the retreat began and it was the Greys' task, as part of 5 Cavalry Brigade, to assist in covering the withdrawal of I Corps.

Patrols and larger formations of German cavalry were employed ahead of the German advance in many places, and the machine-gun sections of the Greys were usefully employed. The cavalry screen's task was to ensure the enemy cavalry and infantry advanced cautiously, and were kept as far away from the withdrawing British infantry as possible. Operating much of the time as troop patrols, alternating with larger parties to cover gaps and flanks, the Greys carried out their tasks effectively during the fortnight of the withdrawal.

'There was reveille long before dawn,' went the routine, 'followed by a slow and tedious march northwards along the congested roads, to take up positions to cover the retirement of the infantry picquets, and then came the long harassing day which ever proved too short for all that had to be done, so that generally it was about midnight before the men could seek repose and snatch some two hours' sleep before the wearisome round began again.'

Other sectors of the BEF's front, however, took the brunt of the German advance. There were few casualties in the regiment, but many narrow escapes.

As the positions of the two armies stabilised on the River Marne the cavalry sent out patrols to check the extent of the enemy positions before the offensive began. On 7 September the village of Rebais was captured by a patrol of the Greys. As the British infantry advanced the cavalry's activities were modified: patrolling became deeper and more dangerous.

Machine-gun sqn of the Royal Scots Greys during the Somme offensive, 1916. RHQ

'We had not proceeded far that morning,' wrote Lt Compton, 'when we came in touch with some mounted Germans. I dismounted my troop and opened fire on the enemy and our fire was returned by some others further away, but these soon mounted and moved off at a trot down the road. We at once mounted and galloped for a point beyond the village where I guessed we should obtain a good field of fire. In this we were successful, being just in time to get into action and obtain a few seconds' rapid fire at them. They were beautifully bunched together and a perfect target, and we killed eight as we afterwards verified.'

Above:
Royal Scots Greys riding through Brimeaux, May 1918. IWM

On 10 September regimental headquarters, while on the march, came across some 300 Germans, and the commanding officer demanded their surrender – an order with which they surprisingly complied. The infantry had moved forward to the River Aisne by the middle of September, and the Greys supported them in fighting for new positions. German artillery was now becoming particularly effective, and at Veilly the Greys came under heavy attack while astride the River Aisne, suffering many casualties. The cavalry was then pulled back into reserve until the end of the month.

The BEF were moved northwards in early October and the Royal Scots Greys were on the march every night. On 13 October German cavalry were encountered, indicating the enemy were also extending their line to the coast. The Greys, like other cavalry regiments, had to fill gaps in the defences, and the regiment spent most of the last week of October in the trenches. On 30 October the Greys moved to reinforce the 3rd Cavalry Division for a time, and returned to the brigade trenches on completion of this task. As the front was still not a continuous line, German troops often turned up unexpectedly and the Greys fought several local battles at close quarters.

In early November the Greys acted as a mounted mobile reserve, but returned to the trenches at the end of the first battle of Ypres. The remainder of the year was spent mainly in reserve, but close enough to the front to be moved quickly into the line.

In February 1915 the Greys moved with the 3rd Cavalry Division to Merville, and took over trenches at Sanctuary Wood which at that time was a quiet sector. In March the battle of Neuve Chapelle began, and the regiment stood by to act in its cavalry role, but was not required. The Greys remained in reserve and continued to train as mounted troops during April. While the second battle of Ypres was being fought, the regiment spent most of the time in the trenches, with the horse-lines nearby. Due to the shelling the regiment had a steady number of casualties.

The period June to October 1915 was spent by the regiment away from the line at Staple and there it trained hard both in cavalry and infantry tactics. The Greys stood by in September during the battle of Loos in the event of the need for cavalry, but again they were not required. In November each cavalry brigade was instructed to provide a dismounted battalion, comprising a regimental headquarters (in rotation) and a 'company' from each regiment. The machine-gun sections were brigaded.

In January 1916 the Greys' Company went with the 5th Cavalry Battalion into the trenches at Vermelles. In February there was heavy fighting in

Below:
Royal Scots Greys halt by the roadside, May 1918.
IWM

conjunction with mining operations, and the company suffered 66 casualties during the two months. After this period the regiment was held in reserve until September 1916.

The battle of Somme was by then in progress, and on 5 September the Greys were moved to the River Ancre. Unfortunately the breaks in the German line that were achieved by the infantry were not sufficient to allow the cavalry to exploit, and the regiment was again not called upon to fight in its primary role. In October the Greys retired first to Morlancourt and then to Vacquerie-le-Boucq, where it stayed until February 1917.

During March and April 1917 the Greys were constantly on the move near the front, ready at short notice to support the infantry. The brigade at one stage was ordered to occupy some ground near Wancourt.

'When the brigade came over the high ground, the regiments were opened out into line of troop columns, on their way to new positions, at the gallop. Fortunately, at the moment of the advance, a heavy snowstorm came on which partially concealed from view the swiftly moving masses of men. It was marvellous how the leaders were able to keep their direction at top speed in the blinding storm, and the way that the troops managed to thread their way through the trenches and shell holes . . .'

After a period out of the line, the Greys then moved to Hamel in May, and went into the trenches near Guillemont Farm. On 10 June the regiment mounted a particularly successful surprise raid on the Germans, killing 56 and capturing 14 prisoners, for 2 Greys killed and 5 wounded.

* * * * *

From July until November 1917 the Greys were away from the line but, as before, were held ready to reinforce or exploit a breakthrough. In late November they sent a battalion headquarters and a dismounted company into a recently captured part of the Hindenburg Line. Moving to the area of Bourlon Wood, the battalion was then attacked by a large German force. The line was held successfuly, but the battalion suffered many casualties before it was relieved. The 5th Cavalry Battalion, with its company of Greys, manned the trenches again in March 1918 at Vermand.

During the German offensive of March 1918 the Greys were in the area of the St Quentin Canal. On 22 March the dismounted company, manning part of the front line, repulsed a German attack while covering a withdrawal. As the Germans advanced, mounted troops were needed more than ever for reconnaissance and holding operations to cover gaps and flanks. The regiment thus had to fulfil both mounted and dismounted tasks. On 1 April 5 Cavalry Brigade were ordered to seize the high ground at Moreuil Wood. The horses were sent back and the advance continued on foot.

'Although the Greys, being on the extreme right of the line, did not have such serious fighting as some of the others, their casualties were severe as they had to move in the open exposed to very heavy machine-gun and rifle fire; nevertheless they successfully attained their objective, consolidated it, and held it until relieved at midnight.'

After a week the enemy's advance seemed to be held by the allies and the cavalry was pulled out of the line temporarily. For the next fortnight, the dismounted company was called on frequently to man the trenches in various parts of the line at short notice.

During the period May to July 1918 the regiment was away from the front. In preparation for the coming allied offensive, the Greys were moved in early August with 5 Cavalry Brigade to the Somme near Amiens. When the offensive was launched the cavalry advanced several miles through the German lines, with the regiment leading its brigade. The Greys were then moved to the Arras area as divisional cavalry, supplying detachments to carry out numerous tasks, particularly mounting local attacks to deal quickly with enemy infantry. In the steady allied advance during September and October the regiment was much occupied in patrolling and liaison duties. On 5 November, in its last action of the war, it mounted an attack over the Sambre Canal which resulted in the successful capture of most of the regiment's objective.

* * * * *

After the armistice on 11 November 1918, the Royal Scots Greys prepared for the march into Germany. They were, however, only used as occupation troops for three weeks before returning to Belgium. There they returned to peacetime duties, resumed riding to hounds and ran off the traditional 'Grey horses' race at a regimental race meeting. In March 1919 the regiment reached England.

SSMs form a human hoop for the Riding Instructor at the Meikleour Show, 1929. RHQ

In 1920 the Royal Scots Greys were sent to the Middle East for two years, and for a time were on active service in Palestine guarding Jewish settlements. In 1922 they began a five-year tour of India – their first visit to the sub-continent – and they were stationed initially at Risalpur, near the frontier, but then moved to Meerut. During the 1930s when other cavalry regiments were mechanised, the Greys remained a horsed regiment. In 1938 the regiment embarked at short notice for Palestine, where the trouble between Arabs and Jews had grown more serious.

THE ROYAL SCOTS GREYS

1939–1971

On the outbreak of the Second World War the regiment was stationed in Rehovot, employed on internal security both in the countryside and towns. The 1st Cavalry Division arrived from England during 1940 and the regiment joined it, but the prospect of action against the Axis powers seemed remote. Apart from training and patrolling, the year provided little opportunity for an active part in the war.

By 1941 the situation was deteriorating in the Middle East, with the activities of the Vichy French in Syria and growing German influence in Iraq. A number of ad hoc forces were formed for specific tasks, and in May the Greys were ordered to provide one such for the invasion of Syria. 'Todcol' was formed for the purpose of supporting the 7th Australian Division, and it consisted of RHQ, A Squadron and the machine-gun troop of the regiment together with B Squadron of the Staffordshire Yeomanry. The 'column' rapidly converted to a motorised infantry role. Operations during the first three weeks of June were particularly gruelling, since Syria was held in strength by the French: the British and imperial troops also had no armoured support. Todcol advanced some twelve miles into Syria to the west of Mount Hermon, but had to give ground in order to prevent the enemy seizing the main road into Palestine. The road was held successfully but there were a number of casualties, and some Greys were taken prisoner. Elsewhere the British invasion was successful: Damascus fell and an armistice was agreed by the end of the month.

Above:
Cleaning tack at camp during the 'Highland March'. RHQ

Left:
The Royal Scots Greys on the march through Glenalmond during the 'Highland March', 1935. RHQ

* * * * *

The Royal Scots Greys have the distinction of being the last operational regular regiment to be horsed cavalry in the British Army. The final mounted parade had already been held in March 1941, and by the autumn the horses had been returned to the remount authorities prior to mechanisation. A number of American light M3 Stuart tanks were issued and armoured training was conducted during the winter months. In February 1942 the Greys rejoined the former 1st Cavalry Division – now the 10th Armoured Division – in Egypt, and some medium M3 Grant tanks were issued in April. In mid-June the regiment was ordered to move forward by rail and transported westwards along the Egyptian coast. Consisting of one medium and two light tank squadrons, the regiment formed up at Mersa Matruh, and prepared to defend that town during the British withdrawal from Tobruk. It thus came as a great disappointment when the Greys were ordered to hand over their tanks to the 4th County of London Yeomanry, The Sharpshooters, and return to Mareopolis in the Delta.

In early July 1942 the regiment was re-equipped with Grants, Stuarts, and Lee tanks, few of which, however, were in a satisfactory conditon. In mid-July the Greys moved forward to the Alamein line and held positions on the Ruweisat Ridge guarding the coastal road and railway line.

For a time there was little German activity against the north of the allied line, as the enemy was chiefly concerned with probing against the south, preparatory to a breakthrough. The Greys were moved at the end of the month to support the New Zealand Division, whose task was to capture the western end of the Ruweisat Ridge from the Germans. This only involved the regiment in a long-range exchange of fire with enemy tanks across a minefield. During August the Greys moved several times, and on 30 August the German armour attacked the British positions at Alem Halfa. The regiment quickly formed up in reserve, and was held ready to plug any gaps or mount counter-attacks in the 7 Armoured Brigade area. On the afternoon of 31 August the Greys motored forward at speed to relieve the Sharpshooters. This action prevented a breakthrough in the southern part of the line, and the Germans and Italians withdrew.

Preparations were made during the next few weeks for the breakout at El Alamein, which involved an advance through the minefields and attack on the enemy armour sited in well-prepared positions. During the night of 23 October the assault formations moved forward under cover of a massive artillery barrage. The regiment succeeded in passing the first minefield during the night, but was in a very exposed position during the following day, as the breaching party had been unable to penetrate the second minefield. Lt-Col Sir Ranulf Twisleton-Wickham-Fiennes, the commanding officer, personally organised the squadrons' defence of the bridgehead covering the gap in the minefield, and sent forward reconnaissance parties towards the second minefield. Enemy artillery fire continued throughout the day, and B Squadron was sent to support the British infantry and clear some residual enemy groups. Towards last light, the regiment fired at a number of enemy tanks moving south along the edge of the minefield. While the main breakthrough of the British and dominion formations was further north, the Scots Greys continued to keep the enemy occupied in the south, which contributed greatly to the eventual success of the battle.

A Grant tank of the Scots Greys in the desert near El Alamein, July 1943. Their task was to guard the coast road and railway from the Ruweisat Ridge. IWM

Within hours of landing at Salerno the Scots Greys were engaged in fighting against enemy armour, 9 Sept 1943. IWM

During the first week of November the regiment moved to the north of the line and passed through Alamein itself. The regiment's next engagement was the capture of an Italian force, which was achieved by a spirited charge. A and B Squadrons then surprised some German tanks, scoring several hits and capturing some others. It was hoped that by a rapid advance the Germans and Italians could be outflanked, but the speed of the Axis troops' retreat put them ahead of the British and New Zealanders' advance along the coast road. Although the going was difficult due to prolonged rain, good progress was made. The Greys had to deal with several stay-behind forces as well as contend with long-range shellfire. In a fortnight they had covered over 400 miles, reaching a position in the desert south of Tobruk. In mid-November they then withdrew to El Adem for maintenance and replenishment. At the end of the month the regiment took over Sherman tanks in position at Agedabia from the 2nd Royal Tank Regiment.

The regiment, with a squadron of the Staffordshire Yeomanry under command, bypassed El Agheila between 12 and 15 December 1942, by taking a wide sweep through the desert undetected by the enemy. The town, meanwhile, was captured by the 51st Highland Division. One hundred miles west the Greys were ordered on 17 December to attack the heavily defended enemy positions to the west of Nofilia and there was hard fighting in the ensuing tank-versus-tank battle. There were losses on both sides and eventually the remaining German tanks succeeded in escaping. The Greys occupied the village and remained there for several days.

In mid-January 1943 the regiment, in support of the New Zealand Division, moved along the coast to Sirte and inland to Bu Ngem. There the Greys were engaged by the enemy during 15 January, and on the following day came across well-sited enemy tanks and anti-tank guns, which held up the advance temporarily. By 20 January the Greys had reached Azizia only twenty miles south of Tripoli; the enemy, however, evacuated both places without a fight.

* * * * *

As the Royal Scots Greys were not included in the permanent order of battle of any particular formation, and had been used during the North African campaign to re-inforce where necessary, they did not take part in the further advance on Tunis or the invasion of Sicily. Thus they remained in Tripoli until Sep-

A Sqn, Scots Greys, firing a broadside on the outskirts of Torre Annunziata, with Mount Vesuvius in the background, Sept 1943. IWM

tember 1943, and during this period the squadrons were in support of separate brigades preparing for the invasion of the Italian mainland. On 3 September the Eighth Army invaded across the Straits of Messina and on 9 September the US Fifth Army landed some 200 miles north at Salerno. The Greys were in support of the latter force.

The first-light landing a few miles south of Salerno was heavily opposed by German artillery, and within hours enemy tanks were moving into the area of the beach-head held by the infantry and supporting squadrons of the regiment. They were soon involved in the fighting at close quarters, mainly at troop level, and casualties were quickly inflicted on both sides. During the first four days the Greys moved between five and six miles inland in support of the infantry, gradually establishing a series of strong positions from which to withstand expected enemy counter-attacks. When these occurred between 13 and 16 September, they were successfully repelled. An example of the painstaking work often required to take out the enemy in detail was that of Corporal Stamper. He carried out a reconnaissance on foot to find a well-concealed enemy tank which could not be by-passed, and brought his own tank forward to a concealed position. Having worked out mathematically the direction of the target from a reference point, he destroyed the enemy tank with his first shot. He went on to knock out two anti-tank gun crews before his own tank hit a mine. He won the MM for his actions. The dangerous situation whereby the Germans nearly succeeded in dividing the US Fifth Army was averted.

While the main allied thrust was made north of Salerno along the axis of the road via Pompei to Naples, the Scots Greys embarked with a brigade to seize Maiori from the sea. This they did on 19 September, and for the next ten days they supported the infantry task of clearing the subsidiary route through the mountains. This prevented the enemy from attacking the main force from the flank, and the Greys reached the plains near Pompei on 29 September, after dealing with some resistance on the way. Passing to the west of Mount Vesuvius they reached Naples on 1 October. For the following week the regiment advanced through the close countryside north of Naples, clearing it of small enemy positions. Most of the enemy armour had withdrawn further north to hold major positions on the River Volturno.

The regiment moved up to the river in the middle

of October, with the purpose of supporting an assault river crossing. The bridges, however, were all blown and the river unfordable by tanks, but the Greys finally crossed on a bridge thrown across the river by the Americans while under fire. The enemy, however, rapidly pulled back and for the following three weeks the squadrons advanced slowly, supporting the infantry in the close and hilly country between the Rivers Volturno and Garigliano. The Greys had to contend with artillery fire and hidden anti-tank weapons along the route, in country that did not favour the use of armour. The period from 24 November to 14 December was spent in positions overlooking the plains around the mouth of the river Garigliano, some thirty miles west of Monte Cassino. In mid-January 1944 the regiment handed over their tanks to the 50th Royal Tank Regiment and returned to England by sea in order to prepare for the Normandy invasion.

* * * * *

The Royal Scots Greys trained in the south of England for the next five months as part of 4 Armoured Brigade, chiefly equipped with Sherman tanks. On 7 June the regiment sailed from Gosport on tank-landing ships, and landed some twelve miles north of Caen over a period of forty-eight hours. The brigade's task was to act as a reserve for the 51st Highland Division, positioned north and west of the city. A major offensive against the enemy was mounted on 26 June which was designed to encircle Caen. Moving forward towards the River Odon, the Greys' squadrons supported infantry battalions in a successful attack on 29 June. They then defended the town of Cheux during a determined German counter-attack.

The Germans, however, were still holding strong positions west of the River Odon, in particular 'Hill 112' where several enemy anti-tank guns were well sited in a wood on the reverse slope. When the Greys and infantry advanced the forward slope was easily occupied, but a deliberate attack had to be mounted against the wood by B Squadron supported by C Squadron – a formidable task for both infantry and armour. There was a fierce battle, the Greys losing several tanks and the infantry being forced back.

'It was now practically broad daylight,' wrote Captain Callender, 'and, in order to get through the gap each tank came into full view of the enemy to the south and south-east. This was a nasty moment, but the risk had to be taken, and everybody got safely in. This wood was no place for eleven tanks, there was hardly room to move, what with infantry in holes in the ground and large trees everywhere . . . By this time armour-piercing shot and spandau bullets were whistling through the wood. It was now obvious that there were two enemy tanks just outside the wood. We did our best to spot them but without success, until I actually saw the flash of the gun which knocked out my own tank, which immediately became a raging inferno.'

Eventually the enemy withdrew and the regiment was relieved. In late July the Greys passed through Caen, in order to support the 2nd Canadian Division fighting south of the city. Again, the Greys had to contend with well-sited infantry and anti-tank guns. During various engagements over a three-day period, the regiment lost more tanks, but the Germans were successfully prevented from mounting a large counter-attack in the area.

On 1 August the Royal Scots Greys were relieved and the regiment moved westwards past Bayeux and southwards towards Vire. 4 Armoured Brigade was to be in support of the 3rd Division, and on 9 August two squadrons supported a successful attack mounted by the King's Shropshire Light Infantry north-east of the town. The following day the whole regiment supported a brigade attack near Vire. There was much confused fighting in the area and during the battle the Greys were withdrawn for a more essential task – the brigade was to assist in cutting off the whole of the German Seventh Army south of Falaise. On 18 August the regiment took up positions on a ridge covering the Falaise gap, half-way between Falaise and Argentan. For the next day-and-a-half the regiment remained in this area engaged in long-range shooting at the enemy columns. Although its own casualties were high, the regiment contributed to the many hundreds of enemy vehicle casualties and thousands of Germans killed, wounded and captured during the retreat.

The Scots Greys rapidly advanced with their brigade to the River Seine, and crossed on 29 August once a bridge-head had been secured. The enemy, although in retreat, still had numerous isolated forces in the area between the Rivers Seine and Somme. There the regiment was engaged with several armoured groups and captured hundreds of enemy infantry and supporting troops. On 1 September the two leading squadrons reached the high ground overlooking an intact bridge over the Somme. B Squadron and the recce troop then seized the bridge, which was discovered to have been prepared by the enemy for demolition. The following day a German counter-attack was repulsed.

On 5 September the regiment crossed into Belgium and took up positions north of the River Escaut, guarding the approach to the bridge at Avelghem. The Germans attacked the village from the north, and with the assistance of the 9th Cameronians, the Greys fought the enemy off for several hours and subsequently occupied the whole area. The brigade then advanced north-east towards the area between Ghent and Antwerp. There was more fighting in the area of St Nicholas and Beveren Waes. Extensive flooding of the land by the Germans, however, imposed some delay on the advance.

The Scots Greys' next task was to support the airborne operation 'Market Garden', and the regiment was given a stretch of the Meuse-Escaut canal to hold. The operation was a failure as the airborne and ground forces never established contact. At the end of September the regiment moved into Holland and occupied Nijmegen 'island' for a fortnight, where the enemy made a number of unsuccessful attacks to dislodge the Greys and infantry. In late October they were moved to the Eindhoven area, and from there the regiment assisted the 15th Scottish Division's liberation of Tilburg, and in the fighting for Rijen on the nearby canal.

Tank crews of the Scots Greys await the order to support an attack on Udem near Goch, 27 Feb 1945, during the allied offensive against Germany, west of the Rhine. IWM

In mid-November the advance towards the River Maas began, and although opposition was light, progress was slow owing to thick woods, waterways and the poor state of the roads. This lasted for ten days and on reaching it, the Greys were given the responsibility of guarding part of the river line, which kept them occupied for the following three months.

In February 1945 the Scots Greys were on the move again, their brigade supporting the allied offensive against the Siegfried Line on the German border. The initial assault on the line was largely successful and the regiment crossed into Germany on 24 February near Cleve. The next major engagement was on 26 February near Udem, where the enemy were in strong positions and well supported by artillery fire. Working closely with the infantry the Greys advanced against various objectives in a night attack. The enemy resisted strongly and accounted for a number of tank casualties. For part of the time the troops of tanks had to work without infantry support, a dangerous task in view of well-sited anti-tank weapons. A few days later the regiment was involved in some heavy fighting on the Siegfried line, south-west of the Hochwald forest. The enemy mortar, artillery and rocket-fire was often intense, and close protection by infantry was necessary for the tank troops to operate effectively. The regiment was then withdrawn to prepare for the Rhine crossing.

The Scots Greys crossed the Rhine by a floating bridge on the night of 25 March and, advancing north-eastwards, met some enemy resistance which was quickly dealt with. They supported the British infantry attack on Bocholt three days later and maintained good progress until reaching the River Ems. There was some delay while awaiting bridges to be constructed, but the only major enemy stronghold in the area was at Ochtrup which had to be cleared. Rheine airfield was captured by C Squadron and the town occupied by the infantry. Crossing the Dortmund-Ems canal caused further delay, but the enemy then withdrew to Hopsten. On approaching the town during the morning of 6 April, the reconnaissance troop reported that the Germans were hurriedly digging-in behind a stream. The routes were confined to roads and trucks and were soon either blocked by vehicle casualties, or made impassable. Enemy mortar and anti-tank fire was kept up all day, and although the leading tank troop with its accompanying infantry had reached a bridge over the stream, they could not advance. Attempts were made to work around the town to find a less dangerous

approach but they were met with gunfire from defensive positions manned by SS troops. During the evening troops of B Squadron and infantry made fresh attempts to enter the town, but then had to probe forward during the night. 'Crocodile' flame-throwing tanks were brought up, and C Squadron of the Greys with two companies of infantry joined at daylight on 7 April. It took the British troops until eleven o'clock before the town was successfully occupied. Further villages to the east were successfully captured, and five days later the regiment temporarily left the 52nd Lowland Division which it had been supporting, and moved independently to the River Aller.

The river line was held in great strength by the Germans, and British progress towards the ports of Bremen and Hamburg was slow. On 14 April the regiment crossed the river at Rethem and began clearing enemy positions around the bridge-head. The Greys' next major objective was the village of Kirchboitzen, and it was successfully captured despite heavy opposition. During the following nine days the regiment advanced north-westwards along the eastern side of the river, with the cooperation of carrier-borne infantry systematically engaging and clearing the enemy. The Germans still had considerable forces in the area including anti-tank weapons and artillery, but could not seriously delay the

A Honey tank of the Royal Scots Greys advances through Wismar, 2 May 1945. A rapid advance of British troops was ordered to this area of the Baltic to ensure the Russians did not occupy it first. IWM

British advance. The Greys continued to advance on Bremen and supported the 52nd Lowland Division's entry into the city. There was considerable chaos during the few remaining days of the war and the regiment was ordered to move rapidly to Wismar on the Baltic to establish a British presence during the last days of hostilities.

* * * * *

After the war the Royal Scots Greys spent seven years as an armoured regiment with the British Army of the Rhine in various stations. In 1952 they moved to Libya, and squadrons served for a time in Egypt and Jordan to garrison the Canal Zone and in defence of treaty obligations. The regiment finally returned to England in 1956. In the 1960s the regiment served in Germany, and squadrons were stationed in Aden, Hong Kong and Bahrein as part of the strategic reserve.

Royal Scots Greys in support of the 52nd Lowland Division's advance on, and occupation of, Bremen, 25 April 1945. IWM

THE ROYAL SCOTS DRAGOON GUARDS

The Royal Scots Greys, unlike all other cavalry regiments, had never been amalgamated, but in 1971 they were ordered to amalgamate with the Carabiniers. The new regiment, however, has yielded none of its Scots character. During the 1970s and 1980s the Royal Scots Dragoon Guards have served in Edinburgh, various stations in West Germany, Northern Ireland, Cyprus, Catterick, Berlin, Belize and Tidworth. The regiment had been allowed to retain an additional squadron, which served independently in various stations until it was absorbed into the regiment in 1976.

In 1978 the tercentenary of the raising of the original troops of Scots Dragoons was celebrated during a week of festivities. The whole regiment mounted in chieftain and scorpion tanks paraded down Princes Street in Edinburgh, preceded by the Commanding Officer Lt-Col Charles Ramsay, his adjutant, trumpeter, the regimental standard and escort, all in full dress and mounted on grey horses. The salute was taken by a former serving officer of the Greys, HRH The Duke of Kent.

Above:
The amalgamation parade of the Carabiniers and Royal Scots Greys took place at the Palace of Holyroodhouse, Edinburgh, 2 July 1971. The familiar figure of HRH The Duke of Kent can be seen in the foreground. RHQ

A troop of Chieftain tanks of the Royal Scots Dragoon Guards on a training area whilst serving with the British Army of the Rhine. RHQ

CHAPTER 3
THE SCOTS GUARDS

THE REGIMENT
1661–1913

The Scots Guards claim antecedents which predate the Civil War and Commonwealth. In 1642 a large contingent of Scotsmen was raised at the request of Charles I for service against the catholic forces threatening the protestant settlements in Ireland. Archibald, 1st Marquess of Argyll was the commander of the royal regiment in this army, although its status as a guard for the protection of the King's person is unconfirmed. The Scots battalions fought in numerous engagements against the King's enemies in Ulster, and those who remained returned to Scotland in 1649 to be formed into one regiment. After the death of Charles I, it reputedly formed the bodyguard for his son Charles II, who landed in Scotland in 1650 to secure the northern Kingdom.

During Cromwell's invasion of Scotland of that year the regiment held Edinburgh Castle for the King, and fought at the battle of Dunbar. When Charles II was crowned at Scone in 1651 the two companies that remained were in attendance, but later that year the King's army was decisively defeated at the battle of Worcester. The Guards dispersed and, during the years until the restoration of the monarchy, no Scots regiments remained in royal service.

In January 1661 the first company of Foot Guards was formed in Scotland for the purpose of garrisoning Edinburgh Castle. By September the following year six companies of the 'Scots Regiment of Guards' had been raised. The two royal castles at Stirling and Dumbarton were also garrisoned by companies of the regiment, leaving three companies for 'field' duties. The distinction, however, between 'field' and 'garrison' companies did not last long.

A contemporary engraving of the Scots Reg of Guards at the Palace of Holyroodhouse, 1685.
National Museum of Scotland

The Scots Guards were thus Household Troops from their formation, but in the regiment's early years the responsibility of guarding the Monarch in England fell to the other two regiments of Foot Guards. During the period in Scotland when royal authority and covenanting factions were drawn into military conflict, the Guards took part in a number of military actions. The first was at Rullion Green in 1666, and in June 1679 Lord Ross's detachment withstood a foray of the Covenanters' army against Glasgow. Shortly afterwards the Guards attacked the Covenanters at Bothwell Brig, and captured the area of the bridge house. The remainder of the Covenanters' army was quickly routed by royal troops.

When Charles II was succeeded by his brother James II, the Scots Regiment of Foot Guards was added to the English establishment; they took precedence after the 1st and 2nd Regiments of Foot Guards – the Grenadier and Coldstream Guards – and soon became known as the 'Scotch Guards'. The regiment was soon augmented to two battalions, and one proceeded to England, where it was brigaded with the other Guards regiments. In 1688 all the royal regiments in Scotland were ordered to move to England in support of James against his son-in-law William, Prince of Orange, and his daughter Mary, the Protestant claimants to the throne. One by one, however, the regiments of the army transferred their allegiance to William and Mary, and one battalion of the Scotch Guards did so readily; the other showed more reluctance, until James lost his nerve and fled to France.

Previous page:
A group of Guardsmen, 1807. Battalions of the three regiments of Foot Guards were usually brigaded together during peace and war. Parker Gallery

The 1st Battalion was sent to Flanders in 1689 to take part in the War of the League of Augsburg. As in virtually all the subsequent wars in which the regiment fought, it was brigaded with other Guards regiments, and often companies of the regiments formed composite battalions, particularly of flank or grenadier companies. The battlion's first battle in the campaign was at Walcourt in 1689. The 2nd Battalion also moved to Flanders in 1691, joining the 1st Battalion in the Guards Brigade, and the following year they both fought at Steenkirk. In 1692 the Scots Guards were in the village of Landen during the battle of that name and, with the Royal Scots and 1st Guards, they bore the brunt of the French attack. After the third charge by twenty-six enemy battalions the British were forced to withdraw. In 1695 the regiment took part in the siege of Namur and assisted in storming the outer defences. The grenadier companies of the Guards then captured part of the fortress, and the town subsequently surrendered.

The two battalions of the Scots Guards returned home in 1697. There was still a certain amount of unrest in Scotland and they remained there until 1709, helping to maintain the peace. A Highland company of the regiment existed at this time, the members wearing highland dress and carrying appropriate weapons. The regiment became known as the 3rd Regiment of Foot Guards soon after the Union of Parliaments, and increasingly were called upon to guard the Monarch in London.

In 1710 the 2nd Battlion joined an expedition to Spain during the War of the Spanish Succession. Although the battles of Almenara and Saragossa were successful, the British troops were outnumbered and surrounded at Brihuega in December 1710. Members of the battalion thus remained as prisoners for the next two years, but in 1719 a detachment of the 3rd Guards returned to Spain with other Guards' detachments to carry out a punitive raid on the port of Vigo, a base used by the Jacobites.

The 3rd Guards remained at home duty until the War of the Austrian Succession broke out, and in 1742 the 1st Battalion went to Flanders as part of a Guards brigade. In the following year it was present at the battle of Dettingen, but was not heavily engaged in the fighting since its task was to guard the King at the rear of the army. In May 1745 the 3rd Guards fought at Fontenoy, where British fire caused great casualties amongst the enemy.

> 'The British muskets, so long shouldered, were levelled,' wrote Fortescue, 'and with crash upon crash the volleys rang out from end to end of the line – first the 1st Guards, then the Scots, then the Coldstream, and so on through brigade after brigade, two battalions loading while the third fired – a ceaseless, rolling, infernal fire . . .'

In the advance, however, without the assistance of the Dutch allies, the British infantry could not break the lines of the much more numerous enemy. The British army was then ordered to retire, and the Guards withdrew in perfect order, though severely harassed by the French.

The 3rd Guards returned to Great Britain during the Jacobite rebellion, but their sole engagement was at the capture of Carlisle, which involved only a small detachment. In 1747 the 2nd Battalion reached the continent and served in various parts of North Germany. It fought with determination at the battle of Lauffeld, holding the village of Vlitingen successfully, until ordered to conform to a general withdrawal of the allied army to the area of Maestricht. In the following year the war came to an end.

When the Seven Years' War began, the 3rd Guards were not immediately required for active service. They took part, however, in an amphibious landing on the French coast in 1758 during which Cherbourg was captured. Two years later the 2nd Battalion returned to Germany and fought in the allied victory over the French at Vellinghausen. In 1762 it formed the left of the line at the battle of Wilhelmstahl and prevented the enemy from outflanking the army, which contributed to another allied victory. The 3rd Guards were in action again at the attempt to capture Melsungen and fought at Amaeneberg in a particularly fierce battle. There the French attacked the allied garrison again and again, and the 3rd Guards suffered severe casualties, as did all British battalions. Peace was declared in 1763 and the 3rd Guards returned to England.

In 1776 the 3rd Guards provided a detachment of 300 men to make up a Foot Guards Battalion for service in the American colonies, where they remained for five years. They fought in engagements at Brooklyn and Brandywine, assisted in the capture of Fort Washington, and successfully defended German Town against the rebels. Further successful engagements against the King's enemies were fought at Freehold, Young's House, the crossing of the River Catawba and the capture of Guildford Court House. The Guards were present at the defence of Yorktown in 1781, where the 8,000 loyal troops (expecting reinforcements which arrived too late), faced 17,000 American and French troops. After a two-month siege the British troops surrendered and, when the peace settlement was concluded, the royal troops were repatriated.

When not serving overseas, the 3rd Guards spent much time on ceremonial duties, guarding the Sovereign and maintaining the peace in the capital. In 1780 there were serious riots against Roman Catholics in London, known as the Gordon riots. For three weeks Household and other troops guarded public buildings as well as the royal family and officers of the Crown.

* * * * *

In 1793 the 3rd Guards went with the Duke of York to Holland to fight the French. The force fought in a number of engagements, the most notable being at Lincelles near Dunkirk.

This print by William Hogarth shows the march of the 3rd Guards towards Scotland, 1745. A detachment assisted in capturing Carlisle from the Jacobites.
RHQ

'The Guards alone were drawn up in the line of battle,' wrote an eye-witness, 'drove the enemy from the town, and in a very short time Ensign John Campbell of Schawfield had the honour to place the "Bloody Flag" (the King's Colour) in one of the strongest redoubts. He and Lord Rollo jumped over the ditch among the very first, each carrying the colours, and gave three cheers, Schawfield halloaing to the men to follow, as eager as I ever saw him in a fox chase.'

Due to the overwhelming numbers of French troops in the Low Countries, the expedition was called off.

In 1798 the light companies of the 3rd Guards formed part of a raiding force against Ostend. The expedition, however, was over ambitious, and the 3rd Guards' companies were quickly surrounded and taken prisoner. In the same year the 1st Battalion joined a Guards brigade which was sent to Ireland at the time of the rebellion.

The following year two complete brigades of Guards, which included the 1st Battalion, the 3rd Guards landed and occupied Helder in Holland as part of a joint British and Russian expedition. British troops then took up positions along the Zupe Canal, which the Dutch and French attacked on 12 September, but they were forced to abandon the attempt. When the Russians arrived, the allies advanced and took Alkmaar, Egmont-op-Zee, Beverwyk and Haarlem. Having achieved limited objectives, the British and Russians withdrew at the end of the year.

In 1800 a brigade of Guards was sent to the Mediterranean to help destroy the French forces which had invaded Egypt. The 1st Battalion, 3rd Guards landed with the main British force on 8 March 1801 at Aboukir Bay, despite the heavy enemy fire from the shore. The British then advanced on Alexandria and reached the enemy lines in front of the city, whereupon the French mounted a direct attack on the British but were stopped by the weight of small-arms fire. The 3rd Guards' flank companies then successfully prevented the French from outflanking the brigade, but suffered nearly 200 casualties in the process. The French, however, were forced to withdraw into Alexandria, and for several months the Guards assisted in the siege. The city capitulated in September 1801 and the 1st Battalion soon afterwards returned to England.

The 3rd Guards remained in England to guard against a possible French invasion, but in 1809 the 1st Battalion was sent to join the army in Portugal. In May the British army crossed the river Douro and met the French at Talavera on 27 July. The French attack on the evening of the first day was successfully withstood, and after two further attacks on 28 July, the enemy lines were broken by British musket fire. The British advanced, but the Guards were then counter-attacked and caught by heavy enemy volleys. With cavalry support the Guards charged the French, and by the end of the day the enemy had withdrawn from the battlefield. It was, however, the only battle in which the 3rd Guards fought during the year, although two light companies of the regiment took part in the unsuccessful Walcheren expedition.

The 1st Battalion was not again involved in any major engagement in 1810, but three companies of the 2nd Battalion were sent to reinforce the British garrison at Cadiz. In March 1811 the Guards fought in the highly successful attack against the French at Barossa, and the victory effectively ended the French threat in that part of Spain.

In May 1811 the 1st Battalion, 3rd Guards was on the right of the line at the battle of Fuentes d'Onor.

'In front were the picquets of the Guards, about 100 rank and file under Lieut Col Hill of the 3rd Guards, which were cut off and surrounded by the French cavalry early in the action, Lieut Col Hill and several men being taken prisoners. Later the light infantry of the Guards, under Lieut Col Guise of the 3rd Guards, took their revenge by breaking up an attack of the French light infantry. Through all the attacks which followed the British line held firm throughout the day.'

Two days later the enemy withdrew. In July the following year they were in reserve at Salamanca, and in 1813 provided part of the storming party at the capture of San Sebastian.

In the same year the 2nd Battalion took part in another expedition to Holland. The only notable operation in which the Guards fought was the storming of Bergen-op-Zoom. They made a successful lodgement in a part of the defences and held it during the night; but as attacks had failed elsewhere, they were withdrawn. The battalion remained for a time in garrison at Antwerp and Brussels.

Meanwhile the 1st Battalion continued to serve with Wellington's army in the Peninsula. It took part in the battle of the Nive holding some high ground, but was not directly attacked by the French. The battalion was more closely involved at the crossing of the River Adour near Bayonne in February 1814, where five companies of the 3rd Guards formed a bridgehead and held it against a determined French attack. The main party of the army crossed over the next day. Although in reserve during the siege of Bayonne itself, the Guards' picquets were attacked by the French at night, and the 3rd Guards and other battalions fought the enemy off. On the conclusion of the peace treaty the 1st Battalion returned to England.

After the return of Napoleon Bonaparte to Paris in March 1815, a division of Guards was formed with the 2nd Battalion of the regiment in 2 Brigade. Hastily assembled, the British army was stationed near Brussels until the French crossed the river Sambre. The Guards division was amongst the troops ordered by Wellington to advance to Quatre Bras, but the light companies were the only members of the regiment who took part in the battle. The army withdrew on 17 June to the area of Waterloo.

The light companies of the Guards' battalions took up a position in a small wood to the south of the walled farm of Hougoumont, to the left of the British line, while the remainder of the 3rd Guards were in the line behind the farm. At the start of the battle the light companies were replaced by German troops; but when the French attacked in strength, the Guards returned to clear the enemy from the wood. At 1pm a further French attack was launched in Hougoumont and the light companies had to fight their way into the farm.

Officer, 3rd Regt of Guards; a contemporary print by E. Hull of 1830, published by Englemann, showing the 'new dress' recently adopted. RHQ

'The enemy, strongly reinforced, pushed through the wood and made a determined attack on the 3rd Guards as they retired on the great north gate. In the hand-to-hand fighting which ensued, two brothers, Sergeant and Corporal Graham of the Coldstream, and Sergeants Bryce, McGregor and Ralph Fraser, and Private John Lister of the 3rd Guards, especially distinguished themselves. Sergeant Fraser, indeed, in order to cover the withdrawal of his men engaged singlehanded the French Colonel Cubières, who was in command of the attacking battalion, pulled him from his horse, and rode back on it into the courtyard. Mingled together, Guardsmen and Frenchmen crushed through the gateway.'

The gates were then closed with a supreme effort by a few men of the Coldstream Guards. The area was now defended by only 2,000 troops, and faced a French corps of 30,000.

The Guards' battalions were all ordered forward for the defence of Hougoumont, which was by now completely surrounded by the French, and during the rest of the day the enemy mounted attack after attack on the farm. At one stage the 3rd Guards launched a foray to clear the orchard to the east of Hougoumont, now occupied by the French with three infantry brigades and artillery, but they failed. Despite catching fire, the farm itself was successfully defended and, when reinforced, the 3rd Guards then recaptured part of the orchard. At the end of the day, when Napoleon's Imperial Guard advanced, the Guards Brigade poured down such accurate fire that the enemy were stopped in their tracks. Shortly afterwards a general advance was ordered by the Duke of Wellington, and the French army began their headlong retreat. The 3rd Guards had over 400 casualties in the battle, but as a measure of their success the Duke of Wellington, writing later, stated that 'the success of the battle of Waterloo turned upon the closing of the gates of Hougoumont.'

* * * * *

After the battle, the battalion was stationed in Paris until 1816, when it returned to London. Apart from the 2nd Battalion's tour of duty in Portugal in 1827, where it helped to restore order after a rebellion, the regiment remained at home duty until the Crimean War. During that period battalions of the regiment served in Ireland, and helped to maintain the peace in London and Manchester at times of civil unrest. In 1831 the name of the regiment was changed to the 'Scots Fusilier Guards'.

Lt R. J. Lindsay defends the Colours of the 3rd Scots Fusilier Guards at the battle of Alma, 20 Sept 1854. Lindsay was awarded the VC for this exploit. Print by A. Laby after A. F. de Prades. NAM

The 1st Battalion joined the Guards Brigade on the way to the Crimea, which was reached in September 1854. On disembarking the army advanced on Sevastopol, and met a Russian army on 20 September holding the River Alma. The Guards at first supported the attack across the river by Codrington's brigade. Called forward hurriedly, the Scots Fusilier Guards in the centre of the brigade forded the river, and with

Wounded soldiers of the Scots Fusiliers Guards recuperate after the Crimean War at Brompton Barracks, Chatham. IWM

Lt-Col The Hon Wenman Coke, MP. Several generations of the Earls of Leicester's family have served in the Scots Guards. Lithograph by C. Baugnier. NAM

fixed bayonets advanced up the hill towards the enemy's redoubt. They halted in front of the Russian line and fired volleys, while waiting for the battalions on each side to conform to their advance. There was some confusion, since the order to retire had been given for another Fusilier battalion, and was partly obeyed by the Scots Fusilier Guards.

'The colour party, consisting of Lieut Robert Lindsay who carried the Queen's colour, Lieut Arthur Thistlethwayte with the regimental colour, Sergeants James McKechnie, Nicholas Lane, William Bryce and Angus McLeod were for some moments isolated and surrounded by the Russians. There were four and twenty shot-holes in the Queen's colour, and the pole was shot asunder, but both officers were unwounded. Lane was killed, McLeod was mortally and McKechnie slightly wounded, but the small knot of determined men stood firm.'

The remainder of the brigade, however, had by now come up in line; all three battalions fired volleys

The Scots Guards march through Hyde Park, 1880, led by the Corps of Drums and Pipes and Drums. Painting after Edouard Detaille. Parker Gallery

and stormed the redoubt together, at the same time as the Highland Brigade mounted its attack alongside. The Russians quickly retreated, leaving open the approach to Sevastopol.

The allies' siege of Sevastopol then followed, and in October the Russians appeared and attacked the British lines at Balaclava. The Guards and Highland Brigades were in positions overlooking the Inkerman valley at the time and were not called upon to take part in the battle. On 5 November, however, the Russians attacked the Inkerman positions and captured some of the British trenches. Three times the Scots Fusilier Guards charged the Russians, and there was very fierce hand-to-hand fighting. The enemy eventually were ejected from the hill, but the Guards were then threatened by the approach of a large force of hitherto uncommitted Russian troops. French reinforcements, however, quickly arrived and the Russians withdrew.

During the winter of 1854–5 the Guards suffered numerous casualties owing to the weather and disease, but in the summer of 1855 the health of the troops improved, and the Scots Fusilier Guards received further drafts. They continued to man the trenches in front of the besieged Sevastopol, until the sudden evacuation of the fortress by the Russians. The peace treaty was concluded in 1856 and the battalion returned to Great Britain in June of that year.

The 1860s and 1870s were uneventful for the regiment. The 2nd Battalion spent two years in Canada during the time of the American Civil War, but the fighting did not spill over the border as had been feared. In 1877 the regiment's title was finally changed to the 'Scots Guards'.

In 1882 the 1st Battalion joined the expedition to Egypt to fight against the Egyptian army in revolt against the Khedive. The Guards Brigade seized the Sweetwater Canal and railway line at Ismailia, and on 9 September joined the remainder of the British troops at Kassassin. Four days later the Scots Guards took part in the night march and surprise attack on the enemy at Tel-El-Kebir. In this decisive battle the Egyptian trenches were rushed and taken at bayonet point, before they could bring down effective artillery and small-arms fire against the advancing British. The Scots Guards were garrisoned in Cairo for a month before returning to Great Britain.

In 1884 an expedition was assembled for the relief of Khartoum, which included the 'Guards Camel Regiment', specially recruited from the three regiments. The expedition failed to reach Khartoum in time, before its capture by the Mahdi and the death of General Gordon. The regiment, however, fought with

determination, particularly near Abu-Klea where the enemy broke into a British square – a rare occurrence.

In the following year the 2nd Scots Guards were sent with the Guards Brigade on another expedition against the Mahdi. They landed at Suakin on the Nile and fought in a number of engagements, including Tofrek and Tamai, where they were involved in fierce hand-to-hand fighting with the dervishes. After a few months, however, the Sudan was abandoned and the Scots Guards returned to England. The regiment remained at home duty until 1899.

* * * * *

In October 1899 the Boers invaded the Colony of Natal and laid siege to Mafeking, Kimberley and Ladysmith. The 1st Battalion of the regiment left England at the end of the month with the Guards Brigade. Reaching South Africa they at once set off for the relief of Kimberley with Lord Methuen's column. Their first action was at Belmont on 23 November, and the Grenadiers and Scots led the brigade attack on the Boer positions in the hills.

> 'In the grey dawn the firing line advanced to within 350 yards of the steep face of Gun Hill looming in front of them. Then heavy fire broke out from the defenders, but the attacking line pushed steadily forward to the foot of the kopje, and after a pause to recover breath and fix bayonets, clambered up the rocks in spite of the well-aimed fire of the Boers who, however, did not wait for the final assault.'

There was fierce fighting for crossings on the Modder River, but the enemy withdrew to Magersfontein near Kimberley, and established a strong position covering the town. In the battle fought on 11 December the Scots Guards were in support, the assault being conducted mainly by battalions of the Highland Brigade, and they were thus spared high casualties. The Guards subsequently covered the withdrawal to the Modder River.

Two months later the division moved to Bloemfontein, and the Scots Guards were sent to make contact with another British division under General Gatacre. Meanwhile the 2nd Battalion of the regiment had been sent to South Africa, and a 3rd Battalion was raised to provide drafts for the two serving overseas. Both battalions, in different brigades, then took part in the advance on Pretoria. The 2nd were in action near Bethlehem in support of the Grenadier Guards, and after following General Prinsloo's commando, took part in the battle at Slaapkrantz in July where he surrendered. The 2nd Scots Guards took part in a number of further actions during the remainder of the year.

These two photographs show a private in marching order and a pioneer sergeant of the Scots Guards c1890. They wear the Egypt Medal and Khedive's Star awarded to both battalions between 1882-5. IWM

The 1st Scots Guards had been in action at Komati Port and Belfast against Louis Botha's commando, and then pursued two other commandos in the border area of Cape Colony and the Orange Free State. In 1901 the battalion operated in the Transvaal, and assisted in the capture of Roos Senekal. Meanwhile the 2nd Battalion were in the area of Harrismith, first in defence, then trekking after further enemy groups. For the last months of the war the 2nd Battalion guarded sections of the railway, while the 1st spent the same period in the Bloemfontein area. Both battalions reached England in October 1902 after peace was declared in May of that year.

In 1906 the 3rd Battalion was disbanded, and for the first time in their history the Scots Guards served overseas during peacetime – the 1st Battalion spending the years 1911 to 1913 in Cairo.

THE SCOTS GUARDS

1914–38

On mobilisation in August 1914, the two battalions of the Scots Guards were both at home duty. The 1st Scots Guards joined the British Expeditionary Force in 1 Guards Brigade of the 1st Division. Taking up a position at Grand Reng near Mons, the battalion was on the right of the BEF and was not seriously engaged by the enemy. During the retreat from Mons the battalion was constantly on the march, and although one of the other battalions in the brigade, the 2nd Royal Munster Fusiliers, were surrounded and overrun, the Scots Guards only fought minor skirmishes. The battalion reached Rozoy at the end of the retreat, and 1 Guards Brigade now comprised two other Scottish battalions, the 1st Black Watch and 1st Queen's Own Cameron Highlanders as well as the 1st Coldstream Guards.

During the subsequent advance on the Marne the Scots Guards were again only lightly engaged in the fighting, and took up strong positions at Pargan near the Chemin des Dames. On 14 September the brigade mounted an attack on the Chemin des Dames Ridge and, during the German counter-attack in the afternoon, Right and Left Flank companies were urgently called from reserve to plug a gap in the line. There

was confused fighting for several hours, and the brigade front line was held, although no further advance could be made: the battalion's casualties were 117 in the battle. On 17 October the 1st Scots Guards moved with the BEF northwards into Belgium.

Meanwhile the 2nd Battalion had left England with 20 Brigade and, reaching Belgium on 7 October, assisted in covering the Belgian army's retreat from Antwerp. At the start of the first battle of Ypres the 2nd Battalion was involved in skirmishing against a German cavalry screen on the Ypres-Menin road. The fighting continued to be very fluid, and on 20 October the Scots Guards and 1st Gordon Highlanders advanced towards Gheluvelt specifically to draw enemy fire and reconnoitre the area. The Germans attacked the neighbouring brigade on 22 October, and the 2nd Scots Guards were sent to support it, only to be recalled to reinforce their own brigade which was also under attack. The enemy shelling was intense and at one stage, when the line was broken, Capt T. Rivers-Bulkeley was sent in with Left Flank Company to fill the gap.

'He never looked behind, with six men he went forward, followed by the Company. He walked right on and was shot at not more than 100 or 200 yards range. His advance was magnificent, it stopped a gap being forced in our line.'

Attacks and counter-attacks continued for many days under constant shellfire. On 25 October a Scots Guards Officer described that

'Never have I been through such a day as it was. It was a veritable hell on earth. There was an incessant shower of shells from 7.30am to 6.00pm.'

In one engagement at this time a company of Scots Guards captured nearly 200 Germans.

The 1st Scots Guards defending positions north-east of Ypres were comparatively lightly involved in the fighting until 27 October when they defeated a German attack, but at a cost of some 240 casualties. Four days later, after an intensive bombardment, the Germans attacked Gheluvelt and, despite the Scots Guards being used to reinforce various other battalions' positions, the town was captured. Other elements of the Scots Guards were defending Château Gheluvelt, and they had to be reinforced by the Worcestershire Regiments. The situation was saved and Gheluvelt itself was re-taken with the assistance of the few remaining members of the Scots Guards. On 11 November the 1st Scots Guards were withdrawn from the line, having by then lost a further 114 killed, 158 wounded and 435 missing. The 2nd Battalion

The 2nd Scots Guards march from the Tower of London, 15 Sept 1914. Their first task was to assist the gallant Belgian troops' withdrawal from Antwerp. IWM

2nd Scots Guards man a rapidly dug trench at Ghent, Oct 1914, before the withdrawal to Ypres. IWM

remained in the Ypres area until 6 November.

During the winter the two battalions spent much of the time in the now static front-line trenches. On 25 January the reinforced 1st Scots Guards were in the line of a major German attack near Cuinchy, after a severe bombardment and the blowing of mines. Although other parts of the line were pressed back, and the flank companies were virtually wiped out, the Scots Guards successfully defended the centre until an attack could be launched. A German witness admitted during the battle that

'there was pandemonium of rifle fire and of machine gun discharges that bordered on the incredible. The hand-to-hand combat had begun almost instantly. The Scots fought like demons. Many of their comrades had been blown into the air with the earth of the trenches.'

The 2nd Scots Guards were involved in the fighting at Neuve Chapelle in the spring of 1915. On 12 March the battalion took part in an attack in which 300 German prisoners were taken; but owing to the companies becoming separated, they failed to take their objectives. Although held in reserve, the 1st Scots Guards were not called upon to assist. The 2nd Scots Guards were again in action at Festubert, and during a fast-moving battle on 16 May the companies took part in the fiercest close-quarter fighting. F Company was overwhelmed, but in the counter-attack the other companies ejected the Germans from an orchard the Guards were defending.

During the early summer of 1915 neither battalion

Officers of the Scots Guards have a hearty meal at Festubert, May 1915. IWM

took part in any major operations. With the raising of the Welsh Guards in 1915, and the formation of new battalions for the Grenadiers, Coldstream and Irish Guards, the Guards Division was formed in which all Guards battalions were consolidated. The 1st Scots Guards were placed in 2 Guards Brigade, and the 2nd Battalion in 3 Guards Brigade; they remained with these brigades until the end of the war.

On 27 September, at the start of the battle of Loos, the 1st Scots Guards formed the second wave of an attack on two objects called the 'Keep' and 'Puits 14 bis' near Hill 70. These objectives were taken despite the intense enemy machine-gun fire in the advance, but the Guards were unable to hold on to the Puits. The 2nd Scots Guards then took part in a brigade attack on Hill 70 itself, also in support, and they too consolidated positions on the objective very close to German trenches. Both battalions defended their positions until relieved on 30 September. On 8 October the two battalions were back in the front line and assisted in repulsing a German counter-attack. On 17 October the 2nd Scots Guards took part in an attack on the Hohenzollern redoubt, where two companies seized some 350 yards of trenches.

The Guards Division spent the winter of 1915–16 in the low ground by the River Lys, north of Neuve Chapelle: there the battalions carried out active patrolling but no large-scale operations. In mid-February 1916 the division moved to the sector north of Ypres, and had a relatively quiet time until April.

B Coy, 1st Scots Guards in the captured 'Big Willie' trench, Oct 1915. IWM

When the British offensive began on 1 July on the Somme, the Guards Division was in reserve behind the River Ancre: the Scots Guards' battalions were frequently on the move, but did not fight until September. On 10 September two companies of the 2nd Scots Guards were sent to reinforce the 1st Welsh Guards near Ginchy for an attack which proved successful, and on the following day the whole battalion relieved the Welsh Guards at Ginchy itself. Then on 15 September the Guards Division launched an attack north of the village. The 2nd Battalion was in divisional reserve, while the 1st was in brigade support. By the time the 3rd Grenadier Guards had reached their objective, the 1st Scots Guards were close behind, and members of the various battalions became mixed. Lance-Sgt McNess

> 'during a severe engagement led his men with the greatest dash in face of a heavy shell and machine-gun fire. When the first line of the enemy trenches was reached, it was found that the left flank was exposed and that the enemy was bombing down the trench. Sgt McNess thereupon organised a counter-attack, and led it in person. He was very severely wounded in the neck and jaw, but went on, passing through fresh supplies of bombs to his own men.'

McNess was awarded the VC for this exploit. The 2nd Battalion was ordered forward later in the day to reinforce the 1st Guards Brigade and was itself involved in some of the fighting.

The advance from the Ginchy area was ordered for 25 September. The 2nd Scots Guards were in the first wave, and the objectives on the German front line were taken quickly. They supported the 1st Grenadier Guards in taking two further lines, together with Right Flank of the 1st Scots Guards. The divisional objective of Lesboeufs having been captured, the 1st remained in possession, whilst the 2nd Battalion was withdrawn into reserve. The division remained in this sector for the rest of the Somme offensive, but there was little further movement. The winter of 1916–17 was spent by the two battalions in the same sector and, although active patrolling and local raiding was conducted, there was little fighting of any intensity.

Much of the summer of 1917 was spent in training for the forthcoming offensive in the Ypres sector. At the end of July the 1st Battalion was moved to the Poperinghe area, and the 2nd near Elverdinghe. When the battle started, the 1st Scots Guards were in the first wave, and they advanced to their first objective without too many casualties; but on their occupying the German line, enemy machine guns and snipers inflicted many casualties before being themselves wiped out. Nevertheless the battalion continued the advance behind the 3rd Grenadiers and 1st Coldstream Guards who had passed through. Meanwhile, the 2nd Battalion had been in reserve, but took the lead after the first German line was captured. The battalion took its objectives, together with a number of German prisoners and established a defensive line. It was relieved at the end of the day, but returned shortly afterwards to the line and remained in or near the front for some weeks. The 1st had by this time been withdrawn in order to be reconstituted.

Neither battalion was much involved in the further course of the battle until October. On 9 October the 1st Scots Guards went into the attack with their brigade. 'The whole attack,' claimed the commanding officer, 'went off just as if it had been done at Aldershot. Every officer and man was splendid, and it could not have been a more brilliant success.' The first objective was taken and the second. There the Scots Guards consolidated their positions to allow the 3rd Grenadier Guards to pass through. Two German counter-attacks during the evening failed, owing mainly to accurate artillery fire and on 13 October the 1st Battalion was relieved. The 2nd Scots Guards moved up to the front and although they were not involved in any fighting, they suffered a number of casualties from artillery fire and mustard gas. Two of the platoons were attached to the 1st Grenadier Guards and took part in a number of skirmishes over a two-day period, before both battalions went into reserve.

In November the Guards Division moved to the Cambrai sector. On 23 November the 2nd Scots Guards took up positions in the recently captured Hindenburg support line, three days after the battle began. They then moved forward to relieve units of the 51st Highland Division near Bourlon Wood; at the same time the 1st Battalion advanced to Flesquières Ridge on the Hindenburg Line. On 24 November the 2nd Scots Guards had to clear part of Bourlon Wood.

> 'It was a very dark night and the units in the wood had become very much mixed up. German patrols and machine guns were holding the highest part of the wood, and the latter were firing down the side which runs from north to south through the centre of the wood.'

The Scots Guards had a very difficult time and suffered many casualties, but so did the enemy, who were prevented from breaking out of the wood. Meanwhile, to the south the 1st Scots Guards were taking part in the assault on the village of Fontaine. Unfortunately the leading battalions had failed to clear the village of enemy snipers and machine guns, and the Scots Guards suffered many casualties before occupying it. When the enemy subsequently counter-attacked Fontaine, the battalion successfully repulsed them. Sgt McAulay was awarded the VC for taking command of C Company when all the officers had been killed or wounded.

Although the Guards Division was withdrawn from the battle on 29 November, it was recalled urgently the following day to an area well to the

Two Scots Guardsmen in the trenches at Ypres, April 1916. They appear to be priming some Mills No. 36 grenades, still in the inventory of British ammunition in the 1980s. IWM

south of the previous fighting. The 2nd Scots Guards fought in support of 1 Guards Brigade in retaking Gouzeaucourt village, Gauche Wood and Quentin Ridge. The Scots Guards then left the immediate vicinity of the fighting and went into reserve in early December 1917.

In the new year the 1st Scots Guards went to the River Scarpe sector, and the 2nd Battalion was nearby at Roeux to the west of Arras. It was a quiet sector at the time but the terrain was particularly muddy. There the battalions remained in and out of the line until late March 1918. When the Germans launched their offensive along a fifty-mile front on 21 March the Guards Division was in reserve near Arras. Both battalions were ordered to take up positions on the line south-east of the town, which they did two days later. The enemy artillery fire gradually increased but the Scots Guards were not directly attacked. On 25 March the Scots Guards were ordered to withdraw, the 2nd Battalion being under considerable enemy pressure. The withdrawal was for only a short distance in this sector, where the main German activity was heavy shelling.

Throughout April and May the Guards Division remained in the Arras sector, and in June went into reserve for training. July was spent at the front, and patrolling and raids were the chief activities while preparations were made for the coming allied offensive.

At dawn on 21 August the 1st Scots Guards formed up in an assembly area near Ayette, and advanced to take two objectives: all resistance was overcome and 100 prisoners were captured. On 23 August the battalion again advanced, supported by some tanks, and captured Hamelincourt. By the end of the attack three miles had been gained, 400 prisoners and numerous machine guns taken, for some 200 battalion casualties.

The 2nd Scots Guards were called forward with 3 Guards Brigade on 24 August. In their attack on that day, resistance was greater than had been experienced by the 1st Battalion and progress towards the objective of St Leger was slower. The enemy used numerous machine guns to good effect, and could only be defeated by shelling. The St Leger area was not cleared until 28 August.

On 3 September the 1st Battalion rapidly advanced five miles, and the 2nd a similar distance. German resistance, however, was stiff, but steady progress was made towards the Canal du Nord and Hindenburg Line. Preparation to assault these two obstacles (the canal was dry) took until the end of the month. On 27 September the 1st Scots Guards were in the leading wave of the assault while the 2nd Battalion was in the second; both battalions achieved their objectives. The enemy put up strong resistance in the Hindenburg Line support area, but were quickly overcome; the Scots Guards remained in the area ready to resist any possible counter-attack. On 7 October the battalions both advanced again in the wake of leading formations.

During the final four weeks of the war, the two battalions conformed to the allied advance. Much of the movement was lightly opposed, but some major positions were defended in considerable strength by the Germans. The intensity of the fighting increased, particularly from the beginning of November, as the Guards Division approached Mauberge. The towns and villages still had to be cleared of the enemy, and the German artillery bombardment and machine-gun fire continued to cause casualties. After hostilities ceased on 11 November, the Scots Guards marched into Germany as troops of occupation.

The Scots Guards returned to the United Kingdom in early 1919 and resumed peace-time duties. In 1927 the 2nd Battalion was sent to Hong Kong, and in the following year to the British garrison at Shanghai. In 1935 the 1st Scots Guards went to Egypt and the 2nd Battalion moved to Palestine for a short tour in 1936. Two years later it returned to the Middle East, where it was serving when the war began.

This period-piece photograph shows members of the 1st Scots Guards climbing onto transport during the 1930s. IWM

THE SCOTS GUARDS

1939 to the present

The 1st Battalion of the regiment was the first in action during the Second World War. In April 1940 it joined the expedition to Norway, and landed 50 miles from Narvik, which had already been captured by the Germans. As part of 24 Guards Brigade the battalion was sent to hold positions at Mo. In mid-May the Germans attacked in greatly superior numbers and forced the battalion to withdraw to avoid being surrounded. After four days of fighting in the rugged snow-covered terrain, the brigade was ordered to march northwards to Bodo, more than 100 miles to the north, within the Arctic Circle. On the first day they experienced, according to a participant, a 'long dreary road . . . harassed by aircraft. Arrived dead-beat, welcome rum ration and slept on floor. Total 15-hour battle and 18–20 mile route march.' The chief difficulty lay in withdrawing through a belt of snow stretching for twenty miles.

'Through this barrier there was but one narrow road kept open by snow-ploughs and lined by high, perpendicular snow falls,' wrote Captain Ellinger '. . . one well-aimed bomb would completely stop all motor-transport. To pass the snow-belt with a battalion would require both skill and luck in avoiding observation by the enemy. To try to cross the snow-belt while an action was actually going on would surely spell disaster.'

Faced by a German mountain division the withdrawal continued, with the Scots Guards continually fighting rear-guard actions, as they moved on foot or by road transport. On 31 May the Scots Guards embarked on ships of the Royal Navy and were moved to a secure area before the final evacuation to the United Kingdom. The battalion had lost nearly a hundred men as casualties and prisoners during the brief campaign.

* * * * *

The 2nd Battalion, Scots Guards spent the first eighteen months of the war in garrison duties in Egypt, and manning positions on the border with Libya. Then in the spring of 1941 the German and Italians attacked the British troops in Libya and forced a withdrawal. The Scots Guards, as part of 22 Guards Brigade, were moved to Matruh to assist in blocking the German advance. On 15 May the battalion took part in a highly successful attack with the 4th Royal Tank Regiment and the 2nd Battalion, Rifle Brigade on objectives at Sollum; three days later the battalion defended Halfaya Pass nearby, capturing more than 400 enemy troops.

In mid-June the battalion was again in action during operation 'Battleaxe'. At 4.40am on 16 June the Scots Guards mounted an attack on Musaid, personally led by the Commanding Officer Lt-Col B. Mayfield.

'We were advancing when a heavy fire was opened up . . . The noise was terrific . . . After a momentary pause, the line advanced at a steady double through the fire. After doubling seventy-five yards, the outer defences were reached, a few enemy were bayoneted, some shot, others knocked on the head.'

Later in the day the battalion recaptured Sollum.

Fighting on the border continued during the summer of 1941. The 22 Guards Brigade was converted to a motor brigade and in November took part in the advance to Sidi Resegh. The fighting was intense and the Germans, while suffering numerous casualties of tanks and men, successfully blocked the British for three weeks. By mid-December the brigade was in a position south of Tobruk at the time of its relief, and on 7 January 1942 occupied Agedabia.

The Scots Guards were subsequently ordered to withdraw to the Gazala Line owing to increased German pressure, and in May established 'Box' positions near the 'Knightsbridge' junction. On 27 May the Germans launched their heaviest attack, and fighting continued for several days. On 3 June the Scots Guards took up a position on the Rigel Ridge overlooking Knightsbridge itself; German pressure continued and the main battle was fought on 13 June.

At 2pm two columns of German tanks, followed by two hundred lorries carrying infantry and towing guns were seen approaching; it was the main thrust of 21st Panzer Division. Although the defensive

A charge of the 2nd Scots Guards during training in Egypt, 30 April 1941, shortly before moving to block Rommel's first offensive. IWM

minefield delayed the enemy advance for a while, the infantry skirted the minefield and attacked Left Flank, F and G Companies. They were followed by the tanks and, despite the work of the battalion's anti-tank guns, F and G Companies were overrun. But eleven enemy tanks had been destroyed and a further ten crippled, five of them by Lt I. Calvocoressi's No 17 Platoon which took the full force of the attack. Other troops and some tanks came to the assistance of Left and Right Flank as well as battalion headquarters. The ridge positions were therefore held for as long as possible, until the order for withdrawal came. The Scots Guards lost over 300 casualties, but General Rommel's own judgment of the Guardsmen in this battle was of their 'tremendous courage and tenacity'. The remaining members were formed into a composite battalion with the Coldstream Guards, and they had the important task during July of assisting in guarding the Alamein Line. But the Scots Guards were not involved in the breakout from Alamein, because in July they were reinforced and reconstituted as a full battalion, and then spent five months training in Syria.

The battalion rejoined the Eighth Army in Tunisia in March 1943 near the Mareth Line. The Scots Guards' position was at Medenine, and the battalion's anti-tank weapons were sited to counter the expected armoured thrusts. The enemy attack was launched on 6 March, and the anti-tank guns of the battalion accounted for some fourteen tanks by midday. In all, more than 50 enemy tanks were destroyed by the Eighth Army, and the enemy's attack completely failed. The 2nd Battalion, Scots Guards remained in the area during the British assault on the Mareth Line, and a month later supported the 51st Highland Division's attack on Wadi Akarit. Then on 19 April the battalion entered and occupied Enfidaville.

Men of 2nd Scots Guards move up behind Matilda tanks during July 1942. The battalion had lost over 300 casualties the previous month during Rommel's second offensive, successfully blocked by Gen Cunningham's Eighth Army. IWM

Meanwhile in March the 1st Battalion, Scots Guards had landed in Algeria with the First Army. At first they were only involved in sporadic fighting to the south-west of Tunis, but in April they took part in the final offensive. On 20 April the Germans attacked the 5th Grenadier Guards on a ridge east of Medjez. B Company, 1st Scots Guards under Capt The Lord Lyell moved up to reinforce them, and thence to assist the Duke of Wellington's Regiment. At dawn on 23 April the British 1st Divison advanced north-east in the direction of Tunis, its objective being the Jebel Bou feature. The 1st Scots Guards met heavy opposition and suffered numerous casualties, particularly in Left Flank Company. 'I had to think twice,' an eye witness commented, 'to realise it was real – the scene in the half-light – smoke drifting about – tanks on fire – shells exploding – traces from AA. I shall never forget my first view of real fighting.'

Intense fighting continued for four days and the advance progressed slowly over the twelve miles of hills to the Jebel Bou. At one stage battalion headquarters was nearly overrun, and the casualties were high. On 27 April Lord Lyell led an attack of four men onto a gun emplacement and personally killed some of the enemy gun crew and stampeded the others, before

being killed himself. For this exploit he was awarded the VC. The Scots Guards finally gave up their advanced position on 5 May, having been in action for nearly a fortnight under constant artillery fire.

The 2nd Scots Guards had in the meantime been advancing on Tunis from the east and were engaged in sporadic fighting. The city capitulated on 8 May, and the battalion had an active role in clearing residual enemy groups. Both battalions then began training for operations in Italy.

* * * * *

The 2nd Battalion, Scots Guards landed at Salerno with 201 Guards Brigade on 9 September 1943. On the following day a daylight attack was mounted on the village of Battipaglia, and the Scots Guards, supported by the Scots Greys, captured their objectives of the railway and factory area. During the night part of Right Flank was cut off and captured. For the remainder of the month the battalion was not committed to any further heavy fighting, but in mid-October the Scots Guards carried out a diversionary raid over the River Volturno, and acted as flank guard to the 56th Division as it advanced north over the mountains.

By the end of the month they had reached the area of Monte Camino, and 201 Guards Brigade was given the task of launching a frontal assault on a series of mountain summits. This entailed route marches over the most difficult terrain: F Company, supporting the Grenadier Guards had to face eight German counter-attacks on one day, and required reinforcements from the other companies to hold the ground gained. The fighting for Monte Camino continued throughout November and on 5 December the battalion captured Acquapendola Ridge after a particularly arduous and dangerous march. By 9 December the whole area had been cleared by the allies, and the advance towards the River Garigliano begun. During January and

Led by a guide, a patrol of 1st Scots Guards pass through Castel di Sangro, 21 April 1944. IWM

Above left:
The 1st Scots Guards had landed in North Africa with the First Army, Nov 1942. Here Capt The Lord Lyell wins the VC at the battle of Djebel Bou, Tunisia, 27 April 1943, when knocking out a German gun emplacement at the cost of his own life. RHQ

February 1944 the 2nd Scots Guards manned part of the front line, which was by now static due to the winter conditions.

Meanwhile the 1st Battalion, Scots Guards had taken part in the allied landing at Anzio on 22 January 1944. They were unopposed at first, but on 25 January the battalion advanced with its brigade, 24 Guards Brigade, and contact with the enemy was made. The Germans carried out frequent raids on the brigade front line and progress had to be made cautiously. Then on the night of 29 January the 1st Battalion mounted its first major attack of the campaign to clear the main road fifteen miles north of Anzio. There was very heavy fighting throughout the night: the German artillery fire was very effective and their tanks and anti-tank guns had to be defeated in detail. By dawn the enemy had retreated, and positions were rapidly consolidated to defeat possible counter-attacks.

The following night Left Flank was holding a feature known as Point 105; they were first attacked at 4am, but managed to eject the enemy infantry and some tanks in support. They were again attacked at dawn and reported at 7.15am that the enemy were in full retreat. Ten minutes later company headquarters went off the air, having reported that they were 'surrounded, and looked like being overrun'. Three officers and forty-two rank and file were killed, the remainder were taken prisoner by the overwhelming number of enemy who swarmed over the position. On 31 January the feature was re-taken by C Company, but the Scots Guards had lost more men that day than on any other during the war.

There was constant activity by both sides during the first week of February, and on 10 February the Germans launched a major attack against the battalion. Battalion headquarters were threatened by enemy tanks and had to be withdrawn, and there followed some very close-quarter combat before the battalion was relieved. It then spent several weeks in reserve.

The decision for the 2nd Scots Guards' return to the United Kingdom was made during the spring of 1944. A new company, known as S Company, was formed at this time from drafts from England and acted as an independent company attached to the Coldstream Guards. It fought at Monte Pacciano, Monte Cassino and in numerous other engagements during the year.

The 1st Battalion was not involved in the battle for Monte Cassino, but took part in the advance to the River Arno during the early summer with the South African Division. The Germans had established various strong points designed to delay the allied advance, and the battalion had frequently to mount swift local attacks in order to maintain the momentum: in one month the Scots Guards covered more than 150 miles. In July the battalion captured the major strongpoint of Castel di Brolio, and advanced with its brigade into the Chianti mountains for the capture of Monte San Michele, where the Scots Guards were given close support by South African tanks. Fighting in the mountainous country was extremely difficult and much of it was at very close quarters. In early August the allies reached Florence, by then evacuated by the enemy.

In September the battalion advanced north towards the Gothic Line twenty miles from the city, but the enemy had abandoned the line and established defensive positions further north. On 30 September a battalion attack was mounted on Monte Catarelto,

Searching the ruins of Monte Cassino in May 1944. S Coy of the Scots Guards served with the Coldstream Guards during the Italian campaign. IWM

and it took all day before the Scots Guards managed to take all their objectives. During the night the Germans sent fighting patrols against the company positions, and counter-attacked at dawn on 1 October: Left Flank had to withdraw and two other companies were threatened with being outflanked, but they held out until the enemy withdrew. Further advance was hampered by the appalling weather, making the terrain even more difficult to move through. During the winter months the line remained static, ten miles south of Bologna, and there the Scots Guards spent much of the time manning forward positions and conducting patrol operations.

In April 1945 the 1st Battalion, Scots Guards which had been joined by S Company, moved to the

Adriatic Coast in order to take part in an operation at Lake Comacchio in support of the Royal Marines. Fighting continued for a week for crossings over the various associated canals: seizing the Fossa Marina and Val D'Albero Canals were their most difficult tasks, and both involved fighting at close quarters and relying on intimate tank support amid built-up areas. During the last days of the war the Scots Guards continued with the Allied advance to the River Po and, after the German surrender, they assisted in garrisoning Trieste which came under international control.

* * * * *

The first element of the Scots Guards to fight in the Normandy campaign was X Company, the only remaining Company left from the disbanded 4th Battalion. The company was attached to the 3rd Battalion, Irish Guards, and landed at Arromanches on 23 June 1944. At first they had a defensive task near Caen, but then took part in operation Goodwood – the attempted break out. After advancing in the wake of armoured troops, the Company took up positions at Cagny before being relieved on 22 July.

In the meantime the 3rd Battalion, Scots Guards reached Arromanches as part of 6 Guards Tank Brigade in the Guards Armoured Division. They had been converted to armoured troops in September 1941, but had to wait until July 1944 before going into action in their tanks. They moved inland and reached a concentration area near Caumont on 29 July. The 3rd Scots Guards' task was to support the 2nd Argylls' attack on the Bois du Homme in the second phase of the attack.

'We advanced,' wrote a Company Officer, 'with the infantry right round us to protect us from Bazooka men and snipers . . . each hedge was practically a tank obstacle anyway, as they were always on top of very high earth banks. As we came through a hedge we made the infantry look first to see if there was a Panther in the next field . . . if not we settled down to a quarter of an hour's speculative shooting up of the next hedge. HE into any likely looking place and Besa everywhere . . .'

To maintain the momentum, however, the tanks had to go on ahead of the infantry and casualties overall were high before the final objective was reached.

X Company reached the same area during the first week of August, and on 3 August the 3rd Scots Guards advanced southwards. Three days later the battalion was ordered to attack the Estry Ridge. The village was very strongly held by infantry, anti-tank weapons and tanks, and under constant artillery cover. Progress was therefore slow, although troops of Left Flank managed to reach the village. The Germans, however, successfully defended Estry and the Scots Guards was diverted to attack another feature nearby on 11 August. The village of Chênedollé was captured after some severe fighting.

Tank crews of the 3rd Scots Guards brew up during a halt near Celle, Germany, 11 April 1945. IWM

The allied break-out from Falaise and subsequent rapid advance gave X Company a respite from fighting. They crossed the Seine on 1 September and advanced into Belgium with the Welsh Guards. They reached the Albert Canal east of Brussels on 7 September, where contact was made again with German troops. At Hechtel the company was involved in capturing the village, a task which succeeded after five hours of fighting, and at the end of the month X Company reached Nijmegen Island.

In the meantime the 3rd Battalion, Scots Guards were moved by tank transporter, and reached an area near Eindhoven by 30 September. Their first major operation in Holland was the attack on Tilburg. Considerable difficulty was encountered in crossing the River Aa, but the town was assaulted by the Seaforth, Glasgow Highlanders and Cameronians with Scots Guards support. The battalion spent November taking part in operations to clear the countryside west of the River Maas. During December the Scots Guards were moved south in order to assist the Americans fighting the Germans in the Ardennes, but in the event they were not needed. In January 1945 they were moved to Geilenkirchen, but returned to Nijmegen in early February during a quiet period. Meanwhile the 2nd Battalion, Scots Guards had left Scotland and joined the Guards Armoured Division in January 1945.

In February 1945 the 3rd Scots Guards took part in operation Veritable, in support of the Argylls and HLI. On 8 February they advanced against Kranenberg and, three days later after much hard fighting, reached Cleve, having penetrated the Siegfried Line.

A week later the battalion motored south-east, meeting very heavy resistance: the accompanying infantry had difficulty in keeping up with the tanks which made the advance extremely dangerous. The Scots Guards were ordered back to Cleve, and then lifted the 5th Cameronians to Goch, south of the Reichswald Forest. From Goch they advanced eastwards, and were involved in more heavy fighting in support of the Glasgow Highlanders, Seaforth and Gordons. In early March, X Company supported the Lincolns attack on Winnekendonke held by a most determined German parachute battalion. The attack was carried out with utmost speed and bravery, and was entirely successful.

The 2nd Scots Guards and X Company were then brought up to the same area, but were not much involved until early March, when they attacked Bonninghardt, five miles from the Rhine. Enemy artillery and machine-gun fire was very heavy and the fighting intense. The village was captured, but when advancing east the companies had to fight a running battle for most of the following day. Preparations for the Rhine crossing began once the Germans had been cleared from the west side of the river. X Company was then disbanded and its members absorbed into the 2nd Battalion.

The bridge-head was established on the east bank of the Rhine during 24 March and the 3rd Scots Guards' tanks were ferried across on the following day. On 27 March the battalion, as part of 6 Guards Armoured Brigade, advanced east of Wesel and supported the American infantry's attack on Dorsen. The brigade group made good speed, often moving under cover of darkness, occupying the towns and villages on the route to Münster, which was reached on 2 April.

The 2nd Battalion, Scots Guards were meanwhile with the tank squadron of 2nd Welsh Guards further to the north. They crossed the Rhine at Rees and travelled north-east along the German Dutch border to Enschede, arriving there on 30 March. Despite the danger from enemy fire and the delay caused by blown bridges, the battalion made good progress mounted on the Welsh Guards' tanks, entering Germany at Nordhorn on 2 April. They frequently had to dismount to clear villages and woods of possible enemy resistance. The approach to Lengerich in particular was held in some strength by the enemy, and had to be cleared in detail by Right Flank.

After fighting through a German ambush, tanks of the 3rd Scots Guards with jocks of the HLI on the move along a cratered road near Uelzen, 14 April 1945.
IWM

HRH The Duke of Gloucester inspects a detachment of the 2nd Bn, Scots Guards at the laying up of the old Colours at Glasgow Cathedral, 1956. The detachment commander is Maj George Nickerson. RHQ

Meanwhile the 3rd Scots Guards had advanced to Osnabruck and were heading for the Minden on the River Weser. Rapid progress was made to Celle and the momentum of their advance overwhelmed much of the resistance, but blown bridges caused delays from time to time. On 14 April the Scots Guards and HLI were ambushed in the woods near Uelzen and there followed some bitter fighting over the next two days, during which the Scots Guards' tanks were particularly vulnerable to Germany infantry and artillery fire. A week later the 3rd Scots Guards were ordered to advance with the 5th Division to Lübeck on the Baltic coast, and thence to Lütjenburg in order to ensure a British presence to demarcate the border with the Russian occupied zone.

The 2nd Scots Guards spent the last weeks of the war advancing due north from Nienburg on the River Weser to Cuxhaven on the North Sea coast; their major battle was fought at Visselhovede held by German Marine troops. Although the town was captured, the Germans infiltrated back and launched a particularly effective counter-attack: but eventually the town was cleared by the Scots Guards and the advance continued. There was still considerable enemy resistance in various towns and villages, and artillery fire was often heavy. The battalion's casualties for the last month of fighting were 242.

* * * * *

When the war ended the 1st Battalion remained in Trieste for two years, and the 2nd in Germany, while the 3rd Battalion was disbanded in Germany in February 1946. In 1947 the 2nd Battalion took part in the revived ceremony of the King's Birthday Parade, and in the following year sailed for Malaya to assist in the Emergency.

There the Scots Guards were based near Kuala Lumpur, with companies detached to various parts of Selangor state. During the early part of the operations, the Scots Guards sent numerous patrols into the jungle, hunting for groups of bandits and dominating the area to prevent them from operating freely amongst the population. The battalion had a number of successes and in August 1949 the Scots Guards took part in a major sweep operation which lasted for two months. On 25 September F Company was involved in some close-quarter fighting when three terrorists were killed, but the same number of Guardsmen, including an officer, were killed. After two months in Singapore, the battalion returned to the Malayan jungle and operated first in Pehang State and then again in Selangor. Another major operation was conducted near Kejang and a Left Flank patrol killed and captured members of a notorious gang who had killed several members of the security forces. The 2nd Scots Guards remained in the country until April 1951.

The two battalions of the Scots Guards served in the United Kingdom, West Germany, Cyprus and Kenya during the 1950s and '60s. During the '70s and '80s they have visited Northern Ireland for emergency tours on numerous occasions, and served eighteen-month tours as roulement battalions.

In April 1982 the 2nd Scots Guards were mobilised to take part in the recovery of the Falkland Islands after the Argentinian invasion: with 5 Brigade they

Top:
1st Scots Guards en route for the Malay-Thai border, 1964. IWM

Above:
HM The Queen, Col-in-Chief, inspects a guard of the Scots Guards during the Queen's Birthday Parade. HQ London District

Far left:
'Shining Parade' for recruits of the Scots Guards. The familiar 'target indication' landscape and the regimental cap star seem to be the only permitted wall decorations in this austere barrack-room. IWM

The Regimental Colour of the 1st Scots Guards being uncased ready to be trooped during the Trooping of the Colour ceremony to mark the Sovereign's official birthday, June 1987. HQ London District

first trained at Sennybridge in Wales and then embarked on 12 May on the liner *Queen Elizabeth II*. After landing at San Carlos on the West coast of East Falkland Island on 2 June, the Scots Guards were re-embarked on *HMS Intrepid* and landed at Bluff Cove, fifteen miles from Port Stanley. There the battalion remained in dug-in positions for a week, and shot down at least two of the aircraft which attacked the support ships *Sir Galahad* and *Sir Tristram*.

The first phase of the British attack on the Port Stanley area was the seizing of Two Sisters and Mount Harriet; the last remaining major feature west of Port Stanley was Mount Tumbledown. On 13 June the 1st Battalion, 7th Gurkha Rifles on the left and 2nd Scots Guards on the right attacked Tumbledown in a silent night attack. A diversionary attack had been launched first, and G Company in the lead of the main attack crossed the start line at 9pm. By 10.30pm the Scots Guards were on the western part of Tumbledown, and the other two companies passed on to take further enemy positions. Argentinian small arms fire and artillery, however, was effective, and dealing with enemy positions well dispersed around the rocky landscape in the dark was difficult. The top of the mountain was cleared by Left Flank, but the leading section suffered three casualties from the eastern-most shoulder of the mountain, which had yet to be taken by Right Flank. The whole mountain was occupied by the two battalions by 8.15am, and the cease-fire took effect a short while later. The Scots Guards remained on the islands until late July, and were the last Task Force battalion to return to the United Kingdom.

Centre:
With fire support and airlift helicopters overhead, men of the 2nd Scots Guards dig in on East Falkland Island, June 1982. IWM

Left:
This photograph shows the 2nd Scots Guards advancing by Mount Harriet, 13 June 1982, during the final phase of the Falklands' campaign. IWM

Above:
A pikeman of Hepburn's Regt, 1633, later the Royal Scots. Foot soldiers of the time wore body armour. Modern watercolour by Douglas N. Anderson. RHQ

Left:
Officer of the Scots Regt of Foot Guards. Watercolour by Maj R. A. Wymer. RHQ

Below:
Sir Robert Douglas recapturing the colours of his regiment the Royal Regt of Foot, later the Royal Scots, at the battle of Steenkirk, July 1692.
Engraving from Cannon's Records

Far left:
A field officer of the Earl of Mar's Regt, later the Royal Scots Fusiliers, in 1685. Four years later the regiment went over to King William's cause, although Mar's son, the sixth earl, commanded the Jacobite army at Sheriffmuir in 1715. RHQ

Left:
Drummer, 25th Edinburgh Regt of 1707. Drummers wore yellow jackets during this period. Watercolour by R. Simkin. RHQ

Below:
The Royal Regt of Foot, later the Royal Scots, during the siege of Namur in 1695. Watercolour by R. Simkin. In the same siege the 25th Regt, later King's Own Scottish Borderers, lost 500 casualties when a mine was exploded under them by the defenders. RHQ

Above:
A troop of Scots Dragoons on patrol in the highlands in the late 17th century. Watercolour by Lionel Edwards. RHQ

The Cameronian Regt at the battle of Blenheim, Aug 1704. British infantry and cavalry fought with ferocious gallantry at this decisive battle. Watercolour by R. Simkin.

Defeat of Spanish troops and Jacobites at the battle of Glenshiel, 1719. Soldiers of the Royal North British

Dragoons and Royal North British Fusiliers round up prisoners. Watercolour by Lionel Edwards. RHQ

Top left:
A grenadier of the Royal North British Fusiliers, 1742.
Engraving from Cannon's Records

Top right:
Soldier of the 3rd Foot Guards showing the uniform worn in 1745. NAM

Right:
A private of the Black Watch in the uniform of 1745. It was in this year that the regiment fought with great bravery at the battle of Fontenoy. From a watercolour of 1932. Rusk family

Opposite page
Top left:
A grenadier of 1st or Royal Regt of Foot, the Royal Scots. A copy by C. C. P. Lawson of an oil painting by David Morier, who painted similar figures of every regiment of the army in 1751 for the King.
National Museums of Scotland

Top right:
A soldier of the 26th Cameronians of 1751. Watercolour by R. Simkin. RHQ

Below: RHQ
Numerous British regiments fought in the wars to protect the King's German possessions during the mid-17th century, and Minden in 1759 was the most decisive of their victories. Here the 25th Edinburgh Regt repels French cavalry. Watercolour by R. Simkin.

GR

Left:
A grenadier of the 42nd Royal Highlanders in 1751. A painting by C. C. P. Lawson after David Morier, whose original painting is in the Royal Collection.
National Museums of Scotland

The 25th Regt, later King's Own Scottish Borderers are shown in this oil painting by an unknown artist, during their tour of duty in Minorca in 1771. NAM

CHAPTER 4
THE ROYAL SCOTS
(The Royal Regiment)

HEPBURN'S REGIMENT

1633–78

In 1625, John Hepburn, of the family of Athelstaneford, raised a regiment of Scotsmen for foreign service. It formed part of the Green Brigade of Gustavus Adolphus, King of Sweden, and fought at the battle of Leipzig and elsewhere during the Thirty Years' War. A comment on the precarious life of a soldier in foreign service was given by Colonel Robert Monro who served with Hepburn's Regiment.

'Since then we are sure we cannot live long, and uncertaine if we live at all, being like leaves on trees, we are in the spot of every puffe that bloweth, and with the least guste, may be shaken from our life and nutriment; we travell, we study, we fight, that labour may pay us the losse of our ill expended time, while Death whiskes about us like Pegasean speede, flies unawares upon us, and with the kicke of his heele, or the dash of his foot, we are driven down to dust, and lie there.'

Eight years later he formed a new regiment from Scotsmen already in French service, and Charles I and the Scottish Privy Council authorised Hepburn to raise a further 1,200 recruits in Scotland. This regiment was known as Le Régiment d'Hebron, which later became the First Regiment of Foot, the Royal Scots. It has thus served without interruption since 1633.

During the ensuing forty years it took part in numerous campaigns in the French service. Hepburn was killed in 1636 and command passed subsequently to Lord James Douglas, later the Earl of Dumbarton. It was as the Earl of Dumbarton's Regiment that it finally returned to the service of the British Crown in 1678, having had two short periods of home service in 1662 and 1667, and in 1684 its name became The Royal Regiment of Foot. Successive colonels of the regiment were the Duke of Schomberg (1681), Sir Robert Douglas (1691), Lord George Hamilton (later the Earl of Orkney, 1692), and James St Clair (1737).

THE FIRST OR ROYAL REGIMENT OF FOOT

1678–1881

When it reached England in 1678, the regiment comprised twenty-one companies, in two battalions. The following year it moved to Ireland, and sixteen of the companies embarked in 1680 as reinforcements for the British garrison at Tangier. On two occasions during the year the regiment made determined attacks on the Moors, who were constantly threatening the town. In 1683 it was decided to withdraw the garrison and Dumbarton's regiment returned to England.

In 1685 five companies of the regiment were with the King's army in the West Country during the Duke of Monmouth's rebellion. At the battle of Sedgemoor they were on the right of the royal line, and successfully repulsed the rebels, albeit losing many casualties. The battle was decisive and the rebellion collapsed.

The Earl of Dumbarton, however, was a catholic and when, in late 1688, the army's loyalty to James was put to the test, the Royal Regiment stood by the King. On his departure, Dumbarton also left for exile in France, but his regiment remained in England. In 1689 William III, by now virtually accepted as King of England, but not yet of Scotland, required the regiment's service in Holland, but part of the regiment refused and set off without authority for Scotland. They were followed by a large number of troops loyal to King William who overpowered them on the way. The mutineers were treated leniently, and thereafter the Royal Regiment fully supported the new Monarchy.

Previous page:
Storming of the Taku Forts, 1860. The Royal Scots are among the eight regiments which carry this battle honour won during the second Chinese war.

The 1st Battalion of the regiment went to Holland in June 1689 to fight in the War of the League Augsburg, and took part in an engagement at Walcourt, causing severe casualties amongst the French. Joined by the 2nd Battalion, they remained in the Netherlands during 1690 and 1691. The regiment was present at the Siege of Mons, and in 1692 fought at Steenkirk. During the battle the French attacked first with vastly superior numbers and, with the Royal Regiment on the right of the line, the British troops held for a considerable time. Eventually they were ordered to retire, and during the retiral, the Colonel, Sir Robert Douglas, personally recaptured a regimental colour previously lost to the enemy; but in doing so he was mortally wounded.

In 1693 the regiment fought at Landen and successfully repulsed the French, although the whole allied army was eventually forced to withdraw against a more numerous enemy. Two years later the allies besieged the French fortress at Namur, and in July the regiment was amongst one of the assaulting parties which attacked the fortifications, and forced their way eventually into the town after several days' fighting. In 1697 the Royal Regiment returned to

England on the conclusion of the war and remained there until the War of the Spanish Succession broke out in 1702.

The regiment's first engagements were during the sieges of Venlo and Ruremond in 1702. Then in 1704 the Royal Regiment accompanied the Duke of Marlborough's march to the Danube. The Bavarians were holding positions on the Schellenberg Hill overlooking an important bridge on the river, and the two battalions of the regiments were part of a force sent to attack it. The task was particularly difficult and required much hand-to-hand fighting, but eventually the allies succeeded in dislodging the enemy. A few days later, during the battle of Blenheim, one battalion was part of the attacking force on the village on the right of the French line, while the other was brought up subsequently as a reinforcement. A large part of the French infantry was trapped in the village and faced successive attacks by the British infantry, while the rest of the French line was broken by cavalry. In due course the French surrendered.

The following year the regiment was back in the low countries and was involved in the engagement at Helixem, which resulted in a further defeat over the French. In 1706 the two armies faced each other at Ramillies. The 2nd Battalion was with the British right who attacked first, a large part of the allied army being held in reserve out of sight. The 1st Battalion joined later, clearing a village of the enemy as the French line collapsed. After the battle the French withdrew and the Royal Regiment spent many weeks occupying various fortified towns.

Two years later the two armies had manoeuv- opposing positions on the river Scheldt at Oudenarde. During the battle the regiment fought with the main part of the allied army and the French were forced to withdraw after several hours of fighting. During the summer the allies laid siege to Lille, where the regiment formed part of the covering force. In September the regiment provided a battalion to guard a supply train and, after an engagement at Wynendale, it successfully defeated a large French force attempting to capture the train. At the end of the year the regiment helped to storm and capture Ghent.

On 11 September 1709 the two armies faced each other again. The French were holding some high ground at Malplaquet, south of Mons, and a very fierce battle was fought after a heavy artillery bombardment early in the day. The two battalions of the regiment were launched into the attack upon the French right, who were entrenched by a wood. The positions were captured after some determined fighting and the battle went on all day until the French withdrew. It was the last major battle and for the final three years of the war the regiment took part in only one more engagement, the capture of Bouchain. It returned to England in 1713.

The regiment remained at home duty for many years, some of which were spent on detachment duties in Ireland, their purpose there being to maintain public order. In 1742 a battalion of the Royal Regiment was sent to Jamaica to reinforce a British expeditionary force against the Spanish islands in the Caribbean. The expedition was disastrous for the British: thousands of soldiers were lost through disease and there was little actual fighting. Few members of the regiment survived to return to England.

During the War of the Austrian Succession the 1st Battalion of the Royal Regiment was sent to the continent and arrived in the aftermath of the battle of Dettingen. In 1745 it was present when the allied army attacked the French at Fontenoy, near Tournai. The battalion was in the front line of the allied right.

'Both flanks of the advancing British infantry were exposed to a murderous enfilading fire. Nevertheless, the British marched forward unconcerned. All alike moved as if they were at review. The trenches a thousand yards ahead vomited fire, but the British made no reply. The ground was dotted with scarlet forms, dead and dying, but as each man fell the ranks closed up.' Thirty yards from the French, 'The order came to fire, and fire they did by battalions. The French withered under the hail of lead; and as the British marched on three hundred yards into the French camp

Private of the Grenadier Coy, 1st or Royal Regt of Foot in 1751. Watercolour by Douglas N. Anderson. RHQ

nothing could withstand them. The cavalry of the enemy hurled themselves on the British ranks only to stagger back broken to shivers.'

The British infantry thus fought with great determination and would have defeated the French had the allied troops not failed on other parts of the battlefield. Eventually the Royal Regiment withdrew with the remainder of the British troops, having lost a third of the battalion as casualties. Later in the year the battalion fought a successful engagement near Ghent, but when the French successfully captured the town the survivors were taken captive. Later they were released and repatriated.

The 2nd Battalion was sent from Ireland to England in July 1745, soon after Prince Charles Edward Stuart landed in Scotland to raise his rebellion. Two newly raised companies were already stationed in the highlands and on the march to Fort William they were overwhelmed by the Prince's army. The battalion was present at the battle of Falkirk when the highland army's charge broke the nerve of the royal infantry, who left the field in some confusion. In April 1746 the Royals fought at Culloden and repulsed the wild charge of the highland army. The rebels were quickly defeated and those who fled the battlefield were pursued relentlessly by the Duke of Cumberland's troops.

The 1st Battalion took part in a brief expedition to France in September which attacked Quiberon. Returning to the Continent in 1747 the battalion then fought the French at Hulst in Holland on two separate occasions. In the second engagement the Royal Regiment advanced steadily in face of the French and inflicted severe casualties. The enemy withdrew and the remainder of the British force moved back to their garrison in South Beveland. After that the regiment took no further active part.

In the 1751 reorganisation the Royal Regiment, as the senior regiment of the line, was given the title 'The 1st or Royal Regiment of Foot'. At the time the regiment was on home service, but in 1757 the 2nd Battalion was sent from Ireland to fight in North America against the French colonists. The following year it took part in the successful capture of Louisberg on the Missouri River.

In 1760 the battalion provided detachments to fight the Indians who were attacking the settlers, while the remainder were present at the surrender of Montreal by the French. In 1761 and 1762 companies were sent to the Caribbean, taking part in the capture of Dominica and the storming of Fort Moro in Cuba – which resulted in the surrender of Havana. Meanwhile, the two remaining companies assisted in expelling French soldiers from St John's, Newfoundland. In 1763 the regiment was re-united in England.

The Royal Regiment was on home service for some years but provided garrison troops for Gibraltar in 1768 and Minorca in 1771. In 1780 the 1st Battalion served with the expeditionary force to the Dutch Caribbean island of St Eustatia which quickly surrendered. The following year, however, it was garrisoning the island of St Christopher when it was captured by a large French force. The battalion reached England later in the year on exchange.

* * * * *

The regiment served in various home stations thereafter, and when the French revolutionary war broke out in 1793, it was divided between Jamaica and Ireland. The 2nd Battalion was then sent in the same year as part of the British garrison defending Toulon against the French republicans. There was continuous fighting for four months, and during the evacuation at the end of the year the battalion covered the withdrawal. The force then moved to Corsica and, having secured the beach-head at Gulf San Fiorenzo, the battalion was heavily involved in the fighting for the nearby forts. Members of the regiment assisted in manhandling artillery pieces up the cliffs before the attack on one of the redoubts, and were in the front line of the attacking party which successfully captured it. The French were thus ejected temporarily from the island, but in 1796 the British evacuated Corsica. After staging in Portugal, the battalion reached England in 1799.

Meanwhile, the 1st Battalion of the Royal Regiment had gone to the assistance of the French royalists in St Domingo. There they fought in several engagements against the republicans, but the battalion again lost many men through disease; when it returned to England in 1797 it was less than 200 strong. Moving to Ireland in the following year, its ranks were made up by substantial numbers of Irish militiamen.

In 1799 the 2nd Battalion was part of a force sent to liberate Holland from the French and, landing near Helder, the fort was quickly captured. During the latter part of this campaign, the Royal Regiment fought successfully at the battle of Egmont-op-Zee, but the whole force withdrew shortly afterwards and returned to England.

In March 1801 the 2nd Battalion with a force under Sir Ralph Abercromby reached Aboukir Bay, with the purpose of capturing Alexandria and Cairo from the French. The enemy strongly resisted the British landing and the battalion was involved in some hard fighting on the beach. During the British advance towards Alexandria the battalion was in the centre and when the French attacked the British positions in front of the town, the battalion held firm in face of heavy fire at close quarters. It then took part in the successful advance and occupation of Cairo, and returned to Alexandria, which fell to the British after several months of siege.

3rd Bn, the Royal Scots resist French cavalry at the battle of Corunna, 1809. Contemporary watercolour by D. Dighton. RHQ

The battalion was then withdrawn to Gibraltar and reached the West Indies in 1803, where the 1st Battalion had already been stationed for two years. The most notable expeditions in which the Royal Regiment served were those against the South American mainland and the French islands of St Lucia and Tobago, which were both captured. Again disease severely reduced the battalion's strength. At this time two further battalions had been raised at home, and later in 1812, the suffix 'Royal Scots' was officially added to the regiment's title.

In 1807 the 2nd Battalion was sent to India, having been made up to strength during a short stay in England. After an eventful voyage the battalion reached the sub-continent, and there it remained until 1816 on garrison duties. The 1st Battalion had embarked for service in Canada in 1812, where the war against the United States threatened to spread over the border. During the next two years detachments of the regiment were involved in fighting the Americans at Sodus, Fort Niagara, Longwood near Delaware and Fort Erie. The most notable engagement was near Niagara Falls in 1814, when an American attack was beaten off by the Royal Scots and other battalions.

Meanwhile the 3rd Battalion of the Royal Scots had joined the army in the Peninsula in 1808. The French successes against the Spanish necessitated the withdrawal of the British to Corunna, and in 1809 the battalion played a part in the battle covering the embarkation. The same battalion joined the Walcheren expedition to the Netherlands later in the year. It was present at the siege of Flushing, mounting a spirited attack there against the French and fought in various engagements before the expedition was abandoned.

Returning to Spain in 1810, the 3rd Battalion's first battle was at Busaco. At a crucial moment the Royal Scots reinforced Sir Thomas Picton's Division, and repulsed the French attack on the British right. In 1811 the battalion played a minor part in the battle of Fuentes d'Onor, and later were present at the siege and assault on Badajos. At Salamanca the Royal Scots were in the centre of the British advance and attack on the French squares; these were successfully broken but the battalion lost many casualties during the battle.

The 3rd Royal Scots were part of a force which attacked the French at Vitoria on 21 June 1813. They captured the ridge on the enemy's flank, and forced the French line to fight facing two directions. The French line broke and the battle proved a decisive victory for Wellington's army. The following month three companies of the Royal Scots mounted a successful attack on one of the forts comprising the San Sebastian defences. The light company of the Royal

Pte Joseph Prosser, 2nd Royal Scots, surrounded by his family. He won the VC for two acts of bravery while in the trenches at Sevastopol, summer 1855. RHQ

Scots fought under Colin Campbell (later Lord Clyde) in the forlorn hope.

'On arriving at the breach,' he wrote, 'I observed the lower parts thickly strewed with killed and wounded. There were a few individual officers and men spread on the face of the breach, but nothing more. They were cheering and gallantly opposing themselves to the close and destructive fire directed at them from the round tower and other defences of each flank of the breach, and to a profusion of hand-grenades, which were constantly rolling down . . . Observing two officers of the Royals who were exerting themselves to lead some of their men from under the line wall near to the breach, I went to assist their endeavours, and again went up the breach with them.'

The battalion's losses were 343 killed and wounded and 135 taken prisoner. The British attacked several more times and eventually were successful, albeit suffering further heavy casualties.

The battalion's final engagement in the Peninsular campaign was at the crossing of the Nive in April 1814. A strong attack was made by the French from the town against the Royal Scots' picquets, causing them to be withdrawn with many casualties. The battalion returned to England at the conclusion of the war.

The 4th Battalion of the Royal Scots meanwhile, had remained as a depot battalion, but in 1813 it saw active service with the expedition to Sweden. Then in 1814 it marched across Germany from Lubeck to Holland and took part in the siege of Bergen-op-Zoom. The Royal Scots entered the town under heavy fire from the French defenders. They were, however, trapped and after losing over a hundred casualties during the day's fighting, the remainder were taken prisoner. They were subsequently exchanged.

The following year the 3rd Royal Scots joined the Duke of Wellington's force, which embarked for the continent in response to Napoleon's renewed campaign. On 15 June they left Brussels and marched by night towards Quatre Bras. There they formed square with other battalions of the Sir Thomas Picton's Division and repulsed several attacks by enemy cavalry, successfully delaying the French advance. At the battle of Waterloo on 18 June, the Royal Scots were in the British centre near La Haye Sainte. A major attack by the French infantry was mounted, during which La Haye Sainte was captured and the British were forced to give ground. The British squares formed and held successive attacks and later in the day the Royal Scots advanced and re-took La Haye Sainte as the French retreated. The battalion remained in France as occupation troops until 1817, during which time the regiment was reduced to two battalions.

* * * * *

The 1st Battalion, the Royal Scots served in the United Kingdom for several years before moving to the West Indies in 1826 and remained as garrison troops in various stations for the next nine years. The 2nd Battalion was in India on active service from the start of the third Mahratta War. In 1817 it was sent with a relief force to Nagpore, where the East India Company's troops had been attacked. Defeating the Mahratta force, the Royal Scots and Company troops then besieged the town. After several attempts to storm the fortifications they finally captured it. At an engagement at Maheidpoor two companies captured some enemy guns. Four native forts were subsequently besieged and captured with the assistance of the Royal Scots, who then went in search of scattered groups of Mahratta troops as the campaign drew to a close.

In 1825 the 2nd Royal Scots served for a short time in the Burmese War which cost them many losses from disease. They assisted in the capture of Ava and the Burmese subsequently negotiated a peace. The battalion then returned to the United Kingdom, and served from 1836 to 1843 in Canada. There it was involved in internal security operations, notably at St Charles and St Eustache. The battalion spent the years 1844–52 in the West Indies.

In 1854 the 1st Battalion, Royal Scots embarked for service in the Crimean War. In September it was present at the battle of Alma, but was not much involved. Later in the month the battalion joined the line during the siege of Sevastopol. During the battle of Inkerman part of the battalion marched rapidly from their trenches to support those British positions facing a powerful Russian assault.

'The Russians charged our troops,' wrote Sir George Bell who served in the regiment, 'with incredible fury and determination. Ninety guns on the field were pouring death and destruction into our ranks; shells exploding fast and furious. Fresh Russian columns were now advancing, before whom our slender line gave way, rallied, charged, retired and returned to the charge against long odds . . . as the enemy gained ground, they drove their bayonets through our helpless wounded who lay at their mercy. It became a hand-to-hand sanguinary struggle, marked by daring deeds and desperate assaults. At every corner fresh foes met our exhausted troops . . . until at length the battalions of the Czar gave way.'

The following year the 2nd Battalion reached Balaclava and joined the 1st Battalion. In September 1855 the final assault was made on the Redan fortification at Sevastopol, with the 1st Battalion forming part of the attacking force. The attack failed but Savastopol was immediately abandoned by the Russians before a fresh attack could be launched.

The 1st Battalion returned to England after the Crimean War and in 1857 sailed for India, while the 2nd Battalion left for Hong Kong in 1858. There were several military expeditions into China for which the Royal Scots provided detachments. In 1860 the battalion embarked on the expedition to north China and, landing by way of the River Peiho, it assisted in the capture of Pehtang and the Taku forts.

Col Holcombe, commanding, surrounded by the officers of the 2nd Royal Scots in Aldershot, 1863. The establishment of the garrison towns at Aldershot and the Curragh was one of the measures of army reform after the Crimean War. RHQ

THE ROYAL SCOTS

1881–1913

The Royal Scots then served in various stations in the United Kingdom and abroad during the next forty years. Overseas stations included India and South Africa. In 1881 the regiment was renamed 'The Royal Scots (Lothian Regiment)', denoting its territorial area, and it adopted trews for the first time. The tartan was initially the government pattern, but in 1907 the regiment changed to hunting Stuart in recognition of its royal status.

In 1899 the 1st Battalion was sent to South Africa at the start of the Boer War. Its first action was in January 1900 at Loperberg, and during the next months the Royal Scots were continually on the march and involved in frequent engagements, the most notable being Labuschnages Nek and Dewetsdorp. The battalion led a force to reinforce Sir Redvers Buller in September, and at the battle of Paardeplatz the Royal Scots advanced with great speed over very difficult country to attack the Boers' line. A volunteer service company served with the battalion for many months and the regiment also provided a mounted infantry section.

In 1901 the Royal Scots were responsible for guarding a section of railway line for four months. In April a company attacked the enemy at Zwaggershoek, and in May a difficult battle was fought by another company at Bermondsey. Marching in search of the elusive Boer groups continued during the next few months and the Royal Scots fought several engagements, including a second encounter at Paardeplatz. During the last part of the war, the battalion covered many hundreds of miles hunting the enemy's dispersed commandoes and on escort duties. In common with most battalions, the hard conditions caused more casualties than enemy action.

Between the end of the Boer War and 1914 the two battalions served in various stations at home and in India.

Pipe-Maj G. S. Allan and pipers of the 1st Royal Scots at Bareilly, 1910. Allan was Pipe-Maj from 1907-30 successively of the two regular battalions. RHQ

THE ROYAL SCOTS

1914–38

The British Expeditionary Force included in its order of battle the 2nd Battalion, the Royal Scots in 8 Brigade. The battalion took up positions in the area of Mons on 23 August, but were ordered almost immediately to withdraw to Le Cateau.

'We held our ground at Le Cateau from an early hour in the morning till half-past four in the afternoon,' wrote Pte Thomas Hunter, 'a terrific fire pouring in on us all the time. The shells dropped on us like rain, many of them bursting in the trenches around. C Company of the Royal Scots got the worst of it there, the shrapnel causing terrible havoc among them. The transport we had was completely destroyed. It was stationed in a farmyard – many wagons containing ammunition and provisions – and when the Germans got the range of it, it was absolutely wiped out, many of the horses being killed and the wagons being blown into the air like matchwood.'

The battalion was then ordered to withdraw to the area of Cambrai in order to conform to the French. The Royal Scots held positions there for two days, and then retired south through St Quintin. The final point reached by the battalion at the end of the retreat was at Meaux on the River Marne.

The German advance had been held by the allies on the Marne by 5 September and the BEF was then ordered to advance. The battalion moved forward to Orly-sur-Marne and Braisne and assisted in ejecting the Germans from the towns. On 13 September the battalion reached the Aisne and, crossing the river, seized the high ground to the north near Vailly. Then for the following seventeen days the Royal Scots held the rapidly dug trenches under relentless artillery fire. When the BEF was redeployed to cover the north of the allied front, the 2nd Royal Scots moved to the area of the La Bassée Canal and Neuve Chapelle. The line then became relatively static and during the winter of 1914–15 the battalion was in the Kemmel sector.

The 1st Battalion reached France from India at the end of 1914, followed by the 8th Royal Scots, a Territorial battalion. In February 1915 the 9th Battalion (Highlanders) also joined the front line, and in April it reinforced part of the line at Ypres during the second battle, in which gas was first used. It remained in this sector for many months.

The 2nd Royal Scots march past Sir Horace Smith-Dorrien, Plymouth, 1913. The following year they served under him in II Corps at the retreat from Mons.
RHQ

In the summer of 1915 the 11th, 12th and 13th Battalions of the regiment reached the Western Front. In September these three battalions fought at Loos, each holding part of the line during massive German counter-attacks and suffering over one thousand casualties between them. Meanwhile the 2nd Royal Scots fought in a diversionary attack near Ypres which unfortunately achieved only limited success. The 8th Battalion, before being converted to a pioneer battalion, held trenches in the Festubert sector.

* * * * *

The 5th Battalion, Royal Scots (known as the Queen's Edinburgh Rifles), took part in the landings on Gallipoli on 25 April 1915. Moving forward in contact with the Turkish enemy over some three miles, the battalion had to dig in short of the objective, Achi Baba Nullah, in face of the most devastating enemy fire. There the line was consolidated and when the Turks attacked on 1 May, the battalion mounted a successful bayonet charge against them. For the remainder of the month the Royal Scots were in and out of the line, mounting local operations and facing enemy counter-attacks.

'We made our way by short pushes up a kind of gully,' wrote Pte Walter Meal, on one such encounter, 'with the continual whiz! whiz! of the bullets over our heads and the shriek of the shrapnel as the shells tore through the air . . . We witnessed the constant stream of wounded, who came struggling down the gully with bloodstained clothing and bandages round their heads, arms and legs. Then came the word for the Fifth to advance by companies. At every rush the enemy's machine guns would open on us, accompanied by a perfect hail of bullets from the riflemen. The struggling lines which kept arriving in the gorge were met by a cheer from their comrades already established there, and digging as hard as they could.'

In early June a limited advance was accomplished, with front-line trenches. In mid-June the Turks mounted a large-scale attack on the brigade front, which the battalion repelled with a highly successful counter-attack.

The 4th and 7th Battalions of the Royal Scots also reached Gallipoli in June 1915. The 7th was much understrength on account of losing 217 killed and 107 injured in the Quintinshill railway accident in the previous month – the worst in British railway history. The 4th Battalion manned the trenches at first, but in late June took part with the 7th Battalion in an attack on Gully Ravine and Achi Baba. Casualties were heavy but the Royal Scots gained some ground. The 5th Battalion, held in reserve on a different part of the line, was hurriedly called forward to attack in the same sector against almost impossible odds; they lost more than 300 casualties for little gain. The three battalions remained in the trenches at Suvla until the withdrawal from Gallipoli at the end of 1915.

The 1st Royal Scots had been withdrawn from the Western Front in December 1915 for service in Salonika on the Bulgarian front. For the first half of 1916 there was little fighting, but from positions in the Struma valley they assisted in capturing Bala and Zir from the enemy in September. The battalion spent the following two years in and out of the line, and during the allied summer offensive of 1918 mounted raids and diversionary attacks in the Vardar sector. In this theatre most of the battalion's casualties were caused by disease.

Jocks of the 5th Royal Scots cleaning rifles after coming out of the line at Suvla, Gallipoli. In one attack in June 1915 the battalion lost over 300 casualties. IWM

The 6th Battalion, the Royal Scots were sent to Egypt in early 1916. Their task was to defend British garrisons from the Senussi. These tribesmen were quickly defeated and the battalion did not long remain in the country before leaving for the Western Front. The 4th and 7th Battalions meanwhile had reached Egypt from Gallipoli with the 52nd Lowland Division, and were employed in the Suez Canal defences for several months. In August 1916 they fought against the Turks at the battle of Romani on the Sinai coast where the enemy was decisively defeated. The Royal Scots then advanced with the British and imperial troops along the coast into Palestine.

The two battalions did not take part in the first battle of Gaza, but in the second battle the 52nd Division acted as fire support troops. The two offensives failed to dislodge the enemy and the battalions remained in the area for most of 1917 in static positions. On 31 October the third battle of Gaza was fought which involved both battalions. The 4th Royal Scots were particularly successful in seizing the fortifications at El Arish. During the subsequent advance on Jerusalem, the Royal Scots fought hard for the capture of positions at Burkah and Brown Hill, and took and held part of the Nebi Samwil Ridge. Later in December 1917 the brigade mounted a surprise assault over the River Auja, which contributed to the final removal of the Turks from Palestine. In April 1918 the two battalions were hurriedly withdrawn from the Middle East for service on the Western Front.

In 1916 the 15th, 16th and 17th Battalions, the Royal Scots had been sent from the United Kingdom to France. In the same year the 5th Battalion arrived from Gallipoli and the 6th from Egypt; due to the depletion of their numbers these two battalions were amalgamated.

At the start of the British offensive on the Somme on 1 July, the 15th and 16th Battalions attacked in the La Boisselle area and captured three strong points. Between them they lost over 1,100 casualties, but held their ground until relieved on 3 July. On 14 July the 2nd, 11th and 12th Royal Scots attacked in the Longueval sector. The German forward positions were captured, but in the village itself the enemy put up a fierce resistance and the Royal Scots could not keep possession of their gains.

9th (Highlanders) Bn, Royal Scots marching in wet weather along the Amiens-Albert road, Sept 1916.
IWM

Subsequently, the 2nd Royal Scots attacked south of Guillemont, while to the north, the 9th (Highlanders), 15th and 16th Battalions fought for several days in the front line at High Wood, and the 8th Battalion was working in the same area behind the line on pioneer tasks. Meanwhile the 13th Royal Scots launched an attack on Martinpuich and extended the line forwards despite numerous casualties. During the autumn all eight battalions manned the front line from time to time, the heaviest fighting

12th Royal Scots on a daylight reconnaissance patrol at Meteren, 23 June 1918. This part of the Ypres sector had been lost to the Germans during their spring offensive, March 1918. IWM

being at the Butte de Warlencourt and at Serre on the River Ancre. The offensive, whilst not in itself greatly effective, resulted in the German withdrawal to the newly established Hindenburg Line during the spring of 1917.

On 9 April 1917 the battle of Arras began and during the next six days the British front was pushed forward some distance. The eight battalions were all involved in the fighting, taking most of their objectives. Later in the month the Germans launched a series of determined counter-attacks and four of the battalions, the 9th, 13th, 15th and 16th, sustained very heavy casualties.

In the next offensive in August 1917 the 9th and 13th Battalions were initially involved in the attacks in the Ypres area on Passchendaele. Little ground was gained, and other battalions of the regiment also met with little success in September and October in the same sector. Captain Henry Reynolds won the VC during this battle.

'On 20 September,' read the citation, 'Captain Reynolds' company was approaching its final objective when it suffered heavy casualties from enemy machine guns and from an enemy pill-box. Captain Reynolds organized his men, who had become scattered. Then alone he made for the pill-box, scrambling from shell-hole to shell-hole; all the time he was under heavy machine-gun fire . . . Reynolds then crawled right to the entrance and forced a phosphorous grenade inside, setting fire to the post. Three enemy died and the remaining eight surrendered with two machine guns. Later, though wounded, Captain Reynolds continued to lead his company against another objective, which he captured with seventy prisoners and two more machine guns.'

Two battalions were present at the battle of Cambrai on 20 November, the 8th and 9th Royal Scots. The latter captured much ground at Fontaine.

When the Germans launched their final offensive against the British line in March 1918, all the Royal Scots' battalions were heavily involved over a long period. The 9th Battalion, which held its positions successfully, was nevertheless almost entirely wiped out, and the 11th, 12th and 13th Royal Scots held their trenches under the most determined German attacks for several days. In April the 15th and 16th Battalions suffered severe casualties on the withdrawal to Bailleul and subsequently had to be disbanded. The 12th Royal Scots held their line for six days in the area of Kemmel.

During the spring of 1918 the 4th and 7th Battalions reached France, but they were not immediately involved in the fighting. When the allied offensive was launched in the summer in the French sector, the 8th, 9th and 13th Royal Scots were rapidly moved to support the advance from the Marne. The 13th Battalion launched a surprise raid in early August as a diversion, while the 9th Royal Scots suffered very heavily yet successfully forced the enemy to retreat after launching a frontal assault on them. On 8 August the renewed British offensive began and the 5th/6th Battalion took part in the attack against the

Expecting gas, a Lewis gun team of the 12th Royal Scots in action, Ypres sector, during an attack, 25 June 1918. IWM

Amiens sector. The 11th and 12th Royal Scots successfully pushed the enemy off Hoegenacker Ridge, and soon all along the front the Germans began a full-scale retreat to the Hindenburg Line.

By late August the 2nd, 4th, 5th/6th and 7th Royal Scots were all advancing steadily. The 2nd Battalion met the most resistance in the Ancre valley, and were counter-attacked later while holding positions on the Somme. The 4th and 7th Battalions assaulted German positions near the Hindenburg Line at Quéant, and captured them successfully. Other battalions of the regiment held various sectors and were kept fully occupied as mounting pressure was placed on the enemy all along the line.

The final allied offensive was launched in late September. The 5th/6th Royal Scots attacked the Hindenburg Line by the St Quentin Canal. They met the fiercest resistance in the village of Sequehart, which changed hands on 3 October several times, but was finally held. The 4th Battalion, however, met

Troops of occupation. A picquet of the 5th/6th Royal Scots near Solingen, Germany, 15 April 1919. IWM

little resistance on the Canal du Nord sector and advanced swiftly. Likewise, the 11th and 12th Royal Scots advanced from Ypres with ease, although the 17th Battalion found its advance more strongly resisted in the same sector.

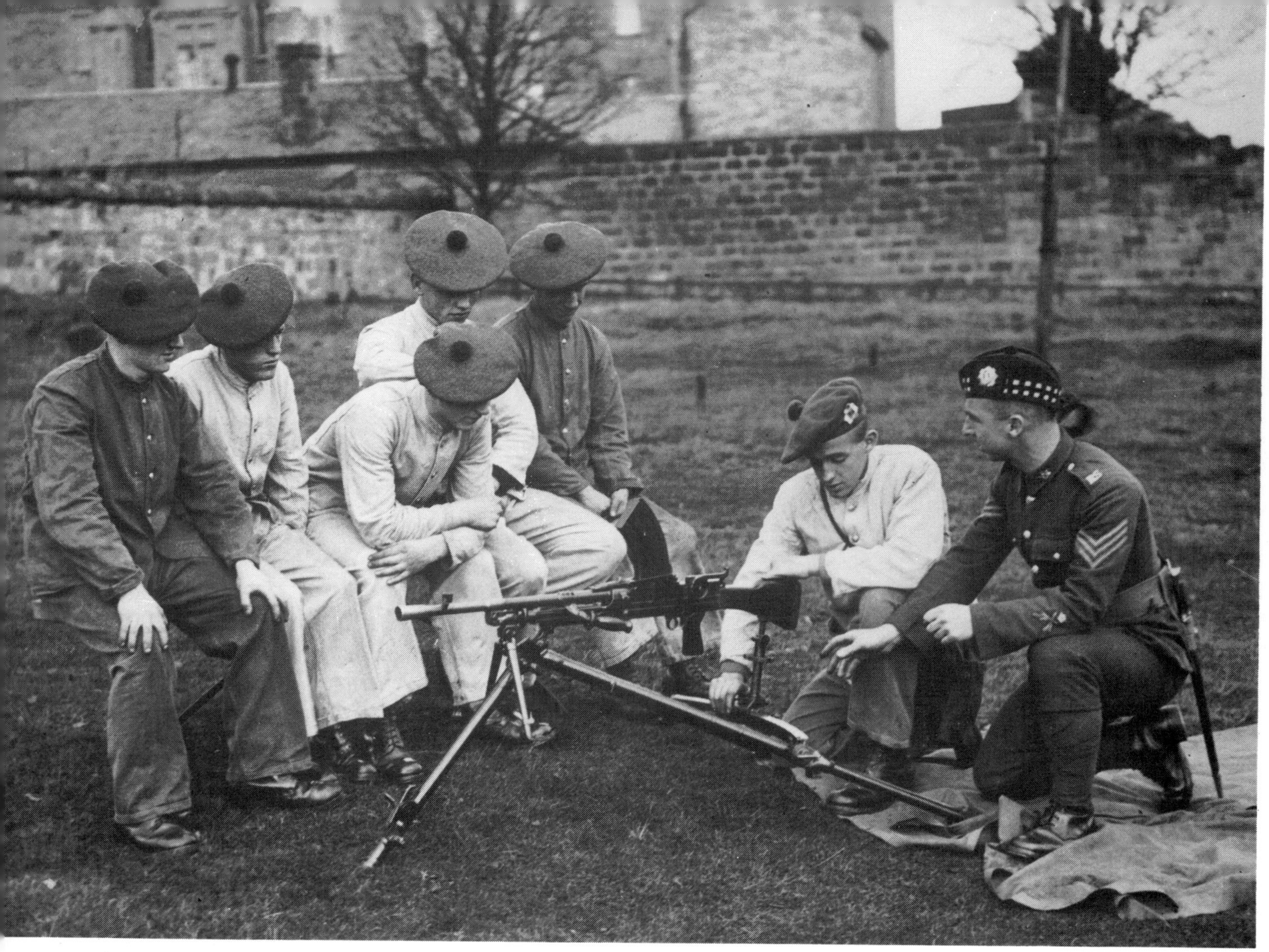

The soldier behind the Bren gun is shown how to calibrate it for fixed-line shooting by an instructor at the Royal Scots Regtl Depot, c1930. RHQ

1st Royal Scots gymnastic display at Shorncliffe, 1934. RHQ

By mid-October the Germans had withdrawn along most of the front. The 11th and 12th Battalions, however, were held up near Courtrai and on the River Lys, and the 2nd had many casualties fighting near Cambrai. The 5th/6th Royal Scots had to force strongly held German positions on the Sambre Canal and Hoogmolen. But the allied advance continued and on 11 November the armistice came into effect.

* * * * *

At the end of the war the 1st Battalion Royal Scots returned to Scotland temporarily, re-formed and spent three years stationed in Rangoon. There followed tours in India and Aden. It then spent the period 1926 to 1937 at various home stations, followed in 1938 by internal security operations in Palestine, mainly against Arab guerrillas.

Meanwhile the 2nd Battalion had spent four years in Ireland leading up to the time of the formation of the Irish Free State. The Royal Scots were much involved in security duties, there being no reduction in tension and crime. In 1926 the battalion moved to Moascar on the Suez Canal, followed by tours of duty in China and India. Stationed in Quetta and then Lahore, the Royal Scots were often involved in assisting the civil authorities. In 1938 the 2nd Battalion moved to Hong Kong as garrison troops.

THE ROYAL SCOTS

1939 to the present

On the outbreak of war in 1939 the 1st Battalion mobilised and went to France on 30 September with the British Expeditionary Force. Reaching the Belgian border, the Royal Scots took up positions near Lecelles on the right of the British line. In the ensuing weeks the battalion improved its defences and awaited events, but in December it took over part of the Maginot Line for a month, before returning to Lecelles. When Germany invaded Belgium on 10 May 1940 the Royal Scots were moved by road to Wavre, south of Brussels, covering the River Dyle. Their positions were bombed and shelled and, as the Germans advanced rapidly, the battalion was ordered to withdraw to the river Lasne on 16 May.

During the next ten days the 1st Royal Scots withdrew through the chaos of Belgium, frequently in contact with the enemy, until they reached the Escaut Canal. In their new position near Calonne they were attacked in strength by the Germans, but then quickly launched a counter-attack. The Germans crossed the Escaut but were successfully held up for a time by the battalion, who had by now lost some 200 casualties. On 23 May the battalion was ordered to withdraw to the Lys, as the Germans were threatening to cut off the British from the south and west.

At first held in brigade reserve, the Royal Scots then made contact with the enemy crossing the La Bassée Canal. Their last orders were to hold a battalion position at La Paradis, where on 27 May the Germans launched a determined attack supported by armour. There was close-quarter fighting through the village as the Royal Scots resisted against overwhelming numbers. Le Paradis was eventually captured, and those Royal Scots who had remained were taken prisoner. Only a few reached the evacuation beach at Dunkirk.

The 7th/9th Battalion, Royal Scots as part of the 52nd Lowland Division, moved from the United Kingdom to France in June 1940 in the vain hope of holding a second front. Landing at St Malo on 12 June, the Royal Scots were sent to the area of Le Mans. Three days later, with the division already under attack, they were ordered to withdraw and re-embark at Cherbourg. This was achieved without casualties and the battalion returned to England.

* * * * *

In the meantime the 2nd Battalion, Royal Scots were guarding the mainland border of the New Territories in Hong Kong. At first there had been fear of Chinese attack across the border, but as the Japanese forces consolidated their territorial gains in China, there grew the likelihood of a Japanese invasion of Hong Kong. Defensive positions along the mountainous border were improved in earnest over a period of months, although Britain was not actually at war with either the Chinese or Japanese, and border patrols of the Royal Scots were sent out by night from November 1941.

On 8 December 1941 war was declared, and the following night Japanese patrols probed the British defensive line. They were engaged by the Royal Scots immediately and artillery fire was called down. The Shing Mun redoubt, key to the whole defensive line, was only held by one platoon owing to the scarcity of troops to cover the border. It was captured by the Japanese after a desperate resistance by the Royal Scots. Other positions were held but the battalion was withdrawn over very difficult country the following day to new defences. Japanese troops continued to advance, and the Royal Scots and the two other battalions defended the New Territories as long as possible. They fought off many attacks during the next few days, but suffered numerous casualties before the evacuation to Hong Kong island was ordered.

The 2nd Royal Scots were then positioned to the west of the island covering the approach from Kowloon. The Japanese, however, unexpectedly invaded the eastern part of the island by night after shelling and bombing it heavily. Here the island was only lightly guarded and the enemy quickly advanced towards the centre. The Royal Scots moved rapidly to cover the mountain gap in the centre, the possession of which would enable the Japanese to divide the island in two. The Japs reached it first and, despite numerous attempts by the Royal Scots to dislodge them, remained in command of the gap. The battalion, severely depleted, took up positions on Mount Nicholson in order to protect as best it could the western half of Hong Kong island. For a week the Royal Scots fought hard but, after withdrawing westwards, they were firmly ordered to resist to the end. There was a lull on Christmas Eve as the Japanese prepared for their final assault. A Company comprised now only fourteen men, and D Company was half that number. Early on Christmas Day a Japanese attack on the Royal Scots' positions was repulsed: during a so-called two-hour ceasefire the enemy used the time to move troops closer, and continued to mortar, shell and bomb the British positions. This went on for five hours. C Company was withdrawn to a police station under fire, and no sooner had they arrived when it was attacked with incendiary bombs and destroyed. The other companies remained under fire in their positions all afternoon, preparing to fight until over-run in a final attack. It was therefore with some surprise and anguish that the remaining members of the Royal Scots received the order to surrender. The battalion's survivors were taken into captivity, and only a few lived through the ordeal of the next four years.

* * * * *

After Dunkirk the 1st Battalion, Royal Scots was re-formed in England during 1940 and sailed for the east in April 1942. It was stationed at Poona in India for the remainder of the year and trained hard for jungle operations. Burma had been successfully invaded by the Japanese in 1942, but in March 1943 the battalion crossed the border with 6 Brigade in the first Arakan campaign.

The first encounter with the enemy was in a brigade attack against the heavily defended positions near Donbaik. The Japanese could not be dislodged, despite continuous harassing attacks by companies of the Royal Scots and other battalions. The brigade was then withdrawn north to defend the border with India which was under threat. The battalion reached a position near Indin on 26 March and B and C Companies were immediately rushed to the town to prevent the Japanese reaching it and cutting the route. The enemy, however, were rapidly advancing down the hills in greatly superior numbers, and overwhelmed a bridge guard. As the remaining companies moved up during the night, there was a running battle all around the battalion area, and casualties were very high. The other battalions in the brigade concentrated in the Royal Scots' area and, under cover of some excellent shooting by the Royal Artillery, what was left of the brigade fought their way out. The decision to evacuate was then taken, and the 1st Royal Scots, whose effective strength had been reduced by half, acted as rear protection battalion. The battalion reached India overland in late May 1943.

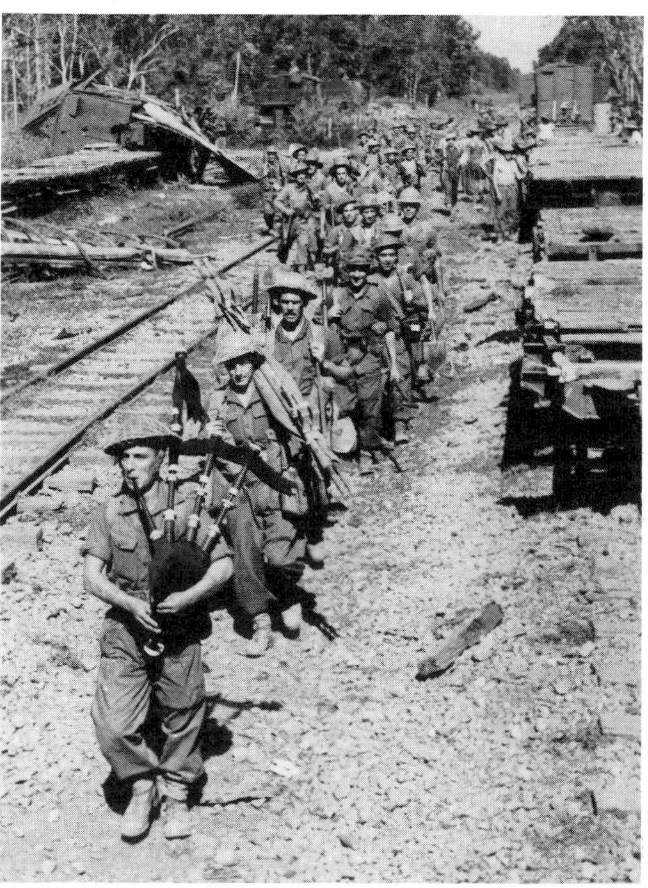

In March 1944 the Japanese mounted a major offensive eastwards across the Chindwin River into British India, their immediate objectives being Imphal and Kohima. The British 2nd Division was moved to the area of Kohima, which by the first week of April was almost cut off by the Japanese. The 1st Royal Scots took up positions in the hills twelve miles from the town. Their task was to mount fighting patrols to divert the enemy, and for several days there were many hard-fought encounters. The Royal Scots then moved through the jungle and mountains to clear the Japanese from the hills to the west. The enemy resisted strongly and the close-quarter fighting was often intense. The battalion, however, defended its bases in the hills successfully, and gradually succeeded in clearing the Japanese from theirs. Kohima had in the meantime been saved in one of the most desperate battles of the war.

The Royal Scots were then moved southwards to capture positions overlooking the road used by the Japanese as their escape route. The battalion was involved in much further fighting, before supporting a brigade attack which cleared the enemy from the area. From positions in the jungle and hills, the Royal Scots then spent many weeks systematically patrolling and fighting parties of Japanese left behind west of the Chindwin.

In early 1945 the 1st Royal Scots were moved a hundred miles eastwards to the area of Shwebo on the Mandalay railway. The town was held by the Japanese and the Royal Scots had to occupy outlying positions first. This enabled them to mount an attack on Shwebo itself which was successfully taken. Advancing through the flat Irrawaddy plains, the battalion then attacked a strong position at Ywathitgyi on the river on 31 January. Only part of the town was taken before nightfall. During the following day the difficult task of clearing the enemy was resumed and, although under heavy Japanese artillery fire, it was eventually accomplished.

The British and colonial troops' advance on Mandalay followed. For the next five weeks patrols of the Royal Scots fought several engagements, and captured two important objectives as they progressed southwards. In late March Mandalay fell. The Royal

A piper leads the 1st Royal Scots into Pinwe, Burma, St Andrew's Day 1944. IWM

Soldiers of the 1st Royal Scots prepare for the battalion attack on Ywathitgyi on the Mandalay railway, 31 Jan 1945. IWM

Scots were withdrawn by air to India for special training for the planned assault on Rangoon; but this city was occupied more easily than expected and the battalion remained in India.

* * * * *

In May 1942 the 12th Battalion, the Royal Scots had been re-formed as the 2nd Battalion, in place of the original 2nd Battalion lost at Hong Kong. In April 1943 the 2nd Royal Scots were moved to Gibraltar as garrison troops, but in July 1944 they reached Naples as reinforcements for the allied army fighting in Italy. As part of 66 Brigade the battalion joined the front on the River Arno. In late August probing attacks were mounted by the Royal Scots across the river. The Germans, however, immediately launched counter-attacks on the British positions which were defended successfully, but the line remained static for a time.

The Royal Scots then moved by way of Florence to positions close to the heavily defended Gothic Line. There they conducted patrols against the German positions prior to the brigade advance. Fierce fighting took place amongst the wooded hills and continued for a day-and-a-half before the Germans were forced off their position. The Royal Scots then launched a night attack on Pratone, but were held up by determined German resistance. With US troops' assistance, the Gothic Line was successfully penetrated, involving a further period of intensive close-quarter combat over the rugged mountainous country. There was a major German position on Monte Paganino, and the Royal Scots spent many hours during 19 September attempting to fight their way up the mountain side; they finally succeeded in ejecting the Germans with a dawn attack the following day.

For three weeks the 2nd Royal Scots advanced slowly northwards, with forward patrols being sent out to detect enemy strongholds. There were several major engagements, including those at Presiola and Monte Gamberaldi. In November the Royal Scots took over positions at Monte Grande and Castellaro, where they were subject to the most determined German counter-attacks and artillery bombardment. They remained in the area north of Florence until January 1945, patrolling and harassing the enemy who were secure in their positions in the depth of winter. The 2nd Royal Scots were then withdrawn with their division, and moved by sea to Palestine at the end of the month.

* * * * *

Meanwhile the 8th Battalion, Royal Scots had

The two photographs show the 8th Royal Scots moving along a road near Tilly-sur-Seul, and attacking across a cornfield, 28 June 1944. IWM

Opposite:
A section of the 8th Royal Scots move forward to block German counter-attacks near Liesel, Holland, 2 Nov 1944. IWM

Royal Scots line a ditch at Moostdijk, 6 Nov 1944. IWM

landed with the 15th Scottish Division on the Normandy coast on 16 June 1944, and moved immediately to positions near Caen. This town was heavily defended, and the Germans mounted the most furious counter-attacks shortly afterwards on the British line. The Royal Scots went into action to the west of the town during operation Epsom on 26 June and captured their objectives. During this action and the subsequent enemy artillery bombardment their casualties were very heavy.

In the southwards advance towards the River Odon, through the so-called 'Scottish Corridor', the battalion had to face numerous well-concealed enemy positions supported by armour. At Haut du Bosq the battalion was attacked and nearly overwhelmed by a superior number of Germans.

D Company, under Major Cadzow, had been ordered to advance towards a railway line and occupy an orchard and group of houses. On reaching these positions, the enemy shelled and rocketed the area intensively, and attacked it with tanks. Withdrawing for a while, D Company counter-attacked the orchard, supported by tanks and anti-tank weapons. The enemy shellfire continued and the company by now was weak in numbers. Reinforcements were sent up, and eventually D Company was relieved by the Royal Scots Fusiliers. Major Cadzow received the MC for his determination and leadership.

In mid-July the battalion was in action on the River Odon and it successfully captured Gavrus and Bougy, also clearing part of the woods alongside the river. The enemy, however, still occupied numerous positions, seriously delaying the British by counter-attacks and ambushes.

On 23 July the Royal Scots moved to Caumont and a week later a divisional attack was mounted to the south of the town. During German counter-attacks the battalion held their positions against infantry and tank thrusts, and advanced again when the enemy withdrew. The bocage countryside greatly favoured the German mobile defence and progress was slow, and at Estry the division was held up by very strongly defended enemy posts. The 8th Royal Scots were the spearhead battalion ahead of the division, and they were ordered to launch a battalion attack on the town, but the Germans rapidly withdrew. The battalion was then pulled back from the

line for three weeks in order to be brought up to strength for future operations.

In late August the 8th Royal Scots crossed the Seine, and within a few days reached the Belgian border. There was little resistance until the allies had reached well east of Antwerp, and the first defensive line taken up by the battalion was on the Meuse-Escaut Canal. On 14 September the battalion was ordered to capture the bridge at Aart, which was achieved but not without some difficulty. The Germans counter-attacked in great strength both during the night and on the following day, when some of the battalion positions were captured. The bridge-head over the canal, however, was held by the Royal Scots until further reinforcements reached the area, and massive artillery fire eventually defeated the enemy. A week later the battalion reached Eindhoven and fought in the region of Best and Fratershoef for several days.

The 7th/9th Battalion, the Royal Scots reached Belgium from England in October 1944 with the 52nd Lowland Division. The task was the seizure of the Scheldt estuary, thus enabling the port of Antwerp to be opened for allied resupply. The battalion's first objective was to clear the heavily defended town of Flushing on Walcheren island, in the wake of the seaborne landings on 1 November. The advance on the town was met with strong resistance, but the most formidable task facing the Royal Scots was the assault on the headquarters at the Hotel Britannia guarded by more than 600 Germans. After fierce fighting at close quarters, the hotel was captured by the battalion. Then for several days the Royal Scots patrolled the town, dealing with further enemy posts and bringing in prisoners. On 6 November a company entered Middelburg and accepted the surrender of over 2,000 Germans – achieved by a mixture of bluff and bravado on behalf of the Company commander.

The 8th Battalion had meanwhile reached Tilburg in Holland and moved forward to meet German counter-attacks in the area of Liesel. In early December the battalion took part in the capture of Blerick with armoured support, and cleared the town of remaining Germans. For the ensuing two months the Royal Scots spent much time guarding areas on the west bank of the river Maas, and awaiting the drive to the Rhine through the Siegfried Line defences.

In mid-February 1945 the 8th Royal Scots moved to the recently captured German town of Cleve and advanced to Goch. The town was believed to be only lightly held by the enemy, but when A Company, led by Major McQueen, bridged an anti-tank ditch, they were subjected to heavy fire for several hours in an exposed position. B and C Companies attempted to pass over the ditch but they, too, were held up. In the evening D Company went into the town, despite heavy resistance, and during the night the battle raged amongst the houses. At dawn C Company, under Major MacIntyre, also entered the town and the two companies began clearing the northern part of the town, taking some 200 prisoners. During the morning the companies were counter-attacked by the Germans, but they held while British troops entered other parts of the town. Major McQueen won the DSO and Major Fife of D Company the MC for their leadership during the battle. The next major objective was the high ground overlooking Schloss Kalbeck, strongly defended and set in a wooded area. The Royal Scots accomplished this, despite very heavy enemy mortar and artillery fire.

Meanwhile the 7th/9th Battalion, Royal Scots had also spent a period guarding the west bank of the River Maas. In late December they withdrew from the line in order to train with armoured troops. They then took up positions on the front near Gilrath, prior to the forthcoming attack on the Roer salient. The enemy launched numerous attacks on the British line and the Royal Scots conducted frequent patrol operations. In mid-January operation 'Blackcock' was mounted and the battalion advanced steadily, defeating numerous German holding positions before attacking the town of Heinsberg with the 4th KOSB. This was a formidable task, and the Germans maintained heavy and accurate artillery bombardment as the two battalions approached. Clearing the streets and houses was accomplished rapidly before the Germans could retaliate. The Royal Scots were next delayed at Kasteel Blijenbeek, a mediaeval fort which was held in great strength by Germans. The enemy brought down heavy artillery fire on the battalion's approach routes, and the area had to be extensively patrolled. Eventually the fortress was bombed and rocketed from the air.

In early March the two battalions of the Royal Scots prepared for the Rhine crossing. The 7th/9th took up positions guarding the west bank near Wesel, while the 8th Battalion trained for the assault which took place on 23/24 March. The battalion met with determined resistance from ground troops on landing, as well as considerable artillery fire. During the day the Royal Scots cleared a number of positions as the British troops consolidated on the east bank. The following day they advanced through wooded country prior to assaulting Heisterhof on the River Issel. This town was captured, but the companies holding it faced constant counter-attacks which, in view of their shortage of ammunition, put the Royal Scots in a dangerous position. They were subsequently relieved.

The 7th/9th Royal Scots crossed the Rhine in the wake of forward formations. In early April 1945 they had reached the area of Ibbenburen, where intense

3ins Mortar detachment practise firing, Korea 1953. The 1st Royal Scots manned the Armistice Line for several months. RHQ

This photograph shows a patrol of the 1st Royal Scots in the Radfan mountains, Aden, 1964. RHQ

enemy resistance had held up the British advance on Osnabruck. The defile in the wooded Teutoburger hills was cleared of remaining German troops in a brigade operation. The attack on Barnstorf, led by the machine-gun carrier platoon, was the battalion's next major battle. Advancing across the north German plain, the town of Soltau also had to be cleared. There, working with armoured troops of 7th Armoured Division the 7th/9th Royal Scots, under severe artillery fire, mounted assaults from two flanks on the Germans.

The town was captured but the enemy still held strong positions in the vicinity and had to be ejected. In the advance on Bremen, the battalion captured several villages and in the port itself the Royal Scots still met resistance before it eventually came under full British control.

The 8th Battalion had meanwhile moved from the Rhine bridgehead towards Hanover and the River Elbe at Artlenburg. In the assault crossing of the Elbe on 29 April the battalion was under heavy enemy artillery fire in what proved a most difficult operation. Nevertheless the battalion seized its objectives north of the river and set about clearing the woods and outskirts of Hamburg, before the final surrender of the German forces.

* * * * *

After the Second World War the 7th/9th and 8th Battalions, the Royal Scots, remained for a short time as occupation troops. In the meantime the 1st Battalion was still serving in India, and the 2nd in Palestine where internal security duties had to be undertaken in various towns during the period leading to formation of the State of Israel. Subsequent battalion tours were spent in Jordan and Malta, followed by duty in Trieste. The 1st Battalion, Royal Scots, had moved temporarily to Singapore and Borneo as garrison troops in 1946, but returned to India in early 1947. They were in Karachi during the transfer of rule to the new state of Pakistan, and returned to Scotland at the end of the year. The two battalions were amalgamated in February 1949 as the 1st Battalion.

In 1953 the battalion moved from Berlin to Korea during the final stages of the Korean War, but by the time it reached the front, hostilities had ceased. After some months manning the armistice line, the 1st Royal Scots embarked for service in the Canal Zone in Egypt during the final months of British occupation. On the withdrawal from Egypt the battalion was sent to Cyprus at the start of the Eoka troubles. There the Royal Scots were responsible for the protection of a large area of countryside. Constant searching and patrolling against terrorist groups and arms smugglers kept the battalion fully occupied during its tour. The 1st Royal Scots also took part in the temporary occupation of the Suez Canal after the Anglo-French invasion of 1956. This was an unpleasant and thankless task, and there were several incidents before the battalion was withdrawn. After a short period in Scotland the 1st Royal Scots returned to Berlin in 1958.

The Royal Scots served in Aden, Cyprus, West

Ken Howard's watercolour depicts soldiers of the 1st Royal Scots on crowd-control duties in Belfast in the early 1970s. RHQ

A mechanised battalion on exercise in West Germany, 1979. Members of the 1st Royal Scots double forward under machine-gun support from the armoured personnel carriers, suitably named Corunna and Kohima. RHQ

Germany and the United Kingdom during the 1960s and 70s. They were one of the first battalions called in to assist the civil authorities in Northern Ireland. During the past eighteen years they have returned there on many occasions. In 1983 the regiment celebrated the 350th anniversary of its formation. Among the regimental festivities was a parade held adjacent to Holyroodhouse, which was attended by HM The Queen and HRH the Colonel-in-Chief Princess Anne, the Princess Royal.

Opposite page:
21st Royal North British Fusiliers hold the Barrier at the battle of Inkerman, Nov 1854. Oil painting by Marjory Wetherstone. RHQ

CHAPTER 5

THE ROYAL HIGHLAND FUSILIERS

(Princess Margaret's Own Glasgow and Ayrshire Regiment)

The infantry amalgamations of 1958–9 included that between the Royal Scots Fusiliers with the Highland Light Infantry (City of Glasgow Regiment). The Royal Scots Fusiliers, long associated with the county of Ayrshire, already had a second battalion in 1881, so had been unaffected by the amalgamations of that year. The HLI, however, had been formed in 1881 from two former regiments, the 71st and 74th Regiments, the former having been a light infantry regiment since the Peninsular War. The HLI had had strong connections with Glasgow for many years.

PART I
THE ROYAL SCOTS FUSILIERS

21ST REGIMENT
(Royal Scots Fusiliers)
1678–1881

The dangerous year of 1678 saw the final recall of the Earl of Dumbarton's Regiment (later the Royal Scots) from foreign service, and the commissioning by the convention of Estates of Charles, fifth Earl of Mar, to raise a new regiment of foot in Scotland. Their purpose was to root out and destroy the various groups of armed Covenanters who were posing a growing threat to the central authority of church and state.

Mar was an experienced commander. By all accounts the regiment, from which descended the Royal Scots Fusiliers, was recruited swiftly, drawing its recruits from a wide area. Although the royal colour was scarlet, the regiment was initially dressed in local grey cloth (like a number of hastily formed regiments) – hence its soubriquet the 'Earl of Mar's grey-breeks'. The Lieutenant Colonel was William Ramsay, third Earl of Dalhousie. Early in the history of the regiment the soldiers had been supplied with flintlock 'fusils' rather than matchlocks. These weapons were easier to handle and faster to fire.

After the success of the Covenanters at Drumclog on 1 June 1679, and their defeat by the Duke of Monmouth's Scots army at Bothwell Brig on 22 June at which Mar's regiment fought, the 'killing times' began in earnest. To be a Covenanter was interpreted by the royalists as treasonable: the Covenanters believed that the monarchy was the devil incarnate. Each side grew more extreme in attitude.

The task of the Earl of Mar's regiment was to garrison various towns with detached companies, and to assist the troops of dragoons to seek out and destroy the Covenanters' 'conventicles' – their open-air gatherings for worship.

In September 1688, the Scots Army had been ordered by James to march to England. The regiment – known temporarily as Buchan's after the Earl of Mar's successor, Col Thomas Buchan – stood for King William at the time of the 'Glorious Revolution'. The new King appointed Francis O'Farrell in command, and the regiment was sent to France to fight in the War of the League of Augsburg in early 1689.

The first action was at Steenkirk in August 1692. The regiment was in the centre of the British line in this hastily planned battle. The infantry attacked the more numerous French in force, and after much fierce fighting the enemy line was broken, and they withdrew from the battlefield.

The following year the French advanced on the allied army at Landen. The enemy infantry attacked several times and the close-quarter fighting lasted for some hours. The allied centre was penetrated first by infantry and then by cavalry which forced the British right, defending the village of Laer, to withdraw in face of more numerous French troops. In 1695 O'Farrell's regiment was besieged while holding the fortified town of Deinse; the Colonel surrendered the town, for which act he was later court-martialled. When the regiment was subsequently released the command passed to Robert Mackay, soon to be replaced by Archibald Row. In 1697 the regiment returned to Scotland.

When the War of the Spanish Succession broke out in 1701, as a consequence of Louis XIV succeeding to the possession of the former Spanish Netherlands, the British resumed the struggle to prevent the French seizing Dutch territory.

Row's regiment reached Breda in 1702 and with the rest of Marlborough's troops, it took part in garrison duties and minor sieges for the next two years. The regiment's most notable exploit was the capture of Limburg.

In mid-1704 Marlborough set off for the Rhineland in order to defeat the Elector of Bavaria's army. The French army followed, and attempted to cut off the

British allies near Blenheim on the Danube. The Scots Fusiliers were on the left of the allied army, one of five battalions in General Archibald Row's brigade. A large part of the French infantry was massed inside Blenheim village and the brigade led the attack on it. They crossed the 150 yards towards the enemy palisade at a steady pace under the strictest orders to reserve their fire. A murderous volley was fired into the British infantry at thirty paces. On reaching the palisade, Row struck it with his sword and the brigade fired. The Scots Fusiliers rushed at the enemy's defences and tried to find a weak spot and force their way in. A second volley was fired by the French and more than half the regiment were by now dead or wounded. French cavalry then charged down onto them and captured the colours, although they were recovered. Other British and allied infantry then attached the palisade and Marlborough sent in his cavalry. The French infantry by now were trapped in the village by the British infantry and the encircling cavalry and surrendered; the remaining enemy troops fled from the battlefield. The Scots Fusiliers' casualties were very high, but they had played an important part in Marlborough's victory.

The war was resumed against the French in the Low Countries in 1706, and Marlborough attacked the French army at Ramillies on 23 May. The regiment, now commanded by Viscount Mordaunt, was heavily involved in the capture of Ramillies village in the centre. The outcome of the battle was that the French army was defeated and the remnants withdrew, leaving a number of nearby garrisons in allied hands.

The French resumed hostilities in 1708, and the British and allies held the line of the river Scheldt, with the army deployed near Oudenarde, but the regiment, serving on the left of the British line, was not greatly involved in the fighting. Later in the year during the siege of Lille, the Fusiliers played a major part in the attack on the town, which finally surrendered after a stiff fight.

In 1709 the regiment – now known as the North British Fusiliers since the Union of Scots and English Parliaments – took part in the final battle of the war at Malplaquet. The British Infantry attacked in the centre through wooded country but were held by the French, but a second assault and subsequent cavalry charges forced the enemy to withdraw. Further manoeuvring and sieges followed before the Treaty of Utrecht was signed in 1713. The regiment was given the suffix Royal in the same year, and returned to Britain in 1714.

In 1715 the regiment was part of the Duke of Argyll's force at Sheriffmuir, the battle fought against the Jacobites near Dunblane. The regiment sustained heavy casualties inflicted by the rebel highlanders under the Sixth Earl of Mar, the son of the regiment's founder: although the outcome of the battle was indecisive the rebellion itself failed.

The regiment remained in the United Kingdom until 1742, when it embarked for service in the War of The Austrian Succession against the French. In June 1743 the Fusiliers took part in the Battle of Dettingen where they formed part of the front line and faced a furious attack by the French Household troops, both cavalry and infantry. The British first line was penetrated by French troops, but they were quickly cut down. George II, who was personally present at the battle, mentioned to the Colonel of the Scots Fusiliers, Sir Andrew Agnew, 'So, Sir Andrew, I hear the cuirassiers rode through your regiment today.' 'Ay, please your Majesty,' Sir Andrew was reported to have replied, 'but they did'na gang back again.'

Two years later the British, Dutch and Austrians attacked the French at Fontenoy on the River Scheldt, and the Fusiliers were in the front line of the British centre. After an initial advance on the French line, which was hidden by a crest, the British succeeded in penetrating it, whereupon they had to face attack after attack by the French cavalry and infantry. After appalling losses the British slowly withdrew under fire, since the Dutch allies on the left had refused to advance in support. The British then disengaged from the enemy and marched off. Garrisoned at Ostend three months later the Fusiliers, severely depleted in numbers, had to surrender, but were allowed to march out with the honours of war. They returned to Scotland at the end of 1745, by which time the rebel Jacobite army had begun its withdrawal to Scotland.

The Royal North British Fusiliers were present first at the capture of Carlisle from the rebels. Part of the regiment then garrisoned Blair Castle on the route between Perth and Inverness: the remainder went with the Duke of Cumberland's force which was marching between Aberdeen and Inverness. On 16 April 1746, outside Inverness, the battle of Culloden took place, and the Fusiliers were in the front line facing Clan Chattan. Outflanked by cavalry, attacked by infantry from the front and under artillery fire, the highlanders were quickly overwhelmed by Cumberland's steadier troops. The battle effectively ended the rebellion.

In 1747 the Royal North British Fusiliers returned to the Continent. There they took part in the defence of Lauffeld, and the regiment distinguished itself in the British charge in an otherwise disastrous allied battle. Returning to the United Kingdom in 1748, it was stationed in England for three years, followed by nine years in Gibraltar. In 1751 it was ranked as the 21st Regiment, and in 1761 it took part in the capture of the French island fortress of Belle Isle off Britanny.

The 21st was sent to Halifax, Nova Scotia in 1776 and was soon involved in fighting the rebel colonials. In July 1777, the regiment served under General

John Burgoyne when the Americans were forced to abandon Ticonderoga. Advancing southwards into New England, Burgoyne's force attempted to gain Benus heights near Saratoga, but were attacked strongly by the Americans. The 21st and two other British regiments held, but at great cost of lives. Moving to a defensive position, the British were then surrounded by a force five times their strength, and Burgoyne was forced to surrender. The regiment virtually ceased to exist and the officers who later reached Britain had to recruit energetically to restore it to its establishment strength, which was accomplished by 1782.

* * * * *

Seven years later the regiment was back on the American continent, serving in Nova Scotia until 1793. It then set off to the West Indies, the first mission being to capture Martinique from the French. Owing to mistaken plans for cooperation with French royalists, it was not possible to take St Pierre, the chief town held by the French republicans, and the British force withdrew to Antigua. There the regiment suffered severely from disease, and the companies were subsequently dispersed for tasks on various islands. In early 1794, three companies of the 21st accompanied General Sir Charles Grey for another attempt to capture Martinique. This time it succeeded, with the three companies distinguishing themselves at the capture of Fort Royal, the final objective of the expedition. St Lucia was captured in a similar fashion, but seizing Guadeloupe proved a much more formidable and costly enterprise. The French, however, re-invaded the island in strength in June 1794, and the companies of the 21st had to withdraw from the island after losing many of their number.

The regiment, though severely depleted served on for a further two years in various stations in the West Indies and finally reached Scotland in 1796. It remained there before moving to Ireland in 1800. In 1804 a second battalion of the 21st, Royal North British Fusiliers was raised.

The 1st Battalion reached Messina, Sicily in July 1806 where a sizeable British garrison was serving. The following year the battalion was sent to Alexandria, but the whole garrison soon withdrew and returned to Sicily. The French were threatening to invade the island from bases on mainland Italy. In 1809 a British expedition, which included the 21st, was mounted against the French at Scilla on the mainland. The fortress was held in great strength and the British had to withdraw to Sicily. In July 1810 a French invasion of the island did take place and the regiment fought in a number of engagements, which eventually led to the ejection of the French troops from Sicily. After further service in Sicily the battalion landed again on the Italian shore in March

Officer and sergeant, Royal North British Fusiliers, 1846.

1814 and marched northwards, forcing the French to withdraw. The enemy finally surrendered at Genoa in April.

In the meantime the 2nd Battalion had served at home until 1813, when it took part in Sir Thomas Graham's expedition to Holland. That country was under French occupation and the British force attempted to capture Bergen-op-Zoom, an important fortified town on the Scheldt estuary. It proved a difficult place to attack, being surrounded by water dykes and salt marshes. Part of the town, however, was captured; but despite the most determined fighting the British had to withdraw. The battalion had suffered heavy casualties, but remained for some months in Holland. It was disbanded in 1816.

The 1st Battalion moved from Genoa in 1814 and eventually reached Chesapeake Bay in August to fight in the war against the United States. The British force comprised three brigades, and marching along the Potomac river they reached Bladensburg, five miles from Washington. The 21st and other infantry battalions mounted a direct attack on the Americans' position and forced them to withdraw. The capital was entered and the public buildings set on fire. The British force cleared the countryside between Washington and Baltimore before returning to the coast. The 21st then sailed for Jamaica ready to join the expedition to New Orleans. Landing in December

1814, the brigade attacked an American force holding the road to New Orleans on 8 January. The 21st lost nearly half their numbers as casualties in this engagement. A few weeks later, news of the peace treaty reached the two armies and the regiment re-embarked to return home.

* * * * *

The Royal North British Fusiliers spent the next thirty-nine years on peacetime duties in the United Kingdom, the West Indies, Portugal and India. Then in 1854 they embarked for the Crimea as part of the 4th Division. The Fusiliers' first task was to man positions near Sevastopol. During the battle of Balaclava they were called on as reinforcements, but the battle ended before their arrival. In November 1854 the Russians attempted to break the British siege positions by a daring attack, known as the battle of Inkerman. The enemy force numbered some 25,000 men, while at first ony 3,600 British troops could be deployed to face them.

They fought a running battle against advancing enemy columns. 'My great anxiety,' wrote Cpt Haines (later Field Marshal Sir Frederick Haines), 'was to steady and keep them together, and the thick brush through which we advanced tended much to break our formation.' Two Russian columns were checked before the 21st withdrew and held the Barrier, a key part of the Home Ridge position. Later in the battle a detachment of the 21st and men from other battalions attacked Shell Hill and the effectiveness, particularly of their rifle fire, was to cause the Russians to withdraw from the battlefield.

The siege of Sevastopol continued throughout the winter and spring of 1855. The regiment faced numerous Russian attacks; it mounted one itself on the Quarries in early June and a major assault later in the month. The regiment remained in the Crimea until May 1856.

The 1st Battalion served subsequently in Malta, the West Indies, Scotland, Ireland and, from 1869 to 1881, in India and Burma. In the latter year the official title of the regiment became the 'Royal Scots Fusiliers' and tartan trews of government pattern (later slightly modified) became part of the uniform. It remained in the United Kingdom until 1895.

The 2nd Battalion, raised in 1858, had been sent to India in 1863, and also served in Burma before returning to Scotland. In March 1879 it reached Durban, South Africa soon after the British catastrophe at Isandhlwana. The battalion advanced from Pietermaritzburg with the British force and, leaving a garrison detachment behind, advanced to the area of Isandhlwana Hill. Lord Chelmsford's army was then attacked by Cetewayo's Zulus near Ulundi on 4 July.

The 21st were at the corner of the square which was in the line of the Zulu advance. The cavalry entered the protection of the British square and the

21st Royal North British Fusiliers man the trenches in front of Sevastopol, 1854-5. Watercolour by Orlando Norie. RHQ

infantry closed ranks, with the two foremost ranks kneeling. Cetewayo's élite warriors advanced 'with clanging shields in a huge wave, regardless it seemed, of the hail of rifle bullets or fire from the nine pounders. But the impis did not get to within thirty yards of the infantry, which poured out that terrible and unremitting fire.' Cetewayo's army of 15,000–20,000 fled from the battlefield after only twenty minutes of fighting, and the British victory brought the war to a rapid end.

In 1880 the first Boer War broke out and the battalion was deployed in various places. Two companies garrisoned Potchefstroom and, when attacked by a Boer force seven times their number, they had to abandon part of the town. Eventually, when the food gave out they surrendered on honourable terms. Other detachments served in the defence of Pretoria and Rustenburg for the duration of the war, and in 1881 the battalion sailed for India.

THE ROYAL SCOTS FUSILIERS
1881–1913

In 1885 the 2nd Royal Scots Fusiliers served in the campaign against the Kingdom of Upper Burma – the British holding Lower Burma at the time. Mandalay was captured without difficulty, but the battalion spent much time in detachments skirmishing against Burmese infiltrators in the south. The 2nd returned to India in 1886 and remained there until 1899, when it was sent to fight in the second Boer War.

The 1st Battalion meanwhile served in India from 1896, and the following year took part in the Tirah campaign on the North-West Frontier. Part of the battalion fought to hold Ublan Pass, and other detachments fought in the hills between Dargai and Maidan, helping to clear the area of enemy tribesmen. The battalion remained in India until 1910.

The 2nd Royal Scots Fusiliers initially were part of the Fusilier Brigade in the South African War. Four companies fought to protect some British guns at Colenso on 15 December 1899, but when General Buller gave orders for the guns to be abandoned, many of the Scots Fusiliers were captured. A month later Buller attempted to clear the route for the relief of Ladysmith, and the Scots Fusiliers were involved in the attack on Vaal Kranz. In February 1900 they were part of the assaulting troops which captured Hlangwane and Green Hill and forced their way north of the Tugela. The Fusilier Brigade captured various positions, the most difficult being Pieters Hill. This was hotly contested by the Boers and, for a time, the Scots Fusiliers could only hold part of it. The Boers subsequently withdrew from the Tugela and Ladysmith was relieved. A small detachment of mounted infantry of the battalion also helped to relieve Mafeking in May 1900.

The battalion was involved in various tasks during the later stages of the war, and was instrumental in the successful defence of the Frederikstad area in October. It remained in South Africa until early 1903. The 1st Battalion also served a tour of duty in South Africa, from 1910 to 1914, when for a time they were involved in internal security duties in the mining region.

Left:
Volunteers of the 3rd Militia Bn, Royal Scots Fusiliers crossing Groot Oliphant River, South Africa, with MacKenzie's column. Lord Cassilis is in the foreground. RHQ

Right:
The custom of a Scottish regiment finding the royal guard continues to the present day, whenever the Royal Family is in residence at Balmoral Castle. The Royal Scots Fusiliers in full dress provided the guard, June 1891. RHQ

A sergeant of the Royal Scots Fusiliers c1890. He wears the distinctive fusilier bearskin and fusil badge. IWM

Royal Scots Fusiliers halt on the march near Ghora Dakka, India, Oct 1897. RHQ

THE ROYAL SCOTS FUSILIERS

1914–38

The 1st Battalion, Royal Scots Fusiliers went to France with 9 Brigade of the British Expeditionary Force in August 1914, and were first in action on 23 August at Jemappes, near Mons. Enemy cavalry advanced at 6am to within 500 yards of the Fusiliers' outposts north of the canal. They withdrew and some four hours later a large number of infantry advanced on the canal. A determined attack was mounted on the Royal Scots Fusiliers, who had pulled back their forward posts. As the Germans approached the battalion engaged them with heavy machine-gun and rifle fire. British artillery fire was also coming down on the enemy and for some four hours the Scots Fusiliers effectively delayed the enemy amid the ruins of the village. The enemy, meanwhile, had made made better progress on other parts of the British front, so in the afternoon the bridges were blown and the battalion ordered to withdraw.

During the retreat across Belgium, the battalion was divided into two detachments in the Le Cateau area on 25 August, where the 3rd Division made a major stand. The 1st Royal Scots Fusiliers put up a spirited defence, but the withdrawal soon continued, and the battalion finally reached position on the River Aisne. Once stabilised, the British counter-attacked German positions overlooking the river. The battalion successfully captured an objective on 14 September, but the casualties were heavy. The battalion manned the line until the BEF was moved onto the allied left flank in October to block the way to the channel ports.

The battalion were in the trenches in the area of Aubers, and on 18 October took part in a brigade attack on Herlies. It became impossible for the battalion's objective to be captured and, after sustaining heavy casualties, the Scots Fusiliers had to withdraw. A staff officer described a visit to the battalion:

> 'We came into the field occupied by the Royal Scots Fusiliers. Here they were drawn up, erect and grim as usual, but what a different regiment from the one which had swung out of Lyndhurst Camp less than five weeks before! That magnificently smart regiment of once a thousand men was now reduced to about seventy men, with a junior subaltern in command. The men were mostly without caps, coats, or even putties, war-stained and ragged, but still full of British pluck and pride, with a "never say die" look upon their faces, which made the heart swell with pride at being connected with such splendid specimens of manhood.'

The 2nd Royal Scots Fusiliers had reached France in the same month and took up duties in the line to the east of Ypres. A strong German attack on the line took place at Polderhoek on 22 and 23 October; and on 24 October the battalion was outflanked but continued to hold its positions. The battalion's strength was by this time reduced by half, more than 500 being killed or wounded; depleted companies remained in position until 30 October. The 1st Battalion assisted in the counter-attack near the Menin road on 11 November, which contributed to the successful blocking of the German advance on the town of Ypres. From then onwards the line stabilised and the two battalions were gradually brought up to strength during the winter.

In the early part of 1915 the 1st Battalion was in the line south of Ypres, while the 2nd Battalion took part in the attack that was launched against Neuve Chapelle in March 1915. There the Germans quickly counter-attacked, and the 2nd Battalion was under constant attack and bombardment in their forward positions.

In May the 2nd Battalion took part in the attack on Festubert; having reached their objective, the Fusiliers were subjected, in error, to heavy artillery fire from British guns. On 15 June they attempted to attack Givenchy with the 4th Camerons, but without success. The 1st Battalion suffered its first enemy gas attack on 22 April in their position on the Ypres salient. It mounted a successful local attack at Bellewaarde in May, but the battalion casualties in that action were over 400.

The newly raised 6th Battalion, Royal Scots Fusiliers reached France in May 1915, and the 7th Battalion in July. With fresh troops, an offensive was planned along the whole front in September. The 1st Battalion attacked from their position near Ypres, while the 2nd, 6th and 7th were involved in the area south of La Basée. In the first day, the 1st Battalion's objective was taken, but could not be held. The 6th Battalion was used in the area of Haisnes, but that village proved to be held too strongly by the Germans. The 7th Battalion was in reserve, but was sent forward to Loos and occupied Hill 70. A German counter-attack was made in strength and, without the expected relieving troops, the British position had to be evacuated. The battle of Loos achieved only a small advantage for the British.

* * * * *

Two Territorial battalions of the Royal Scots Fusiliers, the 4th and 5th, reached Gallipoli on 6 June 1915 as part of 52nd Division. They were at once put in the front line. A month later they took part in the attack on the Turkish positions north of Cape Helles, forming up with their brigade facing the enemy centre, with companies in reserve. The attack achieved some advance of the line, but at great cost and leaving the Turks still in possession of the high ground.

The two battalions then spent much time in the trenches of Gallipoli, constantly under fire and in the most arduous of conditions of terrain, heat and disease. The 5th Battalion mounted a diversionary attack on 19 December, when the Anzac and Suvla sectors were being evacuated, and fierce trench fighting continued to the end of the year. In January 1916 the whole force of 35,000 and over a hundred guns were secretly evacuated, and the remainder of the 4th and 5th Battalions moved to Egypt.

* * * * *

During 1916 the four battalions of the Royal Scots Fusiliers in France spent their time in manning the line and training for the next great offensive. The 1st Battalion took part in an attack on 25 March in the St Eloi sector. The 7th Battalion mounted two counter-attacks on the Hohenzollern redoubt on 11 and 12 May to relieve the 13th Royal Scots, but were beaten back. The 6th Battalion was commanded by Lt-Col Winston Churchill during the early part of 1916, but in May 1916 the battalion was amalgamated with the 7th to form the 6th/7th.

At the start of the Somme offensive on 1 July, the 2nd Battalion was serving on the extreme right of the British line, and their brigade's task was the capture of Montauban. The objective was taken, but the wooded area to the east, Trones Wood, was successfully defended by the enemy. On 14 July the 1st Battalion mounted an attack from the Montauban area, the brigade objective being Bazentin-le-Grand. The 2nd Battalion was called upon to support the 1st, and working together the position was successfully taken. The 1st was then moved to the front near Longueval. On 31 July the 2nd Royal Scots Fusiliers took part in a fresh attack in the Trones Wood area. This again was unsuccessful, although an objective at Guillemont was held for a time. The battalions' casualties during the month had been 633 from a strength of 770 all ranks.

2nd Bn, Royal Scots Fusiliers relax as best they can in the trenches at La Boutillerie, winter 1914-15. IWM

The 6th/7th Battalion was in action on 12 August south of Martinpuich and achieved some gains. A month later a well-planned and executed attack was mounted; Martinpuich itself was taken and the line pushed one mile east, the battalion playing an important part in this action. In November, the 1st Battalion lost over 200 casualties in their final attack of the Somme offensive in the Serre sector.

By March 1917 all three Royal Scots Fusilier battalions were in the area of Arras, the central position from which a new British offensive was launched on 9 April. On this day the 6th/7th Battalion attacked the enemy holding Railway Triangle, and the assaulting formations along the front captured several German lines. The 1st Battalion was initially in reserve, and when the Fusiliers advanced they were held up by the German machine-gun fire. The following day they moved forward and captured the next German line. On 11 April the 6th/7th Battalion took part in the capture of Monchy, and five days later they assisted in the successful attack on Guémappe, but had to face determined German counter-attacks. On 23 April the 2nd Battalion went into the attack on high ground near Cherisy but were stopped short of their objective. The battalion suffered severe casualties. The 1st Battalion's attack on Infantry Hill south-east of Monchy, on 3 May, resulted in nearly 300 casualties.

The third battle of Ypres began on 31 July, and the 6th/7th Royal Scots Fusiliers attacked the third German line near Frezenberg, the first two having been passed through by other battalions. The Fusiliers were held up by German firing still coming from the second line, then a German counter-attack from the front, and the battalion was reduced to about 150 strong. Meanwhile, in the same action the 2nd Battalion's objective was the second German line in the area, appropriately named 'Stirling Castle', 'Glencorse' and 'Inverness' woods. The battalion's attack was held up in front of the woods, but it managed to hold against the inevitable German counter-attack. Third Ypres was not a successful battle, but it continued until November with localised attacks against limited objectives. The three Scots Fusilier battalions took part in a number of these attacks, the most notable one being the 1st Battalion's on 20 September, which resulted in its capturing much of the ground by Hill 40, near Zonnebeke. The casualties were 437 in this intense engagement.

* * * * *

The 8th Battalion, Royal Scots Fusiliers had spent a short time in 1915 on the Western Front, but in December they reached Salonika to serve on the Bulgarian front. During 1916 they manned the line at various places, and in May 1917 the battalion was in support under French command during the allied battle at Dorain. The attack was not successful. In September 1918 the allies attacked again, the major part being played by the Serbians and French. A diversionary attack was mounted around each side of Lake Dorain with French, Greek and British participation, including the Royal Scots Fusiliers. The enemy then counter-attacked with great ferocity, and due to the lack of support from the allied formations, the British brigade had to withdraw. The 8th Battalion lost over 400 casualties in the battle. The remainder of the battalion then took part in the pursuit following a general Bulgarian withdrawal – a result of the main allied attack. Shortly afterwards an armistice was agreed in this theatre.

1st Royal Scots Fusiliers in the well-prepared defences at the village of St Eloi, South of Ypres, April-May 1915. IWM

* * * * *

The two battalions serving in the 52nd Lowland Division which had fought at Gallipoli, had been in Egypt since February 1916. They manned the Suez Canal defence line from the same month, just as plans were being made for it to be extended eastwards into the Sinai desert. The Turks, however, who had hitherto not attacked the canal defences, mounted an attack

An officer of the 76th Macdonald Highlanders in the act of 'fronting' with his sword. The 76th served from 1777-84 and fought in the American colonies.
National Museums of Scotland

Maj-Gen John Small of Dirnanean, Perthshire, served with the Scots Brigade, 42nd Royal Highlanders and 21st Foot before raising the 2nd Bn the 84th Royal Highland Emigrant Regt in America in 1775. He is dressed in the uniform of the 84th. From a miniature.
National Museums of Scotland

Sergeant of the 73rd MacLeod's Highlanders, later 71st Highland Light Infantry, in 1777. Non-commissioned officers continued to carry pikes until the end of the 18th century. RHQ

Top left:
Soldier of the 74th Highlanders of 1787.
Engraving from Cannon's Records

Top centre:
A Gordon Highlander of 1794 wearing the philabeg or little kilt and feather bonnet, which saved many a highlander's skull from sword cuts in battle. Painting by M. Georges Scott.

Top right:
Sir Ralph Abercromby attacked and mortally wounded at the battle of Alexandria on 21 Mar 1801. Highlanders rush to the aid of this most experienced and professional of British generals.

Far left:
75th Highland Regt, or Abercromby's Highlanders, raised at Stirling in 1787, and later 1st Bn the Gordon Highlanders. Modern painting by Douglas N. Anderson. Matthew E. Taylor

Left:
The storming of Seringapatam on 4 May 1799. The 73rd, 74th and 75th Regts all took part in this siege, when the power of the ruler of Mysore, Tippoo Sahib, was finally broken. From Cannon's Records

Top:
92nd Gordon Highlanders attack the French guns at the battle of Mandora near Alexandria in Mar 1801. Watercolour by R. Simkin. RHQ

Top right:
Highlanders man a picquet, 1807. A coloured engraving by J. A. Atkinson. RHQ Queen's Own Highlanders

Right:
Officer, sergeant and private of the 93rd Highlanders, (later 2nd Bn Argyll and Sutherland Highlanders) of 1810. The regiment was serving in Cape Colony at the time. Watercolour by R. Simkin. RHQ

Far right:
The 26th Cameronians at the battle of Corruna, January 1803. Watercolour by H. Oakes-Jones. RHQ

Left:
Piper George Clark of the 71st Highland Light Infantry continues to cheer his comrades by playing the pipes, despite being wounded, at the Battle of Vimeiro in 1808. National Museums of Scotland

Right top:
The 42nd Royal Highlanders beset by French Lancers at Quatre Bras on 16 June 1815. Marshal Ney with the left flank of the French Army failed to defeat the smaller British force. Oil painting by W. B. Wollen. RHQ

Right below:
The charge of the Scots Greys and 92nd Gordon Highlanders at the battle of Waterloo. This oil painting by Stanley Berkeley is based on exaggerated accounts of the battle, but is nonetheless a striking painting of an incident which took place during the glorious British and allied victory. RHQ

Below:
The death of Col Cameron of Fassifern at Quatre Bras, 16 June 1815, while commanding the 92nd Gordon Highlanders. Watercolour by R. Simkin. RHQ

Sgt Ewart captures the standard of the French 45 Regt at the battle of Waterloo 1815. RHQ

Below:
The Royal Scots Greys capture the French guns at Waterloo, 18 June 1815. RHQ

on a position at Dueidar on the new railway, held by a company of the 5th Royal Scots Fusiliers; but a detachment of the 4th Battalion marched quickly to their assistance and the Turks rapidly withdrew.

The British line was extended further eastwards and in late July a major battle was fought at Romani, where the enemy were lured to attack the well-prepared positions of the 52nd Division. The defence held and a counter-attack was successfully mounted; half the large Turkish force became casualties or were taken captive. This allowed the British to advance eastwards without further hindrance, which they did in October with the 52nd Division leading. By the end of January 1917 British and dominion troops entered Palestine. In the same month the 12th Battalion of the regiment was formed in this theatre from the dismounted Ayrshire and Lanarkshire Yeomanry regiments, which had been amalgamated earlier.

None of the three battalions took part in the first battle of Gaza, but the 4th and 5th Battalions fought together in the second battle which began on 19 April. Their brigade took several objectives, the most desperate fighting being for Outpost Hill. After several attacks on the hill which the Turks beat off, two companies of 4th KOSB joined up with companies of 5th Royal Scots Fusiliers.

> 'Despite all they had been through, the Borderers and Fusiliers were ready for another assault. When all was ready Major Forrest (KOSB, the Scottish international rugby player) led his men forward. This charge of men from almost every unit in 155 Brigade was a most inspiring sight. Under a murderous fire, which struck down many, they rushed up the hill. About fifty Turks saw them coming, leaped from a ravine and bolted away into the cactus hedges on the western slope. Major Forrest was mortally wounded as he entered the works.'

Thus was the hill captured and held for a while in face of fresh enemy counter-attacks.

The position had to be evacuated eventually during the night, the battle for Gaza by this time having been lost. The third battle of Gaza in November 1917 was successful, chiefly due to the actions of the cavalry. The 12th Battalion of the regiment was engaged in the latter stages of the battle.

In the pursuit of the enemy, the 4th and 5th Royal Scots Fusiliers took part in a number of assaults on successive enemy positions, including the important ridge at Katrah overlooking the railway line to Jerusalem. On 24 November the two battalions were ordered to seize a brigade objective at El Jib. This was defended with great determination by the Turks and, although nearby Nebi Samwil was taken, the El Jib position was successfully held by the enemy. A few days later the battalions had to resist enemy counter-attacks in the El Burj area, which they did successfully despite casualties. Meanwhile, the advance on Jerusalem was pressing ahead and the 12th (Ayr and Lanark Yeomanry) Battalion captured a hill of 1,000 feet at Beit Iksa. The holy city was entered by General Allenby's troops on 11 December.

* * * * *

By early 1918 the three battalions of the regiment on the Western Front had been made up to strength. The German forces, however, had been greatly increased by armies released from the Eastern Front after the treaty with the Russians. The German offensive began at 4.45am on 21 March. Virtually all sectors of the British line had to give way to a greater or lesser extent. Casualties were heavy, particularly amongst the 2nd Battalion on the River Lys, and the

Sketch of an unknown soldier of the Royal Scots Fusiliers drawn in hospital by HRM, 1918.

1st Battalion near the Clarence River. The 6th/7th Battalion was employed piecemeal in a number of sectors during these desperate days of fighting, and those few who survived were absorbed in May 1918 into the 18th Cameronians. Meanwhile, the 2nd Battalion, serving in the South African brigade, was particularly successful in holding the ridge overlooking Kemmel, despite the weight of enemy troops attempting to assault their positions. The German offensive was finally held, although much ground had been lost.

In the spring of 1918 the 11th Battalion, Royal Scots Fusiliers arrived in France from the United Kingdom while the 4th, 5th and 12th (Ayr and Lanark

Yeomanry) Battalions arrived from Palestine. The line had stabilised by this time, and the only engagement at this time involving the Royal Scots Fusiliers was the capture of Meteren by the 2nd Battalion and South African troops on 19 July.

With the success of the French Army at the second battle of the Marne of July 1918, the next British offensive began. The 1st, 2nd and 5th Battalions were early involved in successful advances in the Moyenneville and Beaucourt sectors, and the 4th and 5th Battalions broke through the Hindenburg Line. Quéant was captured with the assistance of the 4th Battalion, but further south the 1st Battalion had heavy casualties. On 15 September the 4th and 5th Battalions helped to capture Moeuvres, and then withstood a strong German counter-attack. The 1st were again in action on 28 September, together with the 11th and 12th Battalions, for assaults in the sector south of Dixmude.

During October all six battalions of the regiment were in action as the momentum of the allies' advance increased, and there were numerous engagements at battalion and company level. Most were successful, but casualties continued to be heavy until the armistice was finally declared on 11 November.

* * * * *

In 1919 the New Army and Territorial Force battalions returned to peacetime stations and were reorganised or disbanded. In December the 2nd Battalion, Royal Scots Fusiliers left England for service with the British Military Mission in Russia. When they landed at Novorossiysk on the Black Sea in March 1920, the White Russian army was already withdrawing on the port and the decision to embark the British force had already been taken. The Scots Fusiliers carried out various guard tasks in the town, and then assisted in the evacuation as the Red Army advanced. They were amongst the last British to leave.

The 1st Battalion, in which was incorporated the 3rd Militia Battalion, spent three years in Ireland during the last period before home rule. It was a most unpleasant time for the Scots Fusiliers, because they had to show the utmost restraint under conditions of grave public disorder. The battalion had a wide area of responsibility, the companies detached to various places in King's and Queen's counties. In April 1922 the battalion reached Glasgow, having been the last troops to garrison the Curragh.

The battalion then spent some years in the United Kingdom, followed by the years 1932 to 1936 in the Middle East. Part of the time was spent in Palestine helping to prevent a terrorist war between the Arabs and the increasing number of Jews. The 2nd Battalion served for ten years in India before moving to Shanghai in 1931. China was in some state of turmoil at the time, with Chinese and Japanese troops engaged in sporadic fighting. The Scots Fusiliers' task was the maintenance of a British presence and to guard British interests in the event of major disturbances.

THE ROYAL SCOTS FUSILIERS
1939–59

When war was declared on 3 September 1939, the 1st Battalion was stationed in India and the 2nd in Edinburgh. In October the 2nd Battalion reached a position on the Franco-Belgium border near Lille, as part of 17 Brigade of the British Expeditionary Force. The Scots Fusiliers maintained their part of the line and trained for the coming hostilities. When Belgium was invaded on 10 May 1940, the whole of the BEF advanced eastwards in order to secure the line of the Albert Canal, but to the south the Germans were advancing swiftly westwards through the Ardennes.

It was several days before the Royal Scots Fusiliers were in action, and they were kept constantly on the move. On 17 May they were in defensive positions on the Charlroi Canal and were attacked from the air. After being ordered to withdraw they took up positions on Vimy Ridge, only to be ordered to withdraw on 22 May towards Arras. There they mounted a counter-attack and in the ensuing brigade withdrawal formed the rear guard. On 26 May the battalion formed a position on the east bank of the Ypres-Comines Canal. The Germans attacked in great strength and after holding for some hours, the battalion withdrew across the canal. There they were ordered to stand and cover the BEF's final withdrawal to Dunkirk, but the battalion was surrounded during the night and again attacked on the morning of 28 May. The Brigadier had ordered the Scots Fusiliers to hold the position until at least 9am when a counter-attack could be mounted to relieve them. The forward companies, however, were cut off and battalion HQ moved into a farmstead to be better protected from enemy fire. But battalion HQ was itself totally isolated and no counter-attack came. Time and again the enemy attacked the Scots Fusiliers' positions, but they held out until about 11am. Ammunition had virtually run out and the companies' strength reduced to only a few men each. All positions were then overrun and the commanding officer, who had been wounded himself, ordered his men to surrender.

The 6th Royal Scots Fusiliers, a territorial battalion commanded by Lord Rowallan, had been with

Royal Scots Fusiliers Bren-gun training 'somewhere in England'. IWM

the 51st (Highland) Division from 1 May manning part of the Maginot Line. The Fusiliers were withdrawn from their positions before the line was overwhelmed, and moved by rail. Eventually a battalion position, east of Dieppe and on the River Bresle, was established. Enemy attacks began on 4 June. During the next few days they intensified, with German armoured columns appearing west of the river. On 8 June a withdrawal was ordered from divisional headquarters, and new positions were established at Belleville the following day. Since there was now the strong possibility of the division being cut off to the west, the 6th Battalion acted as the rear guard during the next phase of the withdrawal. Then began a race between the divison and the advancing Germans to Le Havre. The 6th Battalion fortunately had motor transport and thus embarked speedily at the port on 12 June, reaching Cherbourg by sea the following day. The final evacuation to England took place on 15 June.

The 4th/5th Battalion, Royal Scots Fusiliers also served briefly in France in June 1940, as part of the 52nd Lowland Division. They were, however, evacuated without being involved in the fighting.

* * * * *

The two regular battalions of the Royal Scots Fusiliers took part in the invasion of Madagascar during 1942. The island was held by troops loyal to the Vichy French government, and it was considered important to prevent the Japanese from establishing bases on it. Both battalions landed at different times on 5 May, their task being to assist in the capture of the northernmost promontory. The 1st Battalion, serving in 29 Brigade, landed first, followed in the afternoon by the reconstituted 2nd Battalion in 17 Brigade. During the next three days the French held the two chief towns of Diego Suarez and Antsirane, on either side of the harbour. There was heavy fighting for both battalions before the French surrendered the northern part of the island.

The following month the 2nd Battalion left the island for India. The 1st Battalion, however, remained for a time before moving to Mombasa in Kenya. From there a second invasion of Madagascar was mounted in September. 29 Brigade, in which the 1st Royal Scots Fusiliers still served, captured Majunga, the seaport on the west coast, and allowed the 22 East African Brigade to capture the island capital of Tananarive. The battalion also took a part in the subsequent assault landing and capture of the eastern seaport of Tametave.

* * * * *

The 2nd Battalion spent a short time in India, and

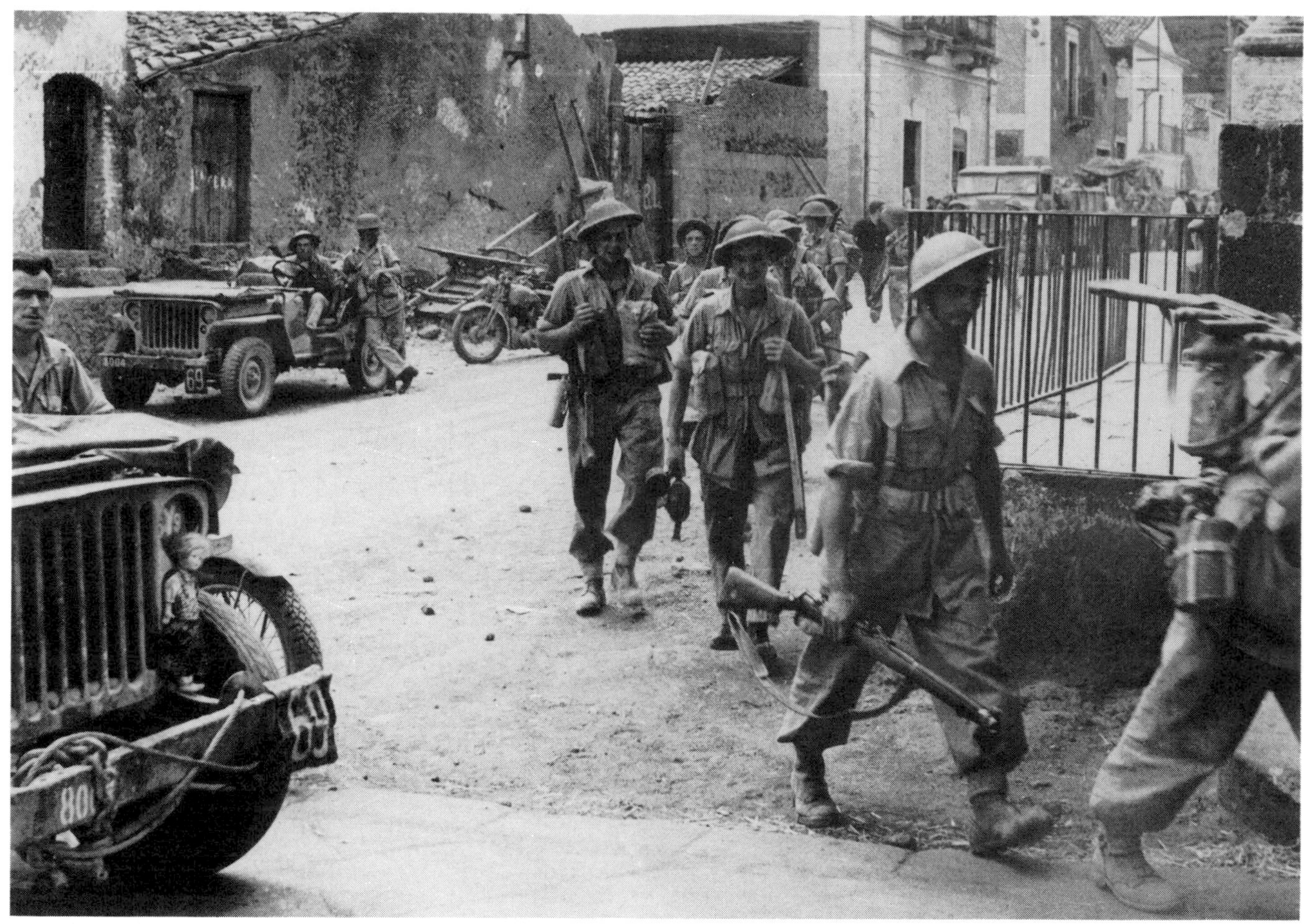

2nd Royal Scots Fusiliers pass through a Sicilian town, July 1943. IWM

in September 1942 left for service with Paiforce in Persia. In early 1943 it moved via Syria and Palestine to Egypt, and in July it embarked for the assault on Sicily.

On landing on 10 July the 2nd Royal Scots Fusiliers were the leading troops of their brigade. At first they took the few Italian positions without much difficulty, but by the afternoon the opposition became more determined. Two deliberate attacks were mounted before the Italians withdrew leaving clear the main objective Syracuse. The next major task was to clear the road to Catania and Messina to the north. German artillery was then encountered on 12 July and the battalion was ordered to mount an attack on the gun positions, in order to clear the route for the brigade advance. The German artillery quickly withdrew. The battalion then re-joined the line of march which effectively sealed Catania from the west, while the main British thrust by-passed it. The town was eventually taken, and preparations for the invasion of Italy began.

The 2nd Battalion, Royal Scots Fusiliers crossed the Straits of Messina with the invasion force on 3 September 1943 and landed north of Reggio. There was little resistance and the Italian troops were surrendering everywhere. In order to speed up progress, assault craft lifted the battalion by sea and landed it some miles further along the coast. The advance then continued on land, partly on foot and partly by motor transport: the American landings at Salerno necessitated the British troops helping to consolidate an allied front 200 miles to the north as quickly as possible. By 5 October the battalion had taken up a position at Foggia near the Adriatic coast. The Germans established a front some thirty miles north in the area of Termoli and stretching southwestwards across Italy.

On 25 October the British offensive began and much of the fighting was against villages and well-prepared positions in the closely wooded mountains. One such was on Mount Macchiagodena and patrols were sent against it by the battalion, followed by company attacks. On 3 November a battalion attack was mounted after a long night march. The Scots Fusiliers assaulted from an unexpected flank and the Germans withdrew hurriedly. This action opened up an important route for the advance. The battalion's next major attack was against Alfadena, as a diversion to the main British assault on the Gustav Line. A series of mountain tops were successfully captured and the town entered on 24 November. It was not possible, however, to move northwards immediately as the Germans held the hills in strength. On 15 December two companies mounted a successful assault river crossing over the Moro River. Heavy fighting continued for some days in the area.

In January 1944 the 2nd Battalion, Royal Scots Fusiliers moved westwards across Italy for operations in the region of the River Garigliano on the allied left, and their brigade mounted an amphibious night assault over this river on 17 January. The crossing was not carried out according to plan, but during daylight the battalion reorganised itself ready for an attack on Mount Argento on 18 January. A Company had to approach the German positions in the dark through a minefield and under considerable mortar fire. When the attack went in over the last 400 yards, a thick wire entanglement was discovered and Lt Brown and some NCOs rushed around looking for gaps under the most intense machine-gun fire from the hill, lit up by parachute flares. No way could be found through the wire, and attempts to cut it failed. The company suffered heavy casualties and had to withdraw through C Company. A German counter-attack was mounted on C Company and it, too, had to withdraw. The battalion lost 140 casualties in the twelve hours of fighting. A fresh attack was planned for the night of 19 January but the enemy withdrew first. Similar fighting withdrawal actions were encountered in the advance on Mount Natale before the line stabilised.

The allied invasion at Anzio took place at this time and the 2nd Royal Scots Fusiliers were sent to reinforce the beach-head on 8 March. The Germans put up the most determined resistance of the campaign so far against the allies, and the battalion had to man the front line for two months opposite German troops holding positions called the 'Fortress' and the 'Claws'. There were constant German and British attacks and counter-attacks, with artillery bombardment from both sides inflicting high casualties.

In May 1944 allied reinforcements arrived and it was possible to mount a break-out from Anzio beach-head. In early June, under allied pressure, the Germans withdrew and Rome fell to the Americans. Later that same month the 2nd Battalion left for Egypt followed by a period of recuperation and training in Palestine.

* * * * *

Meanwhile the 1st Battalion, Royal Scots Fusiliers, after leaving Madagascar, had reached India in early 1943. It then spent a year at Poona, training for further operations. There followed a brief spell in the Arakan region of Burma, where the battalion was involved in some local patrolling from company bases. In June, the Scots Fusiliers were withdrawn to Assam for more training; but in August 1944 they returned to Burma, still as part of 29 Brigade. Their task, which involved them until the end of the war, was to secure the road and railway corridor in eastern Burma which re-supplied British (including the Chindits), American and Chinese troops in Burma and China.

The battalion was flown into the railhead town of Myitkyina and was used initially on guard duties around the divisional dropping zone and other base areas. The battalion then advanced southwards, assisting and protecting the engineers repairing the line. Engagements with the retreating enemy in-

A piper leads an officer and some soldiers into Mawlu, Burma, abandoned by the Japanese after a battalion attack by the 1st Royal Scots Fusiliers in Oct 1944.
IWM

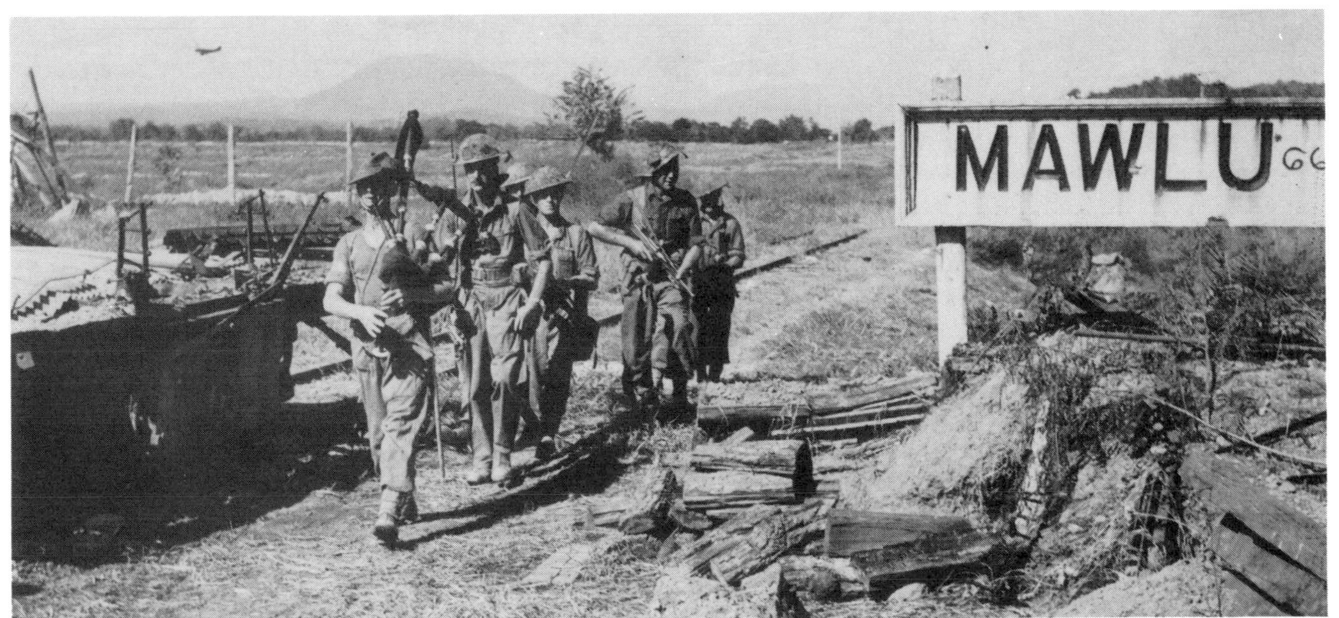

creased. B Company was responsible for the successful capture of Nansankyin and A and C Companies captured Pinbaw, a very heavily defended position.

The British troops gradually moved southwards and the railway was repaired. The battalion's tasks continued to be the close defence and local patrolling around the railway and road, which were by now passing through thick jungle. The Fusiliers then encountered well prepared Japanese positions north of Mawlu on 27 October. A battalion attack was mounted with D and C Companies attacking from the north-east and west and A Company in reserve. Covered by an artillery bombardment, the leading companies reached the outskirts of the town and A Company passed through towards the railway station by last light. The companies dug in during the night, but were shelled, grenaded and sniped at until dawn. By then Mawlu had been evacuated by the remaining Japanese troops, and the Scots Fusiliers immediately set off in pursuit. Over a hundred miles had been covered since the battalion had arrived in Burma, and a short rest was ordered.

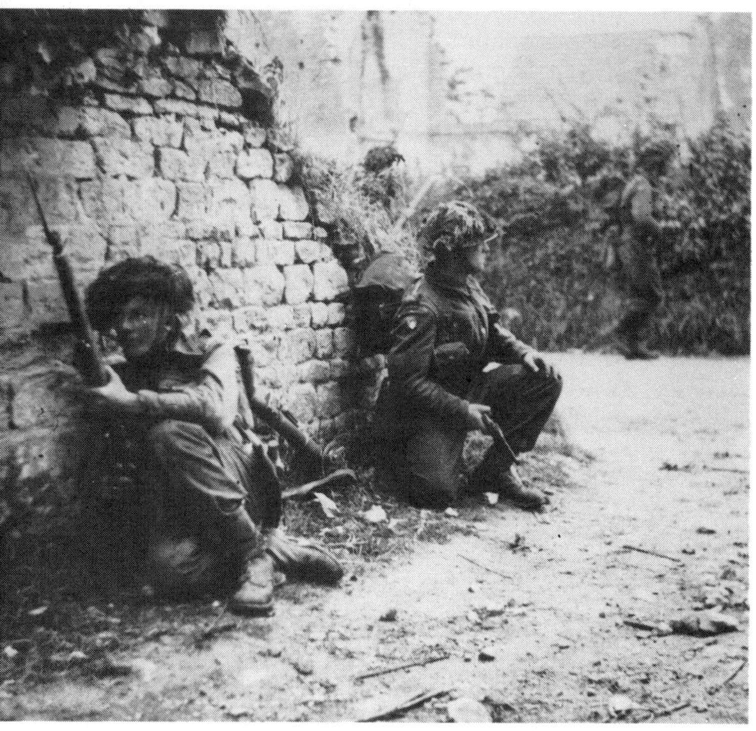

Jocks of the 6th Royal Scots Fusiliers occupy St Mauvieu, June 1944. IWM

The greatest Japanese resistance was encountered at Pinwe which, because of its jungle position, involved a considerable delay. The whole of 72 Brigade was involved at first, then 29 Brigade, and the 1st Royal Scots Fusiliers came under command successively of each brigade. After three weeks of bombardment and probing attacks by the infantry battalions, Pinwe was eventually taken. During the last weeks of 1944 the steady advance to the Irrawaddy and Mandalay continued. That town was still 100 miles to the south, and the Japanese had blocking positions and patrol bases all along the route. Two companies of the Scots Fusiliers were involved in heavy fighting at Sindegang. The battalion's route was then eastwards towards the Mandalay road, and during April and May 1945 the battalion spent much time in patrolling and clearing areas of remaining Japanese troops north of Mandalay. At the end of the month the 1st Royal Scots Fusiliers withdrew from the theatre and returned to India.

* * * * *

During 1944 and 1945 four battalions of the regiment fought in North West Europe, the 6th and 11th Battalions landing in Normandy in mid-June 1944 with the 15th Division. The 6th was in action on the River Odon, west of Caen, on 25 June. Working with armour, they captured St Mauvieu in their first major engagement; and effectively resisted a German counter-attack. Further counter-attacks were concentrated against the divisional area for the next few days. In the middle of July the battalion was involved in the fighting south-west of Caen, and then moved westwards to take up positions beside the Americans, preparing for a breakout. The divisional task was to cover the flank and disrupt the enemy's movement. Fighting in the bocage country was a difficult and slow business, but the battalion kept in close contact with the enemy as they withdrew.

The 11th Battalion had meanwhile reached the front on 15 June, and ten days later took part in 'Operation Martlet', south of Caen. The battalion's objectives in this battle were Fontenay-le-Pesnel and Rauray. In the confusion of smoke and mist there were many close-quarter engagements with the enemy, resulting in very heavy casualties. In mid-August the 11th Battalion was involved in operations to clear the route from Caen to Falaise.

Both battalions moved rapidly forward as the allies approached the River Seine. The 11th Royal Scots Fusiliers' route was through the channel ports, of which Le Havre was the most heavily defended, and by 24 September they had reached the Turnhout-Antwerp Canal. The 6th Battalion moved further south across the Rivers Seine and Somme, past Courtrai and on towards Malines, south of Antwerp. The 6th Royal Scots Fusiliers then moved forward to Aart on the Meuse-Escaut Canal. There had been some very fierce fighting on the canal line and the Scots Fusiliers mounted a counter-attack on Aart which they only temporarily occupied before being forced to withdraw. The fighting for the town lasted from 14 to 18 September. Operations to relieve the airborne troops at Arnhem, the purpose of operations in this area, were frustrated by determined German resistance.

The 4th/5th Battalion, Royal Scots Fusiliers serv-

A group of Royal Scots Fusiliers play cards during a lull in operations in Holland, Oct 1944. IWM

ing in the 52nd Lowland Division, reached Holland from England in mid-October 1944. Their first task was the assault and capture of the two large islands in the Scheldt estuary, Walcheren and South Beveland. The 4th/5th Scots Fusiliers and the 6th Cameronians invaded the latter on 26 October in amphibious craft, and their 'buffaloes' had much difficulty in landing, but most of the troops got ashore after some delay. At first the battalion faced only small-arms fire and steady progress was made in clearing the enemy positions. Later German artillery fire was brought down on the Scots Fusiliers, but the British mortar and artillery counter-bombardment greatly assisted their progress. The division was then ordered to relieve the Canadians by capturing Walcheren island, much of which had been flooded. This was a difficult task, requiring much cooperation between the various battalions, but was eventually successful.

On the Dutch mainland the 6th Battalion in the 15th Division was heading towards Tilburg, and it entered the town on 27 October, meeting very little resistance. But advancing further, they met much more opposition east of Eindhoven and towards the River Maas. One of their major engagements was a successful brigade attack on Blerick on 3 December.

The 11th Battalion was still in the Antwerp-Turnhout area in late October, but then crossed into Holland. Their first two objectives were Wouw and Roosendaal: the Germans withdrew quickly from each, but maintained several positions in the open country in order to delay the British advance. In early December the Scots Fusiliers had to fight for possession of the area known as 'Nijmegen island'. There was much close-quarter fighting, and after the eventual capture of 'the island' they spent a considerable time patrolling the waterlogged countryside. In the early part of 1945 the battalion took part in numerous minor actions in the surrounding areas of Holland north and west of the Rhine, including a number of amphibious operations.

Meanwhile, the 4th/5th Battalion, Royal Scots Fusiliers had moved from Walcheren to the German border, north of Geilenkirchen on the River Roer. In January a corps attack was mounted to capture the Roer area west of the Rhine. The Scots Fusiliers, operating with the Sherwood Rangers and Fife and Forfar Yeomanry, attacked a group of three villages near Echterbosch on 18 January. Each village was a company task, and the Germans, fighting for their own territory, resisted strongly. The following day the Scots Fusiliers advanced from the captured villages, the Germans having decided to evacuate the area. A few days later the battalion mounted a successful attack on Schundorf, in order to relieve the hard-pressed 7th Cameronians.

The 6th Battalion fought during February 1945 in the Reichswald area. Its first major engagement was to support the capture of Cleve, and this required the battalion to seize the heavily-wooded high ground to the west of the town. This they achieved successfully. A week later the Scots Fusiliers took part in a brigade attack on Goch, ten miles south of Cleve. Each company achieved its objective despite the enemy's early successes in holding up the attack.

Once the Roer area had been cleared the British were able to continue the advance towards the Rhine. The 4th/5th Battalion then took part in the fierce fighting around Alpon, which subsequently involved most of their brigade. The battalion attacked from the north at first and other companies followed by attacking on other axes. During the night of 8 March the Germans withdrew from the town itself, but remained in the vicinity in order to inflict further delay. The battalion suffered over 170 casualties in this action.

The 4th/5th Battalion, Royals Scots Fusiliers moved to positions on the River Rhine in mid-March 1945. The 6th Battalion was also moved up and it formed part of the assault crossing on 24 March. On reaching the east bank, the 6th went straight into action. The fighting was very severe and casualties heavy; but by the evening most of the battalions' objectives in the Loh area were taken and they dug in. The following day the Scots Fusiliers advanced from the Rhine and headed for the River Ijssel. On 26 March they mounted an assault crossing over the river which was entirely successful. Their whole

brigade was then subjected to a very strong counter-attack, which was effectively resisted.

The 4th/5th Battalion had also crossed the Rhine as follow-up troops. By 5 April their brigade reached the Dortmund-Ems Canal, and the following day the Scots Fusiliers were ordered to take the town of Hopsten, supported by the Royal Scots Greys. There was very determined resistance by the Germans and the town eventually had to be taken by a brigade attack. The canal was then secured, allowing exploiting formations to proceed swiftly eastwards.

A fortnight later the 4th/5th Battalion was involved in the Weser crossing. It had to mount battalion attacks first on Etelsen and then on Baden, before moving on rapidly for the divisional objective of Bremen, which was captured in late April.

The 2nd Battalion, Royal Scots Fusiliers had earlier travelled from Palestine via Italy and Marseilles to the banks of the Rhine. They, too, crossed the river in March 1945, and their brigade was moved quickly eastwards to pass through ahead of the main British advance across the north German plain. Both the 2nd and 6th Battalions thus reached the River Elbe in late April. The 2nd Battalion had to fight a number of engagements before the river could be crossed; the 6th Battalion's major fighting was for the town of Uelzen. Once the advance continued, both battalions moved rapidly for the capture of Lübeck, which they reached at the time of the German surrender.

The Lord Provost of Edinburgh inspects the 1st Royal Scots Fusiliers at the laying-up ceremony of the Colours, May 1959. RHQ

At the end of the Second World War the 1st Battalion, Royal Scots Fusiliers was still serving in India. During this final period of British rule all troops were heavily involved in internal security duties, and the battalion was first stationed near Delhi, then at Meerut. Additional tasks were the control of refugees and guard duties during the evacuation of British civilians. The Scots Fusiliers returned to the United Kingdom in January 1948, and later in the year a cadre of the battalion moved to Germany to join the 2nd Battalion. Thus the amalgamated battalion was designated the 1st Royal Scots Fusiliers.

The Royal Scots Fusiliers remained in West Germany for some years, which included a tour of duty in Berlin. In 1954 the battalion moved to Penang, Malaya, and there it took part in the latter stages of the anti-terrorist campaign, conducting a number of operational tasks. In May 1958 the battalion was sent to Cyprus for a six-month tour of duty, where it spent part of the time on internal security duties. The Scots Fusiliers returned to the United Kingdom later in the year for their amalgamation with the Highland Light Infantry.

PART II
THE HIGHLAND LIGHT INFANTRY

THE 71ST HIGHLAND LIGHT INFANTRY
1777–1881

For thirty years John Mackenzie, Lord MacLeod, had fought for the Swedish crown. (His father, the Earl of Cromarty, had been out in the 1745 rebellion and had been captured and beheaded in London.) In 1777 Lord MacLeod, a lieutenant-general in the Swedish service, returned to Britain on hearing of the British military defeat at Saratoga. He was one of many who offered to raise regiments at this time, but his was the first Scottish one to be formed, drawing 840 highlanders, 236 lowland Scots, together with 38 Englishmen and Irishmen from Glasgow to the first muster at Elgin. A second battalion was quickly authorised and successfully recruited by George Mackenzie, Lord MacLeod's brother.

Of the two battalions more than half the soldiers were from Mackenzie country, and many of the officers bore that patronymic. The regiment was clothed in the government tartan with red doublets: later the tartan became differentiated by the addition of red and white stripes. Initially the regiment was numbered the 73rd (Highland) Foot.

The 1st Battalion of the regiment, however, did not fight in the American colonies, but after two years at home was sent to India to assist the Honorable East India Company in 1779. On arrival, the highlanders were ordered to discard highland dress and adopt jacket, trousers and headdress similar to company uniform. (Highland dress was reintroduced in 1798, and tartan trews were worn by all except for the pipers. The regiment did not re-adopt the kilt until 1945.)

The 2nd Battalion sailed for the Mediterranean in 1779 and was involved in the sea battle off Cape St Vincent, while helping to man the ships of the Royal Navy. Landing at Gibraltar, the battalion was required to man the defences of the Rock, which was under siege and sporadic bombardment from the Spanish at the time. On one occasion the flank company assisted in a particularly daring attack on a Spanish battery, close to the British forward positions, and helped to destroy it. The battalion's task completed, it returned to Scotland and was disbanded.

The 1st Battalion served in India for eighteen years. The French colonists there were determined to limit British power, and encouraged the Sultan of Mysore, Hyder Ali, and his son Tippoo Sahib, to fight against the British. The British force concentrated at Conjeveram in August 1780 near Madras, and Hyder Ali's army quickly encircled it. The regiment's flank companies were detached with a smaller force, which was then attacked by the main part of the army under Tippoo Sahib. The British force stood up to charge upon charge of cavalry, but was eventually overwhelmed. The survivors, which included Capt (later Sir David) Baird, were kept in captivity and were horribly tortured.

In July 1781 the 73rd Highlanders served under Sir Eyre Coote at the Battle of Porto Novo. When the British attacked, the 73rd were in the centre of the front line, and by a skilful manoeuvre, the front line attacked the enemy's flank: after nine hours of the most desperate fighting, the Mysore army was defeated. Eight weeks later, the British force again attacked Hyder Ali at Conjeveram. Using a similar tactic, the enemy was again defeated, with the 73rd again fighting in the front line.

In September the regiment was once more in action, this time at Sholinghur. The flank companies were used against the enemy flank, and the remaining companies attacked their cavalry. In this action the regiment's casualties were high, but the army of Mysore was again defeated. A few months later Vellore was relieved, with the 73rd playing an important part.

In 1782, the British force was attacked at Arnee from two directions, but by rapid manoeuvre and effective counter-attacking, a British victory was secured. A year later the regiment fought against a combined army of Mysore and their French allies at Cuddalore. The regiment successfully captured seven redoubts, but in the fighting was reduced to half its strength; news of a peace treaty prevented the capture of the fort. The regiment remained on garrison duties and was redesignated the 71st Regiment in 1786.

Tippoo Sahib invaded Travancore in 1790, and it was decided by the British authorities that the war should be taken to Mysore. In early 1791 the British force besieged Bangalore and the grenadier and light companies of the British regiments broke through into the fortress. It was a most remarkable feat and opened the way to Seringapatam, Tippoo Sahib's capital. This town was set on an island in the River Cauvery, but being held in very great strength, the British were not yet ready to assault it.

During the latter part of the year, the 71st assisted in the capture of three important enemy forts. Then in February 1792 the army under Lord Cornwallis, reached Seringapatam and laid siege to it. When a night assault was mounted, the 71st and 74th Highlanders were in the centre column. Much of the fighting was in and around the river, and several of the redoubts were scaled against fierce opposition. The regiment, in company with some native troops, was attacked on 7 February by 3,000 enemy cavalry on the island, but were repulsed. Apart from the main fort itself, the whole town was captured; and eventually Tippoo Sahib agreed a peace treaty.

In 1795 the flank companies assisted in the seizure of Ceylon from the Dutch, who were now allied to the French. Two years later the regiment left India, many of its number, however, being drafted to the 73rd and 74th Highlanders. It reached Scotland in mid-1798 and, due to the shortage of recruits took some time to be brought up to strength.

* * * * *

In 1805 the 71st Highlanders sailed for Cape Colony, which the government had decided should be annexed to the British Crown. The force, which included the Highland Brigade comprising the 71st, 72nd and 93rd Highlanders, secured a beach-head, and the whole force reached the Blueberg Hill on the route to Cape Town. There the highlanders took part in the attack against the main Dutch force, which they defeated without any further fighting in January 1806.

An extraordinary expedition was mounted from Cape Town in the same year, at the instigation of Commodore Sir Home Popham. The 71st Highlanders, with some artillery and cavalry, sailed with the Royal Navy to attack Spanish settlements in South America. On arrival it was decided to seize the town of Buenos Aires. The landing was unopposed and the force reached the city, whereupon the hastily mustered Spanish defenders fled, and the city capitulated. A vast hoard of treasure was captured and prize-money was shared out eventually amongst the victors. After a time, however, the Spanish raised a strong force and attacked the British, who surrendered after a fight. A second British force sent as a reinforcement and who had earlier captured Montevideo, was also outnumbered and captured. The 71st Highlanders and other captives, made a favourable impression on the Spanish, who treated them with much hospitality. Eventually terms were agreed for their repatriation to Britain.

* * * * *

In 1808 the 71st Highlanders sailed to the Peninsula to assist in the defence of Portugal against the French. On reaching the country, the British set off on the march to Lisbon. The first engagement with the French was at Rolica, in which the light company of the regiment took part. Four days later, on 21 August, the battle of Vimeiro was fought. The 71st Highlanders were in a brigade initially posted on the east ridge of Vimeiro Hill and hidden from view. From this position they mounted a suprise flank attack which, despite a determined French counter-attack, resulted in the enemy's defeat and flight. The treaty of Cintra followed, and the French withdrew from Portugal for the time being.

In October 1808 the 71st, serving under Sir John Moore, marched into Spain with the ambitious aim of expelling the French. Half the British force, which included the 71st, passed near to Madrid, but the French army, under Napoleon and numbering 194,000, was also fast approaching the capital. Reuniting the two parts of his army at Salamanca, Moore realised that he was completely outnumbered, and had no option but to withdraw his whole force northwards. With the French hard by, the army reached Corunna in January 1809, depleted in number and in some disorder. The 71st Highlanders were employed first as covering troops at the beach-head, then they were sent as reinforcements to the British left which faced the French main attack. After some bitter fighting the French attack subsided and the British successfully embarked and sailed for England.

In 1808 the regiment was one of a number of regiments that had been given the light infantry role, and from 1810 it became known as the 71st Highland Light Infantry. The pipers retained the kilt; the soldiers their tartan trews and highland bonnet.

In 1809 the 71st joined the Walcheren expedition, numbering some 38,000 troops, whose purpose was to capture the Scheldt estuary. On landing, the brigade in which the 71st served made a quick advance towards Veere and cleared the route of enemy outposts. The fort was captured on the morning of 1 August and, a fortnight later, Flushing was attacked. The 71st's task was to carry out a surprise attack on the eastern part of the town, and two days later it surrendered. The British force remained as garrison troops for the remainder of the year, but suffered a severe epidemic of typhoid fever which caused numerous deaths.

After spending a year recuperating in England, the 71st joined Sir Arthur Wellesley's (later the Duke of Wellington) army in Portugal. The regiment was actively engaged against the enemy during October while manning the picquets near Sobral. On one occasion an attack by a considerable French force was repulsed. During the winter the British army withdrew behind the lines of Torres Vedras, but in the spring of 1811 advanced in pursuit of the French.

The French decided to block the British advance at Fuentes d'Onor. There the enemy succeeded in forcing some British light companies out of the village, which the 71st then were ordered to attack. This they did and swiftly captured the village, whereupon a French counter-attack of four battalions was mounted which, with the arrival of the 79th Highlanders, was repulsed. On the third day of the battle, under pressure the two regiments had to withdraw partially; but with further reinforcements, including the 74th Highlanders, the position was regained and held successfully.

In the autumn of 1811 the regiment operated with Sir Rowland Hill in the Estremadura region, and carried out a highly successful surprise attack at Arroyo Molinos. There followed considerable manoeuvring during the winter, and in May 1812 Hill's force attacked the fortress of Almaraz. The 71st HLI was used in the assault of the outlying Fort Napoleon and, after storming the ramparts, fought at close quarters with the French, forcing them to abandon the position.

During the remainder of 1812, there was much further marching and manouevring of Wellington's army, and later in the year it withdrew to Ciudad Roderigo. Wellington was determined to outmanoeuvre the French, and on 21 June 1813 the battle of Vitoria was fought.

'The 71st were ordered to ascend the heights of La Puebla, to support the Spanish forces under General Morillo. They accordingly advanced in open column, and having formed line, were immediately hotly engaged with the enemy, and upon this occasion suffered an irreparable loss in the fall of their CO, the Hon Colonel Henry Cadogan, who fell mortally wounded while leading his men to the charge. The 71st continued advancing, and driving the enemy from the heights, until the force which was opposed to them became so unequal, and the loss of the battalion so severe, that it was obliged to retire upon the remainder of the brigade. In the performance of this arduous duty the battalion suffered very severely.'

The Heights were captured eventually in fierce close-quarter fighting, and this enabled the River Zadorra to be quickly crossed by a large part of the army. A determined French counter-attack was mounted during this operation, but reinforcements arrived which included the 92nd Highlanders, and the French were beaten off. The victory cost the 71st HLI over 300 casualties.

The campaign continued, and on 25 July the 71st, 50th and 92nd Regiments were attacked in great strength at Baztan Pass. The French were fought off successfully until they threatened to turn the British flank. The three regiments then withdrew and were relieved by a fresh brigade who repelled the enemy. The 71st had suffered 200 casualties in this battle. Subsequently several skirmishes were fought before the French retreated from Spain, and further actions were fought in holding the frontier; the most notable for the regiment was at Roncesvalles.

On entering France the regiment's first engagement was the capture of Cambo on the River Nive, which

The 71st Highland Light Infantry, having fought throughout the Peninsular War, returned to the Continent in 1815. In this contemporary print, they are seen in action at Quartre Bras.

National Museums of Scotland

was lightly held. The campaign in the Pyrenees, however, took many months and Soult made an attack on 13 December at St Pierre near Bayonne. The 71st HLI held a position during the battle on a hill to the left of the British line; again, the French were forced to withdraw from the battlefield. Two months later the regiment fought in the Battle of Orthez.

The final battle of the campaign took place on 10 April 1814 at Toulouse, but the 71st played only a small part. There were only about 75 of the original members of the regiment who had served throughout the Peninsular campaign; more than 300 had been killed and four times that number wounded. In June the regiment moved to Ireland.

The regiment was recalled for service on the continent in April 1815, and in June the HLI was deployed to block the road between the French frontier and Ghent. When Napoleon's purpose and route was known, the regiment was sent towards Brussels and on the night of 17 June was concentrated with the remainder of the army near the village of Waterloo.

The following morning the HLI moved into dead ground by Merbe-Braine on the British right, and during the first part of the battle was engaged by French artillery. When their time came, the regiment was sent to drive off some French troops in the area of Hougoumont farm.

'A heavy fire now commenced upon the retreating enemy, but the *alignement* having been completely deranged by the impetuosity of the advance, Colonel Reynell, with his usual coolness, proceeded to restore order, and had just completed the dressing of the line when the French cavalry were seen advancing. Square was instantly formed, and the 71st with the rest of the brigade, sustained a charge from three regiments of French cavalry, namely, one of *cuirassiers*, one of *grenadiers-à-cheval*, and one of lancers. The charge was made with the most obstinate bravery, but nothing could overcome the steadiness of the British infantry; and after a destructive loss, the French were forced to retire.'

Late in the day the HLI advanced in line with their brigade to attack the French line, and its action in the battle was the capture of some guns of the Imperial Guard. In contributing to the allied victory the regiment had played its part bravely, and its casualties were over 200.

* * * * *

After serving as troops of occupation until 1818, the regiment returned to England. By this time a second battalion, raised in 1804 for home service, had been disbanded. Serving in England and Ireland for the next six years, the 71st HLI then embarked for Canada for the next ten. After a period at home for four years it returned a second time to Canada, where there was considerable trouble from the settlers, particularly those of French extraction. The Americans, too, made several armed sorties and the 71st were kept fully occupied on internal security duties. A second battalion was again formed in 1842 and sent out to be regimented with the 1st in Canada. It remained in Canada when the 1st Battalion moved to the West Indies in 1843.

The 1st Battalion returned to the United Kingdom in 1847 and in 1853 sailed for Corfu to take up garrison duties. In 1855 the two battalions were amalgamated on reaching Balaclava for service in the Crimea. The major battles had already taken place, but soon after its arrival the 71st was part of a force sent to capture and hold the Straits of Kerch at the eastern end of the Crimea. This expedition was highly successful and captured considerable stockpiles of fuel and grain, as well as more than 300 Russian guns. The regiment then mounted several raids on enemy positions and shipping in the area. Meanwhile, a reserve company of the regiment served with the troops besieging Savastopol.

Soldiers of the 71st Highland Light Infantry at skirmishing practice in the 1850s. The bugle badge of light infantry corps is clearly shown on their shakos. Contemporary sketch by Capt A. Grant.
National Museums of Scotland

The regiment arrived in India in 1758. There were still parties of mutinous Indians at large and the regiment joined the Central India Field Force to seek them out. The first action was at Koonch, followed by the holding of the two villages of Diapura and Matra. The highlanders were constantly on the move, and fought several skirmishes against the Indians before taking up peacetime duties at Gwalior.

In 1863 the regiment was sent to join the Ambeyla campaign against the rebellious Sittanas on the North-West Frontier. The plan was to gain the Ambeyla Pass and drive the tribesmen out of their settlements. This, however, infuriated the other Pathan tribes who attacked the 71st HLI guarding the camp at Ambeyla, but were successfully repulsed. When guarding hill-top picquets, the highlanders were frequently attacked. On one occasion a British detachment numbering some 200 soldiers, was overwhelmed by a strong force of tribesmen on 'Crag picquet'. The 71st were ordered immediately to counter-attack. The highlanders climbed up the precipitous and rocky slope as fast as they could, under fire from the enemy who also hurled rocks onto them. Led by their commanding officer, Col Hope, the 71st stormed over the summit. Many of the enemy had fled already, but the highlanders cleared the remainder of the position. For several hours they continued to hunt the tribesmen who still remained in other parts of the ridge. Returning to Rawalpindi at the end of the campaign, the regiment supplied over 200 volunteers to join other highland regiments.

From 1865 until 1881 the 71st HLI served in the United Kingdom, Gibraltar, Malta and Cyprus. The regiment was linked with the 78th Highlanders in 1872, as their recruiting areas were both in the area of Inverness. In 1881 the regiment amalgamated with the 74th Highlanders to form the 1st and 2nd Battalions of the Highland Light Infantry. Both battalions continued to wear trews, Mackenzie being the chosen tartan. Their depot was established in Lanark, which was an unpopular decision, but the 71st had maintained a close relationship from its early years with the nearby city of Glasgow.

THE 74TH HIGHLAND REGIMENT

1787–1881

The Honourable East India Company's war between 1780–83 against Hyder Ali, Sultan of Mysore, has already been described earlier in this chapter. It was decided that the power of Mysore had to be destroyed and four new regular regiments were raised in 1787 specifically to support the company in India. Command of the new 74th Regiment was given to Major General Sir Archibald Campbell of Inverneil. As he was Governor of Madras, the regiment was raised on his behalf by Lt-Col Gordon Forbes, and Campbell's two brothers. Recruiting took place during the autumn, mainly in the western highlands, and many who joined had served in the army previously. At first the highland uniform of red coatee and belted plaid of government tartan was worn.

Four companies sailed to India in March 1788, and the remainder arrived the following year at Poonamallee near Madras. In early 1790 the regiment joined the Bengal brigade as the Madras army set out to fight Tippoo Sahib. For some months the Sultan evaded the British force, but it soon captured the fort of Bangalore from the Mysorean defenders. Then a probing attack on Tippoo Sahib's force outside his capital of Seringapatam was mounted, but was not wholly successful. A number of outlying forts were then attacked; the flank companies of the regiment took one at Pinaga and the whole regiment led the attack on another at Kistuagherry. There the lower fort was taken, but not the upper fort since it proved virtually impossible to scale. In early February Seringapatam itself was attacked. The flank companies of the 74th were in the centre of the assault force, whilst the remainder formed a guard for Lord Cornwallis, the Commander-in-Chief. The highlanders were in action constantly during the battle. Fearing the capture of his fortress, Tippoo Sahib sued for peace and accepted British terms, ceding half his territory.

In 1793 the long war against revolutionary France began, and in India the 74th Highlanders were in action against both French troops and their native allies. The French town of Pondicherry was captured and for a time the regiment occupied it. But Tippoo Sahib was again fomenting trouble against the British, and full-scale war was inevitable.

In early 1799 the British army of Madras marched out with the express purpose of capturing Seringapatam. Tippoo Sahib's force mounted several harrassing attacks on the army as it moved forward, and a battle was fought at Malavelly in March. The 74th were on the right of the army and mounted a spirited attack on the enemy, including their cavalry. The Mysoreans were defeated and the British reached Tippoo Sahib's capital.

Preparations for the siege and attack on Seringapatam were then made, which included building earthworks and the positioning of guns. The 74th were actively involved in this work and had to beat off several enemy sorties. On the afternoon of 4 May the assault on Seringapatam started. The regiment formed part of the right-hand column, and pressed forward through the river to the breach in the walls made by the artillery. Under heavy fire from the defenders, the attacking columns forced their way into the fortress. There was much hand-to-hand fighting on the walls and inside the defences, during which Tippoo was killed; much of the town was destroyed before the fighting ceased. The regiment had played a conspicuous part in the victory.

Although Tippoo Sahib's power had been finally destroyed, there were many of his followers loose in the area, and the regiment's flank companies assisted in a successful attack on a fort at Hollal. The regiment as a whole also took part in several similar actions against enemy strongholds during the following months. The most strongly held fort was at Panjalamcoorchy, and after the two assault companies of the 74th sustained nearly two-thirds casualties, they had to withdraw. Two months later, reinforced by further British companies, they again attacked. This time the attack was successful, but, as before, there were many casualties. Operations of this nature continued for some time before peace was restored.

The 74th Highlanders were stationed at Wallajahbad in 1803, and served for a time with Maj-Gen The Hon Arthur Wellesley (later the Duke of Wellington) in the Mahratta campaign. The first major action was the seizure of Ahmednaggar on 11 August, where the regiment was divided in three parts amongst the besieging columns, which also included the 78th Highlanders. The outer defences were attacked first and, although very strongly held, the highlanders succeeded in scaling the walls and opening the gates. The main fort capitulated on the following day. Wellesley's army advanced to meet the Mahrattas in open battle and on 23 September the battle of Assaye was fought. The Mahratta army numbered 45,000 men, was officered by Europeans, and had a large artillery force of over 100 guns. Wellesley had the southern half of the Madras army, one sixth the strength of the Mahrattas and only 22 guns: the three British regiments in his force were the 74th and 78th Highlanders and the 19th Light Dragoons. Wellesley formed up his army with the 74th in the second line, and attempted to outmanoeuvre the enemy. When the enemy's artillery bombardment began, the two British lines advanced. Wellington's disarmingly honest account of the battle went as follows:

'However, by one of those unlucky accidents which frequently happen, the officer commanding the picquets which were upon the right led immediately up to the village of Assaye. The 74th regiment, which was on the right of the second line, and was ordered to support the picquets, followed them. There was a large break in our line between these corps and those on the left. They were exposed to a most terrible cannonade from Assaye, and were charged by the cavalry belonging to the Campoos; consequently in the picquets and the 74th regiments we sustained the greatest part of our loss.

'Another bad consequence resulting from this mistake was the necessity of introducing the cavalry into the action at too early a period. I had ordered it to watch the motions of the enemy's cavalry hanging upon our right, and luckily it charged in time to save the remains of the 74th and the picquets.'

The 19th Dragoons and Madras cavalry charged to relieve the 74th and the enemy's left wing collapsed. The stand of the 74th Highlanders had enabled the left flank, which comprised the 78th Highlanders, to capture the enemy artillery. Thirteen officers of the 74th died and the remaining five were wounded during the battle, while nearly 400 soldiers were casualties.

Three months later the combined Madras army fought the Mahrattas at Argaum where the two highland regiments were joined by the 94th Foot, the old Scots Brigade. The two opposing front lines, which included the 74th, advanced on each other and fought in bitter hand-to-hand conflict. The Madras army's cavalry then charged and the Mahratta troops dispersed in confusion. Subsequently the enemy withdrew to Gwalighur, which was successfully stormed on 15 December by the 74th Highlanders and other troops. The leaders of the Mahrattas settled for peace soon afterwards, but the 74th spent some months in following and destroying enemy bands who refused to abide by the peace treaty.

The regiment left India in 1805 just over 100 strong and returned to the United Kingdom in order to recruit. Due to a shortage of manpower, it was removed from the highland establishment in 1809, in company with some other regiments, and lost the right to wear highland dress. The following year it went to Portugal to reinforce the 3rd Division under Sir Thomas Picton, where the British army was anticipating an invasion by the French.

This occurred in September and Wellington had lured the French towards his position at Busaco. Two companies of the 74th Highlanders were immediately involved in fighting enemy skirmishers, while the remainder in the front line fought off the advancing French columns. Despite the withdrawal of a Portuguese regiment next to the 74th, the regiment maintained its stand. The French eventually abandoned the attack and withdrew completely from the battlefield.

During the months that followed, the 74th Regiment, still serving in the 3rd Division, marched and counter-marched for long periods, attempting to outmanoeuvre and harass the French. At Fuentes d'Onor on the Spanish border on 3 May 1811 the French attacked, soon capturing the village from the British. The 74th were called upon late in the day to re-take the village, which it succeeded in doing; then

Wellington is cheered by the victors of the storming of Badajos. A piper and men of the 74th Regt (who were dressed as ordinary infantry of the line) are depicted in this painting by R. Caton Woodville. RHQ

the regiment held it for three days before the French finally withdrew. Ten days later the 74th joined in the siege of Badajos for a month, before Wellington decided to abandon it. The regiment was involved in several more actions during the remainder of the year.

In January 1812 the attack on the fortress of Ciudad Roderigo was mounted. The outlying defences having been taken one by one, the 74th were ordered to storm the main fortress. There was much confused fighting in the darkness, but the fortress was captured. In mid-March, the 74th and its division returned to Badajos and the siege was resumed in earnest. On the night of 6 April the assault was lauched on this the most formidable fortress in Spain. The 3rd Division's task was to mount a feint on the citadel, whilst the main attack went in on the fortifications of the town itself. The feint, however, was so effective that it developed into a major assault. The 74th Regiment succeeded in scaling the walls and soon the 3rd Division had seized the citadel. The main attack, however, had foundered during the night, but was resumed at dawn; the breaches were entered and the whole fortified town taken. The sacking of the town was an unfortunate sequel to the victory, but was no doubt a human response to the desperate danger and physical ordeal of the attack.

The British advance through Spain began and by mid-July the two armies were manoeuvring for battle in the area of Salamanca. During the battle, the 74th Regiment advanced from a concealed position and charged the French flank. The whole division formed squares and the British cavalry passed through them to break up the French infantry. This victory enabled the British army to advance and occupy Madrid, where it spent the winter months.

The advance on the French border continued in the spring of 1813. At Vitoria the French army had taken up a strong position, and on 21 June the battle began. The 74th was in the British centre and was given the order to takė the village of Arinez.

Captain M'Queen's account of the battle was as follows:

'At Vitoria,' he says, 'I had the command of three companies for the purpose of driving the French out of the village of Arinez, where they were strongly posted; we charged through the village and the enemy retired in great confusion. Lieutenants Alves and Ewing commanded the com-

panies which accompanied me. I received three wounds that day, but remained with the regiment during the whole action; Davis (Lieutenant) carried the colours that day, and it was one of the finest things you can conceive to see the 74th advancing in line, with the enemy in front, on very broken ground full of ravines, as regularly, and in as good line as if on parade. This is in a great measure to be attributed to Davis, whose coolness and gallantry were conspicuous; whenever we got into broken ground, he with the colours was first on the bank, and stood there until the regiment formed on his right and left.'

In the action some enemy guns were captured, but the three companies of the regiment holding the village were counter-attacked with great determination by the French. The remainder of the regiment came quickly to their relief. Later in the battle there was considerable confusion as the French line began to disintegrate; then the whole British army advanced together and routed the enemy. There was, however, much more marching and manoeuvring before the French finally withdrew towards their own frontier.

On 10 November 1813 the British army arrived at the River Nivelle after a concealed approach. The 74th Regiment's task in the battle was to seize the fortifications of Sarre. The French soon abandoned this position and the regiment captured an important bridge. The result of the battle was a further French withdrawal and a temporary lull in the fighting. In late February 1814 the French held a very strong position at Orthez. The regiment was in action against French skirmishers before the battle and, during the fighting, were forced to give ground until their division was reinforced. The French attack was eventually turned and they left the battlefield.

Painting by Henry Martens shows the 74th Highlanders fighting in the Amatola Mountains in South Africa during the Kaffir War, 1850-53. RHQ

The advance into France continued during the spring of 1814 and the regiment was involved in a fierce action at Tarbes. On 10 April the battle for Toulouse began; the 74th was in the centre and advanced over three miles in contact with the French. The regiment then attacked and overwhelmed the enemy guarding the bridge at Jumeaux. Elsewhere the battle went well for the British. Toulouse was entered by Wellington's army on 12 April, and hostilities ceased immediately.

* * * * *

The regiment was stationed in Ireland from mid-1814, followed by many years in Canada and the West Indies. It was not until 1845 that the regiment again returned to the United Kingdom, and in the same year regained the official title of 74th (Highland) Regiment of Foot, and resumed wearing tartan trews. The Lamont tartan was authorised – government tartan, to which was added a white stripe.

In early 1851 the regiment embarked for service in the Kaffir war in South Africa. From their secure villages in the Amatola mountains, the Kaffirs had periodically attacked the British settlements in the eastern Cape colony over a period of many years.

British troops in the Cape consisted of one cavalry regiment and seven battalions of infantry supported by artillery, engineers and mounted rifles. The regiment's first engagement against the Kaffirs was at Theopolis, but the whole force moved to Fort Hare for operations in the Amatola mountains in June 1851.

The 74th Highlanders' next major action was the assault on the Victoria Heights. The highlanders ascended the steep slope under fire from the Kaffirs, firing volleys as they climbed; this position was quickly taken and the Kaffirs withdrew. Operations thereafter took on the nature of anti-guerrilla bush warfare, concerned with capturing villages, rounding up cattle and destroying Kaffir bands. Occasionally the Kaffirs attacked in force, but more often approached silently in small groups and set upon British soldiers by night. The enemy were particularly intent on keeping possession of the area of Waterkloof, and in an expedition to clear it in November, the regiment was again attacked by a large force of Kaffirs. They were repulsed, but operations throughout the year resulted in a steady number of regimental casualties. This war was quickly followed by operations against the Basutos, who were mounting raids on British settlements on the Orange River.

Death of Lt-Col Fordyce of the 74th Highlanders during a skirmish in Kaffraria. Engraving by Capt W. R. King.

One of the hazards of overseas service was exemplified by the wreck of the troopship *Birkenhead*. This ship struck a reef in Simon's Bay off the South African coast on 26 February 1852, while carrying drafts for the British regiments in South Africa. The 74th Highlanders' draft numbered 2 officers and 72 rank and file; that of the 73rd, 1 and 70; and for the 91st, 1 officer and 60 men. Colonel Seton of the 74th was in command of the troops. During the twenty-five minutes that the ship took to sink, the barely-trained troops assisted in seeing the women and children to the boats, and courageously returned to their line on the decks.

'The situation was now more critical than ever; but the soldiers remained quietly in their places, while Colonel Seton stood in the gangway with his sword drawn, seeing the women and children safely passed down into the second cutter. This duty was speedily effected, and the cutter was ordered to lie off about 150 yards from the rapidly sinking ship. In about ten minutes after she first struck, she broke in two at the foremast – this mast and the funnel falling over to the starboard side, crushing many, and throwing into the water those who were endeavouring to clear the paddle-box boat. But the men kept their places, though many of them were mere lads, who had been in the service only a few months. An eye-witness, speaking of the captain and Colonel Seton at this time, has said – "Side by side they stood at the helm, providing for the safety of all that could be saved. They never tried to save themselves."'

9 officers and 348 rank and file were drowned.

In 1854 the 74th Highlanders reached India and were stationed in the south. They were not actively involved in the suppression of the Mutiny, as southern

A group of 74th Highlanders c1870 showing the Assaye Colour awarded to the regiment by the Honourable East India Company to commemorate the battle. Highland dress of trews was restored to the regiment in 1845; the tartan was Lamont.

India was largely unaffected, although they were occasionally on active duty against troublesome natives. The rest of their tour of ten years was relatively quiet. Service in England, Ireland, Gibraltar, Malta, the Straits Settlements and Hong Kong followed. During this time the 74th was linked with the 26th Cameronians, and the regimental depot was established at Hamilton, Lanarkshire.

In 1880 the 74th Highlanders reached Scotland, moving to Aldershot the following year. The amalgamation with the 71st Highland Light Infantry took place in 1881, although the 2nd Battalion retained in use the number '74th' for very many years. The battalion subsequently adopted trews of Mackenzie tartan, having refused the opportunity of becoming a kilted regiment.

THE HIGHLAND LIGHT INFANTRY

1881–1913

In 1882 the 2nd Battalion, Highland Light Infantry was sent under Sir Garnet Wolseley, to Egypt to contain the revolt of the Arabs against British and French interests. The Highland Brigade, serving in the 2nd Division, landed at Ismailia on the Suez Canal on 9 September, while the Egyptian rebels under Arabi Pasha were in entrenched positions at Tel-El-Kebir, thirty miles west. The British force advanced and, at dawn on 13 September, launched an attack on the Egyptian lines, which were covered by artillery and protected by a deep ditch. The HLI and other battalions endured enemy rifle fire as they advanced, but obeyed orders not to return the fire. The task of crossing the ditch while conforming with other battalions was the most difficult part of the battle.

'On reaching the enemy's works, the centre of the battalion found itself stopped by a ditch, about 9 feet deep by 10 feet wide, and with almost perpendicular scarps. Into this, unseen in the darkness, many of the front line fell, amongst them being Lt Goold Adams, who, along with Cpls Buchan and Adams, succeeded in mounting the opposite face. These pulled others up, and thus collected a small party, which lay waiting for an opportunity to rush over the parapet. The main body of the centre, now reinforced by the second line, was meanwhile swaying backwards and forwards, seeking vainly in the darkness for some means of entry; but the flanks, more fortunate, had found the ditches opposite them shallower, and the parapets lower, and had forced their way in.'

The Egyptians were quickly routed and pursued by the cavalry. The British victory brought the revolt to an end, and the battalion remained in Egypt until early the following year.

The 1st Battalion, meanwhile, remained in the United Kingdom until 1895, after which it served in Malta. On moving to Crete to fulfil a treaty agreement, the battalion carried out the thankless task of peacekeeping until 1898. The 2nd Battalion went to India in 1884, and in 1897 were sent to Rawalpindi to join the Malakand Field Force to fight the Pathans whose attacks against the British had increased. The battalion successfully defeated one such in October 1897, mainly by the application of long-range rifle fire. The battalion's major action of the campaign took place in January of the following year when the force advanced on the Tanga Pass. On reaching it the HLI and two other battalions, mounted a direct attack involving a stiff ascent of the rocks. The action was entirely successful.

In 1899 the 1st Battlion was sent to South Africa on the outbreak of the second Boer War to join the Highland Brigade. Landing at Cape Town, the brigade formed part of Lord Methuen's force which set out for the Modder River in November. It reached the area of Magersfontein on 10 December, near a strong Boer position, supposedly on top of a hill. The battle which followed against an unreconnoitred position, was badly planned. The orders were to attack at dawn and take the position with the bayonet. During the approach march in the darkness the brigade was hampered by the thick bush country, and when deploying ready for the attack, the Boers opened fire at close range from positions at the foot of the hill. Control was lost and the highlanders formed up as best they could and attempted to charge the Boers. Casualties were very high and the highlanders could not approach the hill closer than 400 yards. Throughout the day the HLI and other troops remained in exposed positions and there were even confused orders about the withdrawal in the late afternoon. Thus the battle proved to be a costly disaster. The following day Lord Methuen's force had to withdraw, but established positions on the Modder River. The HLI was later moved to Paardeberg as the Boers withdrew, and spent much time in long-range shooting against the enemy.

By May 1900 the battalion rejoined the Highland

A piper of the HLI demonstrates the sword dance outside a public house. A print of c1890. RHQ

This period-piece of the 1890s shows the 2nd HLI on route march near Aldershot. RHQ

Brigade for the relief of Mafeking and capture of Pretoria. At Heilbron the HLI led the successful attack on the town, but the following month the battalion had to hold the town while being cut off from the rest of the army. Fortunately the HLI were relieved before supplies were exhausted.

In July 1900 the HLI were operating against the Boers in the Orange Free State and Transvaal. They captured a strong Boer position at Retiefs Nek and assisted in the capture of Naauwpoort Nek. In August the battalion marched to Kroonstadt, and was subsequently sent to Bloemfontein to operate independently against the Boers in the Orange River Colony. For the next nine months the Highland Light Infantry trekked through the area, and gradually the Boers' activities dwindled until a peace settlement was agreed. In 1902 the battalion left South Africa for the United Kingdom, but after one year was sent to Cairo and subsequently the Sudan.

The 2nd Battalion had by now returned to the United Kingdom from India and remained at home in various stations. The 1st Battalion moved in 1904 from the Sudan to Meerut in India. They remained there at peacetime duties until mobilisation in August 1914.

THE HIGHLAND LIGHT INFANTRY

1914–38

On 13 August the 2nd Battalion Highland Light Infantry left for France with the British Expeditionary Force. After much marching, the battalion reached Paturages where the German advance on the British line was temporarily checked. The fear of being outflanked necessitated the withdrawal of the BEF from Mons and, although not heavily engaged, the battalion marched some 200 miles in a fortnight.

In mid-September the battalion was engaged during the battle of the River Aisne in the area of Chemin des Dames. During the ensuing month, there was much fierce fighting which prevented a German breakthrough on the Marne and the 2nd HLI was then moved north with the BEF to new positions near Ypres. On 21 October the battalion took part in an attack north of the town, but this was followed by a series of strong German counter-attacks. The battalion front line was opposite Polygon Wood, and on 7 November B Company, holding a trench close to the German front line, was attacked during the dark at

Sgt-bugler Mauchan, and a sgt-piper of 2nd HLI c1890. The elephant badge on the sporran, denoting an Assaye regiment, and the MacKenzie tartan, HLI sett, can be seen clearly. RHQ

4.30am. The enemy rushed in to the trench and the highlanders set about them with bayonets, rifle butts, fists and any other weapons at hand. Lt Brodie, who was awarded the VC in this action, bayoneted four and shot five Germans who had overrun one of the company's Maxim guns, and trained the weapon along the trench before opening fire. 80 enemy were killed and a further 54 taken prisoner in the fighting.

The 1st HLI and the 9th Territorial battalion known as the Glasgow Highlanders, reached France respectively in November and December 1914. All three battalions spent much time in the front line during the winter months. The 1st Battalion, serving in an Indian brigade, took part in an attack to the east of Neuve Chapelle on 12 March 1915. Exposed to fearsome fire from the flank, the highlanders nevertheless advanced and held what ground they had gained, their casualties being more than 250 dead and wounded. Two months later, during the second battle of Ypres, the battalion was in support of the French during a three-day battle on the Ypres-Langemark road.

The 1st HLI and Glasgow Highlanders were in the front line near Festubert during these months, and in May all three battalions took part in the fighting between Neuve Chapelle and Festubert in the attempt to capture Aubers Ridge. Little was gained as the German positions were well constructed and strongly defended. A second attack was more successful, but in a night assault on German front line positions a high number of casualties was suffered, particularly by the 2nd Battalion.

* * * * *

In the meantime the 52nd Lowland Division had embarked for operations in Gallipoli, and three Territorial battalions of the regiment formed 157 Brigade with the 5th Argyll and Sutherland Highlanders. They arrived off Cape Helles on 2 July 1915, and the 5th HLI went straight into the trenches on the first night. The whole brigade subsequently took up positions on the left of the British line, and manned front line trenches for much of the time thereafter.

A major attack was planned for 12 July, and the Territorial divisions were given as their objective the Achi Baba Nullah, a hill which dominated the whole of the central part of the British line. The 7th HLI and 5th Argylls were in the lead with the 5th and 6th HLI in the second wave. The HLI brigade fought the Turks with great determination and at very close quarters. The battalions objectives were taken, but during the night both sides continued to make local attacks and counter-attacks. The following day other formations attacked those parts of the feature still in Turkish hands. Casualties for all battalions were heavy, but some gains had been achieved. During the following months the HLI brigade continued to spend much time in the front line, and the battalions were still mounting local attacks almost to the end of the campaign in December.

* * * * *

During 1915 three new battalions of the Highland Light Infantry reached the Western Front, the 10th, 11th and 12th Battalions. The 12th Battalion was first in action at the battle of Loos in September, and it captured its objective, Hill 70, but was then caught in fire from three sides. After holding the captured German trenches for some hours, the highlanders were ordered to withdraw, their casualties numbering 553 during the battle. Meanwhile the 1st Battalion's objective was near Auchy and its attack met with some success, whilst the Glasgow Highlanders in the same area were held up by devastating fire and the effects of gas. The 10th Battalion similarly was caught by machine-gun fire as they attacked and lost nearly 600 men. The 11th Battalion succeeded in capturing and holding the 'Little Willie' redoubt for two days. The cost to the HLI overall at the battle of Loos was some 2,000 casualties and, as a consequence, the amalgamaiton of the 10th and 11th Battalions was ordered. At the end of the year three new battalions, the 15th, 16th and 17th, reached France.

At the start of the Somme offensive in July 1916 these three battalions took part in the major attack on the German 'Leipzig salient'. The 17th succeeded in their first objective, but the 16th lost over 500 casualties when held up by wire in the open and subjected to devastating machine-gun fire. The 15th HLI had to wait two days in reserve for its attack on the Leipzig redoubt, and when mounted, it only met with limited success, the enemy holding on with great determination.

The 15th HLI were fighting at Ovillers, and the Glasgow Highlanders near High Wood. On one particular occasion the Glasgow Highlanders were ordered to attack the Switch Line with a battalion of the Queen's. As they advanced across the open, the enemy enfilade fire from High Wood caused numerous casualties. One of the companies of highlanders was sent into the wood to destroy the enemy machine-gun posts, but they were prevented by incessant enemy fire. When the other HLI companies reached the wire in front of the enemy line, it was found to be uncut, despite the heavy artillery bombardment, and they had to hold exposed positions for some hours. Meanwhile three platoons had entered the wood, but could go no further. After spending the night in virtually untenable positions, the remnants of the two battalions withdrew, although some of their number had failed to hear the order and remained in no-man's land for a further period of time.

By mid-July some gains had been made along the line, and at the end of the month the 2nd and 18th Battalions joined the line south of Delville Wood. They took part in the capture of the wood, which was a divisional objective. In September the 10/11th and 12th HLI assisted in the successful capture of Martinpuich.

At the battle of Ancre in November, the 2nd Battalion attacked and seized the enemy front line at Beaumont Hamel. The troops, however, were left exposed to fire and there were many casualties. On 17 November the 16th and 17th Battalions assaulted the nearby Redan Ridge, and the 16th were successful in seizing part of the 'Frankfurt' trench, holding it for eight days.

* * * * *

The 1st HLI had left France and reached the campaign in Mesopotamia in January 1916. The purpose of sending reinforcements was to assist in the relief of Kut El Amara. The battalion joined the front line trenches some twenty miles from the town, the intervening area being held in great strength by the Turks. During the following three months, the HLI took part in the gradual advance, but the Turks resisted with great determination. In April a major attack, which included the HLI, was mounted at Bait Isa and some enemy positions captured, but on 29 April Kut surrendered to the enemy.

For the remainder of 1916 and most of 1917 the campaign became static, but in September 1917 the march on Baghdad began. The advance took some months and involved the HLI in much skirmishing and manoeuvre. A successful attack was led by the HLI at Mushak, and this was the last battle before the Turks surrendered on 31 October 1918.

Meanwhile, the 5th, 6th and 7th HLI, still brigaded together, had reached Egypt after leaving Gallipoli. For some months they manned Suez Canal defences, and in May 1916 were sent to guard the garrison of Romani. In July Romani was attacked, but the Turks were beaten off by the British force and pursued across the desert by both cavalry and infantry. During the next few months the HLI Brigade took part in the advance across the Sinai and into Palestine. It fought in the second battle of Gaza in April 1917. All three battalions were in the front line, and advanced onto Mansura ridge. The 7th HLI was then ordered to relieve the adjacent brigade, but the battalion incurred many casualties and was only partially successful.

On 25 October the third battle of Gaza began, and as the Turks withdrew the HLI brigade was sent to prevent the enemy consolidating north of the town. The battalions mounted several swift attacks on the enemy as the advance continued during the next month. The Turks made a final counter-attack on 29 November at Ajalon against the HLI Brigade. The highlanders met them with determined resistance, and there followed bitter hand-to-hand fighting until the enemy withdrew.

Once Jerusalem had fallen, the whole 52nd Division moved northwards to the Auja River. The Turks had formed a strong position holding the river bank, and on 20 December 1917 the HLI Brigade mounted an assault river crossing. The operation was meticulously planned and preparations were carried out as secretly as possible. The 7th HLI crossed the river in coracles which they had built, and seized the enemy positions covering a ford – taking the Turks by complete surprise. The 6th Battalion then crossed the river in a human chain against the current. A bridgehead was quickly established, artillery fire brought down on the Turkish positions and a pontoon bridge rapidly built by the Royal Engineers. The Turks could offer little resistance and those who could abandoned their positions. It was the HLI's last major operation in Palestine.

9th Glasgow Highlanders HLI billeted at Ghyvelde, Aug 1917, play an impromptu game of rugby football.
IWM

On the Western Front the year 1917 had started with widespread harassing attacks on the Germans. The 16th and 17th Highland Light Infantry were in action together during February and held the German front line at Ten Tree Alley on the Somme, while the Glasgow Highlanders carried out a similar attack in February on the Peronne road. In the same month the 2nd HLI had to beat off a large scale attack on its part of the line.

In order to shorten the length of their line the Germans carried out a major withdrawal to the Hindenburg Line which had been prepared and strengthened during the winter. The 2nd HLI led the 2nd Division's advance, maintaining contact with the enemy, a difficult and dangerous task. The 16th and 17th HLI had similar tasks clearing the town of Nesle and Savy.

On 9 April 1917 the battle of Arras began, and the

10/11th and 12th HLI fought in the area immediately to the east of the town. The 10/11th were ordered to capture Monchy and attempt a break-through: the town was taken but there was no opportunity for the cavalry to exploit forward. The 16th HLI fought in support of the French in the area of St Quentin and despite losing many casualties, the battalion took the village of Château Fayet.

The 2nd Battalion meanwhile, was holding Vimy Ridge during the battle and was ordered to mount a battalion attack on Oppy Wood. The HLI achieved their task, but were forced to withdraw when other troops could not protect the battalion's flanks. Both the 10/11th and 12th HLI were also much involved in the battle. The Glasgow Highlanders took part in a brigade attack on the Hindenburg Line, during which there was intense close-quarter combat in the trenches and the battalion held the captured line until relieved.

In June and July there was much troop redeployment along the British front prior to the third battle of Ypres. The 16th and 17th HLI repulsed a large-scale attack on the River Yser sector, and the 10/11th and 12th Battalions took part in the battle for Pilcken Ridge. This included seizing the Frezenburg redoubt, which they achieved with the aid of some tanks. In September the Glasgow Highlanders were moving up to take the town of Gheluvelt, but were

Battle of the Menin Road; members of the 9th Glasgow Highlanders HLI rest on the way to an attack, 24 Sept 1917. IWM

caught in an artillery bombardment: this prevented them from further advance, although they held their present exposed positions. During the last phase of the battle the 15th, 16th and 17th HLI held the line at Passchendaele.

At the start of the battle of Cambrai on 20 November 1917, the 14th HLI came into action for the first time. It took part in a brigade attack in the Bourlon wood area and, at one point during darkness the battalion was cut off and surrounded. Although an attempt to relieve them was made, the remaining highlanders had to surrender, after losing some 440 casualties. Ten days later the 1st Battalion was heavily engaged in captured positions on the Hindenburg Line. The enemy held the second line and mounted several attacks on the highlanders, but they held the German front line until relieved.

When the German offensive was mounted in March 1918, all the battalions of the Highland Light Infantry were in reserve formations. During the British withdrawal the 2nd Battalion was the first in action in support of the 51st Highland Division, and then in the Beaumont-Hamel area. Other battalions were variously engaged. The 10/11th and 14th HLI

were instrumental in holding a divisional flank near Gomiecourt, while the 12th and 18th Battalions were redeployed to support the 9th Scottish Division on the Maurepas Ridge, and helped to cover an orderly withdrawal.

Eventually, the momentum of the German advance over the whole front was spent, but the enemy continued to launch major attacks in some sectors. The British quickly mounted counter-attacks, and in one of them the 15th HLI captured Ayette, having taken the enemy by surpise. During

Top:
Beside a derelict tank, some French soldiers and jocks of the 12th HLI halt awhile on an old battlefield, during the advance on the Menin Road, Oct 1918. IWM

Above:
Assaye Day 1933, the 2nd HLI (old 74th Highlanders) parade the Assaye Colour in India. RHQ

the battle on the River Lys the Germans launched an attack with four divisions, and the 10/11th and 14th HLI were moved quickly to the area to support a Portuguese formation. Such was the ferocity of the fighting that the two battalions virtually ceased to exist. By this time the HLI Brigade of the 5th, 6th and 7th Battalions had reached the front from Palestine.

The German offensive was defeated and during the summer of 1918 the allies launched their offensive. When the battle of Albert began on 21 August the 2nd HLI were given the objective of Behagnies, but the village took longer to seize than expected. Three days later the HLI Brigade mounted an attack on Hénin Hill, and followed on against two further brigade objectives on subsequent days. At this time the 15th Battalion also joined the advance. By the end of the month the British army had re-taken the Hindenburg Line. The momentum of the advance then increased, and battalions of the HLI were constantly in action right up to the time of the armistice on 11 November.

* * * * *

The two battalions of the Highland Light Infantry returned to the United Kingdom at the end of the war and were built up to establishment. The 2nd Battalion were soon sent to Archangel to support the White Russian army, and there they remained for two months, chiefly on dispersed guard duties. The 1st Battalion went to Ireland for a short tour of duty, followed by service in Egypt. The 2nd Battalion also spent a period on internal security duties in Palestine; and then in 1922 it went to assist in the defence of the neutral zone around the Dardanelles. It was later posted to Bangalore in India, and in 1931 was involved in restoring order during the riots at Cawnpore.

While the 1st Battalion served in Malta and Egypt, the 2nd Battalion remained in India, and took part in operations against the Pathans on the North-West Frontier to preserve British military control. This involved much marching and picqueting, and there were numerous minor actions in which the battalion took part. The 2nd HLI moved in 1938 to Palestine and resumed the same type of duties they had carried out during the previous tour.

Right:
Lorried infantry of the 2nd HLI photographed just prior to the battle of 'Knightsbridge', south-west of Tobruk, June 1942, during Rommel's second offensive. IWM

Manning a picquet and signallers of 2nd HLI at rest during operations in Waziristan, North-West Frontier, 1933. RHQ

THE HIGHLAND LIGHT INFANTRY
1939–59

On the outbreak of the Second World War, the 1st Battalion moved from Scotland to France as Corps troops with the British Expeditionary Force. Its first task was on pioneer duties in various parts of the defensive line. When German troops attacked Belgium in May 1940, the battalion was moved forward to positions near Tournai. Though not at first in contact with the advancing German army, the HLI dug in on the River Scarpe; but during the last week of May the battalion was ordered to withdraw as the enemy swung to the north to outflank the BEF. From then onwards, the battalion was constantly in action, acting as brigade rear-guard for much of the time. At one stage in the withdrawal the battalion was itself surrounded by mechanised enemy troops, but managed to fend off the attack and extricated itself. The battalion was fortunate in reaching Dunkirk with fewer casualties than many battalions, and was evacuated.

157 Infantry Brigade, with the three Territorial battalions of the regiment, the 5th, 6th and 9th (Glasgow Highlanders), had landed in June 1940 at Cherbourg as part of the 52nd Lowland Division. The brigade quickly moved forward to positions near Evreux on 13 June: but Paris had fallen to the Germans, and as there was no future in establishing a second front, the division was withdrawn and re-embarked for England on 18 June.

* * * * *

The 2nd Battalion was serving in the Middle East throughout 1940, and in December moved to the Sudan. There was a mounting threat to British troops in both the Sudan and Egypt, and after the failure of the Italians to capture British East Africa, they began to withdraw into Eritrea, whereupon British and Indian troops, including the 2nd HLI, advanced into the country. In their first action the HLI forced the withdrawal of the Italians holding Abu Gamel Ridge in early January 1941, and continued to harass them in numerous actions over very rugged terrain.

The town of Barentu, however, was held in strength by the Italians during March 1941, and they caused many casualties to the battalion during an

A Coy of 2nd HLI land on the Italian mainland near Reggio, Sept 1943. IWM

attack on the town. Part of the Keren escarpment was still in enemy hands and blocking the route to Asmara. The HLI formed up on 15 March behind Cameron Ridge, which had earlier been captured by the Cameron Highlanders, ready to take two objectives, the 'Pinacle' and a fort. C Company in the lead was halted in the open by a tremendous weight of fire from the enemy. Some of the highlanders managed to work their way forward close to the enemy, but were unable to dislodge them from amongst the rocks. A and C Companies were also held up in the same area, as the enemy's full weight of fire was directed on the battalion. The highlanders remained in the open most of the day before being ordered to retire. The objectives were taken that night by a full brigade attack. Ten days later, the HLI took its revenge when, in a silent approach through a railway tunnel, it surprised a whole Italian battalion who quickly surrendered. The 2nd HLI were the first troops into Asmara after the disintegration of the Italian army, and in early May the battalion fought at the last Italian-held town, the seaport of Masawa.

The 2nd Battalion HLI remained in the Middle East with the 5th Indian Division, and in April 1942 moved to the Western Desert. At Gambut the battalion provided troops for the defence of the Army Headquarters. At the start of the German offensive, the battalion was first in action at Bir El Tamar, and then at the battle of the 'Cauldron'. The German armoured attacks were successful all along the British line during the week beginning 5 June, and in the confusion the HLI were forced to withdraw to El Adem. Tobruk fell on 20 June and, during the British withdrawal over the next month, companies of the HLI were involved in many delaying engagements. They were then withdrawn, and remained as garrison troops in Cairo until the end of 1942. In early 1943 the battalion moved to Palestine to train for the invasion of Sicily and Italy.

On 10 July 1943, the day of the invasion of Sicily, the 2nd HLI landed on the island and captured an enemy battery in its first action. During the Sicilian campaign the battalion's task was to hold the beachhead area as a 'beach brick'. This involved unspectacular and mainly administrative tasks, but the battalion carried them out enthusiastically and efficiently. Similarly during the the invasion of the Italian mainland, the HLI was one of the first battalions on shore, and it remained in various coastal localities.

In September 1943, 2nd HLI was withdrawn from Italy first to Egypt and then to Syria, for mountain training. In May 1944 it was sent to Vis, an island off Yugoslavia, to support the partisans. There was much

A patrol of the 2nd HLI on Vis island, Yugoslavia, Sept 1944. The battalion assisted the partisans against German troops on the mainland. IWM

patrolling work to be done, also amphibious raids on various islands and mainland ports. In September the HLI were moved to Greece after the withdrawal of German troops. The battalion's first task was internal security, but then to fight the Communist guerillas attempting to establish power in the country. There were numerous localised engagements in the countryside and fighting in Athens itself, before the Communists were defeated.

In January 1945 the 2nd HLI returned to Italy and practised skills in high altitude patrolling. In March they were again in action against the Germans in the mountains near Belvedere. At the end of the war the battalion served in occupied Austria for a short while before returning to Greece and Yugoslavia, where they were to remain until 1947.

* * * * *

The allied invasion of Normandy in June 1944 included three battalions of the Highland Light Infantry, the 1st, 10th and 2/9th (Glasgow Highlanders). The 2nd Glasgow Highlanders were first in action on 26 June during a divisional attack to secure bridges on the River Odon, south-west of Caen. The Highlanders succeeded in capturing their objectives, but with heavy casualties. The 10th Battalion passed through the same area, but was held up short of its objective by a heavy artillery bombardment. During the next few days, the battalions fought in close cooperation to clear the area, suffering frequent German armoured counter-attacks.

Meanwhile the 1st Battalion HLI arrived, and joined the other two battalions near Cheux. The advance of the British troops in the area, however, was met with determined resistance by the Germans and progress was slow. All three battalions were engaged in the heavy fighting on the line of the River Odon until mid-July. A rapid operation was mounted south of Caumont by 15th Scottish Division in which both 10th HLI and the 2nd Glasgow Highlanders were heavily involved. The 10th HLI were moved forward to the start line of an attack but were machine gunned and mortared in Lutain Wood. After a time the highlanders cleared the area and mounted the tanks of the 4th Coldstream Guards for an assault on Hervieux. The enemy were ejected from this objective. Meanwhile the Glasgow Highlanders went into the attack with the 4th Grenadier Guards' tanks onto Quarry Hill. The tanks were held up by enemy anti-tank guns and the highlanders had to dismount and take the hill on foot. During the ensuing days these two battalions spent much time mutually supporting

Above:
6 HLI advance through snow on the Dutch-German border, Jan 1945. IWM

Below:
Souvenir hunters of the 9th HLI; Ptes McIvor, Harton and Mills in the village of Kranenburgh, near the Siegfried Line, Feb 1945. IWM

various tank squadrons in the bocage countryside to the south-west and south of Caen.

The 1st Battalion in the meantime were operating further to the south, helping to clear the route to Falaise. Progress was gaining momentum and, despite fierce German resistance, the allies outflanked and surrounded the enemy in the Falaise area during August.

By the end of the month all three battalions had crossed the River Seine, meeting only light resistance as far as the Belgian border. Fighting through Belgium was more hazardous, and the HLI battalions frequently had to deal at company level with enemy delaying parties. By 18 September the 2nd Glasgow Highlanders and 10th HLI had reached east of the Albert Canal, and the 1st Battalion near Tilburg in Holland. Progress was swift, and in late September 1944 the 10th HLI and 2nd Glasgow Highlanders crossed the Escaut Canal. The 6th Battalion mounted an attack on Best, and were delayed, but the 2nd Glasgow Highlanders and two other battalions then joined them for a brigade attack which resulted in heavy casualties. The brigade was relieved, but Best remained in German hands.

In the meantime the 52nd Lowland Division had landed on the Continent, its task being to link up with the airborne operation at Arnhem. When this failed, the division's task was altered to capture the Scheldt estuary and open up the port of Antwerp. 157 HLI Brigade, comprising the 5th, 6th and 1/9th (Glasgow Highlanders), reached the front in October 1944, and on 27 October mounted an assault on South Beveland, led by the 5th HLI. The three battalions advanced westwards towards the causeway to Walcheren, and met heavy resistance. The 1st Glasgow Highlanders supported an attack of the Canadians in an attempt to establish a bridgehead on Walcheren island, joined to South Beveland by a causeway. Crossing the West Scheldt in landing craft the highlanders were resisted with great force, having to dig in on a precarious position. The Germans counter-attacked, but the situation was relieved by an aerial attack by RAF Typhoon aircraft firing rockets. During the night the 6th HLI came up along the causeway and reinforced the bridgehead. On 4 November the 5th HLI and Cameronians crossed over to the island, made contact with the bridge-head troops and advanced into the German garrison at Fort Rammekeius: Lt Col R. L. C. Rose of the 5th HLI accepted the German surrender on 5 November, and the Division was then moved inland.

The 1st Battalion Highland Light Infantry was operating in the meantime in the area west of the Maas, and the HLI Brigade joined them near Geilenkirchen. In an attack the 1st Glasgow Highlanders were partly overrun near this town, but with the help of the Sherwood Rangers Yeomanry, managed to extricate themselves. When the German counter-offensive took place in mid-December, the HLI Brigade adopted defensive positions on the River Maas, with the 1st HLI in positions on the same river further up stream. In January 1945 the 1st Battalion advanced southeast towards the Rhine, and the HLI Brigade assisted in the capture of Hargen and Havert en route to the River Roer. Nearly every village and town was held in strength by the Germans, and the HLI battalions met much resistance and were under constant shell-fire.

In February 1945 the 10th HLI were present at the capture of Cleve, and in the same month the 1st Battalion had to fight through the Reichswald forest. This was a formidable task, but by mid-February the area had been cleared. The HLI Brigade mounted a brigade attack on Afferden on the Siegfried Line on 16 Febrary, and fighting continued in this area for ten days. In the meantime, the 10th HLI and 2nd Glasgow Highlanders were also fighting their way to the east of the Reichswald. Frequent German counter-attacks had to be faced by the two battalions. By mid-March the Rhine had been reached, and on 23 March the crossing began.

The following day the 10th HLI crossed the river and met determined German opposition at Wolffskath, which they eventually succeeded in capturing. The other HLI battalions also crossed the Rhine and exploited eastwards, (157 Brigade no longer comprised the three HLI battalions). The 2nd Glasgow Highlanders were severely held up on two occasions, the second time at Wittenhorst which required a full brigade including the 6th HLI, to take it. The 5th Battalion had to clear Rheine and the 6th came across a very strong enemy position covering a defile in the thickly wooded hills at Ibbenburen, west of Osnabruck. The defenders were officer cadets from a German military school, and two companies of the HLI were met by extremely accurate rifle-fire at close range. The whole battalion then became involved and, despite their fewer numbers, the German cadets mounted a very effective counter-attack on the highlanders. It took the battalion and the 7/9th Royal Scots two days to fight through the woods and capture the defile. A second brigade then joined in to clear the whole area. The 1st Battalion went on the capture Verden and continued to advance to the River Elbe. When hostilities ceased the six HLI battalions were dispersed in various different parts of north Germany.

* * * * *

In 1945 the two regular battalions of the regiment served in Egypt and Greece respectively, but the 2nd Battalion reached Scotland a year later and was disbanded. Authority had been granted for the HLI to re-adopt the kilt – which had not been worn by either regiment since 1809 – the tartan being MacKenzie, HLI sett.

This photograph shows the 10th HLI crossing the River Elbe in assault craft, 29 April 1945. IWM

The 1st Battalion moved to Palestine in 1947, and conducted internal security duties in Jerusalem at the height of the Jewish and Arab troubles. There were numerous incidents as both factions operated against British troops, but in May 1948 the British army left the country. The HLI remained in the

United Kingdom before returning to the Middle East, where in 1956 it took part in operations against Eoka terrorists in Cyprus. The following year the announcement was made that the amalgamation would take place of the Highland Light Infantry with the Royal Scots Fusiliers in 1959. The Territorial battalions, however, did not amalgamate but existed separately under their own names until 1967.

Below left and right:
These two photographs show D Coy advancing through the streets and Bren-gun carriers of the 9th Glasgow Highlanders Bn, HLI nr Bremen, May 1945. RHQ

Bottom:
A kilted regiment again; members of the 1st HLI take part in the Nijmegen March, 1958. IWM

THE ROYAL HIGHLAND FUSILIERS
1959–to the present

The regiment was formed at Redford Barracks, Edinburgh in January 1959, and in the past three decades has served in a number of overseas stations, with the British Army of the Rhine and in the United Kingdom. They have spent numerous tours in Northern Ireland on internal security duties. In 1977 the regiment celebrated the 200th anniversary of the raising of the 71st and a year later the tercentenary of the 21st Regiment.

Right:
A patrol of the 1st Royal Scots Fusiliers pays a 'hearts and minds' visit to a village in Belize. RHQ

Below:
Maj P. N. Channer and his Coy march past during the tercentenary parade at Redford Barracks, Edinburgh, 1978, to commemorate the formation of the Earl of Mar's Reg, from which has descended the Royal Highland Fusiliers. RHQ

Overleaf top:
The 'ever-ready' platoon of the 1st Royal Highland Fusiliers react while stationed at Girdwood Barracks, Belfast, 1983. Some members of the two communities in Ulster seem determined to perpetuate their violent antagonism into the twenty-first century. RHQ

Overleaf below:
The anonymity of modern warfare: this photograph shows the Royal Highland Fusiliers on training in Canada during the 1980s. RHQ

CHAPTER 6

THE KING'S OWN SCOTTISH BORDERERS

THE 25TH (EDINBURGH) REGIMENT
1689–1881

When William of Orange landed at Torbay in November 1688, there was in his army a contingent of Scottish expatriates, commanded by David, third Earl of Leven. William's claim to the English throne for himself and his wife was quickly settled, but the claim to the Scottish throne was a separate matter, and Leven was sent to gain the loyalty of the Scottish Estates in early 1689.

Edinburgh was in a state of political disarray. The Castle was held for James II by the Duke of Gordon, while Graham of Claverhouse, Viscount Dundee, was attempting to rally the nobility in the same cause, having the nucleus of an army at his disposal. The Convention of Estates, however, meeting in March 1689, was persuaded to accept the Protestant monarchy and the greater likelihood of a peaceful future, rather than remain loyal to King James. There was a grave fear that Edinburgh would become a battleground between armed extremists of both sides, whatever the outcome, and on 18 March the Convention gave authority to Leven to raise a regiment of 800 men for the defence of the capital. Within two hours of the decision the drums had summoned a new regiment to assemble. Once established, it became known as the Earl of Leven's Regiment or the Edinburgh Regiment of Foot.

Viscount Dundee had raised an army of over 3,000 men by June 1689 and General Hugh Mackay's force, which included Leven's regiment, marched into the highlands to meet Dundee. The battle was fought in the narrow pass at Killiecrankie on 27 July. The Williamite army was smaller than Dundee's and it was defeated convincingly; all but two of the regiments were broken by the charges of Dundee's mounted troops and highlanders. Leven's regiment held their position at first but had to withdraw from the battlefield, which they did in good order. With the death of Viscount Dundee after the battle, his rebel army disintegrated quickly, and the threat to the new monarchy and the Scots parliament subsided.

For the next two years Leven's regiment remained in Scotland to prevent further rebellious activities. In 1691 it accompanied General MacKay to Ireland, where various Irish forces still held part of the country for King James, despite their defeat at the battle of the Boyne. The regiment assisted in the siege of Ballymore and assault on Athlone. At the battle of Aughrim the regiment formed part of the force which broke up an army of some 25,000 Irishmen. The sieges of Galway and Limerick followed, but in the latter, Leven's regiment suffered high casualties.

In 1692 the regiment joined British troops serving in the War of the League of Augsburg. In July King William III, commanding the allies, launched a surprise attack on the French at Steenkirk, meeting initial successes against the enemy. The French, however, counter-attacked and Leven's and other British regiments were nearly cut off. They managed to withdraw from the battlefield, the cause of the defeat being a lack of co-ordination between the allies. Later in the same month the French attacked the allies at Landen. There Leven's regiment formed part of the right wing of the army, which was attacked in great strength and again forced to retire. French losses, however, were more than double those of the allies. The regiment remained in Flanders until 1697, their most notable engagement being the siege of Namur which was defended by some 15,000 French soldiers.

> 'At four o'clock in the afternoon of the 27th July the English and Scots issued from the trenches upon the right, and attacked the point of the advanced counterscarp which enclosed the great sluice of waterstop, near the gate of St Nicholas. In doing this they were terribly exposed to the fire of the counterguard and demi-bastion of St Roch; and the Enemy having exploded a mine under part of the glacis, whereby twenty officers and upwards of 500 men of Leven's were killed, some confusion ensued; but the troops, having rallied, returned to the assault with redoubled vigour, when the Enemy gave way after a desperate resistance. The British now pursued them closely, and effected a lodgment on the foremost covered way, and on part of the counterscarp before the gate of St Nicholas; whereupon the Dutch, also made a lodgement, and by digging some traverses, both were enabled to maintain the positions they had gained.'

On returning to Scotland the Edinburgh Regiment was stationed in various parts of the country. In 1715 it formed part of the Duke of Argyll's army which faced the Jacobite army at Sheriffmuir. The battle was indecisive, but the numerically superior rebel army was unable to proceed towards Stirling and Edinburgh and present a serious challenge to the Hanoverian Crown.

In 1719 the Edinburgh Regiment served in a British expedition to Spain. Landing at Vigo Bay, where many Jacobite exiles were based, the force captured the fort at Ponte Vedra, but withdrew after a few weeks and returned home. After a tour of duty in Ireland the regiment sailed for Gibraltar, where it re-

Previous page:
During the last decade of the 19th century the 2nd KOSB spent much time on active service on the North-West Frontier. The soldiers are wearing government tartan, while the piper wears Royal Stuart. RHQ

mained for ten years. During that time it successfully withstood the Spanish siege of the Rock.

* * * * *

In 1743 the Edinburgh Regiment was sent to the Continent to take part in the War of the Austrian Succession, and joined the British force just after the battle of Dettingen. On 11 May 1745 the regiment fought at Fontenoy in which the French suffered severe casualties, but forced the allies to withdraw. The regiment's casualties were also high and later in the year, due to the ineptitude of the Dutch allies, the regiment had to surrender Ath on honourable terms.

In the autumn of 1745, the Edinburgh Regiment (also known now as Sempill's regiment) was hurriedly withdrawn from the Continent to reinforce the army at home during the Jacobite rebellion. It garrisoned Edinburgh Castle for a period, assisted in the relief of Stirling and moved with the Duke of Cumberland to Aberdeen. In April 1746 the regiment was on the left of the royal second line at Culloden. The furious charge of the highlanders had the greatest impact against this part of Cumberland's army, and Sempill's regiment was soon heavily involved, fighting at closequarters with the rebels. The royal cavalry posted to the left flank of the line then attacked the highlanders, and within a short time Prince Charles Edward Stuart's army was broken. The regiment's casualties were higher than most of the royal regiments, but negligible when compared with the rebel losses. The Jacobite army dispersed, pursued relentlessly by the royal army.

The Edinburgh Regiment returned to the Continent in the summer of 1746. It formed part of the covering force, and a year later fought at the battle of Lauffeld, holding the village of Val on the left of the British line. Forced to withdraw temporarily the regiment, reinforced by others, recaptured the village, ensuring a successful outcome of the battle. In 1747 the regiment served in the defence of Bergen-op-Zoom, where the French laid siege to the town, and in September mounted a large scale attack which the defenders successfully withstood. Eventually the town had to be abandoned and the following year a peace was concluded.

The regiment was numbered 25th Regiment of Foot at this time, and during the period 1749 to 1755 it served in Ireland. In 1757, during the Seven Years' War, the 25th Foot took part in a successful raid on the French island of Aix in the Charente estuary. In 1758 the regiment took part in a similar expedition to

A contemporary oil painting of officers and soldiers of the 25th Edinburgh Regt serving in Minorca, c1770. NAM

St Malo which was less successful. Later in the same year it was sent to defend the King's Hanoverian possessions in Germany.

In 1759 the 25th was one of six battalions of British infantry which withstood successive charges of French cavalry and infantry at Minden.

'The onset of the French Army was extremely furious, rushing with the greatest impetuosity, like a deluge, threatening to sweep all before it. But the undauntedness and good disposition of our Troops checked their career, and made them reel back again; however, they soon rallied, and returned to the charge. Our British Infantry, fought with the greatest ardour and intrepidity, sustaining and repelling the repeated attacks of the Enemy. The soldiers, so far from being daunted by their falling comrades, breathed nothing but revenge;'

The enemy were unable to break the British lines after six hours of fighting and retreated from the battlefield in total confusion, leaving the town undefended.

The regiment remained in Germany until 1763, and took part in four major engagements before the end of the war. At Warburg the enemy were routed by the cavalry and the regiment was involved in the subsequent pursuit and capture of prisoners. At Campen the French were more successful and the allied army had to withdraw. The battle of Vellinghausen was a victory for the British and German armies, the French retreating from the field after suffering heavy losses. During the final battle of the war at Wilhelmstahl, the 25th played only a small part.

The period between 1764 to 1768 was spent by the 25th in Scotland, and from 1768 to 1775 on garrison duties in Minorca. In 1782 the name of the regiment was altered to the 25th Sussex Regiment, as Lord George Lennox was the Colonel at the time and the principle family seat was in that English county. The Sussex designation was retained for twenty-three years – with considerable reluctance amongst the Scotsmen in its ranks. For ten of these years the 25th was stationed in Gibraltar and assisted in withstanding the French and Spanish siege of the Rock in 1782. On its return in 1792 to the United Kingdom, the regiment supplied a number of detachments for service as Marines. Three companies were present at the sea battle in 1794 off Brest, known as 'The Glorious 1st June'.

During the period of the French Revolutionary War, the 25th Regiment provided detachments for service in amphibious operations in the South of France, Elba, Corsica and Spain. They took an active part in the fighting at Toulon, and assisted in the capture of Martella Tower, St Fiorenzo, Calvi, and Bastia in Corsica. One of the detachments prevented a mutiny by sailors on a ship of the Royal Navy.

In early 1795 the regiment, which had been reunited and now possessed a second battalion, left the United Kingdom for service in the West Indies. A major operation was mounted against the rebels on Grenada, who had seized most of the island from the British settlers. At first the detachments of various regiments, including the 25th, did not have much success. Their position on Pilot Hill was held, but was continually beseiged by the rebels. Relief came and the island was cleared by fresh British troops. The 25th suffered numerous casualties during its stay, the majority through disease.

After returning to the United Kingdom, the 25th Regiment was garrisoned in various home stations. In 1799 the regiment accompanied the expedition to Holland, under the Duke of York, in conjunction with a Russian force. During the three months of campaigning the regiment's most notable engagement was at Egmont-op-Zee, where it fought the French in a running battle through several miles of sandhills.

'Major General Moore's Brigade which formed the right as the army in column upon the beach, had the 25th Regiment as its advance guard and approached the French line, drawn up under cover of a ridge of sandhills. Having received the enemy's fire, the brigade charged, by order of the General, and instantly drove the enemy from the first ridge; but in effecting this it suffered severely. The contest continued from ten o'clock in the morning until four in the afternoon, the nature of the ground enabling the French to dispute every inch. They, however, gradually retired towards Egmont-op-Zee.'

The engagement at Castricum was less successful, although the British infantry fought with great determination. As the Dutch did not themselves fight to rid their country of the French, the British force was eventually withdrawn.

In 1801 the 25th Regiment embarked for Aboukir Bay in Egypt as a reinforcement to Sir Ralph Abercromby's expedition. It joined the British force besieging the French fortress of Alexandria. In early September the regiment assisted in the assault on the outlying defences, and the enemy subsequently surrendered the town. The regiment was then sent to Gibraltar, where it remained until 1803 on garrison duties, before returning home for service in England and Ireland.

In 1805 the regiment was redesignated the 25th (King's Own Borderers), which confirmed the connection with Scotland despite its bearing an English county name for many years. Three years later the regiment embarked for further service in the West Indies. As with other infantry regiments, it was frequently divided into detachments for particular tasks on various British islands and to take possession of French ones. The first major enterprise, in which the regiment provided four companies, was the capture of Martinique in 1809. The French forts had to be taken one by one, but after three weeks of fighting, they all surrendered. The 25th assisted in the capture of Guadeloupe the following year; the French

A group of officers of the 2nd King's Own Scottish Borderers, India 1871. RHQ

surrendered quickly and three companies of the regiment remained to garrison the island. St Eustatius was also occupied by the regiment, and in 1815 it had to re-occupy as part of Guadeloupe. Like all British regiments serving in the Caribbean, it suffered many losses, mostly through disease.

Returning to England in 1817 the 25th spent several years in Ireland helping to maintain the peace. From 1827 to 1835 the regiment served again on various West Indian islands. In 1840 it landed at Cape Town and, during a two year tour of duty, provided detachments to fight against the Boers who had attacked British settlements in Natal, then a dependency of Cape Colony.

From 1853 until 1854 the regiment was stationed in India and Ceylon where it was occasionally involved in quelling minor disturbances. A four-year period was then spent in Gibraltar and Malta, and in 1862 it proceeded to Canada. There, in 1866, the Borderers helped to defeat a number of Fenian incursions against various Canadian settlements. In 1875 the regiment returned to the United Kingdom. Meanwhile, a second battalion had been raised by the regiment (the third time in its history) and it served overseas in 1863. Subsequent postings were in Ceylon, India and Aden before it returned to England in 1875.

The 1st Battalion replaced the 2nd in India and in 1878 the 1st joined the Peshawar Valley field force for service in the second Afghan War. The first action in which the battalion took part was the occupation of the Kyber Pass and Fort Jamrud. The Borderers then advanced to clear the Bazar Valley, accompanied by cavalry, artillery and some elephants. This involved dominating the high ground and destroying the fortified villages of the Zakka Khel tribe. The expedition progresed successfully until the British envoy in Kabul was murdered, together with the troops guarding him. The Borderers joined the Kabul field force and, after a night march in January 1880 over very difficult terrain, two columns of the regiment carried out a particularly successful attack on enemy positions near Fort Dakka. Based at Pezwan until the end of the war, the Borderers carried out frequent patrols and marches to keep open the lines of communication.

THE KING'S OWN SCOTTISH BORDERERS

1881–1913

In 1881 the regimental title was changed to that of the 'King's Own Borderers', although for a time the war office had intended it to be named 'The York Regiment, King's Own Borderers', with the regimental depot in York. The KOSB's depot was instead established in Berwick-upon-Tweed. A year later doublet and trews were taken into wear and the tartan adopted for the time being was the universal pattern. (Leslie tartan was authorised in 1900, commemmorating the raising of the regiment by David Leslie, the Earl of Leven.) The word 'Scottish' was added to the regimental title in 1887.

* * * * *

The 1st Battalion remained in India until 1889 when it was sent to take part in the punitive expedition against Upper Burma. Half the battalion of the Borderers was based at Pakokku and thence marched to Kau and Haka through the hills and jungle, subjugating the various tribes as best they could. The battalion returned to India at the end of the campaign and embarked for home in 1891.

In the meantime, the 2nd Battalion had served in Ireland, frequently being called upon to give aid to the civil authorities. In 1888 it embarked for Egypt to take part in the expedition to the Sudan. The Borderers were involved in a number of engagements against the dervishes, the most notable fight being at Gamaizah.

The following year they reached India, and for a time carried out peacetime duties. In 1895 the battalion was sent to join the Chitral relief force on the North-West Frontier. This small tribal state was under British protection, and it had been invaded by Pathan tribesmen from Afghanistan. From the base in Nowshera, the relief force marched north and attacked the Pathans holding the Malakand pass, where the enemy held formidable positions and numbered some 10,000. With the Gordon Highlanders and native regiments, the Borderers assaulted the heights above the pass.

'It was a fine and stirring sight,' wrote an officer on the staff, 'to see the splendid dash with which the two Scottish regiments took the hill. From the valley to the crest at this point varies from 1,000 to 1,500 feet and the slope looks for the most part perpendicular. It was this very steepness which partly accounted for the comparatively small losses suffered from the enemy's fire and the shower of huge boulders which were hurled upon the assailants; but the chief reason was the wonderfully spirited manner in which the men rushed breastwork after breastwork and arrived just beneath the final ridge before the enemy had time to realise that the assaulting columns were at their very feet!

1st KOSB parade in full dress and pith helmets at Dagshai, India 1884. RHQ

Once reached, the attackers took the enemy positions with the bayonet.

Then the march to Chitral began, over one hundred miles distance. The Swat river was successfully forded, albeit under enemy rifle fire. The force met fiercer resistance in crossing the river Pajnkora, but steadily advanced on Mundar, the Pathan stronghold. The British show of force had, however, caused the Pathans to disperse, and the KOSB remained in Mundah while the route was cleared to Chitral without much further difficulty. The 2nd KOSB afterwards returned to peacetime duties in Rawalpindi.

Two years later the 2nd Battalion was called upon to return to the North-West Frontier. The Afridi and Orakzai tribes were in revolt in the Tirah region to the west of the Kyber Pass, and the Borderers joined the Tirah field force at Kohat. The force marched west and crossed the frontier near the Changru Kotal Pass, its purpose being to seize the Dargai Heights. After a formidable climb the 2nd KOSB and a Gurkha battalion reached the enemy positions, causing the tribesmen to flee. The heights were held for a time by the Borderers, but despite being reinforced, the positions proved to be untenable and had to be abandoned. Two days later the enemy had returned in much greater strength, and the heights had to be recaptured, this time by the Gordon Highlanders.

The officers' polo team of the 1st KOSB at Meerut – winners of the Infantry Polo Tournament, 1889. The sport was indulged in passionately by the officers of most regiments and battalions stationed in India. RHQ

The signal section of the 1st KOSB in South Africa during the Boer War. Field communications for the infantry relied on flags, lamps, heliographs and dispatch riders during mobile operations. RHQ

Top:
A picquet of the 1st KOSB on top of 'Commando Nek' during the Boer War. RHQ

Above:
Jocks of the KOSB build a bridge at Colchester in 1906. Most of the traffic then would have been on foot or horse-drawn. RHQ

Opposite page:
Officers and men of the KOSB stand by to act in aid of the civil power outside Harland and Wolff's shipyard, Belfast, Aug 1912. Their presence seems to have been sufficient to prevent civil disturbance on this occasion.

Below:
The 2nd KOSB march to St Giles' Cathedral, Oct 1912 for the ceremony of Laying-up the Colours. RHQ

Slow progress was made by the field force in establishing ts presence throughout the region. The Borderers' duties included piquetting the high ground, guarding the transport, burning villages and attacking enemy positions covering the route. At times they acted as rearguard, and the tribesmen continued to harass the force, particularly by night. The march from Maidan to Swaikot was particularly difficult, as it took place in winter and the weather brought blizzards and freezing conditions. On the conclusion of the expedition the Borderers returned to Cawnpore.

* * * * *

Although not involved in the opening operations, the 1st Battalion, King's Own Scottish Borderers were mobilised for the second Boer War in December 1899. The battalion was soon in action, marching to Paardeberg and along the Modder river in pursuit of Cronje's force. There were many skirmishes and the mounted infantry company particularly had much hard riding and fighting on the way. In March 1900 the Borderers reached Bloemfontein. The hills around the town had to be cleared, and the battalion suffered heavy casualties while assisting in this difficult task.

During the long march to Johannesburg and Pretoria the Borderers were constantly in action, the most notable engagements being the crossings of the Vet and Zand Rivers, and the capture of Kroonstadt. They were present when both Pretoria and Johannesburg fell. In May 1900 they were joined by a volunteer service company of the regiment, and later the Militia battalion. Then in August the battalion successfully dislodged the Boers at Zilikat's Nek in the Transvaal and, with its column, defended Commando Nek from enemy attacks. At Vlakfontein the enemy fired the veldt, forced the withdrawal of some companies of Imperial Yeomanry, and captured two British guns. The volunteer company of the Borderers recaptured the guns with a determined charge.

For a time the battalion guarded part of a railway line, and later spent many months marching in pursuit of the elusive enemy. Their most successful engagement was the capture of a Boer commando at Damboek. In the second year of the war the Borderers guarded static posts on the Mooi River and various other places. The 3rd Militia battalion of the regiment was also employed on the task of guarding lines of communication. On the cessation of hostilities the 1st and 3rd Battalions returned home.

On leaving India the 2nd Battalion spent a period in Burma and Aden before returning to the United Kingdom in 1905. In 1910 it moved to Belfast. In the meantime, the 1st Battalion had been stationed in Cairo from 1906, and five years later embarked for service in India, where it still remained on the outbreak of war.

THE KING'S OWN SCOTTISH BORDERERS
1914–1938

The 2nd Battalion, King's Own Scottish Borderers sailed for France on 13 August 1914 with the BEF. Nine days later they moved to the Mons-Condé Canal near Haine, which advanced elements of the German army had already reached. Enemy infantry attacked the KOSB's trenches on 23 August and the Borderers mounted an immediate counter-attack. That night they were ordered to withdraw in the direction of Le Cateau, where three days later their brigade attempted a delaying battle. Enemy artillery fire caused heavy casualties, but the KOSB kept up sufficient rifle and machine-gun fire to delay the enemy for several hours before the withdrawal was resumed.

'In a dream we marched,' wrote the battalion medical officer Capt Dolbey, 'unconscious of the towns we passed, the village we slept in; fatigued almost beyond endurance; dropping to sleep at the five minute halt that was the reward for each four miles covered. All companies, dozing as they marched, fell forward drunkenly on each other at the halts; sleeping men lay, as they halted, in the roads, and were kicked uncomplainingly into wakefulness again . . .'

Some minor skirmishing against Germans was conducted by the KOSB, and they marched day and night for nearly a fortnight under sporadic long range artillery fire. But the German advance had been checked all along the line by the British and French.

On 13th September the KOSB were called upon to counter-attack on the line of the River Aisne. Companies of the 2nd KOSB took part in attacks on the enemy north of the river at Missy, after crossing the Aisne in hastily-constructed ferries. Once established on the high ground, the KOSB fought hard to hold the ground and suffered heavy casualties. With unaffected honesty a battalion officer, Lt Dalrymple, later reported that 14 September was the 'most awful day of my life: an eternity! 52 men in my company were casualties.'

In mid-October the BEF moved northwards in order to extend the allied line to the Channel. The 2nd KOSB reached the area of Béthune and immediately manned hastily-dug front-line trenches. The Germans soon attacked in great strength and, although they were held, the KOSB and other battalions could not push the line forward. At the end of the month the battalion was moved to the Messines sector in order to take part in a major attack during the first battle of Ypres. The fighting was intense and the Borderers managed to capture much of Messines itself, but from then onwards the line became static.

Remaining in the Ypres salient throughout the winter months, the Borderers' first major engagement of 1915 took place in late April, when they were in support of an attack on Hill 60, beside the Ypres-Comines railway. The attack was successful, but the Borderers were counter-attacked during the night by the Germans who were determined to recapture the hill. There was fierce close-quarter fighting and the Borderers' casualties were over 200; nevertheless they defended positions for twenty-four hours until relieved. A few days later 13 Brigade, in which the 2nd KOSB were serving, launched an attack on Gravenstafel Ridge. The Borderers advanced nearly half a mile to relieve some Canadian troops, and held the forward position well into the night. The battalion's casualties were more than 250 in this action. In the meantime the Germans had recaptured part of Hill 60, and on 5 May the Borderers were ordered to launch an attack on it. Despite their efforts, the Germans remained in possession of the hill and the KOSB suffered many more casualties.

The 6th, 7th and 8th Battalions, King's Own Scottish Borderers reached France between May and July 1915, but were not much involved in the fighting until the battle of Loos in September. The 6th Battalion in the 9th Scottish Division took part in a major attack on the northern end of the Hozenzollern redoubt. The battalion was met by murderous fire as it advanced against the German machine guns through clouds of gas: there were more than 600 casualties and the task proved impossible. 'The finest and grandest old man in the regiment' Pipe Major Robert MacKenzie aged over 60, piped the battalion into the attack before he was wounded in the legs, from which injuries he later died.

In the same battle, the 7th KOSB fought further to the south, and they were played 'over the top' by piper Daniel Laidlaw, and he too was severely wounded, but lived to be awarded the VC for his bravery. The Borderers' advance was initially successful, 1,000 yards being covered and the first line of German trenches captured on the Lens to La Bassée road. In the heat of the battle, however, control and direction had inevitably been lost by divisional and brigade headquarters. The 8th Battalion in support subsequently reached a position just north of the 9th Battalion and together they defended their position until the following night. The cost to the two battalions was over 1,000 casualties, and the small gains of the battle of Loos did not justify the appalling casualty rate sustained by the divisions which took part.

* * * * *

In the meantime, the 1st Battalion King's Own Scottish Borderers had landed at Cape Helles, Gallipoli on 25 April 1905. The Turkish resistance to

the landing built up during the day: 'The line was formed by the mens' packs and with entrenching tools. It never reached what could be called a trench, and was constructed under the most harrassing and ever-increasing rifle fire.' By the evening there was very fierce hand-to-hand fighting, and during the night and following two days the KOSB and other troops defended their precarious positions. The order to withdraw and re-embark was given, as the enemy strength was considered to be too great.

'That any of us got away was due to the gallantry and heroism of the KOSB', reported an officer of the Royal Naval Division. 'It was quite the most gallant part of the landings. The way the KOSB held on for these two days and their final bayonet charges . . .'

Their action assisted in an orderly withdrawal from an impossible beach-head.

The 1st KOSB rejoined the 29th Division, from which the battalion had been detached, further along the coast at Krithia. The fighting there was in a state of confusion and the allied troops were unable to make any progress. The battalion, by now considerably depleted in strength, advanced as best it could but was endangered by other troops' inability to

Borderers refilling belts for machine guns in the trenches at Gallipoli. The 1st, 4th and 5th Bns all fought in the campaign, the two latter with the 52nd Lowland Division. RHQ

conform. The objective, Achi Baba Nullah, could not be reached and the division's casualties were more than fifty per cent in three days of fighting.

During May the line was mainly static but far from inactive. In late June a major attack was launched on the Turkish lines, at Gully Ravine. The 1st KOSB were in support and captured the third line. The casualties were heavy but the advanced positions were defended successfully from counter-attacks for the remainder of the campaign.

Meanwhile the 4th and 5th Territorial Battalions, King's Own Scottish Borderers reached Gallipoli with the 52nd Lowland Division. The division joined the British line immediately, but was not involved in the Gully Ravine battle. On 12 July the 4th Battalion led an attack on the Turkish lines near Achi Baba Nullah, and the 5th KOSB followed in the second wave. The 4th KOSB captured their objectives successfully but the fighting became very confused and the Turks resisted strongly. Eventually the

British consolidated their line but again the casualties were high.

'The strain had been cruel,' commented an officer. 'The sights, the smells, the fog of dust, the noise, the confusion, and the heat had all combined to exhaust brain and nerve and sinew.'

Active trench warfare continued for the battalions, with numerous localised engagements during the following weeks. The 1st Battalion also returned to the peninsula, and in mid-August were sent to the beach-head at Suvla bay. There they acted as a reserve during the major attack on Scimitar and Chocolate Hills by the 2nd Mounted Division and 10th Division – an attack that proved virtually suicidal to the dismounted Yeomanry regiments. The final excavation from Gallipoli took place at the end of the year. The 1st Battalion spent three months in Egypt before sailing for France, and the 4th and 5th reached Egypt in February 1916.

* * * * *

In the meantime the four battalions of the King's Own Scottish Borderers, the 2nd, 6th, 7th and 8th, continued to man various sectors on the Western Front, and to take part in localised actions. The 7th and 8th Battalions in the Loos sector were under strength but remained fully operational. An attack in May on part of the German line known as the Kink resulted in no gain and further casualties, whereupon the 7th and 8th Battalions had to be amalgamated.

The 1st was the only battalion of the regiment to take part in the opening part of the battle of the Somme, which started on 1 July 1916. The Borderers sustained nearly 550 casualties as they and others in their division fighting in the Ancre sector were caught in the open by German machine guns. The men had no alternative but to go on and be killed or wounded, or find cover; to advance was impossible. Late in the afternoon the remnants of the battalion were relieved in the trench they had occupied. They were withdrdawn for some weeks, but in August returned reinforced to the front near Ypres.

The 6th KOSB were initially in reserve at Mametz, but on the night of 3 July they were ordered to take Bernafey Wood. The wood was captured easily, but the Borderers were shelled continuously for five days until they were relieved. On 19 July the 2nd KOSB took up positions in the captured second German line near Guillemont. Their first task was to assist in the capture of the third German line at High Wood, by securing the divisional start-line. Three days later the Borderers were called up in support of an attack on High Wood, but the whole attack failed owing to a misappreciation of the enemy's strength. Further casualties were suffered in a minor attack on 29 July, bringing the total for the ten days to 23 officers and 469 other ranks. The remnants of the battalion were withdrawn for recuperation. The 6th KOSB had meanwhile also suffered further casualties from enemy artillery and had to be sent to a quiet sector near Vincy.

The 2nd Battalion rejoined the front at the end of August and launched an attack on the Germans near Guillemont, but again the enemy machine guns caused numerous casualties. On 25 September the Borderers took part in a very successful attack on Morval when over 700 Germans were captured: it was the battalion's last major engagement of the Somme battle.

The 7th/8th Battalion had joined the line in early August in the Ancre sector, but their first major battle was at Martinpuich in mid-September. The complicated plan worked well as the Borderers and other battalions took their objectives, and the village was captured in the exploitation phase. Battalion casualties were again high. The 6th Battalion then returned to the Somme battle on 18 October to take up positions near High Wood. A participant describes their arrival.

'Men struggled along waist-deep in mud. Unspeakable was the fate of any man who was wounded that night; he sank below the mire, and the men in the rear pressed on all unconscious of the welcome firmness, which momentarily sustained them, was the body of a comrade. Progress could only be made with the greatest exertion; a yard seemed a mile.'

Nevertheless the Borderers were ready for the attack which was launched on 20 October, and all objectives were carried. On the same day the 1st KOSB returned to the front near Fricourt.

* * * * *

In the meantime the 52nd Lowland Division, with the 4th and 5th Battalions, King's Own Scottish Borderers had spent the spring and summer of 1916 in training and guarding the Suez Canal. In September the Borderers were involved in the battle of Romani, when the Turks attacked this most easterly British outpost. Soon after, the division took part in the advance across the desert towards Palestine. El Arish and Rafa were occupied, although most of the fighting was work for the mounted troops.

The Borderers took no part in the first battle of Gaza, but both battalions fought in the second battle on 17 April 1917. Their objectives were at Ali El Muntar, but the Turks had heavily defended positions on all areas of high ground around the town. The 5th KOSB cleared one hill but were met with murderous fire from Outpost Hill, which the 4th then bravely attacked, and carried the lunette redoubt on its summit. The fighting cost both battalions many casualties but Gaza remained in Turkish hands, while the British and Imperial troops adopted entrenched positions in the area. The Borderers remained near Gaza for some months, during which the most notable event was the 4th KOSB's raid in June on a redoubt on the cliff top overlooking the Mediterranean.

In the third battle of Gaza the Borderers were not much involved, but after the victory they played a major part in the pursuit. The 5th KOSB attempted to eject some enemy from a position known as 'Sausage Ridge', but were caught in a fierce fire fight.

The ridge was eventually taken during the night by the 6th HLI. On 13 November the Borderers assisted in the occupation of El Mughar. Their brigade commander, Brigadier Pollok-McCall, reportedly 'snatched up a rifle and bayonet, shouted to the Borderers to follow him, and dashed out into the open. Here, there and everywhere the Borderers, shouting and cheering, jumped out, and there ensued a wild but steady advance in lines across the open for the garden of El Mughar'. A large number of prisoners were taken during this most successful action.

The advance continued, and on 24 November the KOSB took part in the attack on El Jib near Nebi Samwil. The two battalions succeeded in reaching within 400 yards of the objective before the intense Turkish firing made further progress impossible. The Borderers were relieved, and then advanced towards the coast to assist in clearing routes through the hills. Their next operation was the seizing of the River Auja near Jaffa, a masterpiece of surprise and deception by the 52nd Division. The 4th were in reserve but did much good work in preparing the pantoon equipment, while the 5th KOSB provided beach-head parties. Then,

> '60 men of A company rushed the bridge and engaged the Turks in one of the most furious hand-to-hand encounters in the campaign. Sgt Seaton's dash in rushing machine guns was the decisive stroke. The élan of the Borderers carried them past the Turkish garrison. Turning on them the Borderers drove them towards the river, and, as the Turks would not surrender, into it.'

It was the Borderers' last major engagement in the campaign.

* * * * *

All four battalions of the regiment on the Western Front were involved in the battle of Arras. At the start on 9th April 1917 the 6th and 7th/8th KOSB took part in the attack from the town of Arras itself. The 6th successfully advanced half a mile taking all their objectives. The 7th/8th followed in a subsequent wave and established positions some 500 yards beyond their objective near Monchy. Two days later the Borderers attacked the village with their brigade and occupied it, but suffered high casualties. In the meantime the 2nd Battalion was in support of a Canadian formation for an attack on Vimy Ridge, north-east of Arras. This was one of the most successful operations of the battle, and the battalion took its objectives at Bonval and Goulot woods, and probed forward into Vimy village itself. The Borderers remained in the sector for some weeks.

The 1st Battalion took up the defence of part of the front line on the fourth day of battle, but its first attack was not until 23 April, when it captured some enemy trenches. The 6th Battalion was back in action on 3 May against Greenland Hill. Due to the difficulty of co-ordination once the attack had been launched, the Borderers advanced further than the other battalions. Two companies then had to change direction to cover the flank and virtuallly all became casualties. The ground had to be given up. In the meantime the 7th/8th battalion was in support near Guémappe, and on 24 April took part as the second wave in an attack towards Cavalry Farm. The attack, however, came to a halt and the Borderers were unable to pass through 12th HLI, the leading battalion.

At the start of the third battle of Ypres in late July, the same battalion was involved in the assault at Pilckem, north-east of the town. Afer four hours of fighting, the Borderers had gained 1,300 yards of ground. Their casualties were nearly 300, but the Germans did not counter-attack, and the line was consolidated. The 1st KOSB were in reserve during an attack across the Steenbeck near Langemarck which began on 10 August. After waiting for six days under artillery bombardment and mustard gas attacks, the Borderers went into the attack on the 16th. The first objective was taken, then the second, an area dominated by blockhouses shielding enemy machine guns. CQMS Grimbaldeston accounted for the first and CSM Skinner for three more. Skinner, who had to crawl 70 yards 'succeeded in bombing and taking the first blockhouse single-handed; then leading his six men towards the other two blockhouses, he skilfully cleared them taking 60 prisoners, 3 machine guns and 2 trench mortars'. The two men were awarded the VC for their gallantry. The line was subsequently established and successfully defended until the battalion was relieved.

The 6th KOSB were meanwhile in the area of the Menin road, and went into the attack towards the Zonnebeeke redoubt on 20 September. The first objective was taken, and then the redoubt itself was assaulted and captured. The Borderers dug new trenches and suffered enemy artillery fire, but there was no counter-attack before the battalion's relief on 23 September. On 4 October, the 2nd KOSB attacked the area of Polderhoek, just north of Gheluvelt. The battalion advanced through the mud for 500 yards, but was held up and the two forward companies were overwhelmed. The Germans counter-attacked several times, and when the Borderers were relieved, their strength was less than 100. The remaining members of the battalion continued to fight in the sector, mainly on detachment to other battalions, and it was some time before it was reconstituted.

The 6th Battalion was involved in the fighting for the Passchendaele Ridge shortly afterwards. This battle took place in the most appalling conditions of mud and water, and was so totally confused that progress was impossible. The battalion was in reserve, but still suffered nearly 200 casualties, many of them through drowning. Their division was withdrawn soon afterwards.

The 1st Battalion joined the front at Havringcourt in order to take part in the battle of Cambrai on 20 November. The 25th Division was in a follow-up wave and reached Marcoing, capturing a bridge on the Scheldt Canal. The battalion had further casualties on the second day during an unsuccessful attempt to push the line forward. On 30 November the Germans mounted a massive counter-attack, and the Borderers moved up to hold Marcoing, fighting in an unusally open and rapid battle of fire and manoeuvre.

'All units (of the division) working independently by platoons advanced to the east instinctively, acting in accordance with the careful training they had received without any orders and without control. The outskirts of the town were at once cleared and the advancing Germans driven back 2,000 yards,' was the GOC's description in his despatch.

The German shelling had been almost continuous for a week, and persisted until the battalion was relieved on 5 December.

The 2nd Battalion had by this time left the Western Front for service on the Italian front. They spent much time patrolling against the Austrians, but by this stage in the war there was little fighting or movement of the line. They returned to the Western Front in April 1918.

When the Germans launched their offensive on 21 March 1918, the 6th KOSB were in reserve in the area of Cambrai. The British withdrawal started on that day, and on 23 March the Borderers were in the front line. The withdrawal was conducted under full control, and the Germans were unable to penetrate the forward companies. Two days later the Borderers were sent to Albert to defend bridges on the River Ancre, and subsequently a length of the Amiens-Albert railway. The Germans were repulsed time and again, until the momentum of their attacks was dissipated.

The battalion was moved in early April to Hill 60 near Ypres, which it defended for several days until all troops in the line had to withdraw. Later the Borderers fought to defend Kemmel Hill south-west of Ypres, but two companies were overrun. The Germans, however, could penetrate no further as the other companies held fast. The 7th/8th KOSB were in the Arras sector, during the offensive and the battalion had likewise to conduct a fighting withdrawal on 28 March. The German advance was eventually stemmed in this sector, and the 7th/8th remained in the trenches for a further ten days.

The 1st KOSB spent early April on the River Lys sector near Merville, and the 2nd Battalion was nearby. Three companies of the 2nd were nearly overwhelmed during one attack, but the enemy were held off until they could withdraw. Casualties were very high, and by the middle of the month the battalion mustered only about 80. The 6th Battalion at this time were holding ground near the Ypres-Comines Canal, but was ordered to withdraw on 16 April to conform to other troops. The fighting was intense and the Borderers defended their new line until relieved on 20 April. On 25 April, when the Germans launched an attack on the Kemmel area, the 6th KOSB lost its two forward companies and battalion headquarters. The remaining companies withdrew, but then mounted a counter-attack and recaptured some of the ground. With such exploits as this was the German offensive eventually halted.

May and June 1918 were mainly quiet months for the regiment on the Western Front. On 27 May the 1st Battalion carried out a particularly successful raid on a gun position, and aggressive patrol activities increased generally on both sides. A month later the 2nd KOSB launched a battalion attack on the Forêt de Nieppe in order to rationalise the line. In half an hour the objectives were captured but the casualties were over 200. In the meantime the 52nd Lowland Divsion had reached France, and the 4th and 5th KOSB joined the line near Vimy.

A Borderer of the 2nd KOSB mans a newly captured trench, littered with German clothing and equipment, near Merville, 4 July 1918. IWM

The 6th KOSB march past HM King George V at La Bréarde, near Hazebroucke, 6 Aug 1918. IWM

The 7th/8th KOSB was sent with the 15th Division as a reinforcement to the French sector during July. There the battalion took part in the first French attack near Buzancy on 23 July. It was not successful and the Borderers gained little ground while losing over 300 casualties. They held part of the line during the battle for Buzancy itself, and in early August they returned to Arras.

When the final British offensive started, the 2nd KOSB was immediately involved in the fighting near Bapaume, where considerable gains of territory were made and men and equipment captured. The 1st Battalion mounted a set-piece attack on a ridge near Hoegenacker Mill on 18 August, and captured 300 prisoners and 60 machine guns. A month later the Borderers took part in the major assault east of Ypres, when Gheluvelt was captured. The 6th KOSB were also involved in the attack.

The 4th Battalion took part in the capture of Henin Mill near the Hindenburg Line on 26 August. Six days later, during the major assault on the Hindenburg Line itself, the 4th advanced some 600 yards to the first objective, but could get no further. They were relieved on 4 September. Meanwhile the 5th KOSB assisted in the capture of Mount Kemmel, and a month later the battalion took part in the advance over the Ypres-Comines Canal in the direction of Wytschaete. During this battle Sgt M'Guffie won the VC.

'He had to take charge of a platoon in consequence of officer casualties, and was responsible for the capture of several dugouts . . . then . . . with complete disregard to personal safety rushed out singlehanded and cowed a German escort into restoring a party of British prisoners.'

All six battalions of the KOSB took part in the final drive across Belgium during the last five weeks of the war. Most of the fighting was fast moving but the Germans resisted strongly in some areas. When the armistice was declared on 11 November, the 1st and 6th KOSB marched into Germany as occupation troops.

* * * * *

The 1st KOSB spent the winter of 1918 in Germany, but returned to India in 1919. It then served in the Middle East before being posted to Edinburgh. In the 1930s the battalion served in Malta and Palestine, where it frequently took part in internal security duties. The 2nd Battalion served in Ireland after the First World War, and then served continuously abroad, first in Egypt and then Hong Kong, before reaching India in 1939.

THE KING'S OWN SCOTTISH BORDERERS

1939 to the present

In September 1939 the 1st Battalion was at Portsmouth when mobilisation was announced. In early October the Borderers embarked for France with the British Expeditionary Force, and by the middle of the month were manning positions near Lille on the Belgian border. There they remained during the winter until the Germans invaded Belgium. On 11 May they advanced through Belgium to take up positions near Louvain on the River Dyle.

The battalion was not much engaged with the enemy before a withdrawal was ordered. The Borderers moved twenty-five miles westwards to the river Dendre, where they dug in again, guarding two bridges as British formations withdrew through them. By now the enemy were within range and there were some artillery and mortar exchanges. A few days later the Borderers took up fresh positions on the River Escaut. B company had to go to the assistance of the neighbouring battalion, when the Germans formed a bridgehead on the west bank. Most of the heaviest fighting was elsewhere and, while holding successive positions under long-range artillery fire, there was little the battalion could do but conform to the general withdrawal when ordered. The march was exhausting, the situation always confused and the prospects depressing, but it was fortunate that the 1st KOSB reached the perimeter of Dunkirk relatively unscathed. They embarked and sailed for England on 1 June.

Both the 4th and 5th KOSB were sent with the 52nd Lowland Division which formed part of the force intended to hold a second front in France in early June 1940. They reached St Malo on 13 June and were moved by train to the Le Mans area. Two days later since there was no hope of holding the Germans, it was decided to withdraw the division to Cherbourg. The 5th KOSB had the task of divisional rear-guard, and over the next few days it encountered advance elements of the German army. Moving by truck, both battalions reached Cherbourg on 18 June and embarked safely for England.

* * * * *

In the meantime, the 2nd Battalion, King's Own Scottish Borderers were serving in India. In late 1941 they were stationed at Razmak in Waziristan on the

Drums and Military Band of the KOSB c1930. They wear the distinctive Kilmarnock bonnet and trews of Leslie tartan. IWM

North-West Frontier, their task being to operate against Pathan tribesmen who frequently attacked the British stations. The Borderers' major engagement was in the summer of 1942, when the whole British brigade mounted a successful relief expedition to the garrison of Dhatta Khel. They remained at Razmak for a year, and in August 1943 embarked as part of 89 Brigade with the force to fight the Japanese in the Arakan region of Burma.

There was already a British front line established south of Chittagong and the Borderers joined it in October. The line was mainly static at the time, and their first engagement with the Japanese was a well-planned ambush in which they inflicted some 60 casualties on the enemy. Later in the month they conducted aggressive patrols against Japanese positions in the jungle, nicknamed the 'Horseshoe'. After moving to a new part of the front line they fought a major battle. The Japanese were holding positions nicknamed the 'Pimples' along the Mayu Ridge, and the Borderers took part in a night march and daylight attack on a hill named 'Able'. Two companies successfully took their objectives, but the Japanese fire was very heavy, and the battalion's further advance was held up. For two nights the battalion was isolated, unable to advance and short of ammunition, rations and water. It was eventually resupplied, and continued to hold its positions while flanking troops attempted to defeat the enemy on the Pimples. After two weeks the Borderers were relieved.

In early February 1944 the 2nd KOSB were moved to the Wet Valley, their brigade objective being Taung. As the 7th Indian Division, in which the Borderers were serving, advanced through the jungle and hills, the Japanese attacked from several directions and threatened to cut off each of the brigades. The Borderers' task was the protection of 89 Brigade headquarters at Allwynbin. The difficulty was to locate and destroy the enemy forces, and large patrols were sent out with some success. Subsequently they were ordered to move to the divisional 'Admin Box', and there was much fighting on the way. The 'Admin Box' was the administrative area to which the remnants of divisional headquarters had moved. The enemy spent eighteen days attempting to penetrate and destroy the units operating there. The Borderers had the task of preventing the enemy succeeding, and helped to guard vital supplies and equipment as well as to patrol the area. On one occasion while on patrol, C Company was ambushed by a large party of Japanese infiltrators. The Borderers carried out a company attack which, despite suffering many casualties including Major Knox the company commander, broke up the enemy patrol. Similar actions continued for days.

All along the line, however, the Japanese had failed to penetrate and defeat the British and Imperial troops, and the Mayu Ridge was cleared of the enemy by mid-February. The KOSB's task was the seizure of 'Okeydoke' Pass which was achieved on

A long-serving Royal Col-in-Chief Princess Alice, Duchess of Gloucester, inspects the 1st KOSB 'somewhere in England', 1943. Her family have a long connection with the regiment. IWM

23 February and the battalion was sent to make contact with the 5th Indian Division at the Ngakyedak Pass. Subsequently the Borderers occupied 'Massive' Hill, a Japanese stronghold.

As the Arakan campaign was now ended, the 2nd KOSB were airlifted to Kohima on the Indian border in April 1944. The battalion's task was to hold an area of ground covering the Imphal-Kohima road by aggressive patrolling. The Borderers took part in a brigade attack on a hill known as the 'Hump'. After a difficult approach march and ascent up a precipitous slope, the attack went in. The Japanese resisted for several days and inflicted heavy casualties on the British and Indian troops. The Borderers sent in several infiltration patrols, and a fresh brigade attack had to be mounted before the enemy, realising that they were cut off, finally abandoned the position.

The Japanese were by now gradually falling back all along the line, and the 2nd KOSB were given the task of clearing the enemy from a hill-top fort at Ukhrul which was held in great strength. After an exhausting march and several probes against the enemy positions, the Borderers and 4th/8th Gurkhas attacked the hill, but were unable to take it. The Japanese, after resisting for a time, evacuated the fort and withdrew south. Soon afterwards the battalion was withdrawn from the war zone for recuperation and training.

The 2nd KOSB returned to operational service at the end of December 1944 to take part in the march on Mandalay. This lasted for many weeks, and the Borderers frequently met opposition as they progressed through the jungle, plantations and open country. Re-supply was by air, and after one month 168 miles had been covered and the Irrawaddy was in sight. In mid-February the Borderers crossed the river and captured a battalion objective of Nakyo-Aing

Cheerful Borderers of the 1st Bn dig in during the battle for Caen, Normandy, 8 July 1944. IWM

with armoured support from the 116th Regiment (Gordon Highlanders) RAC. There was very fierce fighting spread over a period of two days. During March 1945 the battalion remained on the river line, gradually advancing and holding successive positions against determined enemy attacks and extensive patrolling. In April the advance speeded up and the Borderers blocked the Japanese supply lines at Salin, defeating enemy counter-attacks and capturing much equipment. During the following two months the battalion moved steadily down the Irrawaddy, assisting in clearing out numerous Japanese stay-behind parties. Burma was then evacuated by the Japanese, and in July the 2nd KOSB embarked for Calcutta.

* * * * *

The 1st King's Own Scottish Borderers landed in France on D Day, 6 June 1944. They consolidated inland and took up positions on the second day in a wood near Le Mesnil. During that evening, the Borderers assisted the Royal Ulster Rifles in capturing Cambes Wood. The next four weeks were spent by the battalion in the same area, constantly under artillery fire and attack by armour and infantry.

The 6th KOSB in the 15th Scottish Division meanwhile had reached Normandy on 15 June, and went into action on 26 June for possession of the area of the River Odon. The Borderers were in support of two successive battalion attacks and, when holding the front line the following day, met a furious German armoured counter-attack.

One particular day of fighting is worth recording. On 1 July C Company of the 6th KOSB was in a forward position under shellfire for several hours before daylight. Then a strong force of German infantry and tanks approached and attacked the Company position. Artillery fire was brought down on the enemy and the Borderers engaged them for three hours with every weapon they had, including anti-tank guns. The Germans temporarily withdrew, but returned with six more tanks supported by artillery fire. The fighting continued all morning and most of the afternoon. The forward platoon positions had to be evacuated. A further nine enemy tanks appeared in the woods to the right of C Company, and they were knocked out by artillery fire. The Germans then withdrew, and the Borderers re-occupied their original positions. The battle on this part of the front lasted for several days, the Germans attacking again and again: a general advance was not possible until the Americans could break out from the west.

The 1st Battalion entered Caen on 9 July, after the Germans had been bombed and shelled into evacuating it. The 6th KOSB were in the assault again on 15 July, this time to capture 'Point 113' near Evrecy. This night attack was successful, but the Borderers had to face numerous counter-attacks. The 1st Battalion moved from Caen to the Odon sector at the same time, and was in action at Troarn on 19 July. The Germans were holding the area strongly with well-sited weapons and, in their attempt to seize it, the Borderers suffered over 150 casualties. Meanwhile the 6th continued to hold part of the high ground between the Rivers Odon and Orne, and were in very close contact with the German infantry and armour. 'The enemy,' it was reported, 'was even sharing the same hedge as A Company.'

The 1st KOSB moved in early August to the area of Vire, thirty miles south-west of Caen. The battalion was given objectives, which they took on 7 August, but had to withdraw owing to adjacent battalions being held up. Vire fell to the Americans three days later: this signalled a more mobile phase of the campaign, and the battalion took part in the advance on Flers, Falaise and the River Seine. The Seine river-crossing for both battalions was unopposed.

The 6th KOSB met German resistance again on 15 September on the Meuse-Escaut Canal, near Gheel on the Belgian border. The enemy counter-attacked a bridge-head formed by the 8th Royal Scots, and the 6th KOSB crossed by boat as a reinforcement.

The infantry marches when it is not digging. A sergeant leads his platoon of the KOSB past distinctive Dutch landmarks, Sept 1944. IWM

But this position was untenable and the battalion covered a withdrawal. The 1st KOSB also assisted in the crossing of the canal near Achel on 18 September and led the occupation of the village. The following day the battalion crossed into Holland and moved in the region of Liesel where they conducted probing patrols against the enemy.

In the meantime the 7th King's Own Scottish Borderers landed by glider on 17 September, west of Arnhem, as part of the 1st Airborne Division. The Borderers' task was to hold a dropping zone for the parachute drops on 18 September. They had to face an increasing number of German vehicles and patrols which appeared during 18 and 19 September. After holding the dropping zone, the battalion was ordered to hold a bridge. By 20 September the battalion had been dispersed over a wide area, and had suffered severe casualties in numerous engagements with the enemy. On 21 September the remaining Borderers held a position at a place named the 'White House' near Arnhem. The fighting was intense, with the enemy being fought off at bayonet point on one occasion. The battle raged until 25 September, when the remainder of the battalion, reduced to only 4 officers and 72 rank and file, succeeded in reaching Nijmegen.

During this time the 6th KOSB crossed the Wilhelmina Canal and captured the town of Best, while the 1st were in action in October near Venraij. Both battalions then consolidated on the River Maas. Later in the month the 6th Battalion was moved rapidly to the area of Liesel, to support the Americans fighting against German armoured troops covered by a massive artillery barrage. The town was eventually occupied by the end of the month by the 6th KOSB and four other British battalions.

In October 1944 the 52nd Lowland Division was given the task of clearing the Scheldt islands of Walcheren and South Beveland in order to open up the port of Antwerp for the allies. The 4th and 5th were part of the division and, after landing at Ostend, moved to the Scheldt at the end of the month. Their brigade's objective was Flushing on Walcheren Island. After disembarking from the assault craft, the 4th KOSB had much difficulty in fighting against the enemy in well-protected concrete defences. The 5th KOSB were prevented from crossing the river at the first attempt owing to heavy enemy shellfire, but on landing they immediately set about seizing the Middleburg Canal to the east of Flushing. The battle for the town continued through the following day, and both battalions had to contend with heavy machine-gun and artillery fire. But the Germans were successfully cut off and on 3 November Flushing fell into British hands, while the 4th KOSB cleared the canal linking the town with Middleburg.

Its task accomplished, the 52nd Lowland Division moved to the Maas where the 4th and 5th KOSB joined the allied front line which was static at the time. However, the Borderers carried out aggressive patrolling and faced occasional German attacks. One

such was mounted against the 5th Battalion and some positions were overrun. Reinforcements and tank support restored the situation. Then in early December the 6th Battalion took part in the attack across the Maas against German-held Blerick. In this highly successful set-piece attack the armour led, and the battalion was lifted into the town to clear the streets.

In January 1945 the 4th and 5th KOSB were in the Geilenkirchen area, and were involved in the divisional operation nicknamed 'Blackcock', the purpose of which was to clear the enemy between the River Maas and the Roer. Closely supported by accompanying armour, good progress was made, but they met formidable resistance at Waldfeucht on 22 January. The 5th KOSB entered the village during the early hours. At first it appeared to be unoccupied, but the Germans began to shell the British positions and then enemy tanks and infantry appeared. They attempted to knock out the tanks and fought a close-quarter battle amongst the houses for several hours. Casualties on both sides were high. In the afternoon B Company of the 4th KOSB arrived and fought its way into the village, and for the remainder of the day tanks and infantry moved around in a free-ranging battle. By the time two more companies of the 4th KOSB arrived at midnight the fighting was virtually over, with Waldfeucht in British hands. Shortly afterwards two companies of the 4th supported the Royal Scots in taking the strongly defended town of Heinsberg.

The battle for the Reichswald Forest in February 1945 involved all four battalions of the King's Own Scottish Borderers serving in the theatre. The 6th Battalion reached the Siegfried line in their armoured carriers en route for Cleve, quickly capturing artillery and infantry positions. After occupying Cleve, the battalion moved south to reinforce the 15th and 51st Divisions fighting for possession of Goch. The 4th and 5th, advancing through the Reichswald, were delayed by well-sited enemy positions and devastating artillery fire. An ancient fortress stoutly defended by the Germans, was a further cause of delay until it was destroyed by aerial attack. Several days were then spent fighting through the woods at very close quarters with the enemy. In the meantime the 1st Battalion was fighting through the woods towards Winnekendonk, which was taken subsequently by the Lincolnshire Regiment with the Borderers in support. In early March, as the allies approached the River Rhine, the 4th KOSB were heavily involved in the fighting near Alpon.

These two photographs show Borderers of the 6th Bn moving through a wood and cleaning their rifles after capturing the village of Bislich, 25 Mar 1945. They had crossed the Rhine on the previous day. IWM

The 6th KOSB were the first Borderers to cross the Rhine, which they did on 24 March. A day later the 5th Battalion followed. The 6th Battalion captured Bislich after landing, and were then heavily involved in the attempt to seize a bridge over the River Issel. The Germans mounted a determined counter-attack and overran a company position, but

Borderers on the outskirts of Bremen, 25 April 1945. The 1st, 4th and 5th KOSB all took part in the fighting for this important German seaport. IWM

they were eventually forced to withdraw. The 1st Battalion crossed the Rhine on 27 March and the 4th Battalion a day later. The 1st made rapid progress, but were held up by the German defences on the Dortmund-Ems Canal. The battalion was also involved in clearing the town of Lingen, held by a young soldiers' battalion. At Bramsche the Borderers took a regiment of German anti-aircraft gunners by surprise and overwhelmed them.

The 4th KOSB were with the follow-up formations and did not see any serious action until they reached Ibbenburen, near Osnabruck. There, in the wooded hills of the Teutoburgerwald, the Borderers fought a battle at very close range against cadets of a German battle school. It took the combined efforts of three Scottish battalions to defeat the enemy. The 5th KOSB's main action in early April was the capture of Voltlage, and the 6th Battalion's attack on Uelzen went so well that, despite the town being a brigade objective, the Borderers quickly captured it and held it against heavy counter-attacks.

In the last days of the war the 1st, 4th and 5th

KOSB had to fight against desperate attempts by the enemy to defend Bremen. On 25 April the 1st Battalion crossed the Weser, and the 4th and 5th KOSB also reached the outskirts of Bremen. All three battalions then spent many weeks in helping to restore control and organisation to the shambles that had been the city. To the west, meanwhile, the 6th Battalion was preparing to cross the River Elbe, which it did on 29 April. The crossing was entirely successful, and against light opposition rapid progress was made towards Lübeck to the north-west as the war drew to an end.

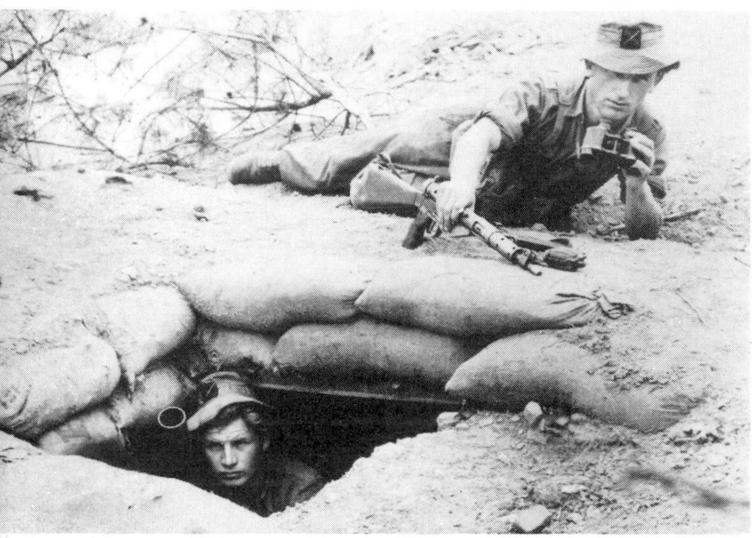

Waiting for targets; mortar section of the 1st KOSB, Korea 1952. IWM

The 2nd Battalion, King's Own Scottish Borderers had remained in India after their withdrawal from the campaign in Burma. Based at Peshawar on the North-West Frontier after the war, not only did they have a role to police the countryside, but also mounted internal security operations within the city during the period of tension before partition and home rule. Their firm control contributed to the minimum of disorder during their two-year tour of duty. In 1947 the battalion was disbanded.

Meanwhile the 1st Battalion had moved to Palestine in 1946 and carried out similar tasks in attempting to keep the peace between Arabs and Jews. Tension was very high and operations included mobile patrols, manning check points, cordon and search and the arrest of illegal immigrants. There was much terrorist bombing and shooting, and the battalion suffered several casualties. In 1948 the battalion sailed for Great Britain.

In April 1951 1st KOSB was sent to Korea to join the UN forces fighting against the North Koreans and Chinese 'volunteers'. The Borderers went into action on reaching the front, but almost immediately the whole UN forces carried out a major withdrawal.

Left forward platoon of C Coy, 1st KOSB just before the battle on the night of 4/5 Nov 1951. A shell lands on the Chinese position in Korea. RHQ

The Commonwealth Division, in which the Borderers served, adopted a sector on the Imjin river along the 38th Parallel, and firm defensive positions were immediately established. In late September there was a general advance, and on 3 October the Borderers' chief battle was fought to gain possession of Hill 355. A new line was set up, which was frequently under attack by the enemy for the remainder of the month. On the evening of 4 November a Chinese division of some 6,000 soldiers was launched against the Borderers' position. Some of the company positions were overrun, but B Company managed to hold, and of those who survived most pulled back, leaving only two platoons in the forward position. Private Speakman led a party of six men forward several times in order to grenade the enemy, which exploits won him the VC. The enemy's attack had failed: they had lost more than 1,000 dead, while the Borderers had 7 killed, 87 wounded and 44 missing. After this battle the Borderers were withdrawn and moved to another sector. They left Korea in August 1952.

After a tour of duty in Northern Ireland, the 1st KOSB embarked for service in Singapore and Malaya. For more than two years the battalion performed internal security and counter-insurgency operations during the 'emergency'. Companies spent much time laying ambushes and patrolling against the terrorists from secure bases in the plantations and jungle. During their operational tour the Borderers had a total of twenty-two contacts, and killed and wounded a number of terrorists.

Further service in Scotland and Berlin preceded a move to Aden. There the battalion carried out internal security duties in the town itself until 1964. A few months after leaving the protectorate, the Borderers were recalled for an emergency tour in the Radfan Mountains 'up-country' from Aden. They operated for three months against Yemeni insurgents, patrolling and picqueting the hill tops.

In 1965 the 1st KOSB were sent on another emergency tour to the Far East. They spent a time in Hong Kong and Singapore, and then moved to Sarawak. There the confrontation with the Indonesian insurgents was in progress, and the companies set up inland bases alongside the waterways. For six months the companies patrolled the border region by river and on foot. After some contacts early in the tour, the insurgency came to an end, although the Borderers continued to patrol the border for a time.

In 1967 the 1st Kings Own Scottish Borderers became a mechanised infantry battalion in Osnabruck as part of the British Army of the Rhine. Three years later they had their first tour of internal security duty in Northern Ireland. During the 1970s and 1980s the 1st KOSB have served in BAOR, the United Kingdom and overseas stations and, like all infantry regiments, have carried out numerous tours in Northern Ireland. Their tercentenary falls in 1989.

Jungle patrol in Sarawak, 1960s. Cpl John Laidlaw and other members of 1st KOSB. RHQ

A section of 1st KOSB photographed in the Radfan Mountains, Aden Protectorate, 1963. RHQ

1st KOSB prepare to seal off a street in Belfast c1970. The Royal Ulster Constabulary are present in force, but clearly expect the soldiers to deal with any violence. RHQ

A Borderer in Belfast. Pte John Clark awaits events on duty, 1975. RHQ

CHAPTER 7
THE CAMERONIANS
(Scottish Rifles)

In the 1881 reorganisation of the army the Cameronians (Scottish Rifles) were formed from the 26th and 90th Regiments. The former had descended from the followers of the Covenanter Richard Cameron, formed into a regiment in 1689, whilst the 90th had been a Perthshire regiment since 1794. A regular battalion of the Cameronians remained in being until 1968 and the regiment is represented at the present time by a company of the Territorial Army and Cadet units.

THE 26TH CAMERONIAN REGIMENT

1689–1881

The regiment originated under perhaps the most unusual circumstances of any in the British army. The Covenanters were a sect of the Presbyterian Church in Scotland, to whom the National League and Covenant of 1638 was the embodiment of the only true religion. In their early years they strongly resisted the characteristics of an hierarchical organisation. As such, the Covenanters drew upon themselves the severest of repressive measures by royalists and episcopalians. The only way that the Covenanters could worship the Almighty in their own way was by the formation of 'societies', who met secretly in the open air at pre-arranged 'conventicles' under armed guard – hence another name for them, the 'hill men'.

In the last years of Charles II's reign and particularly from 1680, when his brother the Duke of York was High Commissioner to Scotland, the Covenanters were hunted mercilessly by the royal troops. The societies formed an association in the same year, called the 'United Societies', to which representatives came from far afield in central and southern Scotland. The followers of Richard Cameron, by adherence to the Declaration of Sanquhar on 22 June 1680, denied King Charles's civil and religious authority: membership of the Cameronian sect was therefore treasonable. Cameron himself was killed at Airds Moss in 1680. When James succeeded to the throne of England and Scotland, and tried to re-establish fully the Catholic Church, Scotland was more sharply divided than it had ever been, even in the years before and during the Commonwealth. In 1689 James II fled to France.

The invitation by the English whigs to William of Orange to assume the Crown of England jointly with his wife Mary, was not immediately copied by the Scots. The situation in the northern kingdom was much more confused, and there were numerous parties vying for political power. In March 1689 the Convention of Estates met in Edinburgh. A large number of armed Cameronians were present in the city, and much pressure was exerted by most presbyterians for the acceptance of the new joint-monarchy, on the condition of a royal guarantee for the protection of the laws, liberties and 'true Kirk' of Scotland. The royal authority of William and Mary was finally accepted by the Lords of Convention on 11 April, and this provoked a brief but intense war in the Kingdom.

The military position in Scotland immediately crystallised with the departure of Graham of Claverhouse, Viscount Dundee, to raise the highlands and north-east for James. The Earl of Leven's Regiment had already been raised for the defence of Edinburgh, and on 19 April seven new regiments of foot were authorised by the Convention, one of which was to be raised by the Earl of Angus. The United Societies General Meeting at first resisted the formation of a regiment from amongst their members, but recognising that their very survival could well depend on the military defeat of Claverhouse and those loyal to the exiled King James, they agreed to the proposal.

Among the eight stipulations on which the General Meeting insisted, were that the officers should be of the choice or consent of the soldiers, and that the regiment should be kept as much separate from other regiments of the army as was possible. The reason was to preserve the purity of the members from the temptations to which soldiers were believed to be traditionally prone. Under the Lieutenant-Colonelcy of William Cleland, and in the name of the Earl of Angus (the eldest son of the Marquis of Douglas), the companies of the regiment were formed up at a conventicle at Douglas, Lanarkshire on 12 May 1689. The agreements between the 1,200 rank and file, their religious leaders and military commanders, were completed two days later.

Thus was raised in a unique fashion a regular regiment of foot from a group of men sworn to uphold their religious cause to the death, for the military service of William and Mary and their heirs. In view of their past history it is ironical that they should so quickly have given their loyalty to the monarchy in 1689, having denied it with such zeal for so many years.

The United Societies, however, soon lost their influence over the regiment. The effects of much active service on the continent, and recruitment from areas other than covenanting country, eventually ensured that the regiment's traditions became more

Previous page:
The Militia on active service in South Africa. F Coy, 4th Cameronians pose by No. 3 redoubt at Kimberley, April 1900. RHQ

truly military. Nevertheless the regiment has always retained a distinct individuality. To the present day its successors have faithfully maintained the conventicles and tradition of issuing a bible to every recruit on enlistment, thus keeping alive the name of a once numerous religious sect and its leader.

* * * * *

Once officially embodied, the Cameronian regiment marched to quarters near Stirling where it received arms, ammunitions and some uniforms. The royal army was divided into two parts; the Duke of Argyll's force, which included the Cameronians, marched to secure the western highlands; and the main force under General MacKay set out for the north. On 27 July 1689 MacKay's force was defeated at Killiecrankie, but the highland army, its leader Claverhouse having been killed in the battle, did not fully exploit the victory. In order to block the road to the south, the Earl of Angus's regiment was ordered to secure the town of Dunkeld, some sixteen miles north of Perth.

There followed some local skirmishing in the hills which surrounded the town, but by the morning of 21 August some 5,000 highlanders encircled the town and attacked the 1,200 defenders. The Cameronians fought with great ferocity amongst the buildings and from behind the dykes. Much of the fighting was at close quarters and the highlanders managed to penetrate the defences.

> 'The assailants then commenced a vigorous attack both on the castle and church; in front of the former Colonel Cleland was killed encouraging his men. Undaunted by their loss the Cameronians kept up a most destructive fire which, together with the flames of some neighbouring houses, effectively baffled all the persevering and gallant attacks of their opponents who, despairing of success, relaxed their efforts at about eleven o'clock, and shortly after withdrew in confusion to the hills . . .'

The highlanders lost some 300 killed while the regiment lost its Lieutenant-Colonel, several officers and fifteen men.

It would be wrong to ascribe the failure of the cause of James II in Scotland wholly to the defeat at Dunkeld, but the spirit of rebellion subsided, and the southern part of Scotland began a period of peace that was to endure, broken only by the brief Jacobite risings in 1715, 1719 and 1745–6.

Like most regiments of the time, the regiment was known by the name of its colonels, sucessively Andrew Monro (1692), James Fergusson (1693), John Borthwick (1705), James Lord Dalrymple (later the Earl of Stair) (1706), George Preston (1706), and Philip Anstruther (1720).

The regiment left Scotland in the spring of 1691 to join William III's army in the Netherlands, where the War of the League of Augsburg was in progress against France. There were two major engagements in which the Cameronians took part. On 3 August William's army mounted an attack on the French garrison at Steenkirk. The Earl of Angus was himself in command in what proved to be an inept attempt to dislodge a superior force. By all accounts Angus's regiment fought bravely, with the colonel and the chaplain, Alexander Shields, in the thick of the fighting. Much of the action was at close quarters amid the hedgerows, trenches and drains in the flat countryside. Reinforcements were not moved up as requested to support the attack and an orderly withdrawal was hampered by French artillery and cavalry. The regiment's casualties depleted its strength by one-third and many of the officers were killed, including the Earl of Angus.

A year later the regiment was part of the force entrenched at Landen. Marshal de Luxembourg with 80,000 French troops attacked William's army of 50,000 on 29 July. The regiment defended the village of Laer and, when driven out, mounted a successful counter-attack. It became necessary, however, to withdraw as the French cavalry had penetrated the allies' main position at Neerwinden at the third attempt. The army withdrew from Landen to a more tenable position out of immediate reach of the French Army: the Cameronians had suffered only minor casualties.

The war continued until 1697, but the regiment was not involved in any further major engagements. In 1699 it returned to Scotland, and was garrisoned in Perth with the task of policing the highlands. The uneasy peace on the Continent was ended in 1701 by the outbreak of the War of Spanish Succession. Great Britain entered the war allied to the Dutch and Austrians, and the Cameronians regiment reached Holland, twelve companies strong, in July 1702.

The British Army spent the next eighteen months in a war of manoeuvre. In the spring of 1704 The Duke of Marlborough moved his forces south through Germany to the Danube. The Cameronians took part in the capture of the Schellenberg, and were in James Ferguson's brigade at the Battle of Blenheim. The brigade mounted an attack on the French right flank holding the village of Blenheim. Four times they charged in face of withering fire, but were unable to dislodge the enemy. Fresh orders were then received, and the brigade took up a blocking position, effectively neutralising the French right wing during Marlborough's main cavalry attack on the French and Bavarian centre. The regiment had sustained considerable casualties in this decisive British victory. Marlborough's army then returned to the United Provinces and Flanders.

The next major battle was in May 1706 at Ramillies, and the Cameronians were part of a diversionary attack under the Earl of Orkney on the French stronghold in the village. This enabled the main allied attack to proceed against an over-extended French right, and the outcome was another victory for Marlborough's army. There followed a series of sieges on French-held towns during the remainder of the year. The battle of Oudenarde, which took place on 11 July 1708, was a hastily-fought affair in which the regiment was under fire but not actually engaged directly with the French.

A year later the allied army made contact with the enemy at Malplaquet, a village just inside the French frontier. Positioned in the centre, the Cameronians with other infantry under the Earl of Orkney, forced a gap in the French line allowing the cavalry, which included the Scots Greys, to exploit and break the French defences. The remaining years of the war were spent in further sieges and manoeuvring, and after the Treaty of Utrecht in 1713 the Cameronians embarked for Ireland.

* * * * *

Just prior to the 1715 Jacobite rising the regiment moved to Chester. As part of a force under Major-General Wills, the Cameronians led by Lt-Col Lord Forrester forced an entry into the Lancashire town of Preston held by the English rebels.

> 'After making their way through the lanes and narrow approaches, they were received with a very heavy fire from the entrenchments and houses . . . During the heat of the action it was discovered that the entrance to the town by the Wigan road was less strongly fortified . . . and Lord Forrester succeeded at the head of his gallant men in occupying two houses. Having accomplished his object, his Lordship . . . drew up one division across the street, whilst with the remainder the houses were secured; by which a tenable lodgement was effected in the rebels' line of defence.'

The town was surrounded, and in due course the rebels surrendered. The Cameronians lost 92 casualties.

After a period of duty in Ireland and service at sea on ships of the Royal Navy in 1726, the Cameronians were stationed in Gibraltar (which had been captured from Spain in 1704) during the siege of 1727. The regiment remained as garrison troops for eleven years on the Rock. During the War of the Austrian Succession from 1738–48 it guarded Minorca against possible attack from France or Spain. In 1747 it was ranked as the 26th in seniority, and was named in 1751 the 26th Regiment (The Cameronians).

During the years 1749 to 1767 the regiment was stationed first in Ireland and then in Scotland. Although it took no part in the Seven Years' War of 1756–63, the 26th supplied drafts for service in other Scots and English regiments. In 1767 the regiment embarked for service in the American colonies, where the army had the task of averting any renewed threat from the French settlers in Canada, and the Spanish from the south. The 26th had been made up to strength over the years by Englishmen and Irishmen, and during this time drew further recruits from the colonies. In 1772 the regiment moved to Canada.

At the outbreak of the American War of Independence in May 1775, the two forts of Ticonderoga and Crown Point, held by small detachments of the 26th, were overwhelmed by the rebels. The more important Fort of St John's was held by a mixed garrison of some 500 soldiers, of which just under half were Cameronians, while the remainder of the regiment was dispersed in detachments elsewhere in Canada. When an invasion of Canada took place, St John's was besieged and cut off. With the surrender by nearby Fort Chambly and the failure of a relief expedition, St John's also had to be surrendered. It was eighteen months before the regiment consolidated and reformed in New York as garrison troops.

After the defeat of the British at Saratoga in 1777, the 26th were sent temporarily to defend Philadelphia, but later returned to New York. Most members of the regiment were drafted to other regiments in 1779 and the regimental cadre returned to Britain to begin the task of recruiting. The proportion of Scotsmen in the regiment then increased substantially, due to the efforts of the new colonel Lord Adam Gordon. The years 1783–7 were spent by the 26th in Ireland.

In 1787 the Cameronians returned to Canada and remained there until May 1800. The duties of the British troops were to man the forts and prevent the Americans, Indians and French partisans from seizing territory held by the Crown, and these tasks were successfully fulfilled. Followed by a brief period in England, the 26th left for service in Egypt as a reinforcement, and landed at Aboukir in July 1801. The regiment took part in the capture of Alexandria from the French which, compared with the previous fighting in the vicinity, was an easy task.

Returning to Britain in 1802, the regiment was brought up to strength when the resumption of war became inevitable. A second battalion was formed in Scotland, and both battalions were sent to Ireland. In 1805 the 1st Battalion embarked for service on the Continent in support of Austria, but nearly one-third of the regiment was lost at sea when one of the transports sank. After a few weeks stationed in Westphalia, the expedition was recalled as a consequence of the defeat of the Austrians at Austerlitz.

In 1807 French troops had entered Spain and Portugal and the Cameronians were part of the reinforcements sent to northern Spain under General Sir David Baird in late 1808. After much manoeuvring during the winter, the British Army was forced to retreat to the port of Corunna. The French mounted an attack on the British positions on 16 January. The Cameronians, as part of the reserve, took part in an attack on the flank of a French column attempting to break the British right. The line held and, during a period when French attacks had subsided, the British force succeeded in embarking on the transports bound for England.

Six months later the battalion embarked with the Walcheren expedition, the largest expeditionary force yet mounted in the war. The purpose was to occupy the islands in the Scheldt Estuary, which was accomplished with some difficulty. The force remained in the Netherlands for six months, but was stricken by disease from which very many died. The French threat did not materialise and the expeditionary force was subsequently withdrawn.

After a further period in England and the Channel Islands, the Cameronians reached Portugal in July 1811. Under Sir Arthur Wellesley (later Duke of Wellington) the British Army was seeking to force a French withdrawal from Spain. As much as one-third of Wellesley's troops were unfit for duty owing to sickness and the rigours of forced marching, and there was little fighting at this time. Having spent several months with the 1st Division in Spain, the 26th was withdrawn and sent to guard Gibraltar. There it remained until 1822.

* * * * *

Following a tour of duty in Ireland, the Cameronians reached India in 1828. They served first in Madras then in Meerut, and proved to be a most efficient regiment. These were years of relative tranquillity, and it was not until 1840 that the regiment was called upon for active service again, this time to fight in the first China War. The 26th was part of a force designed to exert military pressure on the Chinese in order to force trading concessions, rather than achieve military conquest. Chusan and Fort Chuenpee were captured and Canton and Hong Kong blockaded, but the force was reduced by half due to disease. In May 1841 Canton was captured, and the Cameronians were instrumental in preventing a successful counter-attack by the Chinese on the town.

The political settlement that followed, however, was neither conducive to peace nor to favourable trading, so the war continued. A second expeditionary force, including the 26th Foot, proceeded to recapture Chusan and siezed Ningpo, and from there the force moved to the Yangtse Kiang. Having taken Chinkiangfu the expedition sailed up river to Nanking. The show of force was sufficient to persuade the Chinese to make a favourable peace with Britain.

In 1843 the regiment reached Britain and served tours of duty in England and Scotland before spending the years 1845–50 in Ireland. Then followed tours of duty in Gibraltar, Canada and Bermuda. After further home service, the 26th sailed for Bombay in 1866.

The 26th Cameronian Regt, 1866. Two years earlier it had been in action in support of Lord Napier's expedition to Magdala, Abyssinia.

Two years later it was involved in support of the Abyssinia expedition during which Lord Napier captured Magdala. The Cameronians remained in India until 1875. After home service they moved to Malta and then Gibraltar for a short time, before returning to Scotland.

In 1871 the Cameronians had been linked under the Cardwell reforms with the 74th Highlanders. The Depot was established at Hamilton, Lanarkshire, and was shared with the 73rd and 90th Regiments. Under the 1881 reorganisation the 26th was linked with the 90th, and the name of the new two-battalion regiment was settled as 'The Cameronians (Scottish Rifles)'. This incorporated the light infantry role and traditions of the 90th, and retained the name of the 26th which was, by then, nearly two centuries old.

THE 90TH PERTHSHIRE LIGHT INFANTRY

1794–1881

Thomas Graham of Balgowan, later Lord Lynedoch, took up military service late in life. Having seen aspects of the 'reign of terror' in France at first hand, Graham volunteered for active service in 1793 with the Toulon Expedition. Early the following year, after personally applying through the Home Secretary, Graham was commissioned to raise a regiment – the 90th Regiment of Foot, or Perthshire Volunteers. The regiment was to be clothed in the uniform of infantry of the line.

Recruiting was successful, and by May 1794 the offer to raise a second battalion was accepted. Command of this battalion went to Alexander Hope, Graham's cousin, but it was not long in being. It fed recruits to the first battalion and served on board ships of the Royal Navy in 1795, before being transferred to the Admiralty as Marines.

The 1st Battalion had been warned for service on the Continent in June 1794, but was diverted instead to the south of England. Then, with three other regiments, including the 78th Highland Regiment, the 90th embarked and landed on an island in Quiberon Bay off Brittany. This futile expedition resulted in no fighting, and the troops returned to England at the end of the year.

The regiment was then sent to garrison Gibraltar and in late 1797 sailed with the expedition for the recapture of Minorca. The flank companies of the various regiments under Graham covered the disembarkation and succeeded in distracting the Spanish forces. The remainder of the force, including the other companies of the 90th, landed and compelled the Spanish to surrender. It was during the period spent in garrisoning Minorca that officers of the 90th, notably Major Kenneth MacKenzie, became interested in the concept of light infantry tactics.

In August 1800 the 90th embarked for the expedition to seize Cadiz, but this was abandoned in late October. After a period of training in Malta, the force sailed for Aboukir Bay and landed on Egyptian soil on 8 March 1801.

Once the landing had been completed, the advance guard comprising the 90th and 92nd Highlanders set off towards the French-held fortress of Alexandria at the head of the two British columns. In the early hours of 13 March the force was hotly engaged by enemy rifle fire and artillery. Col Rowland Hill reported on the 90th's part in the battle.

> 'The light company was advanced and was furiously attacked by the cavalry but McNair, his officers and men were steady and firm, and gave them such a reception with musketry that many were killed and the others thrown into the greatest confusion. We advanced and drove the French from the first position. I then, with the bugle horn, halted the regiment and ceased firing, and correcting our line advanced with the greatest regularity to the second hill, where we were opposed with very heavy fire . . . The enemy continued to withdraw . . .'

The regiment's casualties were heavy, but it continued to advance under musket and artillery fire, causing the French to veer off towards the 92nd on the left. In this their first battle – named after the French redoubt of Mandora – the 90th had shown remarkable courage and steadiness in close-quarter combat under intense enemy fire.

When the French attacked again on 21 March in front of Alexandria itself, the 90th on the left were not seriously engaged. The result of this action, however, enabled the British, despite the death of their commander, Sir Ralph Abercromby, to blockade the town and send part of the force to seize Cairo. The 90th were part of this force and their task was successfully acomplished. During the actual British capture of Alexandria in August, the regiment's task was to assault the defences to the East of the town and prevent the French from withdrawing.

After a few months in Malta, the 90th returned to England. Many of the junior British regiments were considered for disbandment as a consequence of the Treaty of Amiens. But the peace was short-lived and the 90th Regiment was sent to Ireland to join other troops to counter a possible French invasion, and guard against a further insurrection such as had occurred in 1798.

In 1805 the regiment sailed to the West Indies to garrison the island of St Vincent. In 1809 half the

'The last gun at Waterloo' The 21st Royal North British Fusiliers capture a French gun towards the end of the battle. Watercolour by R. Simkin. RHQ

Right:
Private of the Light Company of the 3rd Guards of 1817 in field service order. He wears a bugle badge in his shako. A copy of the original painting by Alexander Sauerwied in Windsor Castle.
National Museums of Scotland

A piper, officer and private soldier of the 74th Highlanders in uniform of the 1840s.
Engraving from Cannon's Records

Top left:
Officers of the 72nd Duke of Albany's Own Highlanders c1840.
From Cannon's Records

Top centre:
Officers and soldier of the 71st Highland Light Infantry in the uniform of the 1840s.
Engraving from Cannon's Records

Left:
A coloured engraving of an officer of the Scots Fusilier Guards skirmishing. Ackermann print of 1845.
RHQ

Top right:
Soldiers of the 73rd Perthshire Regt stand fast during the sinking of the troopship Birkenhead *in 1852. Other Scottish drafts on board were from the 74th and 91st Highlanders. Oil painting by Thomas Henry.* RHQ

Right:
Officers, a lance-corporal and a piper of the 79th Cameron Highlanders at camp in 1853, painted by Eugene Lami. V & AM

D.CUNLIFF

Top left:
A corporal of the 79th Cameron Highlanders by Eugene Lami in 1853. The following year the regiment joined the Highland Brigade for the Crimean War. V & AM

Top centre:
Pipe-Maj James Wilson, 93rd Sutherland Highlanders, painted by D. Cunliffe in 1853. RHQ

Far left:
Officers of the 72nd Duke of Albany's Own Highlanders, 1854. Ackermann's costumes of the British Army. RHQ

Left:
Sgt Andrew Rennie of the 93rd Sutherland Highlanders from a contemporary painting of 1852. As a sergeant-major, Rennie died of fever at Sevastopol in 1855. Matthew E. Taylor Collection

Top:
A contemporary aquatint showing the Scots Fusilier Guards cheering the Queen at a parade prior to their leaving for the Crimea in 1854. RHQ

Right:
This touching scene shows a private of the Scots Fusilier Guards bidding farewell to his wife and child, c1850. RHQ

Top left:
The 1st Royal Regt, The Royal Scots depicted on the approach march to the river Alma, Sept 1854 during the Crimean War. Watercolour by R. Simkin. RHQ

Left:
The 42nd Royal Highlanders at the battle of the Alma, 1854. RHQ

Above:
The 79th Cameron Highlanders at the battle of the Alma, Sept 1854. RHQ

Below:
The 21st (Royal Scots Fusiliers) holding the 'Barrier' at the battle of Inkerman in 1854. Watercolour by Orlando Norie. RHQ

Above:
'The thin red line'; Robert Gibbs's famous painting of the 93rd Sutherland Highlanders facing Russian Cavalry at the battle of Balaclava 1854. RHQ

Below:
Another view of the 93rd Highlanders at Balaclava. The commanding officer Colonel Ainslie is in the foreground. Watercolour by Orlando Norie. RHQ

The 90th Perthshire Regt led one of the two columns of Abercromby's army between Aboukir Bay and Alexandria. The 90th and 92nd Highlanders bore the brunt of the French attack at Mandora and successfully defeated the enemy. Watercolour by R. Simkin.

regiment took part in the seizing of Martinique, and in early 1810 the 90th was part of a similar force which successfully took Guadeloupe and captured the Eagle of the 80th Regiment. A further four years were spent on St Vincent, followed by a few months at Fort Niagara in Canada, to prepare for a possible renewal of hostilities with the United States. The regiment embarked for Europe in 1815 for a brief period as troops of occupation.

It was in the same year that the 90th was recognised as one of six light infantry corps, and was armed and clothed as such on its return to England. Having been away from Perthshire and Scotland for so long, only about one-quarter of the regiment were Scotsmen. It was nevertheless redesignated the 90th Perthshire Light Infantry.

* * * * *

In 1820 the 90th was sent to the Ionian Islands which by treaty were under British protection. It was in Britain's interest to avoid the islanders becoming involved in the mainland Greeks' insurrection against their Turkish rulers. This involved disarming the populace and the 90th was one of two regiments given this task. The regiment remained on the islands for ten years before returning to England, followed by another tour of duty in policing Ireland against civil disturbance.

There then followed ten years of duty in Ceylon, which were mainly uneventful, and in 1846 the 90th reached South Africa after a stormy passage across the Indian Ocean. Based first at Cape Town, the regiment took part in active duty against the Kaffirs. This involved much detached duty in support of frontier posts, and in attempts to destroy the power the elusive Kaffir tribes based in their mountain strongholds of the eastern Cape.

The 90th spent the years 1848–52 in England and 1852–3 in Ireland. It was during this period that Garnet Wolseley, later Field Marshal and Viscount, joined the regiment.

Towards the end of 1854, reinforcements were urgently required in the Crimea. The regiment reached Balaclava Harbour on 3 December and, as part of the Light Division, took up positions in the lines surrounding Sevastopol. It was a terrible winter for the besieging troops, who had to hold their entrenched positions close to the earthworks of the ingeniously engineered Russian defences.

In May 1855 the 90th took part in the capture of the Quarries in front of the Redan, which position was successfully held during a Russian counter-attack. In September the 90th took part in the attack on the Redan itself, but although initially successful,

Left: Officers of the 90th taken at camp in the Crimea.

Below left: Not at their parade-ground smartest. The pioneer platoon of the Cameronians at Crookham Camp near Aldershot c1893. RHQ

Below: The Cameronians (Scottish Rifles). Various orders of dress c1900. RHQ

it could not be held for long. The Russians eventually evacuated Sevastopol and a peace treaty was signed a year later. The British forces left the Crimea, and the regiment was quartered until 1857 in Portsmouth.

Whilst on its way to China, the 90th was diverted to India to assist in the suppression of the Mutiny. One of its first tasks was to disarm two native regiments at Berhampore on 1 August 1857. The next month, part of the regiment joined Sir Henry Havelock's force for the first relief of Lucknow. There was much close-quarter fighting in the surrounding country and inside the city itself. At one time a besieging party of the 90th was surrounded but managed to extricate themselves. The troops then joined those already holding the Residency against the mutineers. Three other companies of the 90th, which had been delayed on the voyage out, assisted in Sir Colin Campbell's relief of Lucknow in November. The whole battalion then took part in the final siege of Lucknow in March 1858. The 90th captured the Martinière College and occupied the Secundrabagh on 11 March. On 14 March six companies seized the Kaiser Bagh palace and four other buildings nearby.

'The day was one of long and continued exertion, and everyone felt that, although much remained to be done before the final expulsion of the rebels, the most difficult part had been overcome. The 15th was employed in securing what had been taken, removing powder, destroying mines, and fixing mortars for future bombardment of the positions still held by the enemy on the line of our advance up the right bank of the Goomtee, and in the heart of the city.'

The city was cleared of the last mutineers by 21 March. The regiment then spent the rest of 1858 rounding up mutineers in the Oudh: casualties during the year amounted to 14 officers and over 300 men.

The regiment stayed in India until 1869, when it was posted back to Britain. Two years later it was linked to the 73rd Perthshire Regiment. In the same year Evelyn Wood VC, later Field Marshal, transferred to the regiment.

In 1878 the 90th went as a reinforcement to South Africa towards the end of the war against the Kaffirs. On 1 January 1879 the British force advanced into Zululand in order to destroy Cetewayo's army. On the news of the British defeat of Isandhlwana, Col Evelyn Wood in command of the column which included the 90th, set up a defensive position on Kambula Hill in order to dominate the area. The enemy attacked Kambula in great strength on 29 March, and during the course of the battle two companies of the regiment counter-attacked a column of Zulus with good effect and forced them to withdraw from the battlefield. In July the Zulus were met at Ulundi by Lord Chelmsford's whole force, and the 90th played a major part in this victory.

Later in the year the 90th Perthshire Light Infantry sailed for India, where in 1881 it became the 2nd Battalion of the Cameronians (Scottish Rifles). For many years the title 'Scottish Rifles' was used by the 2nd Battalion to distinguish it from the 1st Battalion, who tended only to use the title 'the Cameronians'.

THE CAMERONIANS
1881–1913

The 1st Battalion, the Cameronians, the old 26th Regiment, remained in England as the home service battalion until 1894, and it established a high reputation for musketry, while the 2nd Battalion, formerly the 90th, remained in India. These were uneventful years for the regiment. In 1895 the battalions exchanged: the 1st went to India, where it was later to join the 'rifle division' of twelve rifle regiments, and the 2nd Battalion returned to England where it stayed until 1899.

When stationed at Glasgow in October 1899, the 2nd Battalion was mobilised for service in South Africa at the start of the second Boer War. In December the battalion was in the vicinity of the disastrous battle of Colenso, but did not take part. A month later it fought in the battle of Spion Kop, where the battalion attempted to relieve the force holding this untenable position, and showed great bravery. A fortnight later the Scottish Rifles joined in the successful capture of Vaal Krantz and subsequently marched to the relief of Ladysmith.

After taking part in the campaign to recapture Natal, the Scottish Rifles spent some months guarding railway lines. In September 1901 the battalion provided a detachment to follow and destroy the remnants of Botha's commando, and it marched over 1,200 miles through Natal in the ensuing months.

In addition to the 2nd Battalion, the regiment provided a mounted infantry company and some members of the 4th Militia Battalion for service in Lord Methuen's force. They, too, saw action against the Boers on a number of occasions. The Scottish Rifles returned to Scotland in 1904 and remained in the United Kingdom until 1911, when they sailed for Malta. Two years earlier the 1st Battalion had left India for South Africa, and in 1912 it returned home to Glasgow.

THE CAMERONIANS
1914–38

The 1st Battalion was immediately sent to France on the outbreak of war, arriving at a position near Mons on the Belgian border, and on the extreme left of the British Expeditionary Force's line. Under the threat, however, of being outflanked, the battalion was withdrawn from the positions on the Mons-Condé Canal. During the ensuing retreat from the Le Cateau area, the battalion marched many miles, hindering as much as possible the German advance. On 8 September the battalion was in action on the Marne, but in October moved northwards with the BEF to block the German attempt to cut off the channel ports.

The 2nd Battalion reached France from Malta in November 1914, and took up positions in the line near Messines. Other battalions of the regiment, both Territorial Force and new army, followed in due course.

On 10 March 1915 the 2nd Battalion fought in the attack at Neuve Chapelle. After a most intensive bombardment which lasted for thirty-five minutes, A and B Companies advanced at the double across no-man's-land. B Company penetrated the German defences rapidly, despite the failure of the bombardment to cut the wire. Captain Kennedy, writing later, stated 'I have a vague recollection of tearing at it with my naked hands and with the help of my Corporal, dragging away the remains of a knife rest, while a German fired at us from a trench and missed us both . . .' The company took 70 Germans prisoners. A Company, however, on the left were practically wiped out by machine-gun fire. C and D Companies followed through and took the second German line, but were caught by enfilade fire which made holding their positions difficult. Neuve Chapelle was captured in due course but the Scottish Rifles suffered two-thirds of its officers and men killed or wounded in the battle. The 6th Battalion reached the area soon afterwards, and both battalions took part in the attack of Aubers Ridge in May which, despite spirited fighting, met with little success.

The following month the 6th Cameronians seized valuable ground from the Germans at Festubert, but sustained forty per cent casualties before they were ordered to withdraw. The 5th Battalion also reached the line at this time. In July and September two newly formed battalions, the 9th and 10th, reached the front and joined the line at Festubert.

Five of the six battalions of the Cameronians serving in France fought in the battle of Loos during September 1915. The 10th Battalion succeeded in taking its objective, Hill 70, while the 9th Battalion captured part of the Hohenzollern Redoubt. Both positions, however, had to be abandoned subsequently; the 10th Battalion's losses had been particularly heavy. The 5/6th was made up from survivors of the two former battalions, whose strength had been severely depleted during the winter of 1915–16.

The 7th and 8th Battalions, as part of 52nd Lowland Division, left Britain in May 1915 and landed at Helles Beach, Gallipoli, in mid-June. A week later, while preparing for an attack on the enemy at Gully Spur, which dominated Cape Helles, intensive Turkish artillery fire was brought down on the 8th Cameronians in the concentration area and 7th in reserve positions. When the attack went in the 8th was caught in the open and, within five minutes, had lost 400 rank and file and all but one of the battalion officers. The 7th Battalion was ordered forward and it, too, sustained heavy casualties – 14 officers and 258 other ranks. The battalions had to be amalgamated for subsequent operations. In the early hours of 12 July the 7/8th Cameronians were moved up in the reserve brigade for the 52nd Division's attack on the Achi Baba Nullah sector. 155 Brigade was severely cut up in the morning's fighting and the 7/8th Battalion was ordered to assault, with a company of the Royal Scots, part of the enemy's line. The companies worked their way forward along the communication trenches, past wounded and dead Scotsmen, and cleared their objectives with the bayonet. The fighting

Top left: A 1st Cameronians' officer and NCOs look out for enemy snipers in their 'cabbage-patch' trench, La Boutillerie, 5 Nov 1914. IWM

Top right: Soldiers of the 1st Cameronians in trenches, Bois Grenier, near Armentières Feb 1915. IWM

Above: Two Scottish riflemen, Pte George and Cpl Baines wondering what to do with their shovels in a water-logged trench, Bois Grenier 1915. RHQ

Left: B Coy of the 1st Cameronians prepare for a gas attack, 20 May 1915. The Germans first used gas in the previous month.

A rifle inspection of the 2nd Scottish Rifles, Estairs sector, June 1915. RHQ

was intense and confused, the captured trenches giving little cover from enemy fire. The Cameronians linked up with Royal Scots and King's Own Scottish Borderers, establishing the line and holding it against counter-attacks during the night. The cost to the division had been extremely high, but the new line formed part of the front until the evacuation at the end of the year.

* * * * *

On the Western Front the Somme offensive was mounted in July 1916 and lasted until November. Five battalions of the regiment took part, the 1st, 2nd, 5/6th, 9th and 10th. The 9th's first objective was Montauban, which they succeeded in capturing with the 6th King's Own Scottish Borderers. The 2nd Battalion was in reserve at first, but then had to hold the front-line British trenches under heavy enemy bombardment. The 9th Cameronians succeeded in capturing the first and second German lines in the Longueval, sector but in the counter-bombardment had to be withdrawn. The 1st and 5/6th Battalions were in reserve in the area of High Wood and Mametz Wood captured earlier, and the 10th Battalion took part in a successful surprise attack at Martinpuich. The 2nd Scottish Rifles were moved to the Loos salient in mid-July, and the 9th were moved to help hold Vimy Ridge. The 1st and 5/6th Battalions were pulled out of the line to prepare for the October resumption of the offensive.

During the next phase in the Albert area, the 9th and 10th Cameronians held the front at Butte de Warlencourt, while the 2nd attacked the Transloy Ridge on 23 October. The daylight assault had to be postponed due to fog, and the Scottish Rifles advanced behind the creeping artillery barrage. Enemy machine guns caused the advancing line to be held up, but Lt J. Ferguson and two NCOs charged forward and cleared the enemy trench, including three machine guns, with grenades. After occupying this length of German front line trench, known as Zenith, the battalion advanced again to the second-line trench and captured it rapidly. German counter-attacks were repulsed and despite the failure of neighbouring troops to conform, the Scottish Rifles held their gains for several hours. The Germans, however, were reported to be concentrating a large number of troops for a major counter-attack, so the battalion was ordered to withdraw to Zenith. The 1st and 5/6th Battalions, as part of the 33rd Division, had the task of attacking various parts of the front during October with varying degrees of success.

With the lack of overall success of the battle, the battalions took up fresh positions for the winter, some of them formerly held by the French. The 9th Battalion mounted a particularly successful surprise attack in the Arras area, adopting a 'box-barrage' tactic involving close cooperation with the artillery.

In the spring of 1917, the Germans began their withdrawal from part of the front between Arras and the Aisne to the Hindenburg Line. The 2nd Scottish Rifles were heavily involved in harrassing the enemy between Combles and La Vaquerie.

The 10th Cameronians made a bold and successful assault at the start of the battle of Arras on 9 April, capturing an important part of the line and several German guns. On the same day the 9th Battalion advanced one-and-a-half miles and captured numerous enemy soldiers and guns. The 1st and 5/6th Battalions did not meet with the same success in their attacks. Then on 12 April the 9th Cameronians took part in 27 Brigade's attack on Roeux and some chemical works nearby. The advance was carried out without smoke or artillery barrage until the first line was occupied successfully. Then, with artillery cover, the Cameronians advanced again for 150 yards before being held up by intense machine-gun fire. The men remained exposed to enemy fire for the remainder of the day from Roeux railway station and the chemical works, and it was not until after last light that they were able to withdraw. Roeux remained in enemy hands for many more days. The 10th Battalion achieved modest gains in the battle, but the attack on Cavalry Farm by 46th Brigade, which the battalion supported, was not successful.

During the third battle of Ypres from July–September 1917, the same battalions were occupied in the series of attacks and counter-attacks east of the town, which had been reduced to a sea of mud. The 10th Battalion supported a brigade assault on Gallipoli Farm, and the 9th Battalion was involved in the capture of Zonnebeke Redoubt. The 9th also fought for Passchendaele Ridge, which was later occupied successively by the 2nd, the 1st and, in January 1918, the 5/6th Cameronians.

* * * * *

The 11th Battalion, the Cameronians had meanwhile, reached the Salonika front with XII Corps in December 1915 to join the allied force in defending the Greeks from Bulgarian invasion. The campaign was essentially a holding operation, but in May 1917 the British were given the task of attacking the enemy near Lake Dorain. This was part of an allied offensive which proved unsuccessful and the 11th Battalion lost one-third of their numbers.

There was little further action on this front, except raiding expeditions against the enemy lines, until a second allied offensive was mounted in September 1918. The battalion fought courageously during the second battle of Dorain and again suffered heavy casualties: the allied attack succeeded this time, the British battle being the deciding factor. When the armistice was signed in October 1918, the 11th Battalion was sent to Egypt.

* * * * *

The 7th and 8th Battalions meanwhile had been temporarily amalgamated after the withdrawal from Gallipoli to Egypt. In May 1916 the two reconstituted battalions moved to Romani, the easternmost outpost of the Suez Canal defences. In August the Turks advanced, and it appeared that the enemy might outflank the British troops holding Romani, whereupon the two Scottish Rifle battalions were sent to head off this attack by seizing Wellington Ridge south of the town, which they achieved. The Turkish attack failed.

The following months saw the advance of the British and dominion force across the Sinai Desert to El Arish and Rafa. The strategic strongpoint of the Turkish defensive line was Gaza, and the 52nd Division, in which the two Scottish Rifle battalions served, took part in the second battle of that name. The divisional objectives were Mansura and Kurd Hill,

Col C. B. Vandeleur speaks to his officers of the 2nd Scottish Rifles in a farmyard, April 1915. The following month the battalion fought for possession of Aubers Ridge near La Basée. IWM

9th Cameronians man a check-point near Dusseldorf in the British zone of occupied Germany, 15 April 1919. IWM

and they were strongly defended by the Turks. After some fighting the 8th Battalion was ordered to withdraw from contact. The 7th Battalion, at first in reserve, was ordered forward to take up a position against a Turkish counter-attack. The Turks succeeded in holding Gaza.

During the summer the positions of both armies in and around the town were consolidated, and General Allenby's attack on Gaza began on 31 October. The 7th and 8th Battalions of the Cameronians were successful in reaching their objectives of Umbrella Hill and El Arish Redoubts. More casualties from counter-bombardment were sustained in defending these positions than in the assault itself. But the Turks withdrew before they were surrounded, and during November the British infantry took an active part in close pursuit of the enemy.

Both battalions were involved in the close-quarter fighting at Nebi Samwil, but the Turks failed to halt the British advance on Jerusalem. The last major engagement of the two battalions in this theatre was the assault river crossing of the Auja on 20 December 1917, carried out with total surprise: its success helped the rapid advance of the British to capture Jerusalem. In April 1918 the whole of the 52nd Division left for France where it was urgently required.

* * * * *

On 21 March 1918 the Germans launched their great offensive on the allied armies. The 9th Battalion, the Cameronians, were from the start used to plug breaches in the British front line. They then held a section of the defences west of the Crozat Canal, but after losing half their numbers, they to withdrew to conform to other battalions. The 10th Battalion was not initially attacked, but it, too, was ordered to withdraw. The 2nd Scottish Rifles, in reserve, covered the withdrawal of the forward troops and took up positions for a time in the Somme sector. By 1 April, the battalion was reduced to 4 officers and 60 men. Although the whole of the British Army was forced back, nowhere had the line been broken without it being somehow plugged.

After a brief respite another German attack was mounted, and for a while the British were hard-pressed in the Arras sector. The 10th Battalion held on under severe attack and forced the enemy to withdraw. The reinforced 9th Battalion rejoined the line on 2 April in time for the renewed German attack. Despite heavy casualties sustained in the artillery bombardment, the line continued to be held.

The 2nd Scottish Rifles cross the River Sarkhuma, Kurdistan on the border between Persia and Iraq, spring 1923. RHQ

The second German offensive started on 9 April and the situation for the British was the most critical of the whole war. The 1st Cameronians helped to defend the sector opposite the German line at Meteren, and the 5/6th Battalion held a reserve position south of the village. During May both battalions took part in counter-attacks, the 1st Battalion at Kemmel Beek and the 5/6th at Ridge Wood. Both were successful, despite losing one-third of the strength as casualties. On 19 July the 9th Battalion took part in the capture of Meteren. By this time the 7th and 8th Battalions had reached France from the Middle East with 52nd Lowland Division.

An allied counter-offensive on the Marne was planned for July, and the 10th Cameronians were first in action, with the French 87th Division on their right. The attack was, however, held up by the German defences near Rozieres. A similar attack by the 8th Battalion made only moderate progress in the area of Beugneux. The Germans then withdrew on 2 August and were pursued by the French with great success.

The British Fourth Army now mounted an attack on 8 August, followed by the Third Army. The 7th Cameronians made considerable progress in capturing territory from the Germans and reached the Hindenburg Line by 26 August. On 1 September they took part in the attack on Quéant, a key German position. In the Second Army's area, progress was also rapid. The 9th Cameronians assisted in the capture of the Hoegenacker Ridge, before being moved further north as reinforcements. The 8th Battalion moved forward as the Germans withdrew from Bailleul, and took up positions on the evacuated Kemmel Hill.

During the final months, the pace of the allied advance began to increase, and all battalions were frequently in action. In the north the 8th and 9th advanced from the Ypres area towards Courtrai. The 2nd Battalion fought from Avions to Mericourt, and the 7th and 10th from the Arras area towards Mons and Ath. The 6/7th Royal Scots Fusiliers, nominally the 18th Cameronians, fought on the same general axis. In the south the 1st and 5/6th Scottish Rifles advanced from the Quéant-Bapaume area, past Cambrai to Mauberge on the River Sambre. Each battalion had to cross the numerous river and canal obstacles and, with the Germans conducting a fighting withdrawal, British casualties continued at a high rate. In the four years of hostilities 7,106 Cameronians had been killed and some 11,000 wounded. The regiment gained four Victoria Crosses.

When the Armistice was signed, the 8th and 9th Battalions were sent as occupying troops to Cologne. Between the wars the two regular battalions of the Cameronians served in China, Egypt, India, Iraq, Kurdistan and Palestine, as well as in the United Kingdom. Although the 1st Battalion saw no active service the 2nd Battalion was involved in operations during 1923 against the Kurdish rebels in Iraq. This involved much marching and skirmishing against the tribesmen.

Rifle inspection of the Cameronians c1936. Douglas tartan is worn to commemorate the regiment's first Colonel, the eldest son of the Marquis of Douglas. IWM

THE CAMERONIANS

1939–68

When war was declared in September 1939, the 1st and 2nd Battalions were mobilised in India and the United Kingdom respectively. The 6th, 7th, 9th and 10th Territorial Battalions were also immediately mobilised. The 2nd Scottish Rifles reached Cherbourg on 12 September as part of the British Expeditionary Force, and took up positions along the Ypres-Comines Canal during the winter.

When Belgium was invaded by the Germans in 1940 the battalion was ordered to a position south-west of Brussels, but on the withdrawal of the BEF it returned to positions north of Lille. When, on 26 May, the enemy shelled the Scottish Rifles' positions on the Ypres-Comines Canal, the battalion mounted a surprise counter-attack. This caused a temporary delay to the German advance in the sector, but during the next two days the battalion suffered heavy casualties. A fighting withdrawal followed, and the survivors of the 2nd, having by now lost 360 of their number, embarked at Dunkirk on 1 June. The 6th and 7th Cameronians had also served briefly in France in June 1940 in the Cherbourg area but they, too, were evacuated.

* * * * *

The 1st Battalion, the Cameronians, had meanwhile remained in India during the early part of the war. In February 1942 the battalion left Secunderabad to join the force defending Burma after the fall of Singapore. The battalion took up positions at Pegu on the river of the same name, some 45 miles north of Rangoon: it was an important bridge-site and railway junction bordering the edge of the jungle on one of the main routes into India. Fighting against the Japanese at first was localised in company areas and in close cooperation with armour, but observation and information-gathering was most difficult to achieve. After a week the Japanese forced the British troops to withdraw.

Thereafter followed a series of marches with the battalion moving from successive positions and harrassing the Japanese advance as best it could. Some temporary delays were forced on the enemy but the withdrawal continued until mid-April. A divisional counter-attack was then mounted against the Japanese at Yenangyang on the River Irrawaddy; the Cameronians succeeded in capturing their objectives and holding them for a time.

However, the steady withdrawal towards Mandalay continued. In early May it was decided that the evacuation of the army in Burma should not be delayed, and it was then a matter of speed to keep ahead of the enemy. Movement was achieved partly by road and partly by river transport. The Cameronians, by now greatly depleted in number, assisted in guarding embarkation points – such as Shwegyin in the Chindwin River – and establishing blocking positions. The battalion was finally withdrawn on 20 May, having endured fighting against a determined enemy in very severe conditions of both climate and terrain.

* * * * *

In Britain the 2nd Battalion had been reconstituted after Dunkirk and spent nearly two years training for future operations. In March 1942 the battalion, as

The 2nd Scottish Rifles are welcomed by the Sicilians as they enter Fleri, July 1943. IWM

part of 13 Infantry Brigade, left the UK bound for India. In May the brigade was diverted to take part in the campaign in Madagascar against the Vichy French: the purpose was to deny its possible occupation by the Japanese. The battalion landed on 6 May, conducted a successful sweep operation against some resistance and the whole operation was over within two weeks.

After reaching India, the 2nd Scottish Rifles were then sent as part of Pai Force to occupy Persia. The battalion remained in the Kermanshar and Qum areas for the remainder of 1942, and in February 1943 the battalion moved via Syria to the Lebanon, where it began training for its next campaign.

On 1 July 1943 the 2nd Scottish Rifles sailed for the assault of Sicily, and on 10 July they landed, at first meeting little opposition. The battalion moved quickly inland, and later in the day mounted a successful attack on the town of Floridia, supported by a troop of the Sharpshooters, 3rd County of London Yeomanry. There was not much resistance from the Italians and the march northwards continued. On reaching the Catania plain on 18 July German positions were encountered and the brigade in which the Cameronians served mounted numerous attacks at battalion, company and platoon level during the next four days. The brigade then joined the 51st Highland Division for the advance northwards past Mount Etna. The Germans, however, were holding the axis of advance in considerable strength, and the Scottish Rifles had to capture a series of enemy positions. This took a week, from 3 to 10 August, when allied successes to the west allowed the route to Messina to be quickly opened up.

On 3 September 1943 the 8th Army crossed the Straits of Messina and landed on the Italian mainland. The 2nd Scottish Rifles moved inland and met with little opposition. A few days later, in order to conform to the rapid allied advance, they re-embarked and landed a hundred miles further north on the Italian coast at Scalea. The speed of movement on land had to be maintained, and the battalion faced many hard days of marching during the following two months. By early December the whole of southern Italy was in allied hands, but the line remained static during the winter.

In March the 2nd Scottish Rifles were moved again by sea to help reinforce the Anzio beach-head. From their forward positions they mounted several raids and attacks on the enemy during the month, particularly against the strong point known as the 'Fortress'. On 5 June the battalion led its brigade on the approach to the Tiber – the first British troops to

Top:
A platoon of the 2nd Scottish Rifles in southern Italy, 1944. The mountainous nature of the terrain can be seen clearly. IWM

Above:
A Coy of the 2nd Scottish Rifles climbs a slope near Cerro, southern Italy, 1944. IWM

reach the river. Rome was then occupied by the Allies on 6 June, and the following month the battalion left by sea for Palestine.

* * * * *

In the meantime, the 1st Cameronians had been preparing for the recapture of Burma. It had been trained for airborne operations and, as part of the Chindit campaign, it landed on 10 March 1944 inside Burma. The Chindit force had artillery support and was completely re-supplied by air. Divided into two columns the battalion's task was to disrupt Japanese lines of communications, first by forming a 'block' on the road near Hopin, and then moving to a position near Mogaung to carry out raids on the enemy.

After early successes against enemy convoys and installations, the Japanese began a determined drive against the Chindit force. The brigade block was bombarded by artillery and mortars on 20 May; the Japanese then captured the airstrip and attacked in great strength on 25 May. The brigade was ordered to withdraw, and the Cameronians' task was to hold a ridge and cover the withdrawal. Despite attempts by the enemy to disrupt the withdrawal it was carried out efficiently and with heavy Japanese casualties. The march was carried out in torrential rain across mountainous and jungle terrain and with shortages of rations and ammunition. Due to the loss of the airstrip the casualties had to be moved over land. The Cameronians acted as rearguard until the safe area of Indawgyi Lake was reached.

It was a hard four months for the Cameronians. Movement in the jungle was slow, planning and co-ordination difficult, and casualties from enemy action and disease numbered 247 by the time the battalion was withdrawn in July.

* * * * *

Of the other Cameronian battalions the 6th, 7th and 9th Battalions had so far spent the war years in intensive training in the United Kingdom. On 17 June 1944 the 9th Cameronians landed at Arromanches in Normandy and first fought at Haut Du Bosq on 24 June, which town they successfully captured, despite 120 casualties. During the next fortnight the battalion was frequently in action, either holding the line or counter-attacking. During the daylight hours of 10 July, the Cameronians took over the defence of Eterville from the Dorsets. They dug in under enemy artillery fire, and at last light were attacked by a company of Germans. They captured some forward positions which isolated D Company, and there was considerable skirmishing during the night before the enemy withdrew. At dawn, C Company advanced to occupy an orchard which had acted as a concealed route, and this provoked an enemy attack, supported by a troop of tanks. They penetrated the orchard for a while, but a section led by Cpl Lorimer charged and reoccupied the position at bayonet-point. C Company's ammunition was nearly exhausted by this time, but the enemy then gave up the attempt to dislodge the company, having lost more than 100 dead and numerous others wounded. In late July the allied advance gathered momentum, and the Cameronians were in the fighting for the Falaise sector. The Seine was crossed subsequently and the battalion reached the Belgian border on 3 September.

The Germans were attempting to hold various canal lines, and the movement and fighting was sporadic during this period. The enemy, however, held the line of the River Maas in strength, and the 9th Cameronians held positions at Neer for a month. The enemy mounted several attacks in the area, but in late January 1945 the allies launched an offensive to clear the ground between the Maas and the Rhine. The battalion took part in the attack on Galgensteeg Ridge, and in mid-February at Moylands Wood near Cleve. There the Germans put up great resistance, and the battalion's advance was delayed until the enemy could be cleared systematically from the area.

The 6th and 7th Cameronians meanwhile, had landed at Ostend in October 1944 as part of 156 Brigade, in the 52nd Lowland Division. Their task was to proceed east along the coast and clear the enemy from the Scheldt Estuary in order to open the port of Antwerp to allied shipping. The 6th Battalion successfully occupied south Walcheren Island, enabling Flushing to be liberated, while the 7th captured Veere. In November the two battalions were moved to the Maas near s'Hertogenbosch and subsequently to Geilenkirchen.

Centre left: A platoon commander of the 9th Cameronians briefs his soldiers, 25 June 1944. The Cameronians were attacked several times over a period of two weeks while holding these woods at Haut Du Bosq. IWM

From mid-January the 6th and 7th Battalions were kept occupied by attacks on several German villages as the advance progressed gradually eastwards into Germany. A large scale operation, named 'Blackcock', was mounted by the division and the 7th Cameronians launched a battalion attack on three villages during the night of 22 January. B Company quickly seized Locken but C Company met very strong opposition, remained surrounded throughout the night, and fought off numerous attempts to dislodge them from Schondorf. The remainder of the battalion had meanwhile, captured most of Obspringen. At 8.15 on the following morning the Cameronians, joined by a company of 4/5th Royal Scots Fusiliers and a troop of tanks, launched an attack on Schondorf to relieve

Below:
These two photographs show the battle for Rheine. 7th Cameronians crossed the River Ems on 3 April and the Dortmund-Ems Canal a day later. IWM

C Company and eject the Germans from the village. The attack was carried out efficiently with the artillery and tanks giving close supporting fire, and the village was quickly cleared of the enemy. The success of operation 'Blackcock' resulted in the capture of the land between Sittard and Heinsberg. Then on 8 March, 156 Brigade mounted an attack on Alpon, a key position which was heavily defended by the Germans. In the first attack the 6th Cameronians were held up and suffered many casualties. The 7th then mounted a second phase attack on 9 March on Alpon and the enemy subsequently withdrew.

The assault crossing of the Rhine took place on the night of 23/24 March 1945. The 9th Battalion crossed and attacked the village of Rees, encountering strong enemy resistance for a time. The 6th Cameronians cros-sed the Rhine on 29 March, and moved swiftly to join the leading troops in the advance to the Dortmund-Ems Canal. The 9th Battalion, meanwhile, were advancing rapidly towards Minden. Subsequently they cleared the route to Celle and crossed the Elbe on 29 April.

The 7th Cameronians had also advanced from the Rhine, and by 2 April had reached Rheine on the Ems. The battalion had to force a crossing to take the eastern part of the town, which they did successfully. The 7th and 9th Battalions then took part in the advance to, and capture of, the port of Bremen.

The 2nd Scottish Rifles, who had been in Italy until late February, reached Germany in April. They They assisted in clearing various enemy positions, which had been by-passed during the advance. On 3 May they occupied Lübeck, where they stayed until the war ended.

* * * * *

The 2nd Battalion stayed on in Germany for a time while the 1st Battalion remained in the Far East. In 1948 the rest of the 1st Cameronians serving in Malaya were drafted to Gibraltar to join the 2nd Battalion, and the amalgamated battalion was redesignated the 1st Battalion. Subsequently the battalion served in Trieste and Hong Kong before moving to Malaya in 1950. The Cameronians' task was to operate against and defeat the Malayan Races' Liberation Army, more commonly known as the 'bandits'.

The Cameronians reached the Muar area of Johore in May. Divided into company areas, they operated to defeat the insurgency in close cooperation with the Malayan Police. This entailed much patrolling and ambushing deep in the jungle. Often such patrols were of many weeks' duration and re-supply had to be by air. At other times deliberate, coordinated attacks were launched on bandit bases. Public relations activities were also conducted to win over the inhabitants of the villages. The anti-guerrilla tactics became increasingly successful in time. Whole areas were cleared of guerrillas as a result and the Cameronians played an important part in the operations until they left the territory in April 1953.

The 1st Cameronians spent 1950-53 in Malaya. A patrol with their Iban tracker display enemy caps and flag captured when they surprised a bandit camp.
IWM

The battalion was stationed in the United Kingdom and BAOR from 1953 to 1956. In early 1957 the Cameronians reached Bahrein in the Persian Gulf: their task was the guarding of oil installations against sabotage by local arab terrorists. In July the battalion, which was now divided between Bahrein and Kenya, was ordered to assist in putting down a revolt in Muscat and Oman. This involved mobile operations against rebel-held positions, fortified farms and high points in the hills, in support of the Trucial Oman Scouts.

The whole battalion moved to Kenya in 1958 as part of the British strategic reserve force. In that year the situation throughout the Middle East deteriorated and the Cameronians spent some time in Aden before moving to Amman in Jordan as a contingency force. The position, however, stabilised and the battalion returned to Kenya.

The period 1960–6 was spent by the Cameronians, partly in BAOR, then followed by a tour of duty in Edinburgh, where it took part in public duties and in support of the Edinburgh Tattoo. In April 1966 the battalion flew to Aden for internal security duties, and for much of their tour the Cameronians were responsible for the western part of Aden town, the harbour. They carried out mobile and foot patrols, manning check-points and searches. Companies also spent time up-country, based at Habilayn and Dhala. This involved patrolling, piquetting and ambushes to prevent rebels infiltrating and operating freely in the Radfan Mountains.

The Cameronians returned to Edinburgh in February 1967, and later in the year it was announced that the battalion would be disbanded as part of reductions in the regular army. The Cameronians were selected because they were the junior regiment of the Lowland Brigade, having declined amalgamation with any other regiment.

The final conventicle of the 1st Cameronians was held at Castle Dangerous, near Douglas in Lanarkshire, on 14 May 1968 in the presence of the Duke of Hamilton. Among his titles was that of his ancestor, the Early of Angus, who first raised the Cameronians in 1689, The picquets were posted and the service held in the usual manner, after which the regimental flag (as a rifle regiment there were no colours) was lowered for the last time. After nearly 300 years of unbroken service the regular battalion of the Cameronians (Scottish Rifles) ceased to exist.

Jocks of the 1st Cameronians in the Radfan Mountains, Aden 1966. IWM

A mobile patrol of the 1st Cameronians in Aden town, 1966. The internal security situation seriously deteriorated during the last year before the British withdrawal. IWM

The final Conventicle of the 1st Cameronians at Castle Dangerous, 14 May 1968. The ceremonial commemorates that of the original Covenanters, who of necessity had to mount guard whenever they met for divine worship. RHQ

While the regiment presents arms, the regimental flag is lowered at the disbandment Conventicle of the 1st Bn Cameronians (Scottish Rifles). RHQ

CHAPTER 8
THE BLACK WATCH
(Royal Highland Regiment)

THE 42ND ROYAL HIGHLAND REGIMENT

1725–1881

During the late seventeenth and early eighteenth centuries specially-formed companies of highlanders were employed by the Crown as regular soldiers to police the Highlands. After the 1715 rebellion the highlanders had been forbidden by act of parliament to carry arms, so the opportunity for joining newly-raised independent companies to 'watch' the Highlands was attractive to men of spirit. Many of those who joined the ranks were men of local standing, and were chiefly from the whig clans. Four companies were formed in 1725 and two more in 1729. Amongst those commissioned to raise them was Lord Lovat, Sir Duncan Campbell of Lochnell and Colonel Grant of Ballindalloch.

The companies wore highland dress of a dark coat and the philamor or belted plaid, the tartan of which was, according to the instructions, 'as near as they can be of the same sort of colour'. (The strict differentiation of clan tartans is almost certainly of much later date than is popularly believed.) These highlander soldiers were of a quite different appearance to the red-coated, white-breeched soldiers of the regiments of foot, and the name 'The Black Watch' – 'Am Freiceadan Dubh' – dates from their early years.

In November 1739 the Earl of Crawford was instructed to raise four further companies and embody them with the existing independent companies into a regiment of foot. The regiment duly assembled at Aberfeldy in May 1740 and was numbered the 43rd Regiment of Foot. The red coat was adopted and in due course the 'government pattern' tartan was introduced for the belted plaid – the 'philabeg' or small kilt was not taken into use until the latter years of the century.

The regiment continued to be employed as before in the Highlands, but in 1743 it was ordered to march to London. The soldiers' terms of engagement were almost certainly misunderstood by the main gaelic-speaking highlanders, and the possibility of foreign service filled many with alarm. The government, of course, treated them as any other regular regiment of foot, and certainly not as men of a different standing and independent honour. After spending several days in London, more than a hundred of them decided to return to Scotland by a secret route and without authority. This was naturally regarded as mutiny, and after a few days they were surrounded by troops of cavalry near Oundle. The three ringleaders were shot and other deserters were transported or drafted to other regiments mainly serving overseas.

Previous page:
Telephone operators of the 5th Black Watch in a well-constructed dugout, spring 1915. IWM

The value of highland troops was proved at the battle of Fontenoy, where the 42nd Highlanders fought their first battle in 1745.

The Black Watch embarked in the same year for the Continent to fight in the War of the Austrian Succession. The regiment was not involved in any major action in the war until May 1745, when the allied army approached the French positions at Fontenoy, near Tournai. The Black Watch were successful in capturing some French positions in a subsidiary action, but were counter-attacked and ordered to withdraw. The regiment then joined in the main allied infantry attack on Fontenoy itself, which was held in great strength. The French defences, however, could not be penetrated, and when the enemy counter-attacked, the Duke of Cumberland ordered his army to withdraw. The highlanders of The Black Watch, by all accounts, had fought with great bavery and determination in their first battle, sustaining relatively light casualties in a very bloody encounter. Later in the year the regiment returned to England, but did not take in any action during the Jacobite rebellion.

* * * * *

Although intended for service in the American colonies, The Black Watch went to Ireland where it was employed, as it had been in the Highlands, to maintain the King's peace amongst a disaffected population. In 1751 the regiment was re-numbered the '42nd Regiment of Foot' and seven years later the title 'The Royal Highland' was added. (The name 'The Black Watch' continued to be used and was officially added in 1861.)

In 1756 the 42nd reached New York as reinforcements to fight against the French and Red Indians threatening the British Colonies. The regiment was little employed at first although the French had made considerable gains on the Canadian border, and the regiment's first expedition in 1757 – to attack Louisburg – was abandoned. In the following year it joined General James Abercromby's army to capture Fort Ticonderoga, a major French garrison. After crossing Lake George by boat the British force was engaged by enemy skirmishes. During a furious assault on the Fort itself

'The Highlanders rushed forward, cut their way through the branches of the trees with their broad-swords, and made a gallant effort to carry the breastwork by storm, climbing up one another's shoulders, and placing their feet in holes made in the face of the works with their swords and bayonets – no ladders having been provided. The defenders were, however, very numerous, and well prepared, and it was found to be impossible to carry the works; Captain John Campbell and a few men succeeded in getting up; but they were speedily overpowered by superior numbers.'

The fort was impossible to take without artillery support, but before the attempt was abandoned the regiment had suffered more than half its number as casualties.

A second battalion of the 42nd was raised in 1758 and was sent to the West Indies, taking part in the landings on the French islands of Martinique and Guadeloupe. On the latter island, a detachment of the Royal Highlanders waited during a naval bombardment of the fort of St Louis, and 'moved towards the shore in boats. They leaped into the stream up to the middle, and drove the French from their works with fixed bayonets capturing the fort, and hoisting the British Colours'. In 1759 the battalion embarked for the mainland and joined the 1st Battalion.

42nd Royal Highlanders capture Fort Louis, Guadeloupe, 1758. Numerous British battalions served in the West Indies, suffering greatly from disease and occasional encounters with the French. Another Perthshire regiment, the 90th, recaptured Guadeloupe in 1810.

Together they took part in a new expedition to attack Fort Ticonderoga, but this time the French decided to abandon the fort. This, with other British successes at Louisburg, Fort Duquesne and Quebec, enabled the occupation of Canada to progress quickly. Both battalions of the regiment took part in the campaign and after some engagements with the French on the way, Montreal was reached in September 1760. The surrender of the city signalled the end of French rule in Canada.

In 1762 the two battalions of the 42nd with a number of other battalions were sent to Martinique, which was still under French control. The highlanders attacked several French positions in quick succession, and the island was surrendered to the British force. The regiment was also present, though not greatly involved, in the seige of Havana in Cuba. After landing with some difficulty on the island the infantry helped to drag the guns into positions on high ground dominating the city. The Spanish has surrendered after a few weeks, and this effectively prevented any further Spanish interference in British Caribbean possessions.

Towards the end of the year The Black Watch, now a single battalion, returned to New York. The next four years were spent in the American colonies, some of that time fighting against the Indians. The highlanders quickly became as cunning in countering the guerrilla tactics of the enemy, and their most notable battle was the relief of Fort Pitt. When the regiment left America in 1767 many individuals remained as settlers, or to serve in other regiments, including the recently raised Royal Highland Emigrant Regiment.

The 42nd spent the next nine years mainly in Ireland, but returned to America in 1776, where the colonists were now in revolt against the crown. One of the companies was captured on arrival, but was later exchanged. The rest of the regiment took part in the battle of Brooklyn, which enabled the royal army to reoccupy New York, and a successful engagement was fought by the regiment at White Plains. Then approaching Fort Washington by a precipitous route, The Black Watch were asked to mount a feint attack in support of Hessian troops, but the highlanders' blood was up and they themselves stormed and captured the fort.

In May 1777 the regiment was attacked by a strong American force at Pisquata and after losing more than 200 killed, the 42nd forced the enemy to withdraw. Then a successful surprise attack was mounted by the regiment and two other British battalions against a force of Americans under General Wayne near Philadelphia.

'The march was conducted with great secrecy, and soon after midnight the British approached the enemy's left, and bayonetted the piquets and out-guards in an instant. Guided by the light of the camp fires, they then rushed forward, and commenced the work of destruction with the bayonet. About three hundred Americans were killed and wounded, and eighty made prisoners, including several officers; the remainder, being favoured by the darkness of the night, escaped, leaving their arms and eight waggons loaded with baggage and stores behind them.'

George Washington's army then attempted to capture Germantown, which was held by a force including the flank companies of the 42nd, but the British held the town after much hard fighting. The rest of the regiment was in the meantime taking occupation of the fort at Billingspoint, from which the Americans had impeded movement along the River Delaware.

The 42nd continued to fight in minor engagements during the remainder of the war and, when peace came, it was sent to Canada. There the regiment remained until 1789 when it embarked for home service. A second battalion had been raised in 1780, but it became a separate regiment in 1786 and its history is recorded separately.

* * * * *

In Scotland there was much disaffection at this time and The Black Watch took part in peace-keeping duties in Ross-shire and the Lowlands. On the declaration of war with France in 1793, the regiment went with a number of others to Flanders, where it spent only a short time campaigning before returning to England. The following year it again embarked for the Continent, but the expeditionary force achieved very little, suffered greatly during the winter, and subsequently withdrew to Germany before returning to England in 1795. The most notable engagements in which the regiment took part were in the Geldermalsen area against the French.

After a stormy and protracted sea voyage, the 42nd, comprising five companies, reached the West Indies in April 1796: the other companies were sent as garrison troops to Gibraltar. Serving under Sir John Moore, the five companies took part in the capture of St Lucia from the French, which had changed hands twice already. St Vincent was also occupied quickly, but there the French troops and armed negroes caused much trouble in the hinterland for some months. The island of Trinidad was also seized in 1797, and the five companies joined the remainder of the regiment later that year in Gibraltar. A successful attack on Minorca was launched in 1798 in which the regiment took part, and the Spanish quickly surrendered the island.

The 42nd then remained in the Mediterranean and joined the expedition led by Sir Ralph Abercromby to Egypt in 1801. The regiment took part in the dawn landing on 8 March at Aboukir Bay, which was opposed by a strong French force. The 42nd had to defend themselves against a cavalry attack immediately on reaching the shore. The advance from Aboukir Bay to Alexandria was blocked by the enemy, and the French held a well-sited defensive line in front of the town. The first British attack was repulsed and they adopted defensive positions opposing the French.

At dawn, on 21 March 1801, the French attacked the British positions with a strong force, with feints against the left and right of the British line, and the main assault against the centre. The British, however, were ready and fiercely resisted the enemy cavalry. At one stage in the battle the French actually penetrated the line, but were driven off.

'Scarcely had the 42nd time to recover their formation, after the destruction of the first body of French dragoons, when they were required to oppose the attack of another column of infantry supported by cavalry: they met their advancing opponents with firmness, repulsed them with great gallantry, and drove them to the rear. While the ranks of the regiment were in some disorder from this fight, it was charged by another body of French cavalry, when the steady aim of the highlanders again emptied a number of saddles, and, although the ranks were afterwards penetrated by the dragoons, yet the highland soldiers fought manfully, and the enemy gained little advantage. Astonished and confounded at this determined resistance, some of the dragoons galloped forward, and were destroyed by the first of the 28th Regiment; others continued to fight with the 42nd: it was a severe trial of personal firmness and individual courage to the highlanders, each man fighting on his own ground, fronting his antagonist whichever way he presented himself, and maintaining his post so long as strength or life remained.'

The last assault on the British line by the French was beaten off in the fiercest hand-to-hand fighting, during which General Abercromby was mortally wounded. The French withdrew to Alexandria and the regiment joined the force sent to capture Cairo. The French surrendered this town without a fight, and Alexandria surrendered later in the year.

After returning to Britain briefly in 1802 the 42nd then spent three years in the garrison of Gibraltar. In 1808 it joined Sir John Moore's army in Spain, the purpose of which was to assist the Spanish in expelling the French army from the Peninsula. The French, however, had achieved major successes, including the capture of Madrid, before the British troops could join their allies. The enemy advanced with some 194,000 troops against the British, who had less than 35,000, and a retreat was Moore's only sensible option. The retreat to Corunna was a disastrous affair, but the highlanders behaved better than most of the troops. The 42nd was heavily involved in the battle of Corunna, and fought to cover the embarkation. The regiment surprised an advancing French column and, in the charge that followed, chased the enemy down the hill into the village of Elvina. For the rest of the day the regiment fought in and around the village, with other battalions brought in to assist. Eventually the French withdrew and the embarkation was completed.

The regiment had barely had time to recover when it was sent on the ill-fated Walcheren expedition. This served little military purpose: thousands of troops perished from disease in a few months, and the 42nd shared in the suffering.

A new second battalion of the regiment had been raised earlier in the war and, after serving much of the time in Ireland, joined Sir Arthur Wellesley's (later the Duke of Wellington) army in Portugal in 1809. In the following year it was in reserve at the Battle of Busaco, and subsequently manned the lines of Torres Vedras. In 1811 the battalion was present at the battle of Fuentes d'Onor, defeating a cavalry charge in the later stage of the battle. In the following year it assisted in the first part of the siege of Ciudad Rodrigo.

When the 1st Battalion reached Portugal at this time, men of the 2nd Battalion men were transferred, leaving only a small cadre to return to Scotland to reform. The 1st Battalion remained in reserve during the sieges of Ciudad Rodrigo and Badajos. In July 1812 the 42nd was at Salamanca but only came into action towards the end of the battle. Two months later the highlanders played an important part during the siege of Burgos. With the 79th they scaled part of the fortifications of Mont Saint Michael during the night. Despite losing many to the bayonets of the French defending the ramparts, the highlanders captured the fort after forcing the 'gorge'. Burgos itself, however, did not fall to the British and on the approach of a large French force Wellesely withdrew his army to Portugal.

In 1813 the British advanced once more into Spain. The 42nd was with 6th Division which had a flanking role. Thus it did not fight at Vitoria but spent much of its time marching to pursue or to head off French columns. In July the army was in the area of Pamplona and came across a French force of some 30,000. There was a short battle and the enemy withdrew into Sorauren, and held it. Two days later, when the French tried to evacuate the town, The Black Watch took part in a charge against the enemy and then surrounded them. During the battle the French suffered huge casualties, and only half their number managed to escape across the mountains into France.

The British crossed the Pyrenees in November 1813 and reached the River Nivelle, passing over it before the French could bring up a sufficient force to stop them. The Black Watch captured an important French redoubt during the action. The following month the light company of the regiment took a strong enemy position overlooking the River Nive, although the rest of the regiment was only lightly engaged. At the battle of Orthez the regiment was used initially in a diversionary attack, but it then led the division onto the enemy-held ridge where it was attacked by cavalry. The highlanders' volleys broke the cavalry's advance, and on reaching the top of the ridge, the 42nd cleared the enemy positions held by greatly superior numbers.

The regiment took part in the final battle of the campaign in 1814, the capture of Toulouse. The 6th Division, in which the 42nd was serving, had to seize some high ground to the east of the town. This was captured, but the 42nd and 79th highlanders suffered greatly from enemy artillery and small arms fire. The highlanders then charged along the ridge, overwhelmed several positions, and only halted when they realised that they had got far in advance of flanking British troops. The regiment's casualties were very high, only 129 escaping death or wounding, but their action was instrumental in capturing the ridge which largely decided the battle.

The 1st Battalion of the 42nd returned to the continent in the following year with the Duke of Wellington's hastily gathered army. When Napoleon crossed the French border into Belgium, the regiment was sent from Brussels with Sir Thomas Picton's division towards the advancing French. On 16th June the 42nd were in the area of Quatre Bras.

'As the regiment advanced through a field of rye, which reached nearly to the men's shoulders, a body of cavalry was seen approaching, which was supposed to be either Prussians or Flemings, but which proved to be French. The mistake was not discovered in time to complete the proper formation to receive the charge; the regiment, however, attempted to form square, and while in the act of so doing, the French lancers galloped forward with great impetuosity, being assured of victory when they saw the unprepared state of the regiment. The two flank companies of the regiment suffered severely; but the lancers were repulsed with loss. The enemy repeated the charge, apparently in full confidence of an easy victory; but the Royal Highlanders stood back to back, every man fighting on his own ground with determined resolution, until he fell, or overcame his antagonist, and in this manner the regiment repulsed a succession of attacks.'

Their volleys effectively broke the cavalry charges, but the regiment lost many casualties in the fighting and continued to be fired on from a distance until the end of the day.

The 42nd, with the rest of the army, took up positions near Waterloo the following evening. During the battle on 18 June, the regiment was on the left part of the line behind La Haye Sainte. In the early part of the fighting it had to face heavy enemy artillery fire and later in the day some subsidiary attacks. The battalion took part in the general advance when the French army finally broke.

* * * * *

After the battle The Black Watch were stationed in Paris until the end of the year, before returning to Edinburgh. During the long period of peace that followed the regiment served in Ireland, Scotland and England, as well as various stations in the Mediterranean. Later the regiment served in the West Indies and Nova Scotia.

42nd Royal Highlanders; officers of the Bn Coy. Coloured engraving by William Heath, 1827.
Rusk Family

In 1854 the Crimean War broke out, and the 42nd joined the Highland Brigade. For some weeks the regiment stayed in Bulgaria before re-embarking for the Crimea, where it landed in September. The route to Sevastopol taken by the British army's advance necessitated the crossing by the River Alma, and the Russians held strong positions on a ridge overlooking the river. The brigade forded the river and began marching up the slope under heavy Russian artillery fire. The regiment passed through battalions of the Light Division, and on reaching the top of the ridge the 42nd found itself in advance of other regiments of the brigade. After a short delay, during which the enemy fired volleys, the whole brigade charged and the Russians quickly took flight.

When the area of Sevastopol was reached, The Black Watch manned entrenchments on the high ground above the nearby port of Balaclava. Of the

Highland Brigade, only the 93rd Highlanders took part in the battle of Balaclava, the Russian attempt to relieve Sevastopol. Thereafter the 42nd were positioned at Balaclava to prevent another Russian attempt, and remained there throughout the first winter. In the spring of 1855, the regiment returned to the trenches in front of Sevastopol and then took part in the expedition which successfully captured the port of Kerch, from which the Russian Army received most of its supplies.

The 42nd was moved into the Sevastopol trenches again, ready to take part in what was to be a final assault on the fortifications on 9 September. The Russians, however, decided to abandon the fortress during the night. The Black Watch remained in occupation of Sevastopol with the rest of the allied troops until a peace was concluded in 1856.

Drum-Maj and NCOs of The Black Watch, c1860. They are wearing the single-breasted doublet introduced after the Crimean War; Crimean and the Indian Mutiny medals are worn. RHQ

Officers and men of the 42nd Royal Highlanders pose for the camera at Bareilly, 1860. Two years earlier the regiment had been present at the capture of the garrison town from the mutineers. RHQ

A year later the regiment was sent to India where the Mutiny amongst the native troops had begun. On arrival, half the battalion set off with Sir Colin Campbell's force for the capture of Cawnpore. After a forced march, an attack was launched on the city on 6 December and the mutineers were quickly routed. For several days The Black Watch and other British troops pursued the dispersing native troops.

In March 1858, after further encounters with mutineer bands, the regiment reached Lucknow. Although two earlier attacks had relieved the Residency, the mutineers still held the city. After several days of artillery bombardment of the city the 42nd led a bayonet assault with the 93rd Highlanders, and quickly cleared the area of the military college. Rebel guns were captured and the regiment continued to fight against the mutineers well into the following day. While other troops continued to fight in the maze of streets and buildings which comprised the city, The Black Watch occupied the Begum's palace.

The regiment then joined a column to clear the province of Rohilcund, still dominated by the mutineers. Fierce fighting was experienced before the fort of Rhooyah was occupied, and at Bareilly the British force was attacked in great strength by fanatical muslim troops, including cavalry. They were defeated at bayonet-point, and the city eventually fell to the British. The 42nd remained in the province, and early in the following year a company of the regiment, with some native troops, held off an attack by some 2,000 rebels at Maylem Ghat. Eight members of the regiment were awarded the VC during the Mutiny.

* * * * *

The 42nd, with its suffix 'The Black Watch' officially recognised, continued to serve in India in various stations until 1868, when it returned to Great Britain. Five years later it joined Sir Garnet Wolseley's force sent to the Gold Coast to fight in the Ashanti war. This powerful nation had been giving much trouble to the British protected settlements on the coast. On landing, Wolseley's force advanced from Cape Coast towards Ashanti country through jungle and swamp. A large army of the enemy appeared near the village of Amoaful, and the 42nd advanced under fire through densely wooded country at the head of the British force, and captured the Ashantis' positions in the hills dominating a defile. The enemy continued to harrass the army as it marched through the difficult country but when Kumasi was reached, the King of Ashanti was discovered to have disappeared into the bush. His power broken and his capital destroyed, the British force withdrew to the coast, its task accomplished.

The regiment returned to Great Britain

immediately after the campaign ended and remained at home until 1876. After a period in Cyprus and Gibraltar it was stationed in Edinburgh in 1881. During that year it was designated the 1st Battalion, The Black Watch (Royal Highlanders), the 2nd Battalion being the former 73rd Regiment, itself directly descended from a previous 2nd Battalion of the 42nd.

Capt Andrew Wauchope in 1878. Wauchope commanded the Highland Brigade at the disastrous battle of Magersfontein 1899, in which he was killed. RHQ

The Black Watch advance on a village during the Ashanti War, 1873-4. Highland dress would have obviously been impractical during this war.

THE 73RD (PERTHSHIRE) REGIMENT

1779–1881

In July 1779 authority had been given for the raising of a second battalion of the 42nd Royal Highlanders. The following year it was embodied at Perth and, after some training, the battalion was sent to India. There was an urgent requirement to reinforce the East India Company's army, as Hyder Ali the ruler of Mysore had formed an alliance with the French. Under the command of Lt-Col Norman MacLeod the battalion reached India between May 1781 and February 1782.

The battalion's first engagement in the war was against Hyder Ali's son, Tippoo Sahib, at Paniani, where it defeated a large enemy force attempting to capture the fort. Afterwards it joined an expedition which successfully captured several forts and the important town of Bednore. The battalion was then sent to occupy two further forts, which included Mangalore, whereupon Tippoo Sahib laid siege to it. Although for nine months Mangalore was defended successfully by the 42nd against repeated attacks, eventually it was surrendered on honourable terms. The highlanders' gallantry earned them the right to carry Mangalore as a battle honour – a most unusual distinction.

The battalion became a separate regiment in 1786, known as the 73rd Highland Regiment of Foot: the reason was allegedly on account of disputed seniority of officers in the two battalions of the 42nd. It continued to wear the government tartan when appropriate. The regiment remained in India, and three years later war broke out again against Mysore. The force in which the 73rd served achieved some successes, but it took until 1792 before Tippoo Sahib was decisively defeated near his capital of Seringapatam. Thereafter a peace treaty between the East India Company and Mysore was concluded.

When war with revolutionary France broke out in 1793, the 73rd Highlanders took part in the siege and occupation of Pondicherry. Two years later they went on an expedition to the Dutch island of Ceylon; Holland had allied itself at this time with the French. The highlanders took part in the capture of the forts of Trincomalee, Batticaloa and Manaar, followed by the siege and surrender of Colombo in 1796. The regiment remained in occupation until 1799, when it returned to India and joined the army which had resumed operations against Tippoo Sahib.

On 20 April 1799 General David Baird set out in with an army to invest Seringapatam. Four companies of the 73rd took part in one of a number of feint assaults on the fortress town, while the artillery attempted to breach the walls. On 4 May the 73rd, 74th and 75th Highlanders, together with other British and native troops, formed one of the storming columns and broke through a breach in the ramparts. After fierce hand-to-hand combat Seringapatam was finally captured and Tippoo Sahib was killed. The 73rd Highlanders remained as garrison troops for a year.

The regiment returned to Great Britain in 1806, and a second battalion was raised in 1808. As the majority of recruits came from militia regiments outside Scotland, in 1809 the regiment lost its place on the establishment of highland regiments, as well as its highland dress. In the same year the 1st Battalion embarked for Australia, where the battalion's four-year tour of duty in New South Wales was highly successful in bringing law and order amongst the settlers. On completion of this task in 1814, the 73rd moved to Ceylon, where it took part in operations against the local rulers who were harrassing the European settlers. The expedition was successful and Ceylon was ceded to the British Crown in 1815.

* * * * *

In the meantime the 2nd Battalion of the 73rd had remained at home until 1813, when it landed with a force on the Baltic coast and marched through Germany. It fought at Gorhde, charging against a strong French hill-top position, but the enemy fled and the battle was quickly won. Later the battalion joined other British troops in Flanders, and it was from there that the 73rd marched to Brussels in 1815, when Napoleon Bonaparte threatened the peace of Europe for the last time.

The 2nd Battalion was present at Quatre Bras on 16 June, and threatened by French dragoons, it formed squares. Later in the action, enemy cuirassiers charged towards them but, wheeling in front in face of a volley, went on to attack the squares of the 42nd and 44th regiments.

The 73rd were posted on top of the crest in the centre of the British line during the battle of Waterloo. There it formed square with the 30th Regiment, and was exposed throughout the action to artillery fire and cavalry. The French artillery later advanced with the cuirassiers and discharged grapeshot into the British squares, but the British infantry continued to stand their ground and fired volleys at the enemy. Their squares remained unbroken; and even when the 73rd ran out of ammunition at one critical time, they continued to hold the French cavalry at bayonet-point. The battalion maintained its position throughout the day, and the survivors took part in the final general advance as the French withdrew from the battlefield. The battalion was subsequently disbanded in 1817.

The 1st Battalion of the 73rd remained in Ceylon until 1819, where it spent time in the jungle and mountains fighting against native groups conducting guerrilla warfare against the European settlers.

During the long period of peace, the 73rd was stationed in Gibraltar, Malta, the Ionian Islands and Ireland. Then in 1845 the regiment served for some months in the Argentine, protecting British nationals from Spanish settlers in the area of Montevideo. During the following year the regiment embarked for South Africa, where operations against the Kaffirs were being conducted. For eleven years the 73rd took part in the sporadic fighting against the Kaffirs in the veldt and mountains of eastern Cape Colony. The enemy had to be defeated in detail, and on four occasions the regiment joined expeditions to the Amatola mountains and in 1851 relieved Fort Butterworth. Other tasks included punitive cattle raids against the Kaffirs and Basutos. A draft of recruits for the regiment was on board the ill-fated troopship *Birkenhead*, when it ran aground off South Africa in 1852. Forty-six members of the regiment were drowned.

In 1858 the 73rd sailed for India to assist in suppressing the Mutiny. It operated on detached duty for several months in the Oude and Gorakhpur districts, fighting in various engagements against dispersed groups of mutineers. In 1861, the regiment returned to Great Britain, and in the following year its title was altered to the '73rd (Perthshire) Regiment of Foot'.

After duty in England and Ireland, the 73rd embarked for service in Hong Kong as garrison troops. It remained there from 1867 to 1871, then moved via Ceylon to India in 1874. In the 1881 re-organisation it became the 2nd Battalion of The Black Watch, readopting full highland dress with the kilt.

THE BLACK WATCH
1881–1913

The 1st Battalion, The Black Watch embarked in 1882 for Egypt and joined the Highland Brigade for the brief campaign against the Egyptian army in revolt against the Khedive. The British army was transported via the Suez Canal and landed at Ismailia in September. There was little local resistance by the Egyptians, but their main position was a well-defended camp at Tel-El-Kebir.

The Black Watch had four companies in each of the two columns for the night-approach march. Some 18,000 troops took part in the march, and although there was some misalignment as the force neared Tel-El-Kebir, the enemy were largely taken by surprise. They opened fire at a range of only 500 yards, whereupon The Black Watch charged with the other battalions, crossed a deep ditch and took the Egyptian first line at bayonet point. The fighting continued for some twenty minutes, and when the second line was successfully defeated, the Egyptians fled from the battlefield. The rebellion had been crushed convincingly.

The battalion remained in Egypt and took part in the following year in the campaign in the Sudan against the Mahdi. At El Teb the British force had adopted a huge rectangular formation comprising six

Soldiers of the 1st Black Watch after the battle of Tel-El-Kebir, 1882. RHQ

infantry battalions, as an experiment, on the orders of the commander General Thomas Graham. The Black Watch were at the head of this formation as it approached the dervishes' trenches. The enemy frenziedly attacked the British but were severely cut up by the cavalry, and then by the British bayonets in successive charges on the square. Although this formation worked at El Teb, two weeks later at Tamai it nearly proved disastrous. There The Black Watch formed a corner of the formation, and when the highlanders were ordered to charge by the brigade commander against the enemy in a ravine, the dervishes surrounded the battalion and got in amongst the other battalions. The hand-to-hand fighting was intense as the battalion forced its way back to rejoin the others and suffered numerous casualties in the process. The enemy were defeated eventually by rifle fire. The expeditionary force was, however, recalled to Egypt without achieving its object of joining up with General Gordon's force in Khartoum.

Later in the year the 1st Battalion joined another force to relieve General Gordon, which proceeded by boat up the Nile. In February 1885 it fought the dervishes holding a hill dominating the river at Kirbekan. The Black Watch mounted a bayonet charge up the hill, the enemy position was taken, and as they fled they were attacked by the British cavalry and a second British battalion. But the news of the fall of Khartoum and Gordon's death then reached the relief force, whereupon it returned to Egypt.

The two battalions of The Black Watch served in various stations during the following years, including England, Ireland, Scotland, Malta, Gibraltar, South Africa and Mauritius. By 1899 the 1st Battalion was mobilised on the outbreak of the war in South Africa, and landed at Cape Town in mid-November 1899. The battalion joined the Highland Brigade on the Modder River, and on 10 December a dawn attack was launched against Cronje's position on the hill at Magersfontein. Unexpectedly the Boers were at the foot of the hill and fired upon the battalion from three directions. The whole of the Highland Brigade were caught out in the open, in close battalion formations, and were subjected to extremely accurate enemy fire, as well as British artillery fire in error. To advance towards the Boers' positions was virtually impossible, although some members of The Black Watch got close to them. With ammunition expended and having suffered severe casualties, the British troops withdrew later in the day. Black Watch casualties were over 300.

In February 1900 the battalion took part in a successful action at Koodoesberg on the march to Paardeberg on the Modder River. There Cronje's

Before the Ball. A group of officers of The Black Watch photographed in Dec 1912, wearing regimental uniform of a hundred years previously. Col W. M. Campbell is seated on the right, and Lt The Hon Fergus Bowes-Lyon, brother of HM Queen Elizabeth the Queen Mother, is standing on the left. RHQ

column of Boers was effectually cut off, but held a strong position. The Black Watch advanced in extended line leading the brigade across nearly a mile of open veldt, and some picquets were forced to withdraw. It was not, however, possible to attack the Boer position itself with certainty of success, but several days later the Boers surrendered. Bloemfontein was entered and Pretoria subsequently fell to British troops.

In May of that year The Black Watch marched with the brigade in pursuit of the Boers to relieve the Heilbron and, subsequently, to clear the whole of the Orange Free State. At the action at Retiefs Nek in July, The Black Watch succeeded in taking two Boer positions: Prinsloo's commando was then encircled by British troops and he subsequently surrendered. Later in the year the battalion was sent to Ladybrand, where it was based for the next year.

The 1st Battalion, The Black Watch also arrived in South Africa in December 1901. During the final months of the war the two battalions were based in various parts of Natal and the Orange Free State, with detached companies guarding blockhouses and lines of communications. In the period of peace after the Boer War, the battalions were sent to Ireland and India. In the months before the First World War started, the battalions changed over, the 1st being moved to Aldershot and the 2nd to India.

THE BLACK WATCH
1914–38

The 1st Battalion, The Black Watch, joined the British Expeditionary Force on mobilisation in 1914. No sooner had it reached France and taken up a position on 24 August along the Mons to Beaumont road, than the retreat to the River Marne began. During the following fortnight the battalion marched nearly 200 miles, frequently in contact with the leading German troops.

On 8 September The Black Watch led an attack on the enemy in a wood near Sablonnieres. Supported by the 1st Cameron Highlanders, the attack was swift and successful. Similar attacks on the Germans on this part of the front forced them to withdraw northwards to the River Aisne. The 1st Black Watch then took part in a divisional attack on the enemy north of the river on 14 September. The Germans, however, had established strongly defended positions by then, and although the battalion made some gains, the enemy successfully counter-attacked. Shortly afterwards the battalion was moved with the whole of the BEF to extend the front in northern Flanders. There they held positions in the Ypres area, meeting furious German attacks for more than a fortnight. After a lull, the Germans mounted an attack in great strength on 11 November on the battalion's part of the line at Polygon Wood, and The Black Watch suffered a great number of casualties, being almost overwhelmed. A counter-attack was mounted by the remnants of the battalion, which deterred further enemy attempts against the British line for a time.

During the winter the 2nd Black Watch, serving in an Indian division, reached Flanders and went into the front line at Givenchy. The 4th and 5th Territorial Battalions also arrived, and were sent to the area of Neuve Chapelle. In March 1915 the 2nd and 4th

This eerie 'post-card' photograph shows jocks of The Black Watch marching through Béthune, 1915. RHQ

Battalions supported a major attack against Aubers Ridge, which proved unsuccessful. In April there was a fresh attempt to capture the ridge; the 1st Black Watch on this occasion succeeded in capturing their objective but, unsupported on left and right, were ordered to withdraw. On the same day the 2nd Battalion had provided two companies to support an attack in the same sector, and the 4th Battalion also supported a nearby attack. Neither met with success, and casualties were high in all three battalions. A final attempt was made on 9 May against Aubers Ridge. A and B Companies of the 1st Black Watch were in the lead with C and D Companies in reserve.

'As soon as our men topped the breastworks, they were met by a terrific rifle and machine-gun fire, which seemed to come from every direction . . . it did not take more than two minutes for the leading troops to reach the enemy wire. A few gaps existed, and into these the attacking platoons converged; then forcing their way into the German line they began to clear the trenches by hand-to-hand fighting . . . and though the battalion established itself at various points, it was attacked from three sides, being bombed from both flanks, and fired into from the enemy's rear line.

The 6th, 7th, 8th and 9th Battalions, The Black Watch (the last two being 'new' battalions) arrived in France in the spring and summer of 1915. All battalions were involved to a greater or lesser extent in the Loos offensive in September 1915. The 9th Battalion led its division's attack on the Lens Road redoubt which was quickly captured. The battalion fought through to Loos and, with the Seaforth, Gordons and Camerons, took the objective known as Hill 70. During the battle over 700 of the battalion were killed or wounded. The 8th meanwhile were supporting an attack on the Hohenzollern Redoubt, and this too was successful. The 1st Battalion started the battle in reserve, but was soon called in to support the assault on Hulluch. These three battalions were relieved before the enemy retaliated: but when the Germans counter-attacked the Hohenzollern Redoubt, a mixed group of Camerons and 1st Black Watch managed to hold the position against overwhelming odds. In the same battle the 2nd and 4th Black Watch's objectives were on Aubers Ridge. Their brigade made considerable progress in the attack; but due to the failure of flanking formations to conform, they were forced to withdraw.

Three weeks later the 1st Battalion fought once more to regain ground near the Hohenzollern Redoubt. The battalion's casualties were high, and the Germans held the position in too great a strength for it to be captured. At Givenchy the 2nd Battalion, with two remaining companies of the 4th Black Watch, successfully beat off the enemy's counter-attacks. The regiment's overall losses during the battle were such that replacement drafts were insufficient to bring all battalions up to strength, and the amalgamation of the 4th and 5th Battalions was necessary. In December 1915 the 2nd Battalion left the western front for service in Mesopotamia, and the 6th and 7th Battalions were moved to the French sector at Arras.

In the trenches, near Albert, 1915. Members of the 'Auchterarder Coy', 6th Black Watch de-louse their clothing. Many of the territorial and service battalions and their constituent companies were recruited from individual towns or parishes in Scotland. RHQ

* * * * *

During the first half of 1916 the line was relatively static while preparations were being made for the Somme offensive. At the start of the battle on 1 July, the 8th Battalion's assault on Longueval was entirely successful, and elements probed as far as Delville Wood. In the counter-attack the Germans occupied the village for a time, but they were again forced out by the battalion who held it until relieved on 19 July. Meanwhile the 1st Battalion was in action in the area of High Wood.

In September the 4/5th Black Watch fought in the River Ancre sector, and there was much close-quarter combat in the German trenches. Although some gains were made, withdrawal was necessary to conform to flanking units' positions. The battalion was moved to the Thiepeval area, where it captured a German redoubt close to the British line. Again fierce fighting was necessary to dislodge the Germans successfully, and prevent them reoccupying their former trenches.

The 6th and 7th Battalions had been fighting in the Beaumont Hamel area against the Germans' positions, so well sited as to be virtually unassailable. A determined attack, however, was mounted in November, with the 6th Black Watch in the assault and the Gordon Highlanders and the 7th Black Watch in reserve. This time the attack succeeded, and the two Black Watch battalions together captured the enemy positions dominating the village, which enabled Beaumont Hamel to be captured at last.

In April 1917 the Arras offensive was launched. The 9th Black Watch was in action at Monchy le Preux and captured part of the first German line. Their division, however, was held up by the second line entrenched in a triangle of earthworks. Supported by a single tank, the battalion broke through the second line, which enabled the divisional attack to be resumed. The 8th Battalion had a similar success amongst the railway cuttings north of the

Men of The Black Watch rest by a field kitchen after the battle of Bazentin Ridge, 19 July 1916. IWM

The Somme offensive, Battle of Bazentin Ridge. 8th Black Watch relax to the sound of the pipes after the capture of Longueval, 14 July 1916. IWM

River Scarpe. Then the 7th Black Watch relieved the 8th some days later, and during the fighting for the chemical works at Roeux they suffered greatly from enemy machine-gun fire. The 6th Battalion, in support, was unable to pass through the captured positions because of the weight of the German counter-attack. At one stage in the battle near Guémappe the 9th Black Watch were cut off, but most of their positions were held with the most determined fighting. In early May the 8th Battalion suffered nearly fifty per cent casualties in the final divisional attack of the battle.

During the third battle of Ypres all six battalions of The Black Watch serving on the Western Front were involved. The 4/5th advanced 1,500 yards on the first morning of the attack, but could not progress beyond the Steenbeck river. The 7th Battalion advanced a similar distance and captured its objectives. The 6th Battalion passed through them and managed to establish a strong defensive line on the same river, but again the river proved too much of an obstacle.

Soldiers of 11 Platoon breaking camp before resuming duties in the trenches, Mesopotamia 1916. Both the 2nd Black Watch and 1st Seaforth Highlanders fought for two years in this campaign. IWM

Meanwhile the 9th Battalion successfully captured enemy positions short of Frezenburg Ridge, but other British battalions which passed through were unable to capture the further objectives at Passchendaele and Gheluvelt. Later the 9th Battalion was called upon to attack Gallipoli farm at night with two companies, but it took two further days to capture the area of the farm. The fight for Passchendaele Ridge continued, and the 1st Black Watch fought an action on 8 November to expel the enemy from their last positions on the ridge itself.

On 20 November the battle of Cambrai began against part of the Hindenburg Line. The 6th Black Watch were in the leading troops of their division and made considerable gains with the assistance of massed tanks. The 7th Battalion passed quickly through its first objective, but in a subsequent phase was under heavy artillery bombardment. The momentum of the attack could not be maintained and the advance foundered short of the battalion's objective in the area of Flesquières. Patrols the following day occupied the trenches abandoned by the enemy during the night.

* * * * *

In the meantime the 2nd Battalion had been in Mesopotamia since early 1916. Its initial task was to assist in the relief of Kut El Amara, which had been cut off by the Turks. Within two days of arrival the 2nd Black Watch was in action at Sheik Saad on the Tigris River in a hastily-ordered attack, unsupported by artillery or cavalry. The battalion suffered so many casualties that it was unable to get anywhere near the Turkish positions. The battalion's next engagement was an attempt to break through the Turkish positions at Hanna on 21 January.

'As the bombardment lifted, The Black Watch advanced at a slow double, and were at once greeted by a storm of bullets. Despite the heavy mud, despite the losses, perfect order was kept, and after a momentary halt at the irrigation channel every man rose up simultaneously and swept forward into the Turkish trench. There for a few moments the Turks met them hand-to-hand.'

In occupying these trenches, The Black Watch were isolated, but they fought off counter-attacks for two hours until ordered to withdraw. The battalion's strength was now reduced from 900 to some 130 men, commanded by 2nd Lt Stewart-Smith.

The Royal Scots Greys depicted during the charge of the Heavy Brigade at Balaclava, 1854. This action, though less celebrated than the charge of the Light Brigade, had much more influence on the outcome of the battle. Painted by Felix Philippoteaux. RHQ

Below:
The 90th disarm mutineers at Berhampore in August 1857. The following month they fought under Outram at the first relief of Lucknow. Watercolour by Orlando Norie. RHQ

Top left:
Major William Rennie (later Lt-Col), won the VC with the 90th Perthshire Light Infantry during the Indian Mutiny. RHQ

Left:
Lt F. E. Farquharson of the 42nd Royal Highlanders leads an attack on some mutineers' guns at Lucknow in Mar 1858, for which he was awarded the VC. RHQ

Above:
The second relief of Lucknow. The charge of the 93rd Highlanders against the Secundrabagh, on 16 Nov 1857. The battle honour Lucknow was awarded to six Scottish regiments. Oil painting by W. B. Wollen.
Parker Gallery

Col John Ewart leads the 93rd Sutherland Highlanders as they storm the Secundrabagh at Lucknow, Nov 1857. Watercolour by Orlando Norie. RHQ

Various orders of dress are depicted here in a watercolour by Maj R. A. Wymer of the 79th Cameron Highlanders in 1856. RHQ

Drummer Cairns, 'night rounds in guard order', Scots Fusilier Guards. After an oil painting by Drahouet at Windsor Castle. National Museums of Scotland

A group of the 25th King's Own Borderers in the dress worn in Canada in 1866. The regiment was involved in operations against Fenian infiltrators. RHQ

78th Highlanders (Ross-shire Buffs) at camp c1860. From a watercolour by Orlando Norie. RHQ

Top left:
Scots Guards forming square on manoeuvres. The square was practised and used in action until the end of the 19th century, when machine-gun and accurate artillery fire made close formations totally impractical. Watercolour by Orlando Norie. RHQ

Left:
Scots Guards at camp c1865. Watercolour by Orlando Norie. The Scots Guards

Top:
Two officers of the Seaforth Highlanders, late 19th century. Parker Gallery

Right:
'A frozen jock'. A Gordon Highlander on picquet duty during the second Afghan War of 1878-80. The extreme condition of climate is clearly depicted by W. Skeoch Cumming. RHQ

Overleaf:
The storming of the Asmai Heights during the Afghan War of 1879 by the 92nd Gordon Highlanders was a feat of sheer bravery. Watercolour by W. Skeoch Cumming. RHQ

W. Skeoch Cumming
1889

As a consequence the remaining men of the 2nd Black Watch were formed into The Highland Battalion, with the equally depleted 1st Seaforth Highlanders. The Highland Battalion's successive attacks on the Sannaiyat position were carried out with extreme bravery, and although the highlanders continued to fight when other battalions had withdrawn, they were unable to dislodge the enemy. Kut-el-Amara therefore could not be relieved, and the garrison consequently surrendered to the Turks.

Reinforcing drafts soon reached Mesopotamia and the 2nd Black Watch was re-formed. Preparations over the following months were made for a campaign to expel the Turks completely from Mesopotamia. In February 1917, the Sannaiyat position was successfully assaulted, and in the following month Baghdad was entered. The 2nd Battalion was then given the task of clearing the railway line, culminating in a successful attack on Istabulat. The Turks counter-attacked with effect, but The Black Watch charged in again and evicted the enemy from the town. The campaign by now had virtually achieved its purpose.

Two battalions of dismounted yeomanry had been, meanwhile, incorporated into The Black Watch in 1916, the Scottish Horse and the Fife and Forfar Yeomanry. They became nominally the 13th and 14th Battalions of The Black Watch. They had both fought at Gallipoli in 1915, and the 13th subsequently joined the troops fighting on the Bulgarian front in Salonika. The 10th Battalion, The Black Watch, had also served in Salonika since December 1915. These two battalions spent most of the time manning the line, the position of which altered little, and occasionally raiding the Bulgarian trenches. The 10th Battalion fought in the battle near Lake Dorain in 1917, which was inconclusive, and the two battalions were sent hurriedly to France in the Spring of 1918.

The 14th Battalion served in Egypt during 1916 and then took part in the Palestine campaign. The 2nd Battalion also fought in the latter stages, and took part in the battle of Megiddo in September 1918. There The Black Watch, with other battalions, broke through the Turkish lines in a surprise attack, which developed throughout the day into a rout. The cavalry were able to head off the Turks, and pursued those who had at first escaped. A few days later the Turks agreed to an armistice.

2nd Black Watch guard the coast at Arsuz, Syria, Jan 1918. As protection against mosquitos, the jocks have taken to wearing khaki drill trousers and puttees.

IWM

* * * * *

The great German offensive of March 1918 affected all battalions of The Black Watch serving on the Western Front. The 6th and 7th Battalions serving in the 51st Division were in the Cambrai area, and put up determined resistance as the Germans attempted to sweep past the forward positions and penetrate through to the rear. The 4/5th and 9th Battalions in the Arras sector had so many casualties that they had to be consolidated as one in order to resist the German advance. Further south the 8th held firm, but had to fight off Germans who had penetrated behind the line. The 1st Battalion suffered high casualties in the trenches and tunnels of Givenchy when the Germans broke through part of the British line. A and C Companies held forward positions.

'The bombardment had been as intense as any known on the Western Front, and if a few had survived, they could not have made an effective resistance. The light trench mortars and machine guns were buried by the bombardment, and their teams destroyed. Captain Sinclair and a small band of devoted followers waited on the tunnel stairway that faced the front line; they must have come out to meet the attack, in spite of the shell-fire concentrated on their only exit, and were overcome by superior numbers at close quarters. Two days later their bodies were found by the exit where they fell.'

With support from flanking battalions the remainder of the battalion held their positions. The price the Germans paid for their successes all along the front was too heavy, and miraculously they achieved no actual penetration that was not somehow met by the British and allied troops.

In late April a counter-offensive was launched. The 4/5th Battalion fought alongside the Seaforth, Camerons and French troops for the possession of Buzancy, south of the River Aisne. The battle passed back and forth and it took several days for the capture of the village. The 6th Battalion also fought alongside the French in the woods of Champagne during July. Again after several days of fighting, The Black Watch succeeded in capturing a well-defended enemy strongpoint in the village of Chambrécy. In Flanders the 6th and 7th Battalions made rapid advances with the 51st Highland Division, capturing much of the ground that had earlier been lost. In late September, as the British formations advanced, the 1st Battalion attacked the Hindenburg Line and successfully cleared part of the strongest of all German fortifications. In the last few weeks of the war the battalions of the regiment took part in many actions in detail against the retreating Germans, before the armistice brought an end to hostilities.

* * * * *

The two regular battalions of The Black Watch returned to peacetime duties, the 1st in India and the 2nd in Scotland. In 1919 the 2nd was sent to Silesia where it remained until 1924 to guarantee the treaty terms. The 2nd Black Watch then moved to Palestine in 1937, where its task was to prevent violence between the Jews and Arabs. The battalion was kept fully occupied, as the tension had reached a dangerous level. The 1st Battalion returned to Britain from India in the following year. By this time the regiment's title had been altered for the last time; it was now called 'The Black Watch (Royal Highland Regiment)'.

* * * * *

Brief mention should be made of the 1st Battalion Tyneside Scottish, The Black Watch. In the First World War four battalions of Tyneside Scottish were raised in the north-east of England, and all served in France. Notable actions were the Somme in 1916, Arras in 1917 and the German Spring offensive in 1918. The title was revived in 1939 for the duplicate battalion of the 9th Durham Light Infantry. Re-designation and affiliation to The Black Watch followed in late 1939. The battalion fought in France and only 140 men were evacuated at Dunkirk. The re-formed Tyneside Scottish then served in Ireland and landed in Normandy. In August 1944 the battalion was drafted and reconstituted after the war, as an anti-aircraft regiment of the Royal Artillery.

Officers of the 2nd Black Watch at Colchester, c1932. This photograph includes Lts David Rose, H. C. Baker-Baker, Michael Hughes-Young and Capt Purvis-Russell-Montgomery. RHQ

Opposite page:
These two photographs show jocks of the 2nd Black Watch at Saxmundham, Suffolk 1933, during annual manoeuvres. A meal en route and cleaning rifles at camp. RHQ

THE BLACK WATCH

1939 to the present

When war was declared in 1939 the 1st Battalion, The Black Watch, joined the British Expeditionary Force in France. It manned the Maginot Line at first, and was then moved to the area of Lens on the Belgian border. The 51st Highland Division reached France in January 1940 and took up positions in the Saar. The 1st joined the 4th Battalion in this division, while the 6th Black Watch was positioned further to the north with the 4th Division.

The 6th Battalion took part in the advance across Belgium when the Germans invaded that country, and reached a position at Louvain. When it was clear that the Germans were about to outflank the BEF, the battalion was ordered to withdraw. The race across Belgium followed, with the battalion fighting several rear-guard actions. On reaching the Lys Canal ahead of the Germans, the battalion held a bridge while the British 5th Division crossed on its way to Dunkirk. Subsequently, the 6th Black Watch held Nieuport, on the coast to the east of Dunkirk, before being ordered to withdraw for the embarkation.

The 51st Highland Division, having withdrawn from the Saar, was a good deal further to the south, defending part of the River Somme against the German advance. The 1st Battalion fought alongside the French to destroy a German bridgehead at Abbeville, but this proved impossible. On 5 June the 4th Battalion, although in reserve, held off the German advance in the battalion area. The 1st Battalion also defended its position above Abbeville, but then the whole division was ordered to withdraw. The 4th Black Watch took up new positions covering a bridge on the River Bresle, which it held for three days. On further orders it moved towards Dieppe and made ready to defend Le Havre prior to the evacuation of the division. When the division was finally cut off, the 4th Battalion was fortunate to escape to Cherbourg and embarked for England. Although it was later garrisoned in Gibraltar, it did not take part in any subsequent campaigns during the war.

Meanwhile the 1st Battalion was moving back with a French division towards Dieppe, taking up fresh positions each night. At St Valéry the German armoured columns finally overtook and surrounded what remained of the 51st Highland Division. After the French troops had surrendered, the GOC Maj-Gen Fortune ordered the 51st to do likewise. Few members of the 1st Black Watch escaped.

* * * * *

The 2nd Black Watch remained in Palestine until mid-1940, when they were sent to British Somaliland. The Italians had some 200,000 troops in Abyssinia, and during August they launched an attack on French and British Somaliland. The Italian forces included armoured support and they greatly outnumbered the defenders, a single battalion of the King's African Rifles and the 2nd Black Watch. The evacuation of the force was quickly ordered and The Black Watch covered the withdrawal of the KAR in the area of Barkasan. One of the companies holding a ridge above a road block was attacked by the Italians, but they were chased down the hill in a spirited bayonet charge led by Capt David Rose, the company commander. This action saved the situation for some hours, but the enemy forces built up during the day. Although they were in a strong position to attack and overwhelm The Black Watch's positions, they failed to do so; this enabled the battalion to withdraw without further losses. The evacuation was successfully covered, and The Black Watch embarked for Egypt. The Italians were thrown out of East Africa in 1941.

Later in the year the battalion was sent to the island of Crete, where The Black Watch's task was the defence of the airfield at Heraklion. There the battalion remained until May 1941, when the Germans invaded the island from the air. Heavy casualties were inflicted on the German paratroopers as they dropped into the battalion's area, but massive air attacks and parachute landings elsewhere in the island enabled the Germans to build up sufficient forces to capture Crete. The British evacuation was then ordered. Most of the battalion managed to embark on ships of the Royal Navy, but when the convoy was bombed on its way to Alexandria, 103 members of the regiment were killed and many others wounded.

* * * * *

The 2nd Battalion spent a brief period in Syria and embarked for Tobruk in October 1941 to reinforce the garrison. Tobruk was already behind the German and Italian lines, and in November General Auchinleck's offensive from the east was supported by the troops from Tobruk. A combined attack by the 2nd Battalion with a regiment of tanks was mounted on German positions on 20 November. The Black Watch captured the first objective without armoured support against very heavy enemy fire. B Company had taken its objective with the bayonet, but had been severely cut up by machine guns. D Company passed through to the stirring sound of Pipe-Major Roy and other pipers, playing *Highland Laddie* and *The Black Bear*. Later, one wounded officer told of the effect of the pipes in 'kindling the spirit with which the whole attack was carried out'. As the battle advanced, however, the battalion's casualties mounted, and the tanks became disorientated after being held up in a minefield. The CO, Lt-Col George Rusk, restored the situation himself by gathering together a sufficient force of highlanders and tanks to assault and capture the battalion's final objective. Formations from the Eighth Army eventually forced back the Axis troops west of Tobruk. The 2nd Black Watch then left for Egypt, and subsequently for India. (Tobruk fell later in the Axis counter-offensive.)

* * * * *

A new 51st Highland Division and 1st Black Watch had meanwhile been formed in the United Kingdom. The 5th and 7th Battalions also served in the division, and in mid-1942 all three battalions embarked for Egypt. There they trained for the coming offensive, and in October moved forward to positions on the Alamein Line. During the night of 23 October the 1st and 5th Black Watch were assault battalions in the advance of the division through the minefields and wire. They made good progress against heavy enemy fire and captured their objectives, despite losing many casualties. The 7th Battalion in the second wave passed through, and in taking its objective – a hill nicknamed 'the Ben' – suffered very heavy casualties. Part of the ridge on which it dug in was held by the Germans, and the battle in this part remained static for a number of days. The 5th Battalion was similarly holding an exposed position. When the breakout occurred, the 51st Highland Division was one of the leading formations. For some weeks the advance across the desert progressed quickly, and the first major obstacle for the division was at Mersa Brega. Painstakingly the 1st and 7th Battalions mounted a night attack on the village which was heavily mined, but found it had been evacuated just prior to their assault.

In mid-January the same battalions were held up by a strong German position short of Tripoli. A brigade attack was ordered and the 7th Battalion, although in support, managed to outflank the enemy position. The 1st Black Watch were engaged in a fast moving action against a mobile enemy column which suddenly appeared, and the highlanders were

Men of The Black Watch embark for the invasion of Sicily, July 1943. IWM

reinforced just in time to defeat it. The enemy withdrew speedily and evacuated the position; whereupon the rapid advance on Tripoli continued and the town was entered a few days later.

In early March the division had reached the Mareth Line. All three battalions of the regiment were in support during the attack on the line, which developed into a major battle. A month later the advance was again held up, this time by the enemy holding the Roumana ridge. In a brigade assault on the ridge the 5th Battalion was called forward from reserve to relieve the Seaforth Highlanders. This they did, and were engaged in heavy fighting against other enemy positions. The 7th Battalion was involved in a most hard-fought battle in Wadi Akarit, which cut across the Roumana ridge. With the 7th Argylls they fought off enemy attacks, and even though reinforced by companies of the 1st Battalion, intensive fighting continued for several hours. The enemy forced the 7th to withdraw during the night, but by dawn on the third day the enemy were discovered to have abandoned their positions.

The 6th Black Watch reached North Africa and joined the First Army as it approached Tunis from the west, towards the end of the campaign. The battalion fought in two major engagements: a battalion night-attack was mounted against Sidi Medienne, and although the Germans counter-attacked twice, the 6th held the village. The fight for the Enfidaville position was also conducted by night, and the enemy did not put up much resistance against

Top:
A Bren-gun carrier of The Black Watch passes through Palazzolo, Sicily, 14 July 1943. Three battalions of the regiment, the 1st, 5th and 7th Black Watch fought in Sicily, while the 6th joined the campaign on the Italian mainland. IWM

Above:
Anti-tank guns of the 6th Black Watch prepare for action on the Rapido River, Italy, summer 1944. The battalion successfully established and held a bridge-head over the river. IWM

the battalion on this occasion. Clearing the remaining enemy pockets around Tunis was by this time a relatively easy task as the North African campaign drew to a close.

* * * * *

The 51st Highland Division, with the same three Black Watch battalions, the 1st, 5th and 7th, then took part in the invasion of Sicily. Landing on 10 July, they met little resistance at first. The Germans held the town of Vizzini, but the 5th Black Watch carried the enemy positions in a fast-moving attack in cooperation with the Gordon Highlanders. The enemy withdrew across the Catania Plain and took up a strong line at Gerbini. The 1st and 7th Black Watch then fought a three-day battle for the possession of the Gerbini airfield and barracks. The 7th managed to penetrate the airfield defences, but were withdrawn when it was decided to bypass the area to the west. In the meantime the 5th Battalion captured Sferro village which was well in advance of the allied line, and held it while reliefs were brought up. The 1st and 5th were part of a brigade attack in the same area, and met the fiercest resistance from the Germans who inflicted heavy casualties on the highlanders. Eventually the enemy were ejected from their positions, and soon evacuated the island.

In September the allies crossed the Straits of Messina and landed on the Italian mainland. The three battalions of the regiment took part in the rapid and mainly unresisted advance northwards. After a few weeks the 51st Highland Division was withdrawn from Italy to prepare for the Normandy landings. The 6th Battalion, however, which had returned to Egypt after the conclusion of the North African campaign, was moved to Italy in March 1944. There it joined the allied line in the area of the River Liri. It took part in the battle for Monte Cassino, and was then ordered to cross the River Rapido to help establish a bridgehead. By chance, in the fog, The Black Watch penetrated a strong German position, which they then held for two days until other troops caught up, but casualties in this action were high.

The 6th Black Watch continued to fight frequent engagements against the withdrawing Germans as the allies progressed northwards. The fiercest fighting the battalion experienced was in the Po valley in early 1945, where it had to fight in more open country with its numerous towns and villages. The fighting continued until the end of the year, when the battalion embarked for Greece. There it remained for two years, conducting operations against the communists in Athens and the countryside.

* * * * *

The 2nd Battalion, after leaving Egypt, had trained in India to take part in the 'Chindit' operations. The Black Watch were divided into two 'columns', and with a number of other columns, they were airlifted into Burma in March 1944. Their purpose was to disrupt the Japanese rear area, and for five months they operated independently, being resupplied and supported from the air. In April they destroyed a convoy near Indaw and then blew up a fuel depot. Later in the month another large Japanese convoy was attacked.

In May a column laid an ambush as a diversion to cover the movement of other Chindit forces. A large body of the enemy, numbering well over a thousand, approached in the dark, unaware of the presence of the 200 highlanders. At 5.25am The Black Watch attacked the Japs. A fierce fight lasted for some five hours, with individual platoon battles taking place over a wide area. The Black Watch's casualties were heavy, and there was much difficulty in bringing in the wounded. The Japanese losses had, however, been very severe indeed. In the afternoon and evening the remnants of the platoons reported in, but it was not until the following day that the column was reunited. An airstrip was hastily constructed and the wounded flown out. The Black Watch continued to

Guard of Honour, comprised of soldiers of the 7th Black Watch from Fifeshire, April 1945. IWM

A machine-gun post of the 1st Black Watch in Korea. The battalion was attacked on two occasions by hordes of Chinese 'volunteers', but successfully defeated them. IWM

patrol against the enemy in the most terrible conditions of terrain and monsoon climate, losing many casualties through disease. Eventually they linked up with the troops advancing into Burma from India. On The Black Watch's return to India, they were reinforced, and converted to a parachute battalion. The war, however, ended before it was required to be used in this role.

* * * * *

On 6 June 1944 the 5th Black Watch landed with the invasion force in Normandy. It quickly took up a position in the area of Château de Bréville. The Germans mounted furious attacks on the château and over-ran part of the battalion's area, but the battalion managed to eject them. The 1st and 7th Black Watch also reached Normandy and as the 51st Highland Division's sector was on the pivot of the allied advance, the fighting was mainly defensive. The Germans certainly were determined to hold the Caen area, and several British attacks foundered against the heavy opposition and determined enemy counter-attacks. The 5th Black Watch took part in one such unsuccessful assault, on Colombelles.

The 51st Highland Division was moved south towards the Falaise area in July. The 1st and 7th Battalions were carried on armoured vehicles into battle against some German depth positions and overwhelmed them, capturing many prisoners and much equipment. The 5th Battalion then passed through and captured some high ground after crossing the River Dives. Such actions contributed to the major defeat of the enemy in the Falaise salient, and enabled the allies to advance rapidly to the Seine, Paris and the Channel ports. The Black Watch battalions occupied St Valéry during the advance, the town where the original 51st Highland Division had been captured four years earlier. They were also involved in the capture of Le Havre and Dunkirk, but caught up in late autumn with the leading troops on the Maas.

During the Winter months the three battalions of the regiment were in various positions in the low-lying country around the Nijmegen 'island'. Much of the countryside was flooded, and they fought in numerous actions to gain bridges, crossing places and to establish bridgeheads. The most notable success was at St Michelgestel, where the pioneers of the 7th Battalion laid a bridge so that the whole battalion group, and that of the 1st Battalion, crossed undetected by the Germans.

At the end of 1944 the 51st Highland Division was moved rapidly to assist the Americans fighting against the German offensive in the Ardennes. This danger was, however, averted, and The Black Watch joined in the advance on the Reichswald area of Germany. The leading battalions were the 1st and 7th, but the 5th Battalion became heavily involved in fighting against the enemy in Genepp. The Germans defended the Reichswald Forest stubbornly, but even the Siegfried Line defences could not withstand the unrelenting pressure of the allied advance. The 1st and 7th Battalions took part in particularly successful attacks on the line at Hekkens, despite the usual enemy's massive artillery fire.

When the assault over the Rhine was launched on 23/24 March the 1st and 7th were in the leading waves. The 1st Battalion was heavily engaged in taking the villages of Klein Esserden and Speldrop. The Germans counter-attacked with infantry and tanks, and for a time the enemy surrounded some of the

Cpl Allen and L/Cpl Ellis training at Takama battle camp, Guyana in the early 1970s. RHQ

forward elements. After much close-quarter fighting the highlanders held until the remainder of the battalion advanced to join them. The 5th Black Watch, arriving at 9pm, quickly occupied positions near Esserden, and during the following day they were ordered to go to the assistance of the Gordon Highlanders fighting for possession of Rees. By the time the 5th reached Rees and mounted their attack on the northern part, it was already dark. All through the night there was fierce fighting amongst the houses and streets of the town; the enemy had well-placed anti-tank guns so no British armour could assist The Black Watch. It took half the morning for the Germans to be cleared from all the houses.

During the next six weeks The Black Watch battalions were part of the rapid allied advance across north Germany. But they still had to fight against enemy positions in numerous actions on their way to the area of Bremen and Bremerhaven, which they reached by the time of the German surrender.

* * * * *

With the end of the war, the 2nd Battalion was stationed on the North-West Frontier area of India. Preparations were in hand for the independence of India and Pakistan, and The Black Watch had responsibility for maintaining the peace in Peshawar until the end of 1946. They left India finally in 1947, and the battalion was amalgamated with the 1st Battalion in Germany during the following year. The 2nd Battalion was re-formed again in 1951, and served in Germany and British Guiana before being disbanded once more in 1956.

The 1st Battalion, The Black Watch, joined the Commonwealth Brigade in Korea in July 1952. By that time the war had become static, but in August The Black Watch took up positions on the Hook feature. There, in November, they were attacked by the Chinese in great numbers, with heavy artillery cover. Although for a time a company position was partly over-run, the Chinese were repulsed. A second, and even stronger attack followed on 18 November, with two successive waves comprising many hundreds of the enemy. From their deep entrenchments A Company, under Major Angus Irwin, again fought the Chinese as they swarmed over the positions. The commanding officer, Lt-Col David Rose, called for artillery fire into the company area, and when re-inforced by another one-and-a-half companies and a tank, the Chinese were eventually forced to withdraw. Later in the war The Black Watch took part in months of extensive patrolling against the enemy.

The battalion spent two years in Kenya during the Mau Mau emergency. There the main task was to conduct patrols in the jungle around Thika, the Aberdare mountains and around Mount Kenya. The battalion scored some notable successes in an otherwise frustrating series of operations. In 1958 The Black Watch were stationed on Cyprus where, pending independence, the battalion was actively engaged in anti-terrorist operations. It returned to the island in 1966 as part of the UN peacekeeping force, but in carrying out their duties, the detachments were often caught between Greeks and Turks fighting each other.

The familiar pattern of service at home and abroad, interspersed with tours in Northern Ireland, has been the regiment's history in the 1970s and 1980s.

Edinburgh Castle guard present arms on the Esplanade, 1986. RHQ

CHAPTER 9
QUEEN'S OWN HIGHLANDERS
(Seaforth and Camerons)

In 1961 the Queen's Own Highlanders were formed on the amalgamation of the Seaforth Highlanders (Ross-shire Buffs. The Duke of Albany's) and The Queen's Own Cameron Highlanders. The former regiment was descended from the 72nd and 78th Highland Regiments amalgamated in the 1881 reorganisation, whilst the Camerons were the old 79th Regiment, whose royal prefix – Queen's Own – had been granted in 1873 personally by Queen Victoria, and was the only infantry regiment so honoured.

PART I
SEAFORTH HIGHLANDERS
(Ross-shire Buffs, The Duke of Albany's)

72ND DUKE OF ALBANY'S OWN HIGHLANDERS
1778–1881

In 1777 Kenneth MacKenzie, Earl of Seaforth offered to raise a regiment which, for the first seven years of its existence, was titled 78th Regiment of (Highland) Foot. It was re-numbered 72nd at the time when several other regiments of foot were disbanded. This was accepted and recruiting was conducted and chiefly in Mackenzie country; half the number were from the Earl's own estates.

The regiment was embodied at Elgin in May 1778 and although originally destined for service in America it spent three years on garrison duty in the Channel Islands, during which the French sent two expeditions to seize the islands. The first one in 1779 was successfully repulsed by the regiment, but in the second attack the French actually captured St Helier. Four companies, however, with the support of local Militia troops, then surrounded the enemy and forced them to surrender.

In 1782 the regiment reached India after a perilous sea voyage, during which many of the men died of disease. Nevertheless, the regiment was quickly sent to join the army campaigning against the French and their allies the rulers of Mysore, Hyder Ali and his son Tippoo Sahib. The first action in which the regiment took part was the battle of Arnee, only two months after its arrival. During the first part of 1783 the highlanders pursued the enemy forces and occupied the French port of Cuddalore, apart from the citadel itself. Before peace was declared in 1784 the regiment provided detachments which seized the two towns of Palacatcherry and Coimbatore. The regiment's service was further extended: drafts were received from a number of other regiments, and many original members who could have claimed their discharge volunteered to continue their service in India.

Previous page:
First day of the battle of the Somme. A roll call of the Seaforth Highlanders on the afternoon of 1 July 1916, near Beaumont Hamel. RHQ KOSB

In 1789 the army of Tipoo Sahib, who had succeeded his father, threatened the British-protected state of Travancore. Several forts were captured with the assistance of the 72nd, and in early 1791 the highlanders laid seige to Bangalore. On 21 March

'before midnight the order to assault was given, and the 72nd rushed forward towards the works. They were met by a heavy musket fire and made for a breach in the walls, with loud shouts the men flung themselves in. A powerful fire came down on them from the fort, but adjusting the scaling ladders, the highlanders mounted to the parapet, swarmed over and put the enemy to flight with the bayonet . . . with ringing cheers the ramparts were swept clear.'

Then in February 1792 the army marched on Seringapatam, Tippoo Sahib's capital. The 72nd Highlanders were on the left of the line in the initial attack and charged the outer works, forcing the enemy to retire across a branch of the River Cauvery. The 72nd then stormed an enemy encampment on open ground, forded a second river and, having charged the enemy nine times in all, captured one of the forts on the outer defences of the city. The regiment surprisingly had few casualties in this battle, which ended with a peace treaty . A year later the 72nd Highlanders were involved in the occupation of Pondicherry, an important French seaport.

In 1795 the 72nd joined a force sent to take the island of Ceylon from the Dutch, who by this time were allied to the French. The town of Trincomalee

Kenneth MacKenzie, Earl of Seaforth, who raised the 78th (later 72nd) Highlanders, 1778. From a painting by B. Douglas Hamilton, 1773. RHQ

SEAFORTH'S
HIGHLANDERS

To be forthwith raised for the DEFENCE of His Glorious Majesty KING GEORGE the Third, and the Preservation of our Happy Constitution in Church and State

All LADS of *TRUE HIGHLAND BLOOD* willing to shew their Loyalty and Spirit may repair to SEAFORTH, or the Major, ALEXANDER MACKENZIE of *Belmaduthy*; or the other Commanding Officers at Head Quarters at______________ where they will receive *HIGH BOUNTIES* and *SOLDIER-LIKE ENTERTAINMENT.*

The LADS of this Regiment will LIVE and DIE together;—as they cannot be DRAUGHTED into other Regiments, and must be reduced in a BODY in their OWN COUNTRY.

Now for a stroke at the *Monsieurs*, my Boys!
KING George for ever!

HUZZA!

A recruiting poster, 1793. The authorities often did not keep strict faith with the terms of enlistment.

was besieged and occupied, other Dutch settlements captured and Colombo was surrendered to the British after a few months of fighting.

The cadre returned to the United Kingdom in 1797, and the regiment was recruited up to strength over the next few years. A second battalion was raised in 1804 but never served overseas, being disbanded in 1816.

The 1st Battalion arrived in Cape Town Bay in early 1806, as part of the Highland Brigade. The light companies were first to go into action against the enemy, and the regiment skirmished against a party of Dutch troops before a general engagement took place. On 8 January the Highland Brigade advanced on the enemy position near the town.

'Arriving within a hundred and fifty yards of the opposing line, the highlanders levelled their muskets with steady aim, advancing and firing until within sixty yards of their adversaries, when Brigadier-General Furguson gave the word "charge". A loud British shout instantly rent the air, and the heroic highlanders closed with bayonets, upon their numerous adversaries, who instantly fled in dismay, pursued across the deep sands by the victorious Highland Brigade. The Dutch marksmen on the right flank with two guns, keeping up a constant fire, Captain Campbell of the 72nd was detached against them with his grenadier company . . . but they were removed with too much speed to be overtaken.'

The highlanders pursued the Dutch for three miles before their army disintegrated. A subsequent treaty ceded Cape Colony to the British Crown.

The 72nd Highlanders remained in Cape Town for a number of years, sending two expeditions to Mauritius and India. In 1809 the regiment was ordered to adopt the uniform of the infantry of the line, and highland dress was not restored until 1823. In this same year it was given the additional title of the Duke of Albany's Own Highlanders. On account of this royal connection, the regiment was allowed to wear trews of Royal Stuart tartan, Prince Charles Edward sett.

After a period in the United Kingdom the 72nd returned to South Africa. There the regiment took part in the war against the Kaffirs, providing detachments to protect colonial settlements against the marauding enemy tribesmen. This was an arduous campaign fought amongst the mountains and thorn-covered plains of Kaffraria in the eastern cape. The Kaffirs were subdued after many months of fighting.

* * * * *

The 72nd Highlanders were employed on garrison service between 1840 and 1855, and overseas tours included Gibraltar, Canada and the West Indies. They did not take part in the initial stages of the Crimean War, but joined the Highland Brigade at Sevastopol in June 1855. Apart from duties in the trenches, the regiment was sent for a time to support the Sardinian allies on the Tchernaya river. Then in September the final allied attack on Sevastopol began, but the first British attempt to storm the Redan was unsuccessful. The regiment was called forward to hold the front line during the night, and at dawn on 9 September advanced on the Redan only to discover that the Russians had withdrawn after destroying much of the fortress in a series of explosions. The British and French occupied Sevastopol until the peace was concluded in 1856.

Original uniforms of the 78th (later 72nd) Highlanders. From a watercolour by R. Simkin. RHQ

Drummer John Rennie, 72nd Highlanders. Photograph in the series taken in 1856 of 'Crimean Heroes'. IWM

The 72nd Highlanders were sent to India in early 1858 and took part in various engagements against the mutineers in the closing stages of the Mutiny. On one occasion they marched 74 miles in 110 hours. They were also with the force which attacked Kotah, crossing the River Chumbul by boat. The 72nd's column blew up a gate, entered the town and cleared the enemy from the ramparts in hand-to-hand combat. The other gates were forced and the town was swiftly occupied. After the Mutiny the regiment remained in India until 1866 and then returned to the sub-continent in 1871.

In 1878 the 72nd Highlanders joined the field force under General Sir Frederick Roberts assembled for the invasion of Afghanistan in the second Afghan War. With a column of Gurkhas and other native troops they moved across the border and advanced on the enemy holding wooded hills known as the Peiwar Kotal, which lay beside the route to Kabul.

'Across the summit or saddle of the steep ascent the enemy had thrown up a battery of field works, the fire of which could rake the whole pass. On either side of the Kotal, on two steep hills, were guns in battery, which could throw up a deadly cross-fire upon an ascending force. The troops of the Amir occupied the entire line of the upper hills for a distance of four miles, and at either extremity were guns in position to meet any flank attack that could be made, and lofty and more inaccessible hills covered their line of retreat.'

The 72nd and 5th Gurkhas conducted a silent night approach and climbed up the wooded scree, taking the enemy by surprise in two of their stockades covering the head of the pass. They were captured in a fierce fight by the two battalions, and the left flank of the Kotal was now in British hands. Two further attacks were launched by Roberts, and after three days of fighting, Peiwar Kotal was completely cleared of the enemy.

Remaining on the North-West Frontier during a temporary peace the 72nd Highlanders marched towards Kabul in the autumn of 1879, when operations were resumed by General Roberts. When a large body of the enemy, numbering about 15,000, appeared and made to seize a mountain gorge after turning back a charge by the 9th Lancers, the 72nd was ordered to head them off and save some guns.

'We lost no time,' said Capt Lauder of the regiment, 'in obeying the orders of our chief, reaching the gorge in a terrible state of heat and perspiration just four minutes ahead of the Afghans . . . the execution was terrible . . . their onward movement was completely checked.'

They were joined by a detachment of the 92nd Highlanders and from there were able to dominate the approach to Kabul. The battalion remained near the city for some weeks. In early December it was called upon to seize and hold a mountain gorge as a strong enemy force approached. Speed was essential, and when the highlanders arrived they were involved in the fiercest fighting. The gorge was successfully held and the enemy turned back.

Further hill fighting took place over a number of days and the enemy were discovered to be holding the Asmai Heights, which the highlanders were ordered to storm on 14 December. After a stiff climb under fire they swept over the enemy position bayonetting the defenders. Meanwhile, a very much larger force of Afghans, numbering some 20,000, approached and overwhelmed an outpost of the 72nd. The enemy then attempted to retake the Heights but were unsuccessful. Their numbers were increasing all the time in the area, and during the night of 23 December the Afghans mounted their largest attack of all. Miraculously

72nd Highlanders at the Relief of Kandahar, Afghanistan, Sept 1880. The British force marched 313 miles in 22 days. Chromolithograph by R. Simkin. NAM

they were defeated, chiefly by combined artillery and rifle-fire; and after dawn the cavalry pursued the retreating enemy.

The battalion remained in Afghanistan after the battle and in August 1880 it was sent to relieve Kandahar. The force reached the town in twenty-two days, a distance of 313 miles, and attacked the Afghans outside the town. In this battle the 72nd Highlanders fought a spirited flanking action. The enemy were defeated and on their withdrawal the war came quickly to an end.

In July 1881 the 72nd were linked with the 78th Highlanders and became the 1st Battalion, Seaforth Highlanders (Ross-shire Buffs). The additional title of 'The Duke of Albany's was added later in the year, and both battalions of the regiment adopted the Mackenzie of Seaforth kilt.

78TH HIGHLAND REGIMENT
The Ross-shire Buffs
1793–1881

Amongst the many offers to raise new regular regiments for overseas service on the outbreak of war with France in 1793, the first to be authorised in the Highlands was the 78th Regiment. Francis Humberston Mackenzie of Seaforth, a cousin of the Earl of Seaforth who had raised the 72nd (originally 78th) Regiment, was appointed the Lt-Col Commandant. On 10 July, the regiment was embodied at Fort George near Inverness, and by the autumn the 78th had moved to Guernsey to serve as garrison troops.

The following year the regiment joined the expeditionary force for service in the Netherlands and north Germany, a campaign, however, which achieved little military advantage. The 78th Highlanders first mounted a successful attack on the French artillery and infantry laying siege to Nijmegen. At Tuyl they repulsed a French force, and at Geldermalsen beat off a combined cavalry and infantry attack with overwhelming small-arms fire. In April 1795 the regiment returned to the United Kingdom.

A second battalion of the regiment was raised in 1794 by Alexander Mackenzie of Fairburn. This battalion was known as the Ross-shire Buffs, a title which was adopted subsequently by the whole regiment. The 2nd Battalion was sent to South Africa in 1795 as part of an expedition and, on landing, the troops occupied Simons Town when the local Dutch force withdrew. Subsequently the battalion attacked a strong Dutch position near Cape Town and forced the colonists to withdraw. When reinforced by a further three battalions, the British force was able to defeat the Dutch at Wynberg and compel the surrender of Cape Town. Nine months later the 1st Battalion of the 78th arrived in South Africa, and formed into a single battalion, the Ross-shire Buffs, sailed for India at the end of 1796.

The regiment remained in India on peacetime duties until 1803, when the campaign against the Mahrattas started.

In September, the Hon. Arthur Wellesley's army came into contact with the Mahrattas' huge force of cavalry and artillery, which severely outnumbered the British and native troops. Wellesley, showing his masterly *coup d'oeil* for ground and opportunity, ordered an attack on the enemy's infantry and artillery at Assaye, despite being vastly outnumbered. The enemy first attempted to outmanoeuvre the advancing front line, which included the 78th Highlanders. The regiment charged the last 150 yards after firing a deadly volley, whereupon the enemy infantry fled, leaving the guns to be taken at bayonet-point. The 74th Highlanders in the second line then came up in support and, when the British and allied native cavalry charged, the enemy's second line, was forced to withdraw.

A picquet of the 2nd Bn, 78th Highlanders, Ross-shire Buffs, Sicily 1806. In July the battalion fought in the battle of Maida on the Italian mainland. NAM

The 78th then had to repel several enemy counter-attacks:

> 'A desperate fight occurred, the enemy battling with great bravery attacked the 78th on all sides. Thrice the gleaming bayonets of the regiment had to wheel to a new front. Each time a hand-to-hand combat ensued and at moments a three-sided fire fell upon the highlanders.'

The Mahratta army was eventually broken and left the field in great disorder; the casualties of the regiment were surprisingly light. The victory proved decisive and the war ended soon after.

In 1811 the Ross-shire Buffs took part in an expedition to Java, a Dutch island held by the French. The British easily captured the capital Batavia, but the French retired to well-fortified positions at Cornelis. The grenadier company of the 78th was with the assault force which took some outer works in a dawn attack on 26 August. The remainder of the 78th took part in the main attack on the town and were under severe fire from enemy artillery and small arms. A detachment prevented the enemy from opening a dyke and flooding the approaches, and after the most determined close-quarter combat, the French were ejected from the town. The following month the regiment was present at the final battle of the campaign at Samarang.

The Ross-shire Buffs returned to Java in 1812 to fight against a confederation of native rulers. The British force reached Jakarta and mounted an attack on the town, which consisted of a labyrinth of buildings and walled enclosures dominated by the fortress of the Sultan. The flank and rifle companies of the 78th succeeded in overwhelming the enemy artillery, while the main party seized the northern and southern gates. The surrender of the fortress effectively marked the end of the war. The regiment remained in occupation until 1816, and reached the United Kingdom the following year.

* * * * *

A new second Battalion of the Ross-shire Buffs was raised in 1804 at Fort George by General Alexander Mackenzie Fraser. It was garrisoned in Gibraltar and Sicily until 1806, when it landed with a small force on the Italian mainland in order to expel the French from the Kingdom of Naples. After some initial skirmishing, the French were found to be in very strong positions in the hills near Maida. On 4 July both armies advanced on each other. The British musketry and artillery fire was more effective than the French, whose force of 7,000 was far in excess of the British and their Italian allies. The enemy directly in front of the Ross-shire Buffs withdrew, and the highlanders were ordered to halt while the battalions on each side conformed to the advance. The enemy lines were then broken up by the British musketry, and the 78th formed part of the pursuing force which followed the retreat. Notwithstanding this convincing victory, the British force returned to Sicily, disappointed in the failure of the local population to rise against the French occupation.

A piper and corporal of the 78th Highlanders, Ross-shire Buffs. Detail of G. H. Thomas's 'Sketches of British Soldiers', 1861. RHQ

In 1807 the 2nd Battalion, the Ross-shire Buffs, left Sicily for Alexandria. The French had formed an alliance with the Turks, and a force of the enemy held the fort at Rosetta near the city. The 78th provided a strong detachment which, in a dawn attack, captured some enemy guns threatening the British camp. Other detachments which included men of the 78th were attacked by strong enemy forces at El Hamet and, despite forming squares, were overwhelmed. More than 160 were killed and the few surviving wounded taken prisoner. The expedition to Egypt was soon abandoned and the remainder of the regiment returned to Britain.

Although still under strength the 2nd Battalion joined the expedition to Walcheren in 1809. Due to fever the British force achieved little military advantage in the few months' campaign. The battalion returned to the Continent five years later, still under strength, and fought in one notable engagement. The highlanders were attacked by four French battalions at Merxem near Antwerp. After firing volleys with good effect, the 78th charged at the French lines, forcing them to retreat. The battalion remained in the Low Countries until 1816 and subsequently amalgamated with the 1st Battalion.

* * * * *

The Ross-shire Buffs spent the next thirty-nine years in garrison duties at home and abroad, including India, Ceylon and Aden. In early 1857 they joined a punitive expedition to Persia. In the highlanders' first battle at Kooshab the enemy were convincingly defeated, but they took up strongly defended positions at Mohomrah guarding the river junction. While ships of the Royal Navy engaged the enemy batteries the 78th Highlanders were landed with other battalions nearby, but when the British advanced towards the numerically superior Persians, they withdrew in great haste. As the purpose of the expedition had now been accomplished, the force returned to India, where the Mutiny had just begun.

The Ross-shire Buffs' first task was to assist in the formal disarming of some sepoy battalions. Three skirmishes were then fought against the mutineers. In mid-July the regiment, with Sir Henry Havelock's force, met the main force of the mutineers under Nana Sahib holding a village seven miles from Cawnpore, two days after the horrifying massacre of the European inhabitants.

'On they came,' wrote G. M. Trevelyan of the attack, 'the unconquerable British infantry. The grape was flying thick and true. Files rolled over. Men stumbled and recovered themselves, and went on for a while, and then turned and hobbled to the rear. As the last volley cut the air overhead, our soldiers raised a mighty shout, and rushed forward, and then every rebel thought only of himself.'

Ten days later the force had great difficulty in capturing Bashiratganj from the enemy, and reinforcements necessary for the first relief of Lucknow did not arrive until September.

Pipers of the 78th Highlanders, Ross-shire Buffs photographed at Gibraltar, 1865. NAM

The mutineers were ejected from the Alam Bagh palace three miles from the city but they held most of Lucknow, apart from the besieged Residency, in very great strength. When the attack on the city started the mutineers' artillery and small arms fire proved highly effective against the assaulting troops. But

'the British drove the foe across numerous gardens until the canal was reached. They crossed by a bridge and the troops entered the streets and fought forward against a fusillade of fire from the houses. A big force of the enemy hurled itself on the 78th. Hastings of the Regiment sprang to the front, there was a highland rush, and the enemy fled. Again they came and now with guns, and Webster of the 78th called out "who's for the guns?" Again the highlanders rushed, Webster cleaved the gunners right and left, and the guns were taken.'

The 78th were for a time cut off, but fought their way through until they could rejoin the main force on the outskirts of the town. For two days the regiment and other relieving troops fought through the streets and enclosures of the city. Then they mounted a dawn attack on the Kaiser Bagh, the enemy's strongest position, which was successful. The losses of the regiment were 122, more than a quarter of its strength, and the heaviest of Havelock's force, but

Both the 72nd and 78th Highlanders served in the second Afghan War. The 78th Ross-shire Buffs' encampment, 1879. They remained in India for 18 years and spent much of the time on active service on the North-West Frontier. NAM

the regiment were awarded six VCs. Once inside the Residency, the relieving force had to remain to defend it until the second relief expedition was mounted in November. On abandoning the Residence the 78th were ordered to defend the Alam Bagh, and there they remained until Sir Colin Campbell's final expedition succeeded in capturing the city in March 1858. The regiment took part in subsequent operations, notably the capture of Bareilly, and in May 1859 embarked for Scotland.

The 78th Ross-shire Buffs spent the years after the Mutiny in garrison duties in the United Kingdom, Gibraltar and Canada. They returned to India in 1879 and took part in the Afghan War, mainly on guard and picquet duties. In 1881 they became the 2nd Battalion, Seaforth Highlanders.

SEAFORTH HIGHLANDERS

1881–1913

The 1st Battalion, Seaforth Highlanders, left India for Egypt in 1882 to join other British forces sent to quell the revolt of the Egyptian army. The Seaforth were first in action in August at Shaluf on the Sweetwater Canal, and the following month took part in the battle of Tel-El-Kebir.

The army set off on a silent night march on 13 September and as dawn approached the enemy trenches. The Egyptians opened fired with rifles and artillery, and the British charged with the bayonet. The Seaforth Highlanders captured a battery of guns and within minutes the battle was over. The highlanders marched immediately in pursuit of the enemy and reached Zag-a-Zig in the evening. The battle brought the campaign to a successful conclusion and the 1st Battalion returned to England shortly afterwards.

The 2nd Battalion serving in India joined the Hazara or Black mountain expedition on the North-West Frontier in 1888. The purpose was the punishment of two treacherous tribes, the Asakis and Hassanzais, in revolt against British rule. The battalion was divided between two columns which marched through the mountainous country for two

Soldiers of the 1st Bn, Seaforth Highlanders in various forms of dress, 1887. RHQ

months attacking enemy strong points and villages, including the most heavily defended position at Kotkai. A second Hazara expedition had to be mounted in 1891 in which the Seaforth Highlanders again participated. Thereafter the tribes accepted British authority.

Four years later the 2nd Seaforth formed part of a brigade sent to relieve Chitral, which had been attacked by rebel tribesmen. This involved a hard march, and the fort was successfully relieved. The Seaforth Highlanders, however, were not involved in much fighting during this campaign, and in 1897 they returned to the United Kingdom.

* * * * *

The 1st Battalion went to Crete in 1896 and two years later embarked for Egypt. The Seaforth Highlanders immediately on arrival joined in the expedition for the conquest of the Sudan under General Kitchener. The Anglo-Egyptian force travelled by a variety of means south to meet the enemy. Once they had been located on the Atbara river, 200 miles from Khartoum, the British advanced by night and attacked the dervishes' Zariba on the morning of 8 April. The 1st Cameron Highlanders were in the lead, deployed in line, and firing on the move, then the Seaforth in column passed through them on reaching

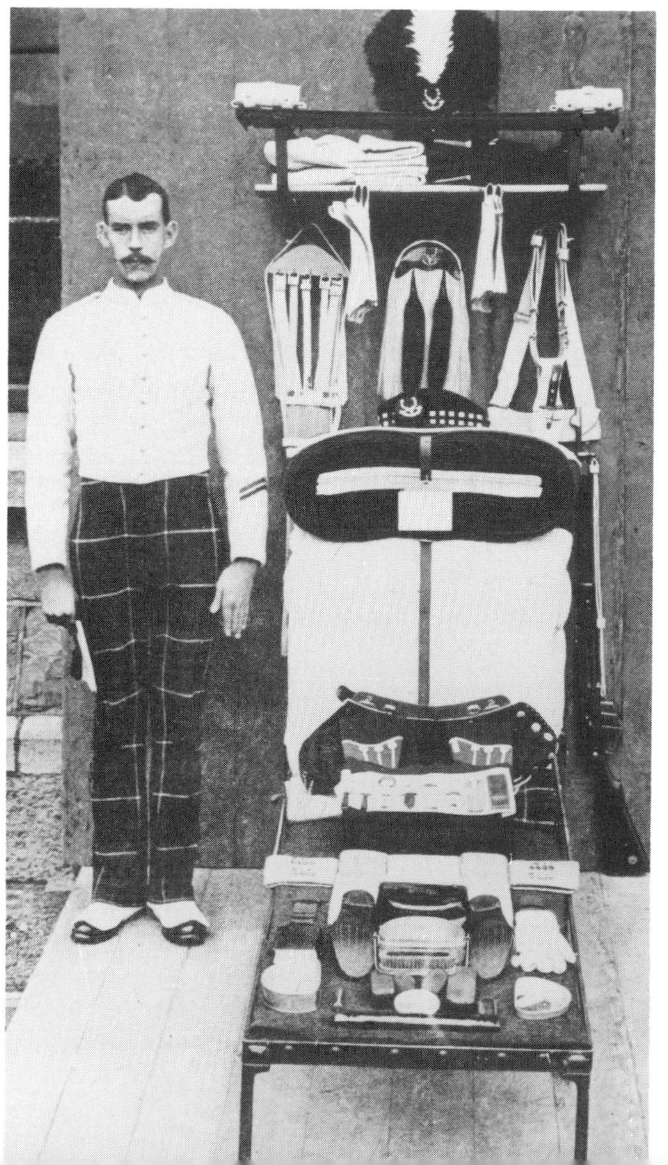

A Seaforth Highlander in 'undress uniform' sets out his kit for inspection, 1896. NAM

the enemy defences. There was considerable confusion in the enemy camp, and the highlanders and other troops fought the dervishes in furious hand-to-hand combat. The enemy were soon overwhelmed and the battle forced the enemy to withdraw gradually to the main position at Omdurman.

Four months later the British reached Omdurman and were attacked by a huge force of the enemy. For the Seaforth Highlanders and other infantry battalions this was a battle involving long-range rifle fire, which proved extremely effective, and contributed to a British victory. Khartoum was later occupied, and the battalion returned to garrison duties in Egypt until 1903.

The 2nd Seaforth Highlanders embarked for duty in South Africa in October 1899 at the start of the second Boer War. On arrival they moved up country and reached the Modder river in early December, where they joined the Highland Brigade. The Boers were besieging Kimberley at the time, and the Boers held Magersfontein Hill. During the night approach march

'Heavy clouds rolled up, burst in peals of thunder, and drenched the Highland Brigade with a torrent of rain. Flashes of lightning illuminated the darkness . . . and men stumbled forward in the darkness which followed and some direction was lost . . . Every man knew what depended on him, for far ahead the Kimberley searchlight cut into the black night . . . It was the mute call of Kimberley.'

But it was not to prove a repeat of Tel-El-Kebir and, as dawn broke, the enemy brought down highly effective fire on the brigade. As the highlanders approached the hill British artillery fire was erroneously directed onto them causing many casualties, and there was

Regimental tailors of the 2nd Bn, Seaforth Highlanders, Dover 1898. RHQ

much confusion. The British were unable to advance close enough to the hill in order to capture it, and the highlanders lay in the open for much of the day until they withdrew to await reinforcements. The battle was one of three disastrous defeats in 'Black week'.

There were several small engagements which involved the battalion during January 1900, and in February it moved with the brigade towards Paardeburg on the Modder River. There the Boers had taken up a strong defensive position. Marching across the open veldt the Seaforth Highlanders were on the left of the brigade line, but the enemy's rifle fire proved too dangerous for the highlanders to approach the

Seaforth and Cameron Highlanders bury their dead after the successful battle of Atbara during the Sudan War, 1898. NAM

positions. There followed a period of long-range shooting between the two armies but the British gradually extended their trenches while, at the same time, surrounding the enemy. The Boers, commanded by General Cronje, held for several days but had to surrender.

The Highland Brigade then marched on Bloemfontein and Heilbron. There were several engagements with the Boers, the most notable for the battalion was at Roodeport when the enemy threatened to surround the column. In July the battalion first took part in the capture of the pass at Retiefs Nek held by General Prinsloo: then the Seaforth Highlanders carried out a successful flanking movement, and the enemy were forced to surrender. Succeeding months were spent by the battalion on the march through the Orange Free State, fighting several more engagements against the enemy.

During the war, reinforcement drafts and two mounted companies were sent from Egypt to South Africa by the 1st Seaforth Highlanders, and the volunteer battalions provided three service companies. At the same time the 3rd Militia Battalion was embodied for service in Egypt, and was stationed there with the 1st Battalion. During 1901 the Seaforth Highlanders serving in South Africa were occupied in more static duties than hitherto, guarding lines of communication and the blockhouse system, as the British Army gradually extended its control until peace was agreed.

* * * * *

The 1st Battalion served in India from 1903, and in 1908 were on active service on the North-West Frontier. Two expeditions were mounted during the battalion's tour, the first against the Afridis and the second against the Mohmands. Both campaigns involved marching through particularly difficult terrain and fighting an elusive enemy.

SEAFORTH HIGHLANDERS
1914–1938

On the outbreak of war the 2nd Battalion, Seaforth Highlanders, joined the British Expeditionary Force when it was sent to France, and reached a position south-east of Mons on 25 August. The battalion was only there for a few hours before the Germans began shelling its positions, and it was ordered to withdraw that same night.

> 'I shall never forget that march,' wrote Major Campion, 'we had not grown accustomed to the sights and sounds of war, which at the commencement of a campaign impress themselves very acutely on the memory. All around our right flank were burning villages . . . We marched all night, passing through Ligny in the early hours of the morning . . . At daybreak we were making arrangements for breakfast when a furious machine-gun fire opened on two regiments of our brigade who were close by. Apparently all night we must have been moving in close proximity to the enemy.'

During the retreat of the BEF from Mons the battalion marched 134 miles in the next 11 days. On 5 September the 2nd Seaforth reached Chevry at the end of the retreat, and spent three weeks fighting for various positions on the Marne.

The battalion was moved subsequently to the new British sector on the north of the allied line, and in October captured the village of Meteren. After that action the battalion spent the rest of the winter in the trenches, as the war became one of static defence. In the same month the 1st Battalion, Seaforth Highlanders, moved to France with the Indian Expeditionary Force. It also manned trenches in a number of sectors during the winter, including Neuve Chapelle and Festubert. In December the Seaforth Highlanders withstood a very strong attack at Givenchy, and sustained heavy casualties.

The first Territorial battalion of the regiment to be sent to France was the 4th. It joined the same Indian brigade as the 1st Battalion in December 1914, and both were involved in the corps attack on the Germans at Neuve Chapelle in March 1915. The attack was launched after an artillery bombardment, and the 1st Battalion was committed from the start, quickly overrunning some enemy positions including the village itself. The two battalions held their captured trenches during the first night, but heavy enemy artillery on the following day caused numerous casualties. After some confusion of orders, the British and Indian troops had to withdraw. During two days of battle the 4th Battalion had lost over 150 casualties. Two months later the same two battalions carried out an attack on Aubers Ridge: again little was gained, and heavy enemy fire forced a general withdrawal to the original line of trenches. In this action the two battalions sustained more than 700 casualties between them.

The 2nd Seaforth Highlanders took part in the second battle of Ypres. In an attack against strong German opposition at St Julien, on 25 April, the highlanders lost 348 casualties, and a week later they suffered more casualties in a German gas attack, but successfully repulsed the enemy. Later in the month they were called from reserve to counter-

Seaforth cobblers at work, France, July 1916. IWM

attack the Germans who had captured some trenches close to Ypres. This was accomplished, but during a whole month of fighting the battalion lost more than 1,000 casualties, many of them being newly drafted. The battalion was moved to the Arras-Albert sector, a somewhat quieter part of the front, and remained there until the Spring of 1916.

Two more Territorial battalions of the regiment, the 5th and 6th, arrived in France in late April 1915. They were posted in May to positions near La Bassée, and in June they took part in an attack on Festubert. The 5th Battalion advanced on the German line while the 6th Battalion gave covering fire from the front-line trenches. Both were shelled heavily by the Germans and many casualties were suffered, particularly by the 6th.

During the remainder of 1915 the 4th Battalion spent part of the time in the Loos sector, but did not take an active part in the battle of Loos itself. The 5th and 6th Battalions were in the trenches in the Laventine sector until August 1915, but then moved to the area of Albert, where they remained until the end of the year.

Meanwhile three new army battalions of the Seaforth Highlanders had reached France between May and July 1915, the 7th, 8th and 9th (Pioneer) Battalions, and in September all three were sent to the Loos sector. On 25 September the two service battalions led their brigades into the attack, the 7th reaching the line of the Hohenzollern Redoubt, and cleared the enemy. The battalions held this line, were relieved for a time, and then returned as a reinforcement. During the three days of battle two-thirds of the battalion were killed or wounded, and the 8th Seaforth Highlanders, fighting for Hill 70 near the village of Loos, suffered over 700 casualties. Meanwhile the 9th Battalion constructed a vital trench system during the battle whilst being under fire much of the time. The 1st Seaforth in the same sector gave continuous fire support from their front-line positions and also suffered many casualties from enemy artillery fire.

The battle of the Somme lasted from 1 July 1916 for over four months, and all battalions of the Seaforth Highlanders took part, with the exception of the 1st Battalion. The 2nd Battalion was first in action, and fought for the village of Beaumont Hamel, losing 500 casualties on the first day. In mid-July the 7th Battalion had nearly as many casualties when it attacked Longueval and Delville Wood with considerable success. The 5th and 6th joined the Somme offensive in late July, and the 8th Battalion took part in the intense fighting around the Switch line in mid-August. Later in the battle the 4th, 5th

Jocks of the 8th Seaforth Highlanders man the front-line trench in the featureless waste near Martinpuich, Somme sector, Aug 1916. IWM

and 6th Battalions of the 51st Highland Division fought in the area of High Wood, where the British front line had been established very close to that of the Germans, and consequently there was much close-quarter action.

In October the 5th and 6th Battalions took part in a major attack on Beaumont Hamel, which the Germans held in great strength. The village had been made into a strongpoint with entanglements, concrete emplacements, dugouts, tunnels and redoubts. The 5th Seaforth were the leading battalion.

'Our artillery,' wrote Captain D. Sutherland, 'opened a terrific barrage fire on the German front line, and over went the infantry; not doubling, not even walking, but wading knee-deep, and sometimes waist-deep, through the morass of sticky mud and water . . . the final objective being a German trench line 200 yards east of the village. The enemy's machine-gun fire and uncut wire in the centre held up the advance for a time, so that the barrage went too far ahead while, owing to the dense fog, direction was lost and the attack split up into small parties. Yet in spite of these difficulties, the first German line was carried easily.'

The battalion thus captured the first line and, after losing many casualties, carried the second and third lines, taking over 600 German prisoners. The remnants of the battalion then resisted several counter-attacks until relieved. The 6th Seaforth Highlanders also successfully captured their objectives but they, too, had numerous casualties. The 5th Seaforth returned to the village a few days later as reinforcements to block further German counter-attacks.

* * * * *

In the meantime, the 1st Battalion had been fighting in Mesopotamia. The task of the mainly Indian Army formations involved in this theatre was to relieve the original expeditionary force besieged at Kut-el-Amara. The Seaforth Highlanders were in action against the Turks within a few days of arrival in December 1915, and the battalion and its division suffered very high casualties. Consequently, little progress could be made towards Kut. Between February and July 1916 the Seaforth Highlanders and the 2nd Black Watch were amalgamated to form 'The Highland Battalion'.

In April the Highland Battalion attacked the Turks at Sannaiyat without success. Returning to the attack some days later, the Turkish position was breached but could not be held. The battalion's casualties were again heavy, and it remained in the trenches, being re-formed as its two original battalions when reinforcements arrived. Kut-El-Amara meanwhile had fallen to the Turks, and it was not until February 1917 that the British and Indian troops broke through the Sannaiyat positions.

'At zero hour,' wrote Captain Lynden Bell, 'the (artillery) storm broke. When nine of the ten minutes had passed, the first line went over. It was immediately followed by the second and third, which merged with it before it had gone 30 yards . . . The Turkish front line . . . no longer bore any resemblance to a trench. In many places it had been blown twelve to fifteen feet wide. The objective – the second line trench – . . . unwittingly passed over it and continued their advance towards the third line, till they reached an old irrigation ditch . . . there they dug in.'

The battle was thus very confused, but the Seaforth and other battalions held their positions through the evening and night, and discovered at dawn the enemy had withdrawn. The force then marched past Kut towards Baghdad, and found the city already evacuated by the Turks. During March and April, the 1st Seaforth advanced north and fought three further actions, but in capturing the town of Istabulat, the battalion lost over 150 casualties. The 1st Seaforth remained in Mesopotamia until the end of the year and reached Egypt in January 1918. Joining the Palestine campaign, the battalion's chief engagement was at Beit Lid in September.

Among the training and home duty battalions of the regiment, the 1st Garrison Battalion, the Seaforth Highlanders had been formed in 1916. In August it was sent to Salonika for garrison duties, and served in the city for some months, but was then sent to the Struma sector. Although that part of the

Bulgarian front was fairly quiet, the battalion remained on trench duties for the next eighteen months until the armistice. It remained in Greece until 1919 when it was disbanded.

* * * * *

In the spring of 1917 three Scottish divisons took part in the Arras offensive on the Western front. Five of the Seaforth battalions, the 2nd, 4th, 5th, 6th and 7th, took part in the initial attack on 9 April, and all seized their objectives. That of the 2nd Battalion marked an advance of four-and-a-half miles, and the 8th Seaforth were in reserve at first, but mounted a highly successful attack at Guémappe on 23 April. The 9th Battalion was also engaged in the fighting, as well as carrying out their pioneer tasks. The 2nd Battalion, however, suffered very heavy casualties on 11 April at Roeux on the River Scarpe. In early May it carried out two further attacks, and by this time virtually all the battalion's officers had been killed or wounded. At the same time the 4th and 5th Seaforth both held positions at Roeux against very heavy counter-attacks.

In July 1917 the third battle of Ypres began. The 4th, 5th and 6th Battalions were all involved in the first attack.

'At 3.50am on 31 July, the bombardment was let loose, guns of every calibre, in their tens of thousands . . . out scrambled the first wave of D Company,' wrote Captain A. H. Macdonald of the 6th Battalion, 'and their direction, in spite of the utter darkness, was infallible . . . The difficulties were appalling. Everywhere were deep water-filled craters, unseen and treacherous: cruel strands of half-broken barbed wire – loosely coiled – and masses of heaped entanglements lay in the path . . . One platoon had been sent out to capture "Fysh Farm". Heavy machine-gun fire caught and halted them . . . orders were signalled successfully – it was still pitch-dark, and the noise was deafening . . . flanking parties ran together and presented themselves at the rear of the stronghold. Its occupants were outwitted and most of them surrendered willingly.'

Other objectives were captured in similar fashion all along the line.

Nearby the 5th Seaforth captured 700 Germans in an attack. The 7th was not involved in the battle, but the 8th Seaforth attacked the enemy line on the Passchendaele Ridge, gaining over a mile of territory. More ground was taken by the battalion the following month, but the casualties were very heavy in both operations. In September the 4th was involved in a divisional attack, and advanced the line by 1,000 yards. The 2nd Seaforth took part in another attack in October on the Passchendaele Ridge and they suffered 457 casualties in the action. The 7th Battalion also fought in the same area, but the battle by this time had achieved little overall advance, despite the most determined fighting during particularly bad weather.

The three Seaforth battalions of the 51st Division – the 4th, 5th and 6th – all took part in the battle of Cambrai on 20 November 1917. Formed up behind the tanks, the highlanders advanced successfully through several German positions. 152 brigade with

Seaforth Highlanders assist French peasants 'tattie howking', Amiens road, Oct 1916. IWM

A section of the 6th Seaforth clear a German dugout on 'Greenland Hill' near the notorious chemical works at Roeux, Arras sector, Aug 1918. IWM

the 5th and 6th Battalions penetrated the heavily fortified Hindenberg Line and captured Ribecourt and Flesquières, taking 600 prisoners, but the 4th suffered heavy casualties in the battle.

The great German offensive began on 21 March 1918, and the strongest attack was in the sector where the 7th and 8th Seaforth Highlanders were holding the line. The 7th Battalion fought for four days and nights, and at times was almost surrounded by the advancing Germans. The 9th succeeded in holding its line at St Pierre Vaast Wood and Hardicourt for a considerable time, inflicting severe casualties on the enemy. The 8th Battalion similarly, held on tenaciously to its positions on the River Scarpe. The 2nd Battalion in the Arras sector, fought off the enemy attack for as long as possible before withdrawing, moving to positions at La Bassée for a time. The 7th Battalion moved to the Ypres and successfully counter-attacked the enemy at Wytschaete.

The 4th and 6th Seaforth Highlanders meanwhile, held their part of line at Beaumont-Morchies during the first part of the German offensive, where they made a most remarkable stand against the heaviest of odds. The 5th Battalion similarly held their front on the Bapaume-Cambrai road for six days. Overall the Germans were successful in forcing the British line back for some miles, but the cost of their casualties was excessive, and it left them little in reserve for the subsequent allied counter-offensive.

In July 1918 the 8th Battalion took part in a brilliantly successful attack at Buzancy on the Marne, in support of the French. The 4th, 5th and 6th Battalions were less fortunate in their support of the French on the River Ardre, but they helped in turning back a strong German counter-offensive. The 5th Battalion, after moving sector in August, successfully captured German positions at Roeux, which had been the scene of bitter fighting a year before.

In the autumn of 1918 the 4th, 5th and 6th Seaforth Highlanders held positions near Cambrai and Quéant, while the 7th and 9th were in the Ypres sector and the 8th at Loos. During the final allied advance, the 5th Seaforth Highlanders carried out a particularly effective attack on Thun St Martin, but their casualties were more than 400. The 4th and 6th reached the area of Valenciennes by the end of the month, and in the hard fighting and rapid movement they each suffered over 300 casualties. The 7th Seaforth fought in a number of actions as they advanced and, by the time they had reached Harlebecke, they had lost 331 casualties. The 2nd, 8th and 9th Battalions also took part in the rapid advance during the last few weeks of the war.

* * * * *

After the war the 1st Battalion, Seaforth Highlanders, returned home, and the 2nd Battalion was stationed in India. The 1st took part in strike duties in 1921 and were sent to Dublin to assist in maintaining the peace during the final period before home rule. In 1920 the prefix 'The' was added to the title, which was retained until 1951.

For some years the 2nd Seaforth Highlanders carried out peacetime duties in India, but in August 1930 they moved to the North-West Frontier. There they occupied positions to deter Afridi tribesmen from threatening Peshawar. In October The Seaforth Highlanders' force crossed the frontier into Afghanistan and set up a base to disperse the dissidents in the border area. Once this was achieved the force withdrew. From 1932 to 1934 the 2nd Battalion was stationed in Palestine, and was joined by the 1st Battalion before returning home.

In 1935 the 1st Seaforth was sent to Mersa Matruh in western Egypt to prevent any possible incursion by Italian troops already occupying Libya. The following year the battalion returned to Palestine, where the trouble between Arab and Jews was becoming increasingly dangerous. In carrying out peacekeeping duties The Seaforth Highlanders suffered several casualties. Between 1937 and 1938 the battalion served in Hong Kong and Shanghai where their task was to guard British interests. The Japanese army had invaded and occupied much of China in 1937, and there was consequently a state of increased tension between Britain and Japan.

From a position on 'Greenland Hill', captured by the 51st Highland Division, a daylight patrol of the 6th Seaforth Highlanders moves forward during the battle of the Scarpe, Arras sector, 29 Aug 1918. IWM

SEAFORTH HIGHLANDERS
1939–61

The 2nd Battalion went to France immediately with the British Expeditionary Force in September 1939, and the 4th and 6th Battalions in the 51st Highland Division reached France in January 1940. When the Germans invaded Belgium in May 1940, the 2nd and 4th Battalions were in the area of Lille. The 6th Battalion, now in the 5th Division, moved first eastwards across Belgium but was then temporarily withdrawn to defend positions on the River Scarpe. Subsequently the 6th Seaforth Highlanders were ordered to take up positions near Ypres on the extreme left of the British line. The battalion then conducted a fighting withdrawal in close contact with the enemy over several days, and those who survived embarked at Dunkirk on 1 June.

The 2nd and 4th Battalions meanwhile were in support of the French holding the Maginot Line in the Saar region. They maintained contact with the advancing Germans, but were withdrawn from action. Returning to fight alongside the French on the Somme the 4th Seaforth was the spearhead battalion of an attack near Abbeville on heavily-defended German positions. They suffered many casualties and were again ordered to withdraw.

The 51st Highland Division was now isolated from the BEF, the remnants of which were embarking at Dunkirk, and The Seaforth Highlanders fought on with great determination. During the night of 8/9 June the 4th Seaforth took up positions covering the River Béthune, south-east of Dieppe. They dug in during the day as other troops passed over the river. During the morning of 10 June the enemy attempted to capture a bridging site by means of a ruse, but machine-gun fire dispersed them. The Seaforth were attacked on other parts of the front, and the fighting grew intense as the Germans attempted to infiltrate across the river. By the evening the battalion was still successfully holding its area and calling down accurate artillery fire against the enemy. However, the whole front was by now untenable and The Seaforth Highlanders were ordered to abandon their positions and move back towards Dieppe, and thence to St Valéry-en-Caux, where most of the Division was encircled. Under orders from their commander Major General Fortune, the 51st Highland Division surrendered to the enemy on 12 June. Most of the survivors spent the war years in captivity, but a new 2nd Battalion was formed for a re-constituted 51st Highland Division in the United Kingdom.

* * * * *

The 1st Battalion, The Seaforth Highlanders, continued to guard the treaty line in Shanghai until 1940. From August until February 1941 the battalion served in Singapore, and then moved to Agra, in India. For several months in 1942 The Seaforth Highlanders were on active service on the Indian border, operating from bases at Kohima and Imphal. This involved constant patrolling, and during the withdrawal they assisted in covering the British and Indian troops as they crossed the border from Burma.

In the same year the 6th Battalion embarked for the campaign against the Vichy French forces in Madagascar. Despite some delay, once the assault troops seized the beach-head, the 6th Battalion and other battalions of 17 Brigade advanced twenty miles inland across the northern tip of the island. They attacked the enemy by night on 6 May at Antsirane, captured the town, and went on to clear other enemy outposts in the area. On the conclusion of the fighting, The Seaforth Highlanders remained in Madagascar for a few months and then proceeded to India. Later in 1942 they moved to Basra in Iraq and thence to Persia to counter a possible German invasion from occupied Russia. During the winter the 6th Seaforth were stationed in Teheran, and were involved in crowd control and other internal security duties before leaving for to Egypt.

Meanwhile, in August 1942 the 2nd and 5th Battalions, The Seaforth Highlanders, had embarked for Egypt with the 51st Highland Division. They were moved to the front at El Alamein. At the start of the battle on 23 October the 2nd were held in reserve, while 5th Battalion established the divisional start line. On 24 October the 2nd Seaforth carried out an attack on a strong German position to establish a bridge-head on the western side of a minefield for the armour to pass through. The battalion held this crucial position for thirty-six hours.

'Operation Supercharge', the breakout from the El Alamein battleground, began on 2 November and involved both battalions. The 5th Seaforth was the left forward battalion and the 2nd Seaforth was in the second wave behind them. An artillery barrage of thousands of guns opened up ahead of the advancing troops. Sometimes in the confusion, blinding dust and dark, the highlanders walked into the exploding shell fire, as well as being met by the machine-gun fire from the enemy: but enemy infantry and tanks in dug-in positions were overwhelmed and the advance progressed some thousands of yards. At dawn a tank battle started in the Seaforth area and the infantry remained dug-in during the day as the armour passed back and forth. During the second night the highlanders were subjected to artillery fire, and at dawn the tank battle resumed; this time the break-through was successful and the two Seaforth battalions continued the advance.

As the pursuit of the German Afrika Corps progressed at great speed, The Seaforth Highlanders were often in action during the next weeks. In January 1943 the 51st Highland Division carried out an attack at Corradini against a major German position. The 5th assaulted from the front while the 2nd attacked the enemy's flank with great effect. Two days later Tripoli fell and was occupied by the division. The advance continued, and the battalions had to hold positions against the German counter-attacks on the Mareth Line while other formations outflanked the enemy. At the beginning of April the Germans holding the Roumana Ridge and Wadi Akarit imposed a further serious delay on the allies. The 5th Seaforth were in the lead in the attack on the Roumana objective supported by the 2nd Battalion, and both battalions then held the captured positions during a heavy German counter-attack. The following month the Germans and Italians were finally cleared from North Africa and preparations for the asault on Sicily began.

in a battle in the region of the Simento River. The 2nd and 5th Battalions were next engaged in the fighting for the Sferro Hills, which were captured during a night attack. When the Germans counter-attacked, The Seaforth Highlanders held for several hours until the enemy withdrew. The 6th Battalion was later involved in the final capture of Catania. The whole of Sicily was in allied hands by mid-August, and the 51st Highland Division, with the 2nd and 5th Battalions, returned direct to England.

The 6th Battalion, The Seaforth Highlanders, remained to take part in the allied invasion of Italy on 3 September. Landing near Reggio the opposition was at first very light, so the advance northwards was rapid. The allied line was consolidated quickly and in October The Seaforth Highlanders moved across, towards the eastern coast of Italy, at Foggia. The

Jocks of the 2nd Seaforth Highlanders dash forward during a 're-enactment' of an attack on the Mareth Line in Mar 1943. The 5th Seaforth also served in the North African campaign with the 51st Highland Division. IWM

On 10 July 1943 the 6th Seaforth Highlanders landed in Sicily and immediately were involved in heavy fighting, actively assisting in the capture of Syracuse on the evening of the same day. The 2nd and 5th Battalions also landed, but at first were held in reserve. On 14 July they met with fierce resistance at Francofonte and, during a thirty-six hour battle, the 5th Battalion mounted several attacks on German positions, which were eventually captured by the 2nd Battalion. Further strong resistance by the Germans at Gerbini Airfield was dealt with by the 2nd Battalion, while the 6th Battalion was heavily involved

Germans were carrying out a fighting withdrawal, and the battalion met fierce resistance in the mountains at Isernia, on the Sangro River and at Ortona near the Adriatic.

In January 1944 The Seaforth Highlanders were then moved into the western part of the front, where preparations to take the Gustav Line were under way, and this involved intensive training for assault river crossings. On 17 January the battalion moved to a start point for a silent night crossing of the Garigliano, near to its mouth and where it was some 100 yards wide. The Seaforth first had to move their

After this battle the 6th Seaforth was moved to a reserve area, only to be subsequently hurried forward in February to assist US troops to hold the Anzio beach-head. The Germans carried out several determined counter-attacks on the part of the line held by the battalion, but they were repelled successfully, and the battalion took part in the advance on Rome. Soon after the 6th Seaforth was withdrawn to Egypt.

* * * * *

In the meantime, the 1st Battalion, The Seaforth Highlanders, had been conducting patrol operations on the north-east frontier of India and during 1943–4 continued, in conjuction with Chindit operations deep inside Burma, in the area of the Chindwin

Pipers of the 6th Seaforth Highlanders play in the early morning near the River Garigliano. The battalion fought in a major engagement to seize a bridge-head in mid-Jan 1944. IWM

A piper leads a section of the 7th Seaforth Highlanders near Mesnil Patry, Normandy, 25 June 1944. IWM

boats, undetected, to the water's edge, but several enemy anti-personnel mines went off and the Germans started firing with machine guns and mortars across the river. D Company managed to get across by paddling hard and then moved up the river bank, dealing with several enemy positions. A Company also succeeded in crossing, but C Company had to be ferried across by another battalion. B Company, coming in from the seaward side was out of contact, and two of its platoons were missing for some time. At dawn the Germans, realising that a firm bridge-head had been established, counter-attacked with infantry and armour. A fierce battle continued for several hours and The Seaforth Highlanders suffered numerous casualties, two of the companies being all but encircled. Reinforcements came up, however, and within twenty-four hours a three-mile bridgehead had been established.

River. The enemy, however, began their invasion of India in April 1944. The 1st Seaforth was sent into the hills west of Imphal to attack the Japanese, who were fast approaching the towns of Imphal and Kohima on the Ukhrul road. The highlanders recaptured the village of Kasom from the enemy, and for two months fought numerous engagements in the dense jungle and mountainous terrain. Imphal and Kohima were eventually relieved and the disruption caused to the enemy lines of communication by British and Indian troops in the surrounding countryside forced the enemy to abandon their invasion. For a time the battalion advanced in pursuit of the withdrawing Japanese, but then returned to India to train for future operations. It did not, however, take part in any further fighting.

* * * * *

The 2nd and 5th Battalions, The Seaforth Highlanders landed, on the Normandy beaches between 7 and 9 June 1944, with the 51st Highland Division. They moved quickly inland across the River Orne and took up positions near Escoville. For several weeks the two battalions held these positions which were on the pivotal eastern flank of the invasion force. The enemy's artillery fire was heavy at times, and many armoured and infantry attacks on Seaforth positions had to be repulsed.

The 7th Battalion also landed in Normandy on 24 June, with 15th Scottish Division, and two days later took part in an attack near Mesnil Patry. The Germans resisted strongly, but by the following day they had been forced to withdraw. On 28 June the battalion was again in action as they advanced on Le Valtru Ridge: there was some difficulty in establishing positions on account of a tank battle raging in the area. On the following day there was a heavy bombardment on the Seaforth and enemy tanks and infantry approached and overran C Company, holding the forward position. Only one platoon was able to withdraw. Then the enemy launched an attack with 4 tanks and about 200 infantry (believed to be SS) onto the village where battalion headquarters was placed. The tanks were destroyed as they entered the village, and burning all night, they assisted as aiming marks for a steady artillery and mortar fire during the night. Both the CO and 2ic were wounded. The 7th Battalion remained in the position through the following day and night, but were only bothered by snipers and patrols before being relieved.

The battalion next took part in the operation for the seizure of the River Odon. It was successfully crossed and a bridgehead established, but the German counter-attack caused heavy casualties and for a time successfully overran the battalion's forward positions. The 7th Battalion subsequently advanced and occupied two positions on Eterville Ridge after losing many more casualties. In mid-July the battalion was moved to assist in the breakout from Caumont.

Signallers of The Seaforth Highlanders wait in the forward area for an attack during the Normandy campaign, June 1944. IWM

The 5th Battalion, The Seaforth Highlanders, took part in the breakout in the Caen sector and, together with the 2nd Battalion, mounted a particularly successful attack on Tilly-le-Campagne. During the subsequent advance towards the Seine the 51st Highland Division took part in a night attack on Le Havre, in early September. The 7th Battalion, meanwhile, had some hard fighting as the brigade spearhead battalion, clearing the towns of Grand Roncherolles and Les Andeleys. The 5th Battalion liberated the town of St Valéry-en-Caux, where the original 2nd and 4th Battalions had been captured four years earlier. Crossing the borders of Belgium and Holland, the battalion had to establish a bridgehead over the Wilhelmina Canal and fight for the possession of Best. The 2nd and 5th Battalions then had two weeks of hard fighting for crossings on the network of canals alongside the River Maas, stoutly defended by the Germans. The 7th Seaforth Highlanders, after a period of rest, were called forward to regain and defend territory in the Nijmegen area, which took them a week. Crossing the Deurne Canal they too reached the Maas, assisting in the capture of Venlo in a major attack.

The 2nd and 5th Seaforth had been moved to meet a German counter-attack in the area of Eindhoven, before advancing to assist in the capture of Venlo. They also exploited forward of a bridgehead in the Uitwaterings Canal, capturing two objectives in the process. In late November they were moved with the 51st Highland Division to hold the Nijmegen 'island'. A month later the division moved yet again, this time to positions to help prevent the Germans breaking through the allied line in the Ardennes. There the 2nd Battalion attacked the Germans at Ronchempey and took Laroche on 11 and 12 January 1945. At the same time the 5th Seaforth captured Merchamps. Both battalions sustained numerous casualties but they managed to link up with the Americans and block further German progress.

The next task for British troops was to clear the area east of the Maas, including the Reichswald Forest and Siegfried Line, which was held in great strength by the Germans, fighting now on their home territory. During operation 'Veritable' the 7th Battalion advanced and seized objectives at Hasselt, Schloss Moyland and Schloss Kaldbeck. The 2nd Battalion took enemy strongpoints at Hekkens and in the area north of Goch, while the 5th captured Asperden village. Together they mounted major attacks in and around Goch, and gradually the ground west of the River Rhine was systematically cleared of the enemy.

On 23 and 24 March the 2nd, 5th and 7th Seaforth Highlanders crossed the Rhine – the two divisions chosen to lead the British assault were both Scottish. The 51st Highland Divisions' objectives were Esserden and Rees, and a bridgehead was quickly established during the dark, once the enemy had been cleared. The 2nd Seaforth Highlanders landed and defended the bridgehead for several days. The 5th Battalion also crossed at first light and exploited eastwards, successfully taking its first objective at Groin against strong German resistance. The 2nd Battalion was ordered forward on 28 March, crossed the Oude Issel River to form a bridgehead, and took further objectives with the assistance of the 5th Battalion. The enemy counter-attacked the 5th, holding bridges on the Rivers Astrang and Issel, but were successfully resisted until armour could move forward in support and the Germans were forced to withdraw. The 5th Seaforth next captured the town of Goldensteht in mid-April and, with the 2nd Battalion, fought for the possession of Adelheide and Gander-Kessee at the beginning of May.

The 7th Battalion meanwhile, after crossing the Rhine, had been fighting for the town of Mehr where German counter-attacks were successfully withstood and turned back. Thereafter the battalion's advance with the 15th Scottish Division, towards the Elbe was rapid and Celle and Uelzen were captured. The 6th Battalion, who had joined the division for the last months of the war, crossed the Elbe with the 7th Battalion, and continued to advance towards Lübeck during the last days of hostilities.

* * * * *

When the war ended, the 1st Battalion, The Seaforth Highlanders, moved first to Malaya and then for a time to Java. Their task was to disarm the Japanese and restore the Dutch colonial administration to the island. The 2nd Battalion remained in Germany, but in 1948 was amalgamated with the 1st Battalion in Singapore.

As the Malayan emergency developed, the 1st Battalion was moved northwards from Singapore, and for three years it played an important part in anti-terrorist operations. As well as providing guards and escorts, the operations involved constant patrolling against the bandits, setting up ambushes and mounting attacks on enemy bases deep in the jungle. The 1st Seaforth killed or captured nearly 100 terrorists for a cost of 14 killed and 23 wounded.

From 1951 to 1954 the battalion was stationed in Scotland, and thereafter served tours of duty in Egypt, Aden and Gibraltar before finally moving to Munster as part of the British Army of the Rhine. In February 1961 the Seaforth Highlanders amalgamated with The Queen's Own Cameron Highlanders to form the 1st Battalion, Queen's Own Highlanders (Seaforth and Camerons).

A Guard of Honour of the 1st Bn, Seaforth Highlanders in the 1950s. The 'Assaye' elephant collar-badge, awarded to the 78th Highlanders to commemorate Maj-Gen The Hon Arthur Wellesley's remarkable victory, is seen in this photograph. IWM

'Flowing to the Sea'. This tranquil watercolour by Sir John Millais PRA shows two soldiers of the 93rd Sutherland Highlanders in a riverside setting.
Southampton Art Gallery

Bugler of the 90th Perthshire Light Infantry, later the Scottish Rifles, in 1880. Watercolour by R. Simkin.
RHQ

Overleaf

Above:

The 90th Perthshire Light Infantry, late Scottish Rifles, repel the Zulu attack at the battle of Ulundi, 1879. Painted by H. Oakes-Jones. RHQ

Below:

A soldier, officer and piper of the Cameronians (Scottish Rifles) of 1882 in their new uniform of rifle green. The Albert helmet was later replaced by a shako. Watercolour by R. Simkin. RHQ

Top right:
The 3rd (Militia) Bn, Argyll and Sutherland Highlanders at church parade in 1885 near Stirling. The 1881 army reforms fully incorporated the Militia into the regimental system. Painting by William Kennedy.
RHQ

Right:
This painting by Alphonse Maire de Neuvelle shows men of the Black Watch fighting across the enemy's trench at the battle of Tel-El-Kebir in Sept 1882. RHQ

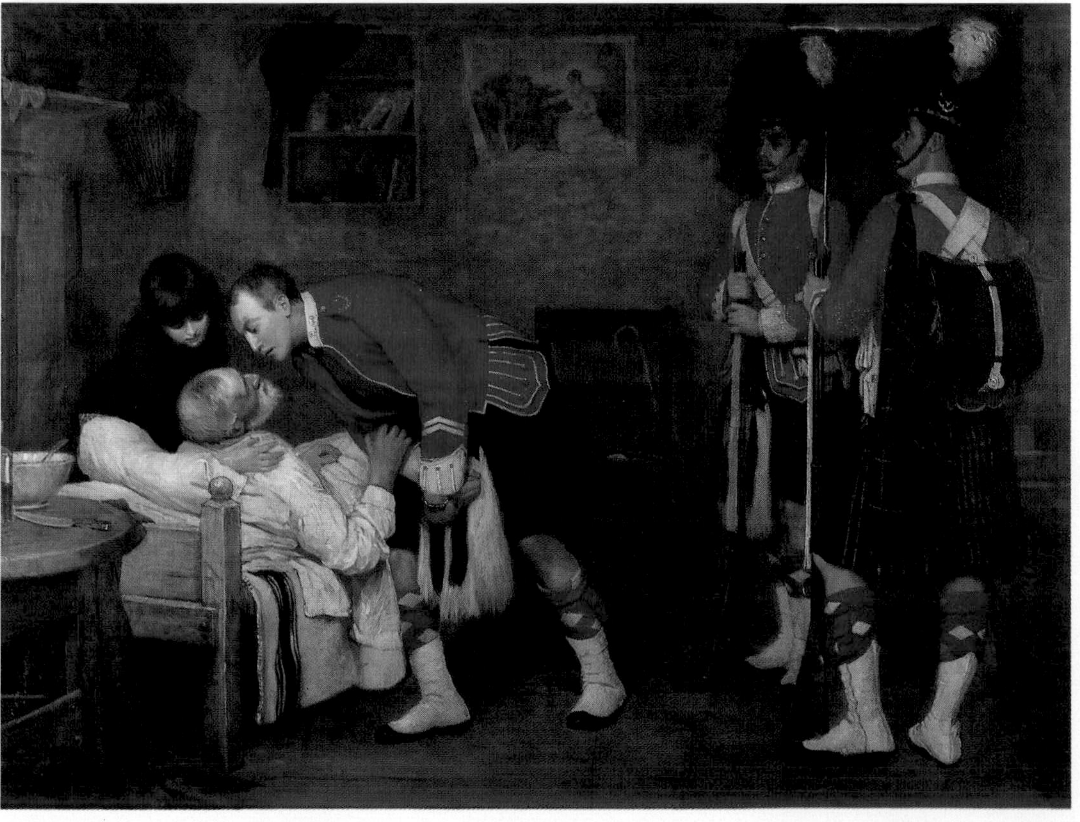

Top left:
Bandsmen and other soldiers of the Gordon Highlanders halt during a march, probably near Chobham, in 1886. Watercolour by W. Skeoch Cumming. RHQ

Opposite left:
'Absent without leave'. A Victorian story-picture, painted by Charles Bartlett in 1889, showing a Seaforth Highlander visiting his dying father.
Astley House Fine Art/Queen's Own Highlanders

Above:
Chobham in Surrey was for a long time a favoured area for military encampments. In this Simkin watercolour, the King's Own Scottish Borderers are depicted showing various forms of dress c1890. RHQ

Left:
A drummer of the Queen's Own Cameron Highlanders c1890. Watercolour by W. Skeoch Cumming. RHQ

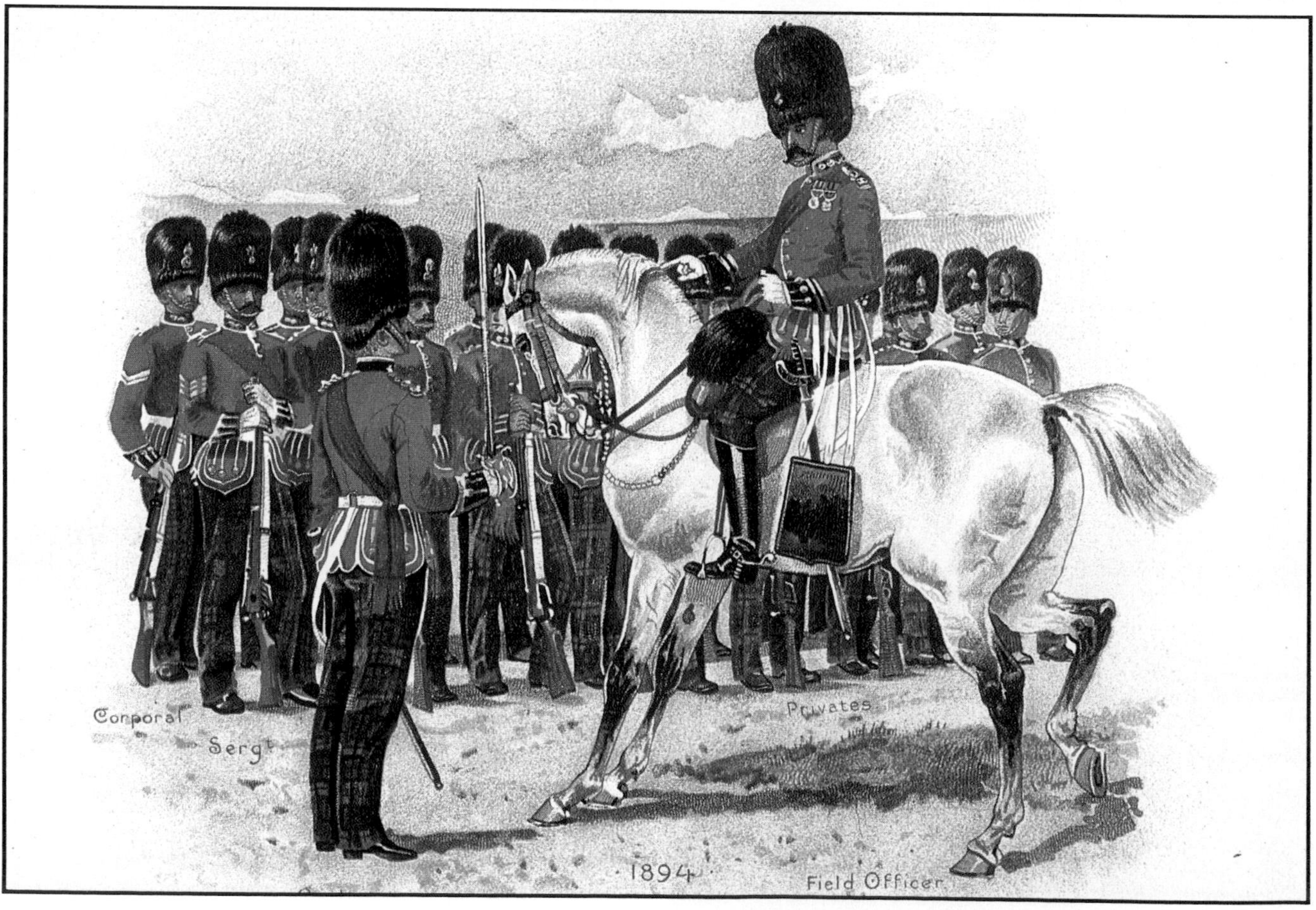

Corporal
Sergt
Privates
1894
Field Officer

Far left top:
'The misfit': tailors' shop of the King's Own Scottish Borderers. The double entendre is clearly implied. Oil painting by Frank Wood. RHQ

Far left below:
A group of Royal Scots Fusiliers in full dress of 1894. They wear the distinctive fusilier bearskin and badge.

Left:
An ensign of the Scots Guards in uniform worn in 1894. Painted by Rodney Player in 1987. Parker Gallery

Below:
The guardroom, King's Own Scottish Borderers. The canteen manager tells the guard of his experiences in battle. Oil painting by Frank Wood. RHQ

The Gordons and Gurkhas seize the Dargai Heights on 20 Oct 1897 on the North-West Frontier, while Piper Findlater continues to play despite serious wounds. RHQ

Officers of the 74th Highlanders, later Highland Light Infantry. Watercolour by R. Simkin. RHQ

PART II
THE QUEEN'S OWN CAMERON HIGHLANDERS

79TH CAMERON HIGHLANDERS
1793–1881

The Queen's Own Cameron Highlanders were one of a number of regiments of foot raised for regular service at the time of the French revolutionary war. Alan Cameron of Erracht was authorised in 1793 to form a Highland regiment, numbered the 79th. Erracht had first seen service in the American colonies. The 79th Regiment was embodied at Stirling on 3 January 1794: they were initially called the 'Cameronian Volunteers' and the majority of the recruits came from Cameron territory in Lochaber. Lt-Col Cameron's mother designed a new tartan and Cameron of Erracht tartan has been worn by the regiment ever since.

The Cameron Highlanders were stationed in Ireland and England during 1794, and were sent in August as reinforcements to Nijmegen during the campaign in the Netherlands and North Germany. This campaign achieved little, and the 79th lost more than 200 men in less than a year mainly from disease and exposure. On the regiment's return there was a threat to divide it up as detachments for drafting to other regiments, but instead it was despatched for garrison duties to Martinique in 1795. There were no enemy operations against the island, but again the regiment suffered hundreds of casualties owing to the climate and disease. After two years the remnants were drafted into the 42nd Royal Highland Regiment, despite Col Cameron's protests, and the regimental cadre returned to Scotland. Fortunately, Erracht was authorised to complete the regimental establishment and the Cameron Highlanders were restored to strength by mid-1798.

A year later the regiment joined the expedition under the Duke of York to Holland and in early October took part in the battle of Egmont-op-Zee. The French, concealed amongst the sand-hills, were put to flight after a bayonet charge and some hard hand-to-hand fighting over a wide area. Casualties in the regiment were light. At the end of October 1799 the 79th sailed for England.

In August 1800 the Cameron Highlanders embarked for an amphibious expedition on the coast of Spain. Landing near Ferrol together with four other battalions they seized the high ground above the harbour, but the expedition was soon called off. Re-embarking, the force reached Cadiz for the purpose of blockading the port from the sea and cutting it off by land. Due to the weather, however, the force did not land but sailed on for Malta. Then on 8 March 1801 the Cameron Highlanders landed at Aboukir Bay with Sir Ralph Abercromby's force and, with the other battalions of the army, began the advance on Alexandria. Their brigade was not heavily involved during the initial fighting, but the highlanders took an active part in repelling the French attacks in front of Alexandria. While the town remained under siege the regiment marched with the force to Cairo, which they occupied after the French surrender. The 79th then returned to the area of Alexandria, which also surrendered in due course.

Subsequent periods of garrison duty were spent on the island of Minorca and in Ireland until 1805. A second battalion was raised in 1805, but remained at home duty until disbandment in 1815. In 1807 the 1st Cameron Highlanders embarked for an expedition to besiege the city of Copenhagen. After a heavy British bombardment, the city surrendered and the 79th occupied the citadel for a brief period. Its mission having been achieved, the British force was withdrawn and returned to England. In the following year the regiment sailed for Sweden, to fulfil a treaty obligation. Due to a dispute, however, the British force never landed and returned to Spithead.

The Cameron Highlanders were then sent to Portugal, where they landed on 26 August 1808 near Lisbon. They formed part of Sir John Moore's army, and advanced into Spain with the purpose of joining forces with the Spanish army. The Spanish, however, were unwilling to take to the field against the approaching French army some 194,000 strong and the only option for the British was to withdraw to Corunna. The retreat was a calamitous affair and the Cameron Highlanders lost 90 dead or captured during the march. On reaching Corunna they formed the defence of the main gate, but they were only partly involved in the battle itself. The regiment embarked safely and returned to England. A detachment of the regiment, which had remained in Portugal, later fought at the battle of Talavera.

The regiment then joined the expedition to seize

French-held garrisons on the Scheldt, but the only successful action in which they took part was the siege of Flushing. Because the British army was severely depleted by fever, the expedition was ordered to return to England after a few months.

In 1810 the Cameron Highlanders reached Portugal to join the 1st Division in the army commanded by Sir Arthur Wellesley, later the Duke of Wellington. They were, however, immediately sent on a subsidiary seaborne expedition against Spain, during which they landed at Cadiz and occupied the town for several months. In August they returned to Lisbon and rejoined Wellesley. At the battle of Busaco on 27 September the French attacked the British army, with the Cameron Highlanders on the right of the line. At first there was fierce hand-to-hand fighting, and a picquet of the regiment was nearly cut off. Later the main French attack was launched against the centre but the British line held, and withdrew on the following day to positions at Torres Vedras. Later in the year the army advanced again and in May 1811 crossed the border into Spain.

Lt-Gen Sir Alan Cameron of Erracht KCB, who raised the 79th Highlanders (or Cameronian Volunteers) in 1793. RHQ

On 3 May the French attacked in great strength the village of Fuentes d'Onor, which was held by the Camerons and 71st Highlanders. During the first day of battle the enemy successfully entered the village, but after much hand-to-hand fighting were ejected. Two days later the French attacked in even greater strength:

'Notwithstanding that the whole sixth French Corps d'Armée was at different periods engaged in the attack, the enemy never succeeded in gaining more than a temporary possession of the village. Its lower portion was, however, completely carried, and two companies of the 79th, which had become separated from the main body in the struggle, were surrounded and made prisoner: but the troops still held the upper and much larger portion, where a bloody hand-to-hand combat was maintained with the French Imperial Guard . . . the highlanders in numerous instances clubbing their muskets and using the butts instead of their bayonets. . . . Colonel Philips Cameron . . . fell from his horse mortally wounded. A cry of grief and revenge arose from the highlanders . . . their comrades of the 71st supported by the 88th Connaught Rangers and 74th Highlanders hurled themselves upon the French . . . [who] were driven with great slaughter from the village.'

Eventually the French retreated, but the regiment had lost well over 200 casualties during the battle.

The Cameron Highlanders were engaged in no major fighting during the remainder of 1811, and were only lightly engaged at Salamanca in July 1812. In September the army reached Burgos, and the light company of the regiment captured part of the outer defences during the initial attack. They continued to fight as part of a light battalion and stormed the 'horn-work' while the main assault on Burgos was launched. The 'horn-work' was captured, but after several attempts by the army to capture Burgos had failed, Wellington ordered a general withdrawal.

For several months the Cameron Highlanders were not involved in any major engagements, but in July 1813 they rejoined the main part of the army in the mountains. During the battle of the Pyrenees the regiment repulsed the attacking French at bayonet point in the village of Oricain. In November, at the battle of Nivelle, the Cameron Highlanders advanced quickly under fire against the French line on some high ground. The enemy were attempting to block the British advance, but were dislodged by the highlanders and quickly retreated. A month later the regiment took part in the battle for the River Nive and again drove the French from entrenched positions, which contributed to the British victory.

The last battle of the Peninsular Campaign was fought at Toulouse in April 1814. Sir Denis Pack's Highland Brigade, comprising the 79th, 42nd and 71st Highlanders, first attacked the French positions on a hill and drove them off.

'About 100 men of the 79th, headed by several officers, now left the captured work to encounter the enemy on the ridge of the plateau, but . . . fell back on the redoubt des Augustins. The Colombette had been suddenly attacked and entered by a fresh and immense column of the enemy, and the 42nd was compelled to give way . . . Both regiments for a moment quitted the works . . . At this critical juncture, Lt-Col Douglas having reformed the 79th, the regiment again charged the enemy, and succeeded in not only re-taking the Augustins redoubt but also the Colombette.'

The action of the brigade played a major part in the victory, and the Cameron Highlanders returned to England soon afterwards.

When the British Army was recalled to the Continent in 1815 the regiment joined Sir James Kempt's brigade in Sir Thomas Picton's division. In the early hours of 16 June the division moved from Brussels to Quatre Bras, and the 79th were on the left of the Britis' line when the French attacked. The light companies skirmished at first, and when some British guns were threatened the regiment was ordered forward to relieve them. The enemy were forced back at bayonet point, and the 79th continued to fire volleys at the French until they ran out of ammunition, and formed square to repel cavalry. The enemy drew off their attack late in the evening, and on the following day the British withdrew to the area of Waterloo.

On the morning of 18 June the Cameron Highlanders were in position near the farm of La Haye Sainte. At about 10.30am

'The French advanced in columns under cover of a tremendous cannonade, which was answered with great spirit by the British artillery . . . Kempt's brigade then deployed into line, threw out its light troops, and advanced to where the artillery were posted . . . until a heavy column of the enemy's infantry, driving them in, advanced direct against that portion of the line occupied by the left wing of the 79th and right wing of the 28th. Picton allowed this column to approach quite close and then, after one volley, we charged at the head of the two regiments and drove back the French down the hill at the point of the bayonet. It was in this charge that the gallant Picton fell. At this moment . . . the union brigade of cavalry came up and . . . charged the broken and flying columns of the enemy.'

Soon afterwards a large enemy cavalry force advanced, and the regiment quickly formed square to repel them, but after a while the 79th were ordered to withdraw as Wellington needed to conserve his forces. When the mass of French cavalry and infantry again advanced and attacked the British centre, the regiment continued to bring down volley after volley of fire, having been re-supplied with ammunition only just in time. By the time that orders were given for the general advance the regiment's numbers had been severely depleted. Nevertheless, the Cameron Highlanders advanced and occupied the original French positions as the battle drew to a close. The regiment's losses during the three days of fighting were 479 killed and wounded, having mustered 776 at the outset.

The Cameron Highlanders remained in France for three years, and from 1818 were stationed in various places in England and Ireland. From 1825 to 1836 the regiment served in Canada where most of the time it was divided into detachments in a number of towns. Occasionally they were called upon to aid the civil authorities in preventing disturbances. On returning to Britain the Cameron Highlanders were

This steel engraving shows the 79th Cameron Highlanders at the battle for the crossing of the River Nive, Dec 1813.

NCOs and men of the 79th Cameron Highlanders pose for the camera in India, 1860. Spats were generally in use from the time of the Napoleonic Wars until the First World War, when they were replaced by puttees. RHQ

employed in similar duties in the north of England at the time of the Chartist riots. A tour of duty was then spent in Gibraltar until 1848, when the regiment returned to Canada: it only remained there for three years on this occasion.

In May 1854 the Cameron Highlanders embarked for service in the Crimea, joining the Highland Brigade under Sir Colin Campbell. They disembarked at Kalamita Bay on 14 September and set off in the direction of Sevastopol four days later. The Russian army was deployed on high ground behind the River Alma and the British army advanced on the enemy in the early hours of 20 September. After fording the river, the Guards and Highland Brigades ascended the ridge, fired volleys at the Russians and charged. The Cameron Highlanders were on the extreme left of the British line:

'Above the crest or swell of the ground,' wrote Kingslake the historian of the war describing the 79th, 'yet another array of the tall, bending plumes began to rise up in a long, ceaseless line . . . and, presently, with all the grace and beauty that marks a highland regiment when it springs up the side of a hill, the 79th came bounding forth . . . It sprang at the flank of the right Sousdal column . . . wrapped in the fire thus poured upon its flank, the hapless column could not march, could not live . . . It broke and began to fall back in great confusion.'

The other highland, Guards and light infantry regiments met with equal success and within fifteen minutes the great redoubt was captured; the remaining Russian troops hurriedly abandoned the battlefield.

On reaching Sevastopol most of the British troops, including the Cameron Highlanders, prepared trench-works in front of the fortified town. On 25 October the Russian army appeared in very great strength with a large number of guns and cavalry and attempted to capture the nearby seaport of Balaclava. The Cameron Highlanders were present at the battle but were not much involved in the fighting.

The regiment remained in the area of Sevastopol during the winter of 1854, extending and guarding the British lines around the town. In May 1855 it accompanied the Highland Brigade on an expedition to capture Kerch and Yenikale, the Russian re-supply ports for their forces in the Crimea. This task was successfully achieved, and valuable stores were captured before the towns were abandoned. The Cameron Highlanders then returned to the trenches at Sevastopol, and in September took part in the second allied attack on the outer defences of the fortress. At first the Russians repelled the assault and held their positions. The Camerons, with the rest of the Highland Brigade, then formed up for a dawn attack, but this was pre-empted by the enemy abandoning and blowing up their defences: whereupon the Cameron Highlanders quickly advanced and occupied the Redan. Until a peace treaty was concluded in April 1856, the regiment remained in the Crimea.

In November 1857 the regiment reached India where the mutiny of the Bengal army had started in May. From Calcutta the Camerons were sent to Allahabad and attacked the mutineers holding Secundragunge: this was easily achieved despite a march of forty-eight miles in less than twenty-four hours. Subsequent weeks were spent moving between various stations and escorting convoys. In March they reached Lucknow which was still occupied by the mutineers, despite being relieved twice the previous year. Part of Sir Colin Campbell's force, which included the 79th Highlanders, attacked across bridges on Goomtee River to the north and gradually forced their way into the town over a period of days. The regiment fought its way from street to street and finally stormed the Residency on 16 March, which was successfully cleared of the mutineers. Three days later the Camerons assisted in storming the Musaghbagh lines and Lucknow was soon completely in British hands.

The following month the Cameron Highlanders were involved in fighting against the enemy at Rooyah fort and Bareilly. Resistance at both places was strong, and near Mahomdie the regiment actually had to form a square to repel cavalry. More casualties, however, were sustained from the heat than enemy action during this period. The regiment continued on the move for the remainder of the year, taking part in various minor actions while British control was gradually restored.

* * * * *

The Cameron Highlanders remained in India for some years after the Mutiny. Their periods of active service included a time spent on the North-west Frontier of 1863 and 1864, guarding the Kyber Pass and garrisoning Rawalpindi. In 1871 the regiment returned to the United Kingdom, and three years later a large re-inforcement joined the Black Watch to take part in the Ashanti Campaign. In 1879 the regiment was posted to Gibraltar.

A group of officers of the 79th Cameron Highlanders with the Regimental and Queen's Colours at Rawalpindi, India. RHQ

THE QUEEN'S OWN CAMERON HIGHLANDERS

1881–1913

When the infantry regiments were reorganised in 1881, after much discussion the War Office allowed the regiment to retain its separate identity as a single battalion regiment, and its title of The Queen's Own Cameron Highlanders. A later plan to amalgamate it with the Scots Guards was successfully resisted.

The following year the Camerons embarked for active service with Highland Brigade in the Egyptian Campaign. Landing at Ismailia, via the Suez Canal, the brigade marched westwards towards the Nile and the enemy encampment at Tel-El-Kebir. The Egyptian rebel troops were holding entrenched positions, and on 12 September a silent night march was ordered followed by a dawn attack with a bayonet charge.

'Just as dawn was breaking two shots were fired . . . Bayonets were at once fixed . . . bugles of the Egyptians rang out, shells screamed above, and a line of fire poured from the enemy's trenches. The 79th moved steadily on in an unbroken line, not a shot was fired in reply; but on the "advance" for the brigade being sounded by Sir Archibald Alison's bugler, drummer John Alcorn of the 79th, Lieutenant-Colonel Leith galloped to the front, waving his sword and crying, "Come on, 79th!" and breaking into double time, to the shrill music of the pipes, and cheering as they ran, the regiment charged the enemy's lines. Private Donald Cameron was the first to gain the top of the trench; but fell dead at once, shot through the head. The trench was now full, and, mounting on each other's shoulders and scrambling up, the front line gained the fiery top. Lieutenant Malcolm jumped down amongst some gunners, one of whom wounded him on the head, but he cut his assailant down with his claymore.

Flash after flash continued along the line until the bayonets of the 79th had done their work. The front line followed the enemy in a confused mass, Pipe-Major Grant playing the *March of the Cameron Men* lustily.'

The first enemy line was quickly overwhelmed, and the regiment stormed a redoubt and put to flight some Egyptian cavalry. It was a most successful and decisive battle, and effectively ended the campaign.

The Cameron Highlanders remained as troops of occupation in Egypt and in 1885 they took part in the expedition to the Sudan, where earlier in the year Khartoum had fallen to the Mahdi's army. The Camerons moved up the Nile by various means of transport, and for part of the time guarded various posts on the river and railway. For some weeks a large force of the enemy moved around the area of Kosheh and Mograkeh, the chief fort, and the regiment was involved in capturing various villages and long-range shooting against the dervishes. In May 1886 the Camerons were relieved, and embarked on river craft for the return to Cairo.

The battalion spent the years 1887–97 in the United Kingdom, Malta and Gibraltar, but then returned to join Kitchener's Anglo-Egyptian expedition, for the reconquest of the Sudan. The Camerons

The 1st Bn, The Queen's Own Cameron Highlanders form square en route from Koroso to Abu Hamed during a tour of active duty in Egypt and the Sudan, 1882-6. RHQ

The 3rd (Special Reserve) Bn, the Queen's Own Cameron Highlanders, formerly the 3rd (Militia) Bn, on the ranges at Fort George, Inverness, c1912. RHQ

The Queen's Own Cameron Highlanders take a rest during a march in the second Sudan War, 1898. NAM

reached the army at Abu Hamed, and a general advance began against the dervishes' camp by the Atbara River. The Camerons were one of the leading battalions in the attack, which was launched from a start line 600 yards from the dervishes' position behind their thorn-bush barricade. As the battalion advanced it brought down highly effective fire on the enemy, and on reaching the stockade allowed the following battalions, including the 1st Seaforth, to pass through and storm the camp. The dervishes quickly fled, but continued to hold the towns in great strength.

In August 1898 the British established a position near Omdurman and on 2 September the dervish army advanced. During the battle the enemy were engaged by artillery, machine-gun and rifle fire at a distance of 2000 yds, which was so effective that they withdrew and abandoned the two towns. The Sudan thus came effectively under the control of the British and Egyptian administration.

The 2nd Battalion of the regiment was formed in 1897 and took two years to complete its establishment of eight companies. The battalion served continuously abroad from 1899 until 1914 in Mediterranean garrisons, South Africa, China and India.

In the meantime the 1st Battalion was sent from Egypt to South Africa in early 1900. As part of 21 Brigade the Camerons joined General Hamilton's column for the march from Bloemfontein to occupy Johannesburg and Pretoria. After the capture of Pretoria the battalion took part in the pursuit of some Boers and attacked them at Diamond Hill on 11 June. The following month the Camerons joined General Sir Archibald Hunter's column which included the Highland Brigade. Their task was to follow and destroy General Prinsloo's force, and the Boers were eventually surrounded at Brandwater Basin. The

Camerons' immediate task was the assault of the Spitzkopf feature, and this action contributed to the enemey's defeat and surrender.

The battalion remained in South Africa until the end of the war, being reinforced by drafts from the 2nd Battalion and a volunteer company. The Camerons also formed a mounted infantry company and, during an action with this company, C/Sgt Donald Farmer won the VC. The second half of 1900 was spent on trek in the Orange River Colony. In 1901 the Camerons adopted a more static role in the Transvaal where their duties, like many British battalions, were the setting up and manning of the blockhouse system and the systematic clearing of the countryside of Boer forces.

In 1902 the 1st Camerons returned to the United Kingdom and served an eventful tour of duty in Ireland from 1904–7. They were called on to give assistance to the civil authorities in Belfast in 1907 during disturbances in the docks and Catholic areas of the city.

THE QUEEN'S OWN CAMERON HIGHLANDERS

1914–38

On mobilisation in August 1914 the 1st Battalion were serving as the resident battalion in Edinburgh Castle, while the 2nd was in India. The 1st Camerons left Edinburgh on 12 August to join the British Expeditionary Force in France, and their first task was the defence of the BEF headquarters during the retreat from Mons, being brigaded with the 1st Scots Guards and 1st Black Watch. At the end of the retreat the Camerons went into the front line on the River Aisne during the British advance. They took part in a major attack on 14 September. The brigade had moved up at first light to positions near the Chemin-des-Dames at Cerny, and A and D were the two forward companies of the Camerons. Both came under small arms and artillery fire as they advanced, and a German attack developed to the left flank at the same time as the Camerons came under fire of British troops from the rear in error. The supporting companies caught up and became mixed with A and D. At 8am a heavy German attack was launched on the Camerons and part of their right had to give ground. There was sporadic fighting all morning and the brigade, rather than be outflanked, was ordered to retire. Another German attack was launched at 3pm and, despite its confusion and lack of contact with other troops, the enemy's advance was checked by nightfall. The battalion suffered heavy casualties, but had fought with great gallantry and resourcefulness. Later in the month battalion headquarters was struck by shellfire and the CO and staff were killed.

The following month the battalion moved north with the BEF and was heavily engaged in the defence of Langemarck and Givenchy in the first battle of Ypres. The fighting became static towards the end of the year and the Camerons manned the line at Béthune and took part in the attacks on Givenchy in late December, which was only partly successful.

In the meantime the 2nd Camerons reached France from India, and in January 1915 joined the line south of Ypres. There they remained for five months and successfully defended positions on Hill 60 during a series of massive German attacks between 21–29 April. At the end of April the Camerons took up positions covering the main road to the east of the town. The battalion fought with great determination, and contributed to the failure of the Germans to capture Ypres. By the end of the battle the 2nd Camerons had suffered 673 casualties.

The 1st Battalion, Liverpool Scottish, a Territorial battalion unofficially affiliated to The Cameron Highlanders and later to be transferred from the King's Regiment, had reached France in November 1914. The battalion was also heavily engaged in the 2nd battle of Ypres during the attack on the Germans at Hooge. The battalion lost over 400 casualties in the action, but the attack was successful.

The 4th Camerons, also a Territorial battalion, had reached France in February 1915, and they too were heavily involved in the battle. Their brigade took part in the attack at Neuve Chapelle which began on 10 March, and the battalion's first task was to hold a mile of front-line trenches to the left of the axis of advance. After a tremendous artillery barrage the attack went in at 7.30am. In the afternoon C and D Companies provided platoons to capture German trenches to the right front of the battalion: their action was entirely successful and they captured 70 Germans. The following day the counter-attack was launched: the Camerons prevented the Germans from breaking through and A and B Companies captured a further 100 enemy. On the night of 12 March the CO, Lt-Col Fraser, was ordered to launch a

Led by the Pipes and Drums, the 1st Camerons march to war from Edinburgh Castle, 12 Aug 1914. Families and well-wishers line the route. RHQ

The 1st Liverpool Scottish encamped at Vlamertinge, near Ypres, Mar 1915. They had joined the front on Nov 1914. IWM

night attack with a neighbouring battalion on an objective at Moulin de Pietre. Moving forward in the darkness to the start line, the battalion made contact with the Devonshire Regiment and waited for the attack. The order, however, was countermanded and the 4th Camerons withdrew to their previous positions. They remained in action for over a week before being relieved.

During May 1915 the 1st Camerons were involved in the unsuccessful attack on Aubers Ridge. The 4th Battalion was more successful in its night attack on Festubert on 17 May and, after crossing half-a-mile of waterlogged country, seized the battalion objective. Unfortunately the Camerons were left exposed and unsupported by other troops, and had to withdraw. A month later they were in action again at Givenchy.

The 5th, 6th and 7th service battalions reached France between May and July, and joined the line soon after arrival. Their first major engagements were during the battle of Loos, which started on 25 September, when five battalions of the regiment took part. The 1st Camerons attacked in the area of Hulluch and, despite severe casualties, captured part of the town. The 4th Camerons were less successful in the area of St Elie and were engaged for a full week of fighting. The 5th and 7th Camerons fought together against the enemy positions on the Hohenzollern Redoubt; the 7th successfully captured Hill 70 with the assistance of other troops.

'Driving the Germans in front of them from a half-finished redoubt on the top of Hill 70, they had pursued them into a group of houses on the southern slopes . . . The strongly wired salient . . . part of the German fourth line, formed a perfect defensive position. Before the highlanders had reached the houses the Germans . . . opened a deadly fire with rifles and machine guns from the upper storeys . . . as they advanced down the slopes towards them. This was the farthest point reached by the division . . . Very few came back to tell the story.'

The 1st Liverpool Scottish in the attack on Hooge, Ypres sector, 16 June 1915. The battalion's casualties for the day were 402 dead and wounded.
RHQ Queen's Own Highlanders

The hill was held but the 7th Camerons' casualties were 588 in the battle. Meanwhile the 5th Camerons fought for three days to hold the 'Little Willie' trench system, but their casualties were 750. Cpl James Pollock was awarded the VC during this battle. The 6th Camerons were in reserve at the start of the battle, but they took part in the attack on Hill 70 losing 400 casualties: the CO, Lt Col Angus Douglas-Hamilton, personally leading his battalion, won a posthumous VC. In the latter stages of the battle the 1st Battalion was again in action near Hulluch.

During the winter of 1915–16 the 6th and 7th Battalions were reinforced, but the remaining members of the 4th Camerons were drafted and the battalion ceased to exist.

* * * * *

The 2nd Camerons had left France in November 1915 with the 27th Division for service on the Bulgarian Front. They were first employed guarding

This oil painting by Joseph Grey depicts the 7th Camerons' advance to capture Hill 70 during the battle of Loos, 25 Sept 1915. The battalion lost 548 casualties in the attack. RHQ

positions around Salonika. In May 1916 the Camerons were moved to the Struma valley where they remained until the end of the war in a mainly holding operation. In the autumn they assaulted and captured Bala and Zir. The 10th (Lovat's Scouts) Battalion, Cameron Highlanders (recently formed from the Lovat's Scouts Yeomanry and 3rd Scottish Horse), joined the same division. Their chief battle was a surprise attack at Salmah in September 1917 when they killed and captured more than 170 Bulgarians. The following month the 2nd Camerons and Scottish Horse (13th Black Watch) mounted a surprise attack on Homondos, and killed and captured over 270 enemy soldiers. In 1918 the 10th joined other Lovat Scouts in France as observer troops. After the treaty with the Bulgarians in September 1918 the 2nd Camerons spent several months in Georgia, Russia, as occupation troops.

* * * * *

During the early part of 1916 the battalions of the regiment serving in France and Flanders were brought up to strength. The 5th Camerons was the first battalion to fight at the start of the Somme offensive in July. They fought for a full week assisting in the capture of Longueval, Delville Wood and Waterlot Farm, and suffered nearly 450 casualties. The 1st Camerons fought for three days during attacks on Bazentin ridge, but by this stage the momentum had been lost.

In August the 1st Liverpool Scottish were in action at Guillemont, during which the Medical Officer Captain Noel Chavasse won the VC for rescuing and treating the wounded. (He received, posthumously, a bar to his VC at Ypres in 1917.) The 6th and 7th Camerons in the 15th Division successfully attacked the Switch Line near Contalmaison in two separate attacks, and on 15 September the 6th fought with its Brigade at Martinpuich. In the same month the 1st Camerons fought alongside the 1st Black Watch at High Wood. In the desperate fighting positions were captured, but had to be relinquished when the enemy counter-attacked in overwhelming strength, inflicting severe casualties.

On 9 April 1917, the 6th and 7th Camerons successfully took their objectives at the start of the battle of Arras, where more Scottish battalions were concentrated than at any other time. In the subsequent fighting they advanced and captured Monchy Le Preux in separate attacks. The 7th continued to hold Monchy with other troops, despite counter-attacks and a steady fire from the nearby chemical works at Roeux: the battalion's casualties numbered 659 during two weeks of fighting. The 6th Camerons, having already fought during the first phase of the battle, received orders on 26 April for a two-company night-raid on Cavalry Farm near Guémappe, while simultaneously other troops from the next brigade were advancing on the farm.

These two photographs show men of the 1st Camerons fighting amid the ruins of Cuinchy, on the La Bassée canal near Béthune, 17 April 1918. IWM

'So terrific was the deafening fire, and so numerous the casualties among the raiders, that when they were twenty yards from the enemy lines, those still alive were obliged to . . . seek such cover as was available. When the fire died down sufficiently A and B Companies of the 6th established six strong points which were completed before dawn . . . At 4.45am the enemy opened an intense fire on the four right-hand posts, from three sides at once, and prepared to attack.'

The two other posts were held during the day and the 6th Camerons were relieved that night. Their casualties in the battle were over 400.

The 5th Camerons fought for possession of the Roeux works on 1 May, but came under British artillery fire in error and lost 300 killed and wounded.

After Arras, three Cameron battalions were moved to the Ypres sector for the third battle of that name. The 6th and 7th attacked Passchendaele Ridge on separate occasions and the line was pushed forward over a mile. In an attack nearby the 1st Liverpool Scottish fought in a particularly successful divisional attack, when more than 630 prisoners were taken. In September the 5th Camerons were also moved to the Ypres sector and took part in another attack on Passchendaele Ridge. The battalion was severely shelled and cut up by machine-gun fire, so the attack failed. Later in the year the 1st Liverpool Scottish had to fight for their trenches against a very powerful enemy attack near Cambrai, and during the fighting the battalion lost 622 casualties, more than half of whom were captured. The 55th West Lancashire Division, in which the Liverpool Scottish were serving, only just managed to hold the line. In the same month, November 1917, the 1st Camerons took part in a successful action at Passchendaele, and captured Vocation Farm.

In March 1918 the Germans attacked all parts of the allied line in their final offensive. The 5th Camerons were on the Somme and lost 400 casualties before they were ordered to withdraw. The 6th and 7th Camerons fought successfully for the defence of Arras, the latter losing 388 casualties. The 1st Liverpool Scottish fought off a heavy German attack in the area of Givenchy and were subsequently amalgamated with the 2nd Battalion, which had been serving in France and Flanders since February 1917. The 1st Camerons also took part in this action, which resulted in the German failure to capture the town of Béthune. In June many battalions in the hardest hit divisions were amalgamated, the 7th Camerons being reduced to a cadre.

In July the 6th Camerons moved with the 15th Scottish Division, to the French sector on the Marne. They took part in the attack at Buzancy in support of the French and captured their objective at Sucrerie. Meanwhile, the 5th Camerons took part in the 9th Division's attack on Meteren, which was captured on 19 July, and in September they assisted in the

Presentation of new Colours to the 1st Bn, The Queen's Own Cameron Highlanders, Calcutta 1923. RHQ

successful capture of the Passchendaele. The 1st took part in the assault at Epéhy on the Somme, when the 1st Division captured hundreds of German prisoners and much equipment. In mid-October the 1st Camerons had a similar success at la Vallée Mulâtre during the great advance. Meanwhile, the Liverpool Scottish had advanced from La Bassée, while the 5th Camerons advanced steadily from Ypres, fighting frequent actions. The 6th Camerons had marched from Loos to St Anne by the time the Armistice came into force on 11 November. The 1st Camerons' final action was an attack over the Sambre and L'Oise Canal, in which 500 prisoners and a large quantity of munitions were captured.

* * * * *

After the war the 1st Battalion was reconstituted in Inverness and left for duty in Rawalpindi in July 1919. Following service in Russia, the 2nd Camerons were similarly reconstituted at home and posted to Aldershot. From mid-1920 until 1922 they served in Queenstown and Cork during the final period before the establishment of the Irish Free State.

Meanwhile, the 1st Camerons had been on active duty in the Kurram Valley on the North-West Frontier, and assisted in internal security duties in Rawalpindi. In November 1925 the battalion moved to Burma, where it remained until 1930 on detachment duty. The years 1930–34 were spent in India, and there followed two years in the Sudan before it returned to the United Kingdom.

The 2nd Battalion spent three years in Germany with the British Army of the Rhine, followed by the period 1926–30 in Edinburgh. In 1935 it embarked for Palestine, and spent some months on active service in aid of the civil power before moving to Egypt for a two-year tour. In 1938 the 2nd Camerons left Egypt for India.

THE QUEEN'S OWN CAMERON HIGHLANDERS

1939–61

The 1st Camerons joined the British Expeditionary Force in September 1939 and took up positions at Aix. During the winter the 4th Camerons reached France and during January 1940 moved to the area of the Maginot Line in the Saar region.

In May the 1st Battalion advanced across Belgium with the 2nd Division to the River Dyle, to meet the German invasion. The battalion's chief engagement during the subsequent withdrawal was a counter-attack on the enemy position on the Escaut River, and on 26 May the Camerons were attacked while holding a stretch of canal at La Bassée. They destroyed enemy recce vehicles and drove off an attack against the battalion on their right. A Company, at only half strength, cleared 300 yards of canal bank of enemy positions in a daring attack. Then at 2.25pm on 27 May about 300 enemy tanks advanced in a divisional attack, 100 of them in the direction of the 1st Camerons. Lt Col Miller's battalion HQ was pounded by tanks at only 80 yards range, but the anti-tank platoon knocked out twenty-one of them, and the depleted companies held their ground for an hour until ordered to withdraw. At Dunkirk the remnants of the battalion embarked for England.

Meanwhile, the 4th Camerons in the 51st Highland Division were ordered to withdraw from the Saar to the Somme at Abbeville. Some delay was inflicted on the enemy, but C Company was overrun and A Company surrounded and captured the following day. The remnants of the battalion were ordered to withdraw on 6 June. The German strength was, however, overwhelming and the 51st Highland Division withdrew to the seaport of St Valéry-en-Caux from where it was hoped the division could be evacuated. On 12 June it was about to be overwhelmed when the GOC ordered the division to surrender.

The 1st and 4th Camerons were re-formed in July 1940 in the UK, and the following month the 4th were sent to the West Indies for an eighteen-month tour. In 1942, they were redesignated the 2nd Queen's Own Cameron Highlanders when the original 2nd Battalion was lost at Tobruk. In the meantime the 1st Liverpool Scottish had provided a contingent to serve in the Norwegian campaign, but the battalion was to remain at home duty throughout the war. The 2nd

The 4th Camerons take over duties on the Maginot Line from French troops. The whole of the 51st Highland Division was sent as a reinforcement to the French army in early 1940, and thus were not part of the BEF which escaped at Dunkirk. IWM

Liverpool Scottish likewise, spent the war in the United Kingdom, first as infantry and then on conversion to an anti-tank role.

* * * * *

The 2nd Camerons moved to Egypt from India on mobilisation in 1939 with the 4th Indian Division. In September 1940 the Italian army advanced towards the Egyptian border and the Camerons' first operation was an attack on Maktila on 22 October. In a much larger action on 9 December, the Camerons took part in the assault on Nibeiwa camp and captured Sidi Barrani on the following day.

Buglers of the 2nd Camerons in Egypt 1940. Tragically the battalion was captured at Tobruk two years later during Rommel's second offensive. IWM

In January 1941 the division was sent to fight against the Italians in Eritrea. After landing at Port Sudan the force advanced to Kassala, and the Camerons led their brigade against an enemy stronghold, a ridge known as 'Gibraltar', near Agordat. On the second day of the battle,

'The main attack,' recorded the regimental journal, 'was timed for dawn on 31 January. Again the battalion was to act as spearhead . . . Under cover of a heavy barrage, C and D Companies advanced, followed by A and B Companies, over the ridge itself. The enemy let fly with everything they had got, but the attack went on unchecked.' Other battalions and armoured troops conformed to the Camerons' advance. 'Nine medium and two light [enemy] tanks were knocked out . . . the Camerons of the right of the line and the Royal Fusiliers on the left, were ordered to make a quarter left wheel to make good the Agordat-Karen road where it entered the gorge . . . No resistance was met . . . Thus ended the battle of Agordat.'

The Italians then withdrew eastwards, but managed to hold and block the road to Keren, until the battalion launched a successful attack on a feature subsequently known as Cameron Ridge. The division made steady progress during the next month in clearing the Italians from a series of strong positions in the mountainous country. The Camerons' final achievement was the capture of twin mountain peaks, Mount Sanchil and Brig's Peak. The Italians in due course were expelled from Eritrea and Abyssinia.

Meanwhile, the Germans had reinforced the Italians in North Africa and the 2nd Camerons returned to Egypt in April 1941. They spent much of 1941 in defensive operations, their most notable battle being at Halfaya Pass. The German strength however, was being built up, and for a time Tobruk was cut off. During the operations to relieve it in December 1941, the Camerons took part in the attack on the Germans at El Gubi, but in the following month the Germans went onto the offensive and forced a British withdrawal. The 2nd Camerons adopted delaying positions at Maraua, El Faida and Carmusa as the Germans approached the Gazala defensive line in front of Tobruk. The Camerons had been ordered to defend the town, but on 19 June the Germans launched a major attack and forced the fortress area of the

Training in the Egyptian desert. The 2nd Camerons on Bren-gun carrier drills in June 1940. Three months later they were in action against Italian thrusts from Libya.

A Cameron Highlander takes an Italian prisoner after the battle of El Alamein, Nov 1942. The 5th Camerons had joined the re-formed 51st Highland Division and this was their first action. IWM

town to surrender. For a further day the 2nd Camerons continued to fight for the outskirts, but as the situation was hopeless, the Commanding Officer ordered fit men to make for Egypt, the rest of the battalion to surrender. This they did in some style by marching into captivity led by the pipes.

* * * * *

The 5th Battalion, Queen's Own Cameron Highlanders joined the reconstituted 51st Highland Division and moved with the division to Egypt in August 1942. Their first action was at the battle of El Alamein on 23 October. The battalion had two tasks: two companies were assigned to give close protection to the Royal Engineers breaching the German minefields, and the other companies were placed under command of 154 Brigade on the left of the division for the actual assault. After the first phase of the battle, the Camerons' companies were reunited and took part in the breakthrough of the German defences, known as operation 'Supercharge'. The battalion was on the left of the brigade and was involved in a hard battle supported by armour during the night of 2 November and the following day. As the axis line crumbled under the weight of the attack, the 51st Highland Division made swift progress.

The 5th Battalion's next major engagement was at Beurat in mid-January 1943, when they were acting as a mobile advanced guard of the division. They entered Tripoli later in the month, but when the division reached the Mareth Line in February the enemy successfully delayed the advance. There the 5th Camerons were given the task of assaulting across the anti-tank ditch to seize an important position held by the enemy. The battalion lost numerous casualties and the task proved too difficult. Other formations, however, succeeded in bypassing the Mareth Line and the advance continued. The next major enemy line was on the Roumana Ridge covering the Wadi Akarit. On the night of 6/7 April the 5th Camerons took part in an assault on the Roumana Ridge, with the 2nd and 5th Seaforth Highlanders. At 3.30am the battalion advanced across the desert and successfully assaulted the Italian and German positions on the ridge. The German 90th Light Division, however, counter-attacked and, together with some Italian troops, fought against A and D Companies. Fierce close-quarter fighting continued all day, but successes elsewhere encouraged those fighting on Roumana Ridge so that by the end of the day its defences were consolidated. A Reuter's report stated of the Seaforth and Camerons 'Their assault is described by military observers as one of the greatest heroic achievements of the war.' After this engagement the battalion was withdrawn and began to train for their next operation – the invasion of Sicily.

The 5th Camerons landed with the 51st Highland Division on the island on 10 July 1943, but were initially held in reserve. During the advance inland the Camerons took the lead and dealt with light opposition for the next two days. On 13 July they assisted the 5th Seaforth Highlanders' attack on German positions at Francofonte, which was entirely successful. Later the battalion met strong enemy positions in the Sferro hills, but again successfully carried their objectives, working in conjunction with the 2nd Seaforth Highlanders. The two campaigns had by this time cost the 5th Camerons over 600 casualties, and they left Sicily to return to the United Kingdom to train for operations in North West Europe.

In the meantime the 2nd Camerons (formerly the re-formed 4th Battalion) went to Egypt in late 1943 and joined the Italian front in February 1944. They were heavily involved in the operation at Monte Cassino and suffered numerous casualties during the battle against the Gustav Line. In the summer the Camerons fought against German positions on the Gothic Line and they continued in action through the autumn, their major action being the occupation of San Marino. Then in November the 2nd Camerons were sent to Greece to assist in restoring order and government, and they remained in the Mediterranean theatre until 1947.

* * * *

The 1st Camerons had been reconstituted after Dunkirk, and had embarked for India in 1942. They were, however, not in action until April 1944 when the Japanese had advanced into India near Kohima. At first the Camerons conducted patrol operations against the enemy surrounding the town, and on 14 April opened the road to the town by destroying a Jap position at Zubza. It was decided that another large patrol would be infiltrated behind the Jap line, to capture Point 5120, which overlooked Kohima. At 2am on 4 May the battalion set off in the dark, and by 5am had seized the western knoll of Point 5120. This enabled the troops to move more freely in the area. Two of the Cameron Companies, however, were by now being subjected to determined Japanese attacks, which continued throughout the day: the enemy managed to remain on part of Point 5120 for many hours, and the Camerons lost 35 killed and 70 wounded and missing. Patrolling continued for several weeks in the surrounding area. Kohima was successfully defended and the Japanese were forced to withdraw. The battalion continued to harass the enemy for the next two months until the road from Kohima to Imphal was again in British hands. The Camerons' total casualties were 283 in these operations, and the 2nd Division, in which the battalion served, was withdrawn from the fighting for several months.

The 2nd Division moved into Burma in November 1944 to join in the reconquest of that country. Crossing the Chindwin just before Christmas, the battalion formed a bridgehead over the River Mu, despite determined resistance by the enemy. The Camerons continued to advance, clearing enemy villages on the way to Shwebo, and on the night of 24 February 1945 the battalion established a crossing point on the Irrawaddy over which the whole division could pass. The 1st Camerons were then involved in the fighting for Mandalay during March, and successfully overwhelmed the enemy at Kyauktalon and Ava in battalion attacks. After the fall of the city, the battalion continued to advance southwards taking part in a clearing operation. At the beginning of May the Camerons returned to India for training in amphibious operations, but were not required to go into action again. They remained in India until early 1946.

* * * * *

The 5th Camerons landed with the 51st Highland Division on the Normandy Beaches on 7 June 1944. Their action during the next few weeks was largely defensive, as the division was on the left of the allied armies and had to wait for the Americans to break through to the south. The Camerons fought in numerous engagements on the River Orne to the west of Caen, and the Germans mounted several large-scale counter-attacks against them during June and July. In early August the battalion took part in operation 'Totalise', the successful breakthrough to Caen and advance towards Falaise. Their most notable engagements were the capture of Lorquichon and Poussy.

A month later, after crossing the Seine, the Camerons entered and occupied St Valéry-en-Caux, where the 4th Battalion had been forced to surrender in 1940. The 5th Camerons were spearhead troops in the division's assault on Le Havre on 11 September, which was followed by a rapid advance across the border into Belgium and Holland. In October the battalion fought successful actions at Schijndel and Vught, and on 4 November carried out an assault crossing of the Aftvaterings Canal. The Camerons continued to advance to the River Maas, and mounted assaults over the Nederwert and Zig Canals in mid-November. In the latter action the battalion faced a very determined German counter-attack after forming a bridgehead; but the Camerons successfully held until the 2nd Seaforth passed through and pushed the Germans back. In January 1945 the division was rushed to the Ardennes to assist the Americans repel the strongest German counter-offensive so far in the theatre. The Camerons took part in several actions in the worst of winter conditions, before the position was stabilised and they could return to Holland.

In early February the 5th Camerons fought against the Germans holding the Siegfried Line in the Reichswald Forest. The battle lasted for a week and the battalion then seized Hervost and Asperden as the enemy withdrew to the Rhine. On 24 March, the Camerons crossed the river with the division in a follow-up wave and, passing through, the leading troops carried out an attack on Mittelburg which the Germans were holding in strength.

As on numerous occasions during the campaign, 5th Camerons take a ride on a Sherman tank during the advance on Tilburg, Holland, Oct 1944. IWM

At '0815 hrs,' states the war diary, 'C Company crossed the start line but met heavy opposition from the area of their first objective. Casualties were inflicted . . . their first objective was secured, despite the presence of a self-propelled gun about 100 yards away. A Company was ordered to go to C Company's assistance,'

with armour, but the task proved too difficult owing to a further number of anti-tank guns. That night after a brief withdrawal by the remnants of C Company, the battalion mounted a second attack on the village, with A and B Companies in the lead. Fighting in the streets continued until 2am, by which time Mittelburg was firmly in the Camerons' possession. Three days later they attacked Isselburg and captured it. The advance north-eastwards was rapid and the battalion fought in a number of engagements, the most notable being the occupation of Adelheide. In the final days of the war the 5th Camerons reached the area of Bremerhaven.

* * * * *

In 1945 the 1st Battalion was sent to Japan as part of the occupation force and in the following year moved to Malaya. There the Camerons were involved in internal security operations until April 1948. Meanwhile, the 2nd Camerons had returned from the Mediterranean in 1947. In 1948 the 1st Battalion cadre returned to the United Kingdom and, on the disbandment of the 2nd, was immediately built up to establishment.

In February 1949 the 1st Camerons embarked for a two year tour in Tripoli. In November 1951 the battalion was moved to Egypt to assist in the defence of the Canal Zone during a time of particular tension in Egypt. Again the Camerons took part in internal security operations in the British-controlled territory, based in Tel-el-Kebir camp.

After returning to the United Kingdom in 1952 the Camerons spent three years in Austria and West Germany. They then served for a year in Korea as part of the Commonwealth Division, whose task was to be prepared to respond to any breakdown of the peace settlement, which fortunately did not occur.

In August 1956 the battalion was sent to Aden for two years with the task of maintaining the security of the town and oil refinery, and patrolling up-country near the Yemen border. In 1958 the Camerons returned to the United Kingdom and were stationed in Dover and Edinburgh. In 1961 they were amalgamated with the Seaforth Highlanders at a ceremony in Edinburgh.

QUEEN'S OWN HIGHLANDERS
(Seaforth and Camerons)
1961 to the present

Shortly after amalgamation the 1st Battalion, Queen's Own Highlanders were sent to Singapore and Borneo, and the following year two companies and Battalion Headquarters were moved by air and sea to quell a rebellion in Brunei. A Company seized Seria airfield from the rebels after being airlanded, and the rebellion quickly came to an end when the battalion occupied Seria itself. The Queen's Own Highlanders remained in Brunei until February 1963 and returned to Borneo for a nine-month tour later in the year, their chief task being to patrol the border with Indonesia.

The period 1964 to 1971 was spent in Edinburgh, West Germany and Berlin, with a nine-month tour in Sharjah in the Trucial States. Their first emergency tour in Northern Ireland was during the winter of 1971–2, and they returned in July 1972 at short notice, at the time of operation 'Motorman'.

In the 1970s and 1980s the battalion has served in the United Kingdom, West Germany, Hong Kong, Belize and the Falkland Islands, as well as Northern Ireland on several occasions.

CHAPTER 10
THE GORDON HIGHLANDERS

The Gordon Highlanders were formed in 1881 from two regiments: the 1st Battalion was the former 75th Stirlingshire Regiment, and the 92nd Gordon Highlanders became the 2nd Battalion. There had been no link between the regiments before, and the decision taken was somewhat arbitrary. The senior regiment had lost much of its highland character when it was removed from the highland establishment in 1809. It was therefore not surprising that it was to some extent eclipsed by the more 'fiercely highland' 92nd.

75TH STIRLINGSHIRE REGIMENT

1787–1881

The regiment was formed in 1787 by Colonel Robert Abercromby of Tullibody, brother of Sir Ralph Abercromby, and embodied at Stirling. Designated the 75th (Highland) Regiment of Foot, it embarked for service with the Honourable East India Company in the following year.

In 1789 the third Mysore War broke out, and the regiment's first action was fought a year later at the storming and capture of Fort Choughaset. At the end of the year the 75th Highlanders fought at the battle of Tervangherry, where 14,000 Mysore troops were routed.

In 1791 a large British and native force was assembled for the siege of Tippoo Sahib's capital of Seringapatam. It was a difficult march through the jungle and mountains with the vast siege train. On arrival, it was decided that the force was not sufficient in strength to invest the fortress successfully, so a partial withdrawal was ordered. The 75th covered the rear and fought off the enemy cavalry which attempted to harass the British force. In early 1792 a much larger force under Lord Cornwallis and Abercromby renewed the march on Seringapatam and laid siege to it. During the fighting outside the walls, on 6 February, a detachment of the 75th Highlanders captured a wooded position held by Tippoo Sahib's elite 'Tiger Battalions', numbering about 2,000 men. The highlanders ran short of ammunition but succeeded in holding the wood by charging the enemy with the bayonet, until reinforced. There they remained until the end of the battle. Tippoo Sahib sued for peace in March and, after ceding half his territory to the British, the siege was lifted.

In 1799 the fourth Mysore War started. The British government had considered that unless Mysore power was completely broken the alliance between Tippoo Sahib and the French would enable them together seriously to threaten British ascendancy in India. In March the flank companies of the 75th Highlanders with the Madras army fought on the action at Peripatum, which forced the Mysore army to retreat to Seringapatam. The regiment's first action on reaching the city was to assist in storming the village of Agrar, which was followed by the seizure of a redoubt close to the city walls. On 4 May an assault on Seringapatam was launched and the 75th provided a forlorn hope and part of the left storming party. The orders for the attack were:

> 'The leading companies of each attack to use the bayonet principally, and not fire except in case of absolute necessity. Shortly after one o'clock in the afternoon, Baird led the columns forward and entered the bed of the river, where they were immediately assailed by a tremendous fire of musketry and rockets . . . Both parties ascended the glacis and the beaches together . . . such was the rapidity of the attack, and the uncompromising bravery of the stormers . . . the forlorn hope, closely followed by the leading companies had in six minutes reached the summit of the breach, and the British colours were soon proudly displayed on the famous fortress of Seringapatam.'

The war quickly came to a close.

In the following five years the 75th Highlanders took part in a number of actions against Indian rulers in revolt against the British. In 1801 the regiment fought at Malabar and Canara in the Madras Presidency and in the following year's campaign in the Gujerat, the highlanders assisted in capturing a number of forts. In 1804 the regiment moved to Bengal and was involved in the attempt to capture Bhurtpore a year later. This fortress was held in very great strength, and on the fourth attempt the highlanders fought with 'an astonishing, even desperate degree of valour', as they tried to scale the wall by driving bayonets into it for footholds. The enemy poured down fire and materials dipped in flaming oil on top of them, and the regiment lost nearly half its number as casualties. A short while later the ruler sued for peace.

* * * * *

The 75th Highlanders returned to Great Britain in 1807 and two years later, owing to the shortage of military manpower in Scotland, it officially ceased to be a highland regiment. After making up its strength the 75th embarked for twelve years of garrison duties

Previous page:
Accompanied by Lt-Col E. G. Hay, Gen Sir Bernard Montgomery makes an informal inspection of the 5th/7th Gordons at Beaconsfield, prior to the invasion of Normandy, 1944. IWM

successively in Sicily, Corsica and Gibraltar. The years 1823 to 1832 were spent at home duty, but in the latter year the regiment sailed to South Africa.

The 75th spent a number of years in the eastern Cape during the almost continual operations against the Kaffirs. In 1834 the guerrilla activities of the natives became so serious that an expeditionary force, which included the 75th Regiment, invaded Kaffraria. The main force of the enemy was quickly defeated, but the Kaffirs continued to harass the British outposts which had to be continuously manned. Detachments of the 75th, some of which were mounted, patrolled and skirmished with the enemy for a number of months, until Major Cox of the regiment concluded a peace personally with the Kaffir chiefs. This gallant officer had carried out the negotiations unarmed in the presence of a large armed body of Kaffirs. The regiment continued to serve in South Africa until 1843, when it returned to Great Britain.

In 1849 the 75th Regiment embarked for India for normal peacetime duties. In May 1857, however, the Bengal army in Meerut mutinied, and the mutiny spread rapidly to other parts. On hearing of this the regiment, which was stationed near Simla, marched a distance of 48 miles in 38 hours to Umballa to join a field force of two brigades. Their task was to march on Delhi and relieve the garrison. On 3rd June they reached Alipur, near the city, and prepared to deal with the outer defensive positions. The mutineers had established an artillery battery at Badli-ke-Serai, and on 8 June the 75th were ordered to capture it. Charging with the bayonet, the regiment carried the position, routed the enemy and enabled other British troops to establish themselves on the Delhi Ridge overlooking the city. For the next three months the mutineers attacked the British lines constantly, but by September a breach in the city walls had been made sufficiently large enough for a British assault. On 13 September the Kashmir gate was blown open and the city stormed at dawn on the following day. The right hand column of four storming the breach was led by the 75th Regiment, and there followed the most desperate hand-to-hand fighting. By the end of the day the northern part of the city was in British hands. For a whole week the fighting continued, and the 75th

'Advanced by breaking through, then posting pickets so as to command the interior of the works, the enemy was taken in reverse with fatal effect . . . with a small party . . . [they] entered the loopholed gorge, and surprised and captured the Burn bastion after slight opposition. Reinforcements arriving, two guns of the captured bastion were turned on the Lahore Gate which was taken early next morning . . . By the afternoon of the 20 September the reconquest of Delhi was complete.'

The 75th Regiment moved towards Lucknow, with a relief column during the autumn, and on the way attacked and routed an enemy force near Agra. At Cawnpore the column joined Sir Colin Campbell's force, and by early November reached the outskirts of Lucknow. The 75th took part in the fighting between 14 and 22 November, when the Residency was successfully relieved and the British defenders, with their women and children, were evacuated to safety. The occupation of the whole city was not possible with the small number of British and loyal troops – some 4,000 against the enemy's 60,000 – so a withdrawal to Cawnpore was ordered.

The 75th Regiment, however, was left in a column under Sir James Outram to hold the area of the Alam Bagh Palace, and on the night of 16 January 1858, the regiment was attacked by five enemy battalions at the nearby outpost of Dungapur. After bombarding the enemy with artillery fire, the regiment allowed them to come within 80 yards before opening fire with their rifles. This naturally required great discipline and nerve, but the tactic succeeded in turning and defeating the enemy. Thereafter the regiment remained holding positions near Lucknow until its final relief in March 1858. The 75th took part in further operations for several months as the British gradually regained control.

The regiment returned to Great Britain in 1862, and in that year the title was altered to include the name 'Stirlingshire', its depot being the county town. For the next nineteen years the regiment served at peacetime stations in the United Kingdom, Gibraltar, Singapore, Hong Kong and Natal. In 1881 it was amalgamated and became the 1st Battalion, the Gordon Highlanders, re-adopting highland dress with the kilt of Gordon tartan.

THE 92ND GORDON HIGHLANDERS

1794–1881

In 1794 the 4th Duke of Gordon raised a new regiment of highlanders mainly from his own estates. The first Gordon regiment to be raised had fought in India in the 1760s, and two fencible regiments had also been in service. At this time of national danger, when invasion was threatened by revolutionary France, there was already a shortage of highlanders to serve in the army. It is alleged that Duchess Jean personally bestowed a kiss and a shilling on many a recruit to assist in raising the regiment. When embodied it was the 100th (Gordon Highlanders) Regiment of Foot, but re-numbered in 1798 as the 92nd.

The regiment remained at home service until 1799 in which year, with the Duke's heir, the Marquis of Huntley, in command, it joined the expeditionary force under Sir Ralph Abercromby for the campaign in Holland. The regiment's first battle was at Egmont-op-Zee, when its task was to guard twenty guns during an approach march through the sand dunes.

'The 92nd was called into action, and coming to the charge at once, a dreadful conflict took place between them and the French, whose cavalry at the same time made a charge upon the British Artillery occupying the beach, between the infantry and the sea, and took a momentary possession of the guns; but the British Cavalry . . . lost not an instant in charging the Enemy, cheered by the British Infantry. The guns were retaken, and the Enemy's cavalry was driven back. The infantry on both sides, which had ceased firing, as if by command, to witness the charge of cavalry, recommenced the action; the action was continued until dusk (about six o'clock), when the Enemy gave way at every point and made a rapid retreat.'

The Gordons' casualties were over 300. The results of the campaign, however, were inconclusive, and at the end of the year the British re-embarked for home.

In May 1800 the 92nd Highlanders embarked for service in the near East, as part of Sir Ralph Abercromby's expeditionary force. The force eventually reached Egypt in March the following year, and landed at Aboukir Bay. The French, holding the fortress of Alexandria ten miles to the west, resisted the landing with artillery as well as cavalry and infantry. Once ashore the 92nd and other battalions held off the enemy cavalry and then charged with the bayonet, successfully seizing some heights overlooking the beach-head. On 13 March the British force advanced towards Alexandria, with the 92nd Highlanders at the head of the left column.

'The British had not advanced,' wrote Sir Robert Wilson, 'out of the wood of the date trees which was in front of Mandora Tower before the enemy left the heights in which they had formed, and moved down commencing a heavy fire of musketry, and from all their cannon, on the 92nd Regiment . . . opposed to a tremendous fire, and suffering severely from the French line, they never receded a foot, but maintained the contest alone, until the marines and the rest of the line came to their support.'

The French cavalry then charged the 90th Perthshire Regiment on the right, whose musket fire at close-quarters range caused the enemy to swing towards the 92nd Highlanders. The 92nd then took the brunt of the charge but beat off the cavalry by determined and effective musket-fire. The redoubt was successfully taken and the British continued the advance.

A week later the French again attacked in great strength, and for some hours the 92nd had to defeat enemy infantry and cavalry charges with musket-fire and the bayonet. Eventually the enemy withdrew into Alexandria. The 92nd remained in Egypt, taking part in the occupation of Cairo and siege of Alexandria, which capitulated later in the year.

The regiment returned for home service and took part in two further expeditions. The first was to Denmark in 1807, under Sir Arthur Wellesley, later Duke of Wellington, where the 92nd Highlanders were in action several times, including the capture of Copenhagen. Their second expedition under Sir John Moore to Sweden was recalled, and they were sent in 1808 to assist in ejecting the French from Spain. The 92nd Highlanders were with Moore's army during his attempt to outflank the French army, but the enemy outnumbered the British by some 194,000 to 35,000. To avoid annihilation the British retreated to Corunna on the northern coast during the winter, fighting rearguard actions on the way. The 92nd's discipline was largely maintained during the terrible march, and at the battle of Corunna they played an active part in repelling the French assaults on the British line. The regiment, having suffered over a hundred casualties, safely embarked for England after the battle.

Like many other regiments lately to have served in the Peninsula, the 92nd Highlanders embarked later in 1809 for the disastrous Walcheren expedition. They lost a high proportion of their number through fever before the expedition was called off, having taken part in little actual fighting.

In October 1810 the 92nd reached the Peninsula again, and joined Wellesley's army behind the line of Torres Vedras, where with the 71st Highlanders, it formed 1 Brigade of the 2nd Division. In the spring campaign of 1811 the 92nd was one of the regiments holding the village of Fuentes d'Onor when, on 3rd May, it was attacked by a large French force of cavalry and infantry. The French were successful in occupying part of the village, but when reinforced, the British forced them to withdraw. The Light Company of the regiment assisted in this action with a particularly spirited charge. The battle lasted for three days, and on 5 May the 92nd Highlanders managed to prevent the enemy cavalry capturing some British artillery batteries.

In October the 92nd, marching with General Hill's division, surprised a French force in a dawn attack at Arroyo del Molinos. The enemy were evicted, but formed up in squares outside the village and gradually moved onto high ground. The 92nd Highlanders advanced towards the French skirmishers, forming a screen in front of the enemy's position, and fought them at close quarters. Another British force took up position at the rear of the enemy, whereupon the French force broke and dispersed, rapidly pursued by the British.

The next significant action in which the 92nd

Highlanders fought was for the capture of a bridge of boats at Almaraz on the River Tagus. On 19 May 1812 a surprise attack was mounted on the three French forts guarding the bridge, and during the action the 92nd Highlanders captured the bridgehead and restored the bridge, which had begun to break up. The French withdrew immediately, leaving the whole area in British hands.

The 92nd Highlanders continued to march and skirmish against the French for the next twelve months. In June 1813 they formed up in the British centre under Wellington's direct command, facing the enemy at Vitoria. Their objective was the capture of the Heights of Puebla in the French centre, and they were assisted by the 50th Regiment. Despite some confused counter-orders, the two regiments fought their way onto the ridge forcing the enemy to give way and relieving the hard-pressed 71st Highlanders.

'The enemy immediately sent a reinforcement of about 7000 men, with some artillery to this point, and made several attempts to recover this lost ground, but was as frequently repulsed by the troops which were opposed to him . . . they covered the remainder of the second division while filing across the Zadorra in its movement to attack the enemy in the village of Subijana de Alava. At this juncture the 92nd was again directed to advance . . . and the French having given way at all points, the battalion continued a rapid pursuit along the Pampeluna road.'

While holding the Pyrenean mountain pass at Maya during the following month, the 92nd Highlanders' brigade was attacked by a French force under General Soult. Although taken by surprise, the brigade flank companies held the pass whilst the other companies attacked the enemy. The enemy strength was such that adjoining passes were abandoned by the British and the Maya pass had to be evacuated. The 92nd's right wing held off a very strong French attack during the withdrawal and brought down deadly fire on the enemy. Despite suffering half their number as casualties, the highlanders then advanced – 'the stern valour of the 92nd would have graced Thermopylae', as one eyewitness commented – and drove the enemy back for over a mile.

During 1813 the French retreated across the mountains into their own country, and on 10 November the 92nd Highlanders captured three French redoubts on the line of the River Nivelle. A month later they captured St Pierre in a successful charge against two French regiments. The French then counter-attacked and the fighting continued throughout the day, before the 92nd mounted a final charge and forced the enemy out of the village. In late February 1814 the regiment played an important part in an attack on the French flank and rear at Orthez, positioned on the ridge above the river. This manoeuvre, with the 92nd Highlanders in the lead, cleared the enemy from the heights, enabled the town to be captured and forced the enemy to withdraw completely from the field of battle. In the final battle of the Peninsular campaign the 92nd captured the first line of trenches at St Cypian, near Toulouse, and held them for the rest of the day while the French were defeated in detail on other parts of the battlefield.

The 92nd Highlanders returned to the continent with the Duke of Wellington's army in the spring of 1815, as a consequence of Napoleon's return from exile. In the early hours of 16 June they were ordered to march to block the enemy's approach at Quatre Bras. During the afternoon the regiment faced a number of infantry and cavalry charges but held its ground. Towards the end of the battle the Gordons attacked a strong column of the enemy, and in the fiercest fighting routed it. The casualties in the regiment were over 300. Although the enemy were checked, the British withdrew to positions at Waterloo.

On 18 June the 92nd Highlanders in Picton's Division were posted behind the ridge in the centre of the allied line, where throughout the day they were under constant fire from artillery.

'The 92nd at this time was reduced to less than 300 men. A column of 3000 French was formed in the position in front of the regiment, which was concealed by the nature of the ground. This was the state of affairs when Sir Denis Pack (Brigade Commander) galloped up to the regiment and called out "Ninety-second you must charge, for all the troops on your right and left have given way." The regiment formed four deep, until within twenty paces, when it fired a volley, and instantly darted into the heart of the French column, in which it became almost invisible, in the midst of the mass opposed to it.'

At the same time the Union Brigade of cavalry took part in the attack, and they did such execution that the French formations were shattered, and they withdrew in confusion. It was with some difficulty that the British regiments were re-formed after such a precipitate charge, but during the afternoon the Gordons formed square and held their ground under the heaviest artillery fire and successive waves of French, losing many more casualties. Napoleon's army had failed to break the British and allied troops, and the Gordons took part in the general advance at the end of the day as the French withdrew from the battlefield.

* * * * *

It was a long time before the 92nd Highlanders saw action again after Waterloo. Like many British regiments they served for many years at home duty in Scotland, England and Ireland. For some time they garrisoned islands in the West Indies, losing numerous soldiers through disease and the climate. In 1834 they served in Gibraltar and, later, on the Island of

Corfu. A stalemate had been reached in the Crimea by the time the regiment arrived there in late 1855, and it took little part in the fighting. The 92nd were sent to India in March 1858 but most of the major battles of the Mutiny were over. They spent the many months in the jungle hunting a most formidable mutineer, Tantia Topee, who successfully waged guerilla warfare against British troops until he was finally captured.

In 1861 the 'Gordon' prefix was restored officially to the regiment, after being in abeyance since 1798. The regiment remained in India, and after five years spent in Scotland and Ireland it returned to India in 1868.

In 1878 war against the Afghan ruler Shere Ali began, and two columns of British and Indian troops crossed the border. The Gordon Highlanders were first in action when a detachment under C/Sgt Macdonald (later General Sir Hector Macdonald) assisted in the capture of Shutagardan Pass. There was a temporary peace when Shere Ali died, but his son Yakub Khan resumed hostilities and murdered the British representative and his whole staff.

A force under General Roberts crossed the frontier again in 1879, and the march on Kabul began. At Charasia the force reached a mountain pass, and Major White led a party of the 92nd Highlanders to capture the enemy positions dominating it. After a very difficult climb under enemy fire the highlanders reached the top, whereupon the tribesmen fled, leaving the hill-top positions clear. Major White won the VC for this action. A short while later Kabul was surrendered to Roberts, but further expeditions had to be sent to various places to fight tribesmen who refused to acknowledge the peace treaty. At Takhtrir Shah two companies of the 92nd ascended a 2,500ft climb to reach the fortified positions from which the enemy were bringing down heavy rifle fire. The highlanders charged over the defences and, using their bayonets, ejected the enemy: Lt Dick Cunningham won the VC for this exploit.

The Gordon Highlanders were also present for the defence of the main British base at Sherpur near Kabul. It was attacked several times during the campaign and, on 23 December 1879, the highlanders helped to defeat a major attack by the Afghans.

In July 1880 the second field force based at Kandahar suffered a desperate defeat at Maiwand, and in August Roberts began a three weeks' march from Kabul to relieve the garrison. On the way the relief column was frequently attacked, and the heat

These two calotypes of 1846, taken by the pioneers of photography in Scotland, David Octavius Hill and Robert Adamson, show soldiers of the 92nd Gordon Highlanders at Leith Fort.

Scottish National Portrait Gallery

and terrain combined to make the march into an ordeal. Kandahar was reached, and the Afghans were attacked by the British and Indian troops. During the battle two companies of the 92nd, showing great bravery, charged and captured some enemy guns. The Afghan army retreated in confusion and the war quickly came to an end.

In 1881 the 92nd Gordon Highlanders left India but were diverted to Durban to reinforce the British troops fighting the first Boer War. A detachment of the regiment numbering 118 all ranks, joined a small expedition to take the Boers by surprise at Majuba, but during the disastrous battle the Boers managed to take up positions dominating the British defences on the hill. The enemy brought down murderous fire for five hours, and of 118 members of the regiment involved, 96 were killed or wounded. In the words of an eye witness: 'I went to the edge of the hill, where so many of the 92nd had been killed. The dead were all shot above the chest.' Such accurate long-range rifle fire had not been experienced before by the British troops. The war came to an end soon after, but the humiliation of Majuba was remembered by the British public for a long time.

THE GORDON HIGHLANDERS

1881–1913

In 1881 the 73rd Stirlingshire Regiment and 92nd Gordon Highlanders were amalgamated, forming respectively the 1st and 2nd Battalions. Highland dress of Gordon tartan was worn by both battalions thereafter, the 1st Battalion having the kilt restored to it after 72 years.

The 2nd Battalion remained at home service for many years, but the 1st joined the Highland Brigade in the expeditionary force sent to Egypt in 1882, to crush the revolt of the Egyptian army. The lines of communication having been secured the British set out from the area of Ismailia on the canal to fight the Egyptian army under Colonel Arabi, camped at Tel-El-Kebir. A silent night march was conducted on 12 September, and at dawn the force advanced close to the enemy before they began to fire. The brigade charged with the bayonet, crossed the ditches and overwhelmed the Egyptian troops within a matter of minutes. The Gordons' casualties were slight, as were those of all the British regiments, but the battle was decisive.

The 1st Gordon Highlanders remained in Cairo after the war, and fought in the Sudan campaign of 1884. They joined the force to the eastern Sudan to capture the port of Suakin on the Red Sea. They marched, when in contact with the enemy, in a curious oblong formation by brigades, as ordered by the expedition's commander. This resulted in unnecessarily high casualties from enemy rifle fire, and difficulty in manoeuvring over broken terrain. At the battle of El-Teb this formation proved most unwieldy when gaps opened, on account of two regiments dashing forward to overwhelm local opposition. At Tamai the square was actually broken for a time, but the Gordons and other regiments successfully beat off the dervishes. Suakim was eventually occupied and the Gordons returned to Egypt.

Later in 1884, however, they returned to the Sudan to assist in the attempt to relieve Khartoum, where General Gordon was cut off by the Mahdi's troops. The regiment was not much involved in the fighting except for Capt Ian Hamilton's (later General Sir Ian Hamilton) D Company at Kirbekan. Khartoum, however, was not relieved, General Gordon was killed, and the Sudan was not reconquered for fourteen years.

The 2nd Battalion, the Gordon Highlanders remained on foreign service first in Malta, and then in Ceylon and India. In 1895 they joined the Chitral Relief Force on the North-West Frontier, when the fort of that name was under siege from Khan tribesmen. The enemy held strong positions, dominating the Malakand pass on the route to Chitral, and the

Under fire from Afridi tribesmen, Gordon Highlanders scramble up the precipitous crags of Dargai before storming the fortified village on top, 20 Oct 1897.

The 1st Gordons wait to move forward during the battle of Paardeburg, Feb 1900, the first major success of the British army in the Boer War. Both regular battalions distinguished themselves in the war.
RHQ

Two soldiers of the 1st Gordons 'port arms' under the eye of some off-duty comrades, South Africa 1900.
RHQ

Gordon Highlanders and King's Own Scottish Borderers were ordered to eject the enemy. The Gordons, divided into three parties, climbed the precipitous hill and forced the gap at bayonet point. As one eyewitness said: 'It was a fine and stirring sight to see the splendid dash with which the two Scottish regiments took the hill.' Chitral was subsequently relieved.

The battalion remained with the field force, taking part in several engagements during the year. The decision was made to mount a much larger expedition to the Afridi tribal area in the Tirah region, and the Gordon Highlanders joined the Tirah Field Force. They assisted in the first attempt to capture the precipitous heights at Dargai on 18 October 1897, but the enemy reoccupied them. On 20 October, the two leading battalions sent to recapture the heights met strong resistance and were still unable to dislodge the enemy. Whereupon the Gordons and 3rd Sikhs were ordered to attack the Dargai Heights.

'The Gordon Highlanders went straight up the hill without check or hesitation. Headed by their pipers and led by Lt Col Mathias . . . this splendid battalion marched across the open. It dashed across a murderous fire . . . followed at short intervals by a second and a third each led by officers . . . Few of the enemy waited for the bayonet, many of them being shot as they fled in confusion . . . in forty minutes [the Gordons] had won the heights.'

Two members of the regiment won the Victoria Cross on this occasion, one of whom was Piper Findlater who continued to play the pipes although wounded in both legs. Further actions were fought by detachments of the regiments at Maidan and Bara Valley, where they were completely surrounded and had to be relieved by a whole brigade of infantry.

Line-up for the start of an inter-company cross-country race of the 1st Gordons. Period-piece photograph, 1912. RHQ

In 1898 the 2nd Battalion reached India and the 1st returned to Scotland. A year later the 2nd Gordon Highlanders embarked for the colony of Natal, which was threatened by the Boers in the Transvaal. The Gordons were sent straight to Elandslaagte when war broke out and, with three other battalions, attacked the enemy on 20 October. The positions were quickly captured and it was reported that 'the charge of the Gordons was a sight to be remembered'. They had to charge a second time to beat off a counter-attack, but during the battle suffered heavy casualties.

The battalion was part of the garrison of Ladysmith when the Boers surrounded and laid siege to the town. Defending Wagon Hill the Gordons fought off a major attack on the defences and several more forays at close quarters. The Gordons remained defending Ladysmith until relieved in February 1900.

Meanwhile the 1st Battalion, the Gordon Highlanders had reached South Africa and joined the Highland Brigade on the Modder River. At dawn on 11 December 1899 the column attacked the Boer positions at Magersfontein Hill. The enemy were unexpectedly holding the foot of the hill, and for most of the day the Highland Brigade was pinned down by incessant and accurate fire. 'If we moved,' remarked one soldier, 'a shower of bullets was the result.' The Gordons could not advance close to the enemy trenches, being held up by wire, and remained in exposed positions, firing back until their ammunition was exhausted. There was much confusion and eventually the survivors withdrew, having suffered much during the heat of the day without water. The battalion was fortunate in having only thirty-one casualties in this disastrous battle.

Joining 19 Brigade, the 1st Gordon Highlanders were involved in an engagement at Reit River early in 1900 while guarding a supply column. In late February they joined in the siege of Cronje's position at Paardeberg, and his eventual surrender signalled the first major British success of the war. Further engagements were fought at Poplar Grove, Driefontein and the occupation of Bloemfontein. During the subsequent advance on Pretoria the Gordons fought engagements at Houtnek – where Captain Towse was awarded the VC for an extremely brave charge with a section of men on a kopje held by 150 Boers – and the crossing of the Vet, Zand and Klip Rivers. A brilliant action was then fought at Doornkop where the Boers attempted to prevent the British march on Johannesburg. The Gordon Highlanders were sent into the attack on the Boer centre and, undeterred by the enemy rifle fire, charged with the bayonet to clear the position. The journalist Winston Churchill described the Gordon discipline: 'Their unfaltering advance, their machine-like change of direction, their final charge with the bayonet, constitute their latest feat of arms the equal of Dargai or Elandslaagte.' The Boers fell back to second positions, before finally fleeing the battlefield. Many of the Gordons' dead and wounded were of the volunteer company. When

Pretoria was reached in early June the battalion had marched 620 miles in less than four months.

Operations continued and in July 1900 the 1st Battalion was ordered to save some guns which had been earlier abandoned. The Boers fire, as accurate as ever, made this task extremely dangerous. The guns were saved and two officers, Capts Gordon and Younger, won the VC for their determined action.

Both battalions of the Gordon Highlanders continued on the march in detachments with various columns for several months. In September 1900 they defended the town of Belfast where, later in January 1901, the 1st Battalion fought off a series of major attacks. During the latter stages of the war the Gordons provided detachments for numerous treks in pursuit of Boer groups, and also mounted soldiers for the battalions of Mounted Infantry. During the war the regiment had taken part in more actions than most and had gained a high reputation.

In early 1902 the 2nd Battalion embarked for a ten-year tour of duty in India, and the 1st Battalion returned to Great Britain.

THE GORDON HIGHLANDERS
1914–1938

The 1st Battalion, Gordon Highlanders embarked for France with the 3rd Division in the British Expeditionary Force, and reached positions on the Mons-Condé Canal on 22 August 1914. At dawn on the following day the Germans attacked in strength and, although they held the line very successfully until the afternoon, the Gordons were ordered to cover the withdrawal of the 3rd Division. By 25 August the Gordons had taken up positions at Le Cateau, and for some hours the German advance was effectively blocked until the enemy artillery concentration proved overwhelming. Part of the brigade withdrew but, apart from A Company, the Gordons failed to receive the order and were cut off. Attempting to withdraw after dark most members of the battalion were surrounded and taken prisoner. Those who escaped were shortly reinforced, but subsequently went into reserve for most of September. In October the reconstituted 1st Gordons were in action again on several parts of the new line which the BEF had established in the Ypres sector.

The 2nd Battalion, Gordon Highlanders, had reached the Western Front from Egypt by mid-October 1914. They were first in action during the first battle of Ypres on 23 October on the Menin Road, where six days later a massive German attack was launched. The battle raged all day, but the enemy were successfully halted by British fire and manoeuvre. For some days the battle remained very fluid and, despite heavy casualties, the 2nd Gordons mounted a number of very effective counter-attacks. As the line stabilised the 1st Battalion fought a desperate battle to gain the Wytschaete Ridge, only to be forced back after losing many more of its soldiers.

A patrol of the 2nd Gordons rest during the first battle of Ypres, Oct 1914. IWM

During the next nine months of the war seven Territorial and new army battalions reached the Western Front – the 4th, 5th, 6th, 7th, 8th, 9th (Pioneer) and 10th Gordons. In March 1915 the 2nd and 6th Battalions fought for possession of Aubers Ridge near Neuve Chapelle. In the battle the 2nd Gordons advanced some 500 yards and held positions until relieved, under the most daunting enemy artillery bombardment. The 6th Battalion followed up, and a further advance was made before they were finally checked: the positions were clearly in view of the Germans, and there the survivors had to remain until they could withdraw under cover of darkness.

In May 1915 four battalions of the regiment fought at Festubert, the 2nd alongside the Scots Guards, while the 6th Gordons were in reserve. Some gains were made in the area of the village by these battalions, while the 5th and 7th Gordons were in action nearby.

In September 1915 the battle of Loos began and five battalions of the regiment were involved in the fighting. The 8th Gordons assaulted the Hohenzollern redoubt early in the battle, and advanced beyond it, taking two further objectives. Under pressure from counter-attacks they withdrew to the German front line. Two days afterwards, on 27 September, they had to retake the redoubt, despite having lost considerable numbers. Meanwhile the 2nd Gordons, advancing across nearly a mile of no-man's-land near Hulluch, quickly seized the front line German trench, but met huge resistance in the support trench. Fifty prisoners were taken there, but the Gordons' discovered that some German guns had been brought up to gun-pits behind – unusually close to the front lines. The 2nd Gordons and 8th Devonshires immediately rushed at them and each captured four guns.

The 8th Gordons were then joined by the 6th, but when the Germans counter-attacked, the two Gordons' battalions were virtually surrounded and had to fight their way back. The 10th Gordon Highlanders with the 15th Scottish Division captured Loos village in an impetuous charge, taking many German prisoners, and the 9th Pioneer battalion assisted the Cameron Highlanders in capturing Hill 70, before having to withdraw under great pressure. While these major attacks were in progress, the 1st and 4th Gordon Highlanders were fighting in a brigade assault in the area of Hooge. This action had the effect of diverting German attention, but the two battalions suffered over 650 casualties between them.

Trench warfare continued throughout the winter without much movement of the line. A notable action was fought in March 1916 when the 1st Gordons in the lead of its brigade took part in a deliberate attack at 'The Bluff', near Ypres. This was entirely successful, but the captured German trenches had to be held under the most appalling artillery fire for more than twenty-four hours.

The 1st London Scottish marching along the Doullens-Amiens road, July 1916. This distinguished battalion was the first of the Territorial Force battalions to go into action on the Western Front – at Messines, 31 Oct 1914. IWM

This photograph shows a company of Gordon Highlanders during the Somme offensive, July 1916. Every man carries a shovel or pick, symbols of the 'Great War for Civilisation'. RHQ KOSB

The London Scottish had formed an association with the Gordon Highlanders during the Boer War, and were officially affiliated in 1916. The 1st Battalion was one of the first Territorial battalions in action on the Western Front during the fighting for Messines in late October 1914. The battalion remained in France and Flanders throughout the war, its most notable engagements being at Messines, Givenchy, Arras and Cambrai.

The 2nd London Scottish went to France in 1916, and served for a time on the Bulgarian Front. It was then moved to Palestine where it fought during the last part of the campaign, taking part in the occupation of Jerusalem in December 1917. The battalion was subsequently recalled to the Western Front.

* * * * *

The Somme offensive began on 1 July 1916, and the 2nd Gordon Highlanders were immediately sent into action opposite Mametz. Half the battalion reached a sunken lane after crossing the German trenches, and were held up by the most devastating machine-gun fire. When reinforced later in the day, the Gordons advanced and took the village, but the day's action had cost them more than 450 casualties. The depleted 2nd were again in action on 13 July and for two days fought for possession of Mametz Wood and Bezantin-le-Petit.

The 1st Battalion, Gordon Highlanders, went into the attack on 14 July in the area of Longueval and Delville Wood. The village was taken but they were held up in the wood by intense machine-gun and artillery fire. For eight hours the Gordons fought on, but after losing over 350 casualties the remainder withdrew and held part of the line for the next week until relieved. In the meantime the 2nd were in action in a similar battle for the possession of High Wood. The 2nd Gordons advanced with four platoons in the first wave and reached the first obstacle, a road. Only one platoon managed to reach the next line, although only 500 yards further. The whole platoon, except for five men, was wiped out in the most intense fire from the wood and the switch trench. The Gordons tried time and again to advance to the wood, but were unrelentingly cut down by fire each time.

Gordon Highlanders repairing a road near Hamel, Sept 1916. Although some Scottish battalions were converted to the pioneer role, most infantry battalions had to share these duties from time to time. IWM

'Finally the survivors, on hands and knees, or even creeping on their bellies, returned to the first road.' The casualties were 29 killed and 233 wounded and missing. The 4th, 5th and 7th Battalions were also engaged in a final attempt to clear the Germans from the wood, until further direct assaults against it proved hopeless.

On the right of the British line the 1st Battalion was again in action in mid-August, attacking an objective near Guillemont together with French troops. The town was not captured at this time, but some progress was made. On 3 September a new general offensive began and a day later the 4th Gordons attacked Ginchy three times, but they were not strong enough to hold the village. East of Ginchy on 15 September the 8/10th Battalion (an amalgamated battalion formed in 1915) assisted in capturing Martinpuich and the 'switch line'.

During the last phase of the battle the 1st, 2nd, 4th, 5th, 6th and 7th Battalions all took part in the action at Beaumont-Hamel and Serre on the Ancre River. The 7th Battalion's dawn attack on Beaumont-Hamel was initially highly successful, but the enemy used the intricate tunnel system to good effect by bringing down machine-gun fire from a number of unexpected positions. The 4th and 5th Battalions advanced to their assistance, and took part in some very heavy fighting before the positions were finally cleared of the enemy. The 6th Battalion also took part in the battle, and the combined casualties of the four battalions were upwards of 700 killed and wounded. Meanwhile the attack of the 1st Battalion at Serre was carried out with great difficulty over the most treacherous mud, but the Gordons advanced as far as the third German line before they were checked.

During the winter of 1916–17 the front remained relatively quiet, although there were frequent local attacks and raids on all sectors. The 8/10th Gordons carried out a particularly successful raid on the Butte de Warlencourt in January when, dressed in white camouflage against the snow, they captured a number of German soldiers and blew up ammunition dumps and trench systems. A similar raid was carried out by the 6th Battalion in March 1917, and in the same month the Germans withdrew a large part of their army to new positions on the well-prepared Hindenburg Line.

In April the British command launched a long-planned attack from Arras on the northern end of the

2nd Gordons march along the Fricourt road, Oct 1916. Lt-Col Turnbull, DSO is on horseback, with Drum-Maj Kenny, VC (Ypres 1914) leading. IWM

new line, in which seven battalions of Gordons took part. The 4th and 5th Battalions fought alongside each other to capture Vimy Ridge, taking the first line on the first day of the battle and then the second line. Although the Germans put up a fierce resistance, they were also cleared from the adjacent lines in a determined attack by the two battalions. To their right the 6th Battalion captured its objectives at Roclincourt despite heavy casualties, but the 8/10th Gordons were held up by heavy fire from well-defended positions at Railway Triangle, before eventually evicting the enemy. The following day the battalion was in support of a brigade attack on the town of Monchy which proved a very difficult task.

The 1st Gordons had started the battle at 5.30am on the first day, and the front waves went forward rapidly, so that the distance between them closed up. The German shells landed well to their rear. Reaching the wire, the Gordons found it well cut by the British gunfire and swept past it to take all but successive objectives within twenty minutes of the start. The Royal Welsh Fusiliers passed through, and at 7.30am the Gordons took the lead again in a further advance. At 5.30pm the battalion attacked the next brigade objective alone, but were severely hampered by enfilade fire which stopped them 300 yards short of the enemy positions. Had they been able to reach them the Gordons would have easily captured these positions, as the wire was cut and the Germans had all but abandoned them. Two days later the battalion was again in action near Guémappe, and their total casualties were 276.

During the second phase of the battle in the area of the River Scarpe, the 7th Gordons were involved in the most severe fighting against odds of four to one. Two complete companies were almost wiped out, but the others made considerable territorial gains and took many German prisoners. In the same area at Roeux the 4th Battalion met similar opposition. In the second phase of the attack the 6th Gordons managed to make gradual progress towards the Roeux chemical works, but a strong German counter-attack forced them to withdraw. They left, however, a well-defended outpost in a quarry which held out until other troops mounted a fresh assault on the enemy. On 21 April the 8/10th Gordons were called forward from reserve to attack Cavalry Farm, but were shelled in the assembly area, and the attack was postponed.

In May 1917 the 2nd Battalion took part in a particularly successful assault on Bullecourt. Later

Off duty 8th and 10th Gordon Highlanders watch a display of highland dancing at Arras, Jan 1918. The swords are cavalry pattern. IWM

in the month the 5th Battalion had to defend the Roeux positions against successive assaults of the enemy and, when relieved, the battalion strength was less than 200. On 15 May in the same area the 6th Gordons were sent to relieve the 5th Seaforth but, joined by the 8th Argylls, all three battalions were engaged in a running battle during the night and well into the following day. Roeux was eventually cleared of the enemy. Then in June the 1st Gordons captured Infantry Hill, a hitherto impregnable position, by means of a surprise daylight attack and without the usual artillery bombardment.

The German spring offensive, 1918. Gordon Highlanders observe the battle while in support of the fighting, 24 Mar at Nesle, Somme sector. IWM

During the third battle of Ypres the 9/10th Battalion were in the assault on Frezenberg, and took two enemy lines by charging with the bayonet. Pushed back the following day by a German counter-attack, the Gordons then recaptured the ground. At the same time the 51st Highland Division was mounting a major attack on the Steenbeck River, where the 5th Gordons were successful in taking two objectives. They were followed by the 6th Gordons who also seized several objectives in successive waves of their attack. The 7th Battalion likewise took three objectives in the area of Hindenburg Farm. Also in the battle the 9th Pioneer Battalion were used to capture two battalion objectives.

In the autumn of 1917 the 4th and 7th Gordons made a significant advance in the area of Poelcappelle, and the 1st and 2nd Battalions also fought nearby, pushing the front forward towards Passchendaele. In October the 2nd Gordons took objectives on the Nordemdhock Ridge in a particularly bold assault under heavy enemy artillery fire. At the end of the month they were in action again at Gheluvelt but, having advanced towards their objective, the casualties were so great that they had to abandon the attempt. The battalion's losses during the month were 660 killed and wounded.

The 51st Highland Division was heavily involved in the battle of Cambrai which started on 20 November. The 5th Battalion was immediately in action in the area of Flesquières, followed up by the 6th and 7th Battalions in the highly successful advance behind the tanks. On the second day of the battle the 4th came into action and it, too, made a bold advance, although by this time the momentum was decreasing. The heaviest fighting was for Fontaine Notre Dame and Bourlon Wood, which the 6th Gordons helped to capture, despite strong resistance.

* * * * *

During November 1917, the 2nd Battalion, Gordon Highlanders were sent to fight alongside the Italian army against the Austrians. It held a sector of the front first at Martello, and from April 1918 on the Asiago plateau. Although the line was mainly static, the battalion spent much time in raiding and harrassing the enemy. The Gordons' most notable battle was at Piave at the end of October 1918. Their task was the capture of part of an island, and under heavy fire they successfully captured their two objectives. The Austrians then began to withdraw hurriedly all along the front, and the 2nd Gordons pursued them, taking hundreds of prisoners as their army disintegrated. An armistice came into effect on 4 November.

* * * * *

On the Western Front the great German offensive began on 21 March 1918 on a front of 50 miles. The 8/10th Gordons were in the area of Monchy near Arras and, despite holding their line bravely with a loss of 300 casulaties, they were ordered to retire. Their stand had nevertheless prevented an enemy breakthrough to Arras. The 1st Battalion similarly held their ground nearby for a week. The four battalions with the 51st Highland Division were in part of the line that had to be gradually withdrawn, owing to the pressure of successive German attacks. The 4th Gordons fought for six days at Demicourt, and lost over 400 casualties.

The 5th Gordons now transferred to the 61st Division, were in the area of Fresnoy-le-Petit on the night of the German attack. At 4.40am the artillery bombardment began, and

> 'The density of falling shells of all calibres was tremendous, and the fire was most scientifically applied . . . In the forward zone . . . battalions had the majority of their men killed, wounded, buried by the heavy French mortar bombs, or at best dazed before the infantry attack.'

The Gordons' sector was the hardest hit and inevit-

HM King George V presents Sgt C. W. Train of the 2nd London Scottish with the VC, Aug 1918. The regiment is affiliated to the Gordon Highlanders. IWM

ably under this onslaught they were overwhelmed. Lt-Col M. F. McTaggart's headquarters was quickly surrounded by 12.30pm, and an hour later only thirty members of the battalion survived the attack.

Nearby, serving in the 61st Machine-gun Battalion, a Gordons' officer Lt E. A. Ker and a sergeant held up a large enemy force with a machine gun until his ammunition was expended. Then for three hours they defended themselves with only their revolvers until finally captured. Ker was awarded the VC for his gallantry.

The 6th and 7th Gordons continued to hold their ground as long as possible in front of Béthune during the offensive, and the 1st Battalion was moved forward on 11 April to the positions held by the decimated 51st Highland Division on the River Lys. By the end of the month, despite huge gains, the enemy offensive had been finally checked.

The next offensive began at the end of May on the French part of the line, and on 15 July the 51st Highland Division was sent to reinforce the French near the River Marne. The 4th Gordons went into the assault on Bois-de-Courton, but eventually took their objective by gradual infiltration. The 7th Battalion, attacking the same wood, also had a long and hard fight. When relieved after successfully carrying its objective, the battalion's losses were over 500. The 6th Battalion made some gains at first but, on the second day of the battle for the wood, were held up. A few days later it took three brigades to capture the area.

The 5th Battalion had absorbed the 8/10th Gordons in June 1918, and in July their division, the 15th Scottish, took part in the allied attack at Buzancy. The Gordon Highlanders carried their objective successfully and assisted in the relief of Jaux, but had to conform to a withdrawal when the Germans mounted a devastating counter-attack. But the failure of the Germans to break through on the Marne signalled the start of the allied offensive.

The 1st Gordons were in the attack mounted against Baupaume on 21 August 1918. For several days the battalion alternated between holding ground and gradually advancing against very strong opposition. Casualties were high, especially amongst the officers. Meanwhile the 6th and 7th Battalions were fighting on the River Scarpe, and making steady progress in pushing the front forward.

In September the 1st Battalion successfully captured Flesquières near Cambrai. This was followed by an attack on Rumilly four days later, in which 800 German prisoners were taken and a counter-attack was beaten off. The Gordons next mounted an assault on the Hindenburg Line, and their objectives were rapidly seized. Shortly afterwards, on 13 October, the 6/7th Battalion (amalgamated at the beginning of the month) took part in a successful advance on the River Selle, but its casualties were very high. During the last few weeks of the war the 1st, 4th and 6/7th Gordons remained in action, and continued to suffer casualties until the armistice finally came into effect.

* * * * *

The 1st, 4th and 5th Battalions of the Gordon Highlanders formed part of the army of occupation in Germany at the end of the war and were joined by three further battalions, the 51st, and 52nd and 53rd comprised of 'young soldiers'. On the return to peacetime establishment of two regular battalions, the 1st was reconstituted in Scotland and subsequently moved to Ireland. The 3rd Militia battalion was reformed as the 2nd Battalion, and was also stationed in Ireland. Subsequent moves saw the 2nd Gordons on duty in Glasgow during the coal strike of 1920, and the 1st moved to Constantinople as part of an allied force. There the Gordons' task was to support Greek and French troops in containing the Turks during a nationalist uprising. Mobile operations and static guards were conducted for several months before peace was restored. After moving to Malta, the 1st Gordons were quickly recalled to man a neutral zone between the Greeks and Turks on the eastern side of the Dardanelles. There they remained until a peace

Marshals Foch and Haig in a jovial mood inspect C Coy, 6th Gordons. The jocks, too, must have been feeling equally cheerful since the Armistice came into force four days earlier on 11 Nov 1918.

settlement was reached.

In 1924 the 1st Battalion moved via Egypt to India, to be stationed at Secunderabad and Belgaum. After a tour of duty in Delhi, the battalion moved to the North-West Frontier where, as usual, the troops were on semi-active service. In 1934 the 2nd Battalion embarked for Gibraltar where it remained, apart from a six-week visit to Egypt, until 1936. In that year the 2nd Gordons moved to Malaya.

HRH The Prince of Wales, in the uniform of the Royal Scots Fusiliers, inspects the Gordon Highlanders after the war. He is speaking to Sgt Bruce whom he remembered from service on the Italian Front, 1918.
RHQ

THE GORDON HIGHLANDERS

1939 to the present

The 1st Battalion, Gordon Highlanders, joined the British Expeditionary Force on the outbreak of war in September 1939. By the end of the month they had reached Arras, and ten days later took up positions south-west of Lille near the Belgian border. There they remained until the spring of 1940. The first Territorial battalion to join the BEF was the 4th Gordons whose role was that of a machine-gun battalion; it was sent with the 4th Division to Roubaix in December 1939. The 51st Highland Division arrived in France in late January 1940, and the 5th and 6th Gordons were concentrated near Béthune. In March the 1st Gordons exchanged with the 6th, who replaced them in the 1st Division.

On 10 May the German invasion of Belgium began. The 6th Battalion moved to positions to defend the River Dyle east of Brussels, and the 4th moved up to a line nearby. On 16 May the 6th were heavily bombarded by enemy artillery and, although relatively unscathed, were ordered to withdraw. The battalion continued to pull back to conform to flanking formations each day. The 4th Gordons were meanwhile fighting rearguard actions to the north of Brussels, and both battalions reached positions to hold the river Escaut by 20 May. After a two-day respite, the enemy bombarded the British positions and again the British were ordered to withdraw. This time the withdrawal was conducted rapidly and, despite taking up a series of positions on the way towards the Channel, the 6th Gordons could only delay the advanced enemy columns and conform as ordered. By 30 May they were on the outskirts of Dunkirk. Although prepared to cover the forward formations as they withdrew, the 6th Battalion was ordered to embark on 1 June. The 4th Battalion meanwhile was used to cover the withdrawal of several different formations, its machine-gun support being frequently required against the German infantry advancing to take the successive river and canal lines. It reached the Dunkirk area on 28 May and also embarked for England on 1 June.

Meanwhile the 51st Highland Division, with the 1st and 5th Gordons, had been serving with the French on the Maginot Line in the Saar region. Both battalions took part in the fighting in support of French formations and continued to be heavily involved for twelve days. They were frequently on the move, often operating at company level against local attacks. The enemy artillery fire was often intense. On 22 May they were withdrawn by road and rail to positions near the River Somme, which were consolidated by 30 May. The Germans were, however, already forming bridgeheads over the river.

The two battalions moved to the front line on 1 and 2 June to the south-west of Abbeville, and both immediately came under artillery fire. On 4 June the 1st Gordons attacked the Grand Bois above Cambron with a French armoured division. Their first objective was quickly taken but elsewhere the French attack failed, resulting in in the Gordons' withdrawal. The following day the Germans launched a massive attack all along the front, and most of the neighbouring 154 Brigade of the Highland Division was surrounded and captured. The 1st Gordons were again ordered to withdraw to fresh positions covering the River Bresle. There the battalion successfully delayed the enemy advance. The 5th Battalion in the same area had not been so heavily engaged and went into reserve.

To the south the Germans were fast advancing and threatening to cut off the 51st Highland Division; and a withdrawal towards Le Havre was ordered. The 5th Gordons established defensive positions covering the River Béthune on 10 June, while the 1st Gordons went into reserve. The 5th had some successes against German forward troops attempting to cross the river, but the route to Le Havre was now cut. The new fall-back position was decided upon at St Valéry, and the very difficult task began of fighting a rearguard action and moving along the congested routes under artillery bombardment. On reaching it the two Gordons' battalions dug in to the east of the town. On 11 June a very strong armoured attack was launched against the perimeter at several points. Soon both battalions were heavily engaged, and during the following twenty-four hours there was intense and confused fighting. Some companies were overrun, while others grimly held on until they were ordered to surrender on 12 June.

* * * * *

The 2nd Gordons in the meantime had served in the garrison of Singapore since 1937, and after Dunkirk they sent back drafts to reconstitute the 1st Battalion. They frequently provided troops for service on the mainland of Malaya, and on 25 January 1942 were moved inland some fifty miles to meet the Japanese advance. A day later they were engaged by the enemy, delaying them until the battalion was withdrawn that night five miles from Singapore Island. Their axis was the main road and during the final days of January the Gordons fought off several probing attacks by the enemy, before being ordered to cross the causeway onto the island.

The 2nd Gordons' initial task was the defence of Changi on the eastern part of Singapore. On 8 February the Japanese crossed over the straits on the north-west part of the island. On the third day the Gordons were ordered to move to the west to take up positions ready to meet the enemy's advance, which by now included armour supported by artillery. The situation everywhere was becoming desperate, and a further withdrawal to the perimeter of Singapore town was ordered. At this point most of the Gordons' casualties were caused by artillery fire and bombing, rather than close contact with the enemy. The cease-fire and surrender came into effect on the evening of 15 February. The survivors remained in captivity on the island until October 1942 when they were moved to camps in Siam.

* * * * *

The reconstituted 51st Highland Division, including the 1st and 5th/7th Gordons, reached Egypt via the Cape in mid-August 1942. In October they joined the British front line already established at El Alamein. The 1st Gordons were in support of the 9th Black Watch on the right of the division, whilst the 5th/7th Gordons were on the left.

The battle of El Alamein began at 10pm on 23 October, and within two hours the 5th/7th had advanced more than two miles. On the right, progress was as rapid, and the 1st Gordons took the lead only to be held up by an enemy minefield at daylight. The fighting had been intense and the battalion suffered many casualties. On 24 October the two battalions held their ground during the day, and advanced again during the night, the 5th/7th taking its objective while the 1st was held up by enemy machine-gun fire. The 1st Gordons took the objective, appropriately nicknamed Aberdeen, on 27 October, after much hard fighting.

From the start of the battle until 2 November the two battalions faced a number of probing and counter-attacks, by the enemy, and were constantly under artillery and mortar fire. After being withdrawn briefly from the front line, the 5th/7th took part in an attack on 3 November with the 8th Royal Tank Regiment on a position near Tel el Aqqaqir. Suffering numerous casualties of tanks and men, the attack could not be pressed forward during the day. That night, however, the Germans withdrew. Then several days were spent in reserve as the battle progressed with other divisions in the lead. The 51st Highland

Valentine tank of the 40th Royal Tank Regt entering Tripoli past crowds of British troops and cheering inhabitants. On the leading tank are members of the 1st Gordon Highlanders with Pipe-Maj George Ramsay piping the while, 26 Jan 1943. RHQ

Gordon Highlanders in action on the Mareth Line, Tunisia, Mar 1943. Both the 1st and 5th/7th Bns served with the 51st Highland Division in the North African campaign. IWM

Division moved again on 15 November and rapid progress was made, with the 5th/7th moving along the coast road past Tobruk and Benghazi, while the 1st Gordons motored across the desert. Contact was made again with the enemy on 4 December, but it was not until 12 December that the Gordons were seriously involved in the fighting. Both battalions probed forward towards El Agheila, but were counter-attacked and forced to fight hard to hold their positions. The enemy then withdrew by night and the advance to the town continued. A month later, and some 220 miles further west, a deliberate attack was launched against the Germans at Beurat where they had hoped to block the Eighth Army. The two Gordons' battalions with armoured and engineer support broke through the minefields, and the Germans withdrew rapidly. The 1st Gordons were amongst the first troops into Tripoli on 23 January 1943, and both battalions remained there in occupation for some days.

The enemy had adopted a new defensive line at Mareth, and when the Eighth Army reached there, the Germans and Italians mounted a number of localised attacks. General Montgomery launched a night-time frontal assault on the Mareth Line and the 5th/7th Gordons were in the leading wave with the 1st Gordons in support. Passing through a cleared lane in the minefield, the 5th/7th occupied part of their objective. The fighting continued for several days before the Germans withdrew on 27 March. They conducted a fighting withdrawal for another ten days before breaking contact. On 10 April both battalions entered Sfax, an important seaport. The next enemy blocking line was east of Enfidaville where the 5th/7th Gordons were heavily involved in the fighting before they were relieved by Free French troops. Then both battalions were withdrawn and began training for the invasion of Sicily.

In the meantime the 6th Battalion, Gordon Highlanders, had been fighting against the Germans and Italians in Algeria since landing there on 9 March 1943 with the First Army. The Gordons' first major battle was on 21 April when the Germans penetrated the battalion position, but were quickly ejected. The following night the battalion launched a deliberate attack on a German position known as Point 144. The objective was captured, but the Gordons had to face a strong counter-attack and artillery bombardment. Nevertheless they held the position for several days as the battle raged around them. The advance into Tunis progressed, and after a period in reserve the battalion was called upon to assist the Irish Guards in occupying Gab Gab Gap and holding it against further enemy armoured thrusts. Soon afterwards, on 12 May, all hostilities in North Africa ceased. The following month the 6th Gordons were involved in an unopposed landing on the small island of Pantelleria off Sicily, and returned to Tunisia for training for their next task.

The 51st Highland Division formed part of the assault troops for the allied landings on Sicily on 10 July 1943. The 1st Gordons landed unopposed just south of Cape Passaro, and the 5th/7th Gordons landed in a subsequent wave. Both battalions advanced northwards, only being opposed by sporadic fire: most of the Italian troops surrendered immediately. The first major German stronghold encountered was at Vizzini, some fifty miles north-east from the landing beach. The 1st Battalion, fighting alongside The Black Watch, successfully captured the town, but the 5th/7th Gordons experienced some resistance as they progressed past Vizzini to seize bridges over the Gorna Lunga River.

The 1st Gordons took the lead north of the river in the direction of Catania and had to deal with more opposition. The 5th/7th Gordons then took over and advanced rapidly through unreconnoitred terrritory. Sferro was the next major German-defended locality, and the enemy had concentrated much armour and artillery to block the British advance. The 5th/7th were first involved in the fighting for the village and on 19 July, the 1st Gordons moved up ready for an assault on the road and railway bridges. Under intense fire on the following day the 5th/7th fought their way across the valley and into the village, and the 1st Gordons established bridgehead positions beyond the captured bridges. Both battalions spent the next three days holding their gains, while the enemy first sent patrols and then more substantial attacking parties against the Gordons. The Germans did not finally withdraw from the area until the end of the month. Allied successes elsewhere resulted in diminishing German resistance as the 51st Highland Division advanced northwards towards the Straits of Messina. In September the two battalions left Sicily with the division, and returned to the United Kingdom.

The 6th Battalion, Gordon Highlanders, left Algeria in December 1943 and landed at Taranto in northern Italy with the 1st Division. After a period of weeks in billets, the battalion moved to the west coast to prepare for action in support of the American operations at Anzio. On 21 January the 6th Gordons embarked for an overnight move by sea, and landed unopppосed five miles north of Anzio. They took part in an advance from the beach-head, suffered from enemy artillery bombardment, but were not involved in any action until 28 January. The division then established a defensive line some fifteen miles north of the town. On 3 February the Germans launched a major attack, and there was fierce fighting as the enemy attempted to penetrate the Gordons' positions. Although the Germans were initially held off, three of the companies were overwhelmed, most of their members being killed or wounded. Little ground had, however, been lost before the remainder of the battalion was relieved. B Company continued to fight in support of various units, and two new companies were formed from drafts which arrived from the United Kingdom. For three months the 6th Gordons continued to man the Anzio Line until the allies' advance absorbed the beach-head. During May and June 1944 the battalion took part in the allied advance on Rome.

In August the 6th Gordons were moved to Florence and were involved in sporadic fighting as the 1st Division progressed northwards from the city. In September the Gordons took up the lead as the division advanced towards the Gothic line. A large-scale attack was launched against Mount Gamberaldi, but on reaching their objective the Gordons found that the enemy had withdrawn. As they advanced they encountered German opposition many times during the following months, most of it at sub-unit level, and the terrain and weather made the going hard. In January 1945 they were taken from the line and embarked for Palestine.

* * * * *

During the Second World War the London Scottish, affiliated to the Gordon Highlanders, formed three battalions. The 1st served in Iraq and fought with the Eighth Army in North Africa, Sicily and Italy. During the Italian campaign their notable battles were the Anzio bridgehead and the penetration of the Gothic Line. The 2nd Battalion remained in the United Kingdom as an officer training battalion. The 3rd Battalion was transferred to the Royal Artillery as an anti-aircraft regiment and it, too, fought in the campaign in Sicily and Italy.

* * * * *

The 9th Battalion, Gordon Highlanders, left the United Kingdom for India in mid-1942. On arrival they were informed that the battalion was to be converted into an armoured regiment – the 116th Regiment (Gordon Highlanders) Royal Armoured Corps. It took nearly a year, however, for them to be issued with the full complement of tanks. Another battalion, the 8th Gordons, had also been converted. It had been a machine-gun battalion, but was transferred to the Royal Artillery as the 100th (Gordon Highlanders) Anti-Tank Regiment. The regiment was also sent to India, exchanging two of the batteries for two already-formed light anti-aircraft batteries from the Royal Warwickshire Regiment.

The 100th Regiment was rapidly sent to Assam when the Japanese invaded India, and established positions five miles from Kohima. For three weeks in April 1944 the gun detachments supported the infantry in preventing the capture of the town, and defeating the Japanese in one of the most hard-fought battles in the theatre.

Both 100th Regiment RA and 116th Regiment RAC supported the British advance through Burma from late 1944, clearing the axis of the River Irrawaddy of Japanese troops. The 100th Regiment's operations were not confined to the artillery role, and it took part in much mobile patrolling. 116th Regiment RAC co-operated closely with British, Indian and East African battalions in numerous attacks. The Japanese resisted strongly all the way, but the Gordons' tanks, working in close support of the infantry, assisted in maintaining the momentum of the advance. By May 1945 the regiment had motored the 1,200 miles to Bangkok, of which 800 had been under operational conditions. It continued fighting in the eastern part of Burma until the Japanese capitulation.

* * * * *

The 51st Highland Division took part in the Normandy invasion and landed during the afternoon of D Day at Courseulles. The 1st and 5th/7th Gordons moved rapidly inland to concentration areas. On 9 June the 1st Gordons moved north of Caen to take over guarding the River Orne and Ouistreham Canal bridges (the most easterly extent of the allied advance), while the 5th/7th Battalion was in reserve behind them. Both battalions were shelled heavily for many hours.

Two days later the 5th/7th Gordons occupied the village of Touffreville, and on 12 June the enemy counter-attacked the company positions but failed to dislodge them. There was no further enemy action against the two battalions until 16 June, when a major armour and infantry attack was launched, chiefly against the 1st Gordons. The fighting was intense and at close quarters, lasting into the darkness. The 5th/7th Gordons' position was penetrated, and it was some hours before the enemy could be ejected.

The Gordon Highlanders remained in the area to the east of the Orne as the fighting for Caen continued to the south. On 9 July the 1st Gordons went into the attack to seize the Colombelles industrial area of Caen, but such was the resistance that it became a full brigade objective. The battle continued for nearly two days and the Gordons seized all their objectives before being ordered back into reserve.

The reconstituted 2nd Battalion, Gordon Highlanders, serving with the 15th Scottish Division, had meanwhile landed near Arromanches on 20 June. Their first task was to establish crossing places on the River Odon, south-west of Caen. During their advance the Gordons were met by murderous artillery fire, and it was with great difficulty that they captured the battalion objective of Colleville. The intense fighting for the bridgeheads continued until 2 July, when the Gordons were relieved. 'Our first introduction to battle has been a very hard test,' reported the commanding officer with typical British understatement. 'We had a week of hell . . . The one thing I can say is that the battalion did all that they were told to do.'

After a respite, the 2nd Gordons were back in action on 15 July over the River Odon, and during a night attack on Evrécy the two leading companies successfully occupied their objectives. But by the time dawn came the follow-up companies were held up in the open. German counter-attacks were faced during the following day, and the Gordons succeeded in destroying a number of tanks while holding their positions. It was not until the evening that the four companies were consolidated, and other units took over the advance.

The 1st and 5th/7th Battalions were on the move again on 23 July and reached positions near Caumont. Their task was to hold the sector until the US troops could force a break-out. A week later the 2nd Gordons advanced and launched an attack to the south-east of the same town. With armoured support they captured their objectives and during subsequent days advanced south-eastwards through the intricate bocage country. The battalion was ordered to occupy Estry, but the village was held in great strength and the Gordons had to dig-in short of their objectives. It was some time before the village was taken, but the Gordons had by then been withdrawn into reserve.

The 1st and 5th/7th Battalions moved from Caumont in early August. Originally their axis was through Falaise, but was altered to Lisieux, and steady progress was made despite enemy artillery fire. The 1st successfully captured Grandchamp on the River Vie, but the eastern bank was thick with Germans and the battle continued for several hours before the Gordons were fully established. Lisieux was occupied on 22 August, but both battalions met considerable resistance subsequently on the route to the Seine. In the meantime the 2nd Gordons had approached the river from the area of Falaise. Their

Anti-tank platoon of the 1st Gordons approach Tilburg, Holland, Oct 1944. Integral anti-tank weapons were highly necessary for infantry battalions in most theatres of war. IWM

1st Gordons man a light machine gun at Nieuwkirk, Nov 1944. The allies were effectively held up by the Germans in the low-lying 'canal country' of Holland after the failure of Arnhem. IWM

2nd Gordons occupy a bunker captured from the Germans during the battle for the Siegfried Line, Feb 1945. IWM

crossing was opposed by the Germans and they sustained nearly 90 casualties at the first attempt.

During the subsequent attack on the Germans at Le Havre the 1st Gordons made good progress against stiff resistance in the forest east of the town, and rapidly captured artillery and infantry positions. Their success enabled other units, including the 5th/7th Battalion, to complete the occupation of Le Havre.

The three battalions of the Gordon Highlanders then made a rapid advance across Belgium to the Dutch border. The 2nd Gordons were involved in the fighting in mid-September for possession of the Scheldt-Maas Canal, which nevertheless was too strongly held by the enemy for the highlanders to force a crossing. They then assisted the Argylls and KOSB fighting to retain a bridgehead at Gheel. At the end of the month the 2nd Gordons broke out from a bridgehead established at Best on the Wilhelmina Canal, but were checked by the enemy in well-defended positions. The battalion then went into reserve.

For most of October the three battalions were fully occupied fighting for territory west of the River Maas. The resistance was sporadic but the highlanders made good progress, reaching Tilburg on 26 October. The final weeks of 1944 were spent in laboriously clearing residual enemy groups establishing a firm line on the River Maas. The 1st and 5th/7th Gordons advanced as far as Nijmegen and took over positions from US troops on the Nijmegen 'island'. The Germans were in strong positions to the east, and when they flooded the region the two battalions of Gordons had to evacuate the 'island'.

In late December the two battalions went with the 51st Highland Division to support the US Army fighting in the Ardennes, and on 7 January they began a clearing operation in the Ourthe Valley, south of Liège. They met only light opposition and, once they had made contact with the US troops, they returned to Holland.

In February 1945 'Operation Veritable' was launched; its purpose was to clear the Germans from the western border to the Rhine, including the Siegfied Line. On the first day the 5th/7th Gordons reached their objective on the edge of the Reichswald Forest, and during the night took advantage of a confused situation, killing and capturing many Germans in a concentration area. On the second day the 1st Gordons took over the lead, but were severely delayed in getting through the forest. They made better progress on the third day against enemy positions alongside the River Maas. Every village, river and other natural feature was defended, and the two battalions, with tank and artillery support, spent the next week fighting for numerous objectives.

On 19 February the town of Goch was attacked by the 1st and 5th/7th Battalions as part of a brigade night attack. The Black Watch entered the town first and cleared some of the enemy positions, but the 5th/7th Gordons passing through had not yet reached their start-line in the town centre when they were fired on. For many hours three of the companies had to fight amongst the streets and half-destroyed buildings, but this delayed the attack of the 1st Gordons, whose task was to take the southern part of the town. In the late afternoon their attack was mounted and they, too, met very strong resistance and the two battalions had by this time suffered numerous casualties. At dawn on 20 February, A and D Companies of the 1st were given the task of capturing a crossroads and a group of houses south of the town, known as the Thomashof. A Company, on entering the Thomashof, was counter-attacked and overwhelmed: there were only a few survivors. Sporadic fighting continued until the Germans finally withdrew on the 22 February.

In the meantime the 2nd Gordons had been fighting further to the north for the high ground to the west of Cleve. Progress there was easier as the enemy put up less resistance, even on the Siegfried Line defences. Crossing the River Niers, the Gordons captured their objectives at Schloss Caldbeck, but by now German resistance was strengthening once more. Other formations took the lead towards the end of the month, and preparations were made for the assault over the River Rhine.

Gordon Highlanders move forwards over the flood bank of the Rhine before embarking for the crossing, 24 Mar 1945. IWM

On the 23 March the 5/7th Gordons were in the first wave of the crossing. On landing south of Rees, their task was to clear the ground one mile from the river bank. This they did, but the countryside was very exposed and dominated by German machine guns. During the first night they advanced, but were held up when attempting to cross a subsidiary river, the Alter Rhine. The 5/7th, following in another wave, succeeded in capturing the town of Rees, but this took until the midday on 25 March. The 2nd Gordons crossed the Rhine further to the south, not without mishap, but their progress after landing was rapid. On 27 March the 1st Gordons reached and occupied Isselburg and the 5/7th conformed alongside.

The 2nd Gordons advanced north-eastwards with the 15th Scottish Division on the axis of Osnabrück and Celle: they met some resistance but their progress was also swift. The most heavily defended locality they encountered was at Uelzen on 15 April, and they were forced to withdraw while another brigade launched an attack against the town. A fortnight later they crossed the Elbe at Artlenburg while under fire, and spent much time clearing the woods to the east of the river before advancing on Hamburg. Meanwhile, the 1st and 5/7th Gordons advanced towards the River Ems. They, too, met isolated resistance and some of the towns had to be fought for. Delmenhorst was strongly defended by the Germans, and the Gordons had to endure heavy artillery fire. After crossing the Weser the 1st Gordons mounted a battalion attack against Barchel, held by a strong party of Panzer Grenadiers, but they quickly withdrew. The last engagement for the 5/7th Gordons was at Ebersdorf on 2 May. When the German surrender came into force the Gordons were moved into the ports of Lübeck and Bremerhaven, where they helped to establish control over the civilian populations.

* * * * *

After the war the 1st Gordons remained in Germany as occupation troops until 1950. The 2nd

Battalion left Germany in September 1945 and, after a short period in Britain, embarked for Tripoli, Libya. There they remained until May 1947 when they returned to Scotland. The following year the two battalions were amalgamated at a ceremony at Essen, where the 1st was stationed.

In 1951 the 1st Battalion sailed for Singapore, and on arrival immediately began jungle training in preparation for operations against the terrorists in Malaya. In May the Gordons moved to the mainland and were given the responsibility for 20,000 square miles of Pehang on the eastern side of the country. The companies were dispersed to various jungle bases and patrol operations were mounted for the next three months. It was exhausting work and D Company's operation in June, nicknamed 'operation Ness', proved successful when a large bandit camp was discovered and attacked. Four terrorists were killed and the camp destroyed. In February 1952 A Company mounted an even more successful operation with the 2nd/7th Gurkha Rifles. The force carefully established a cordon around the terrorists' base and in the attack killed eight and wounded two.

The Gordons spent a year in Scotland before being sent to Cyprus in 1955. On reaching the island they had to build their own camp, appropriately named 'Aberdeen Camp'. The battalion was involved immediately in anti-EOKA operations at the height of the troubles. The Gordons had to deal with riots as well as bombings, murders, weapon searches, ambushes and routine foot and vehicle patrols. After a very eventful tour they returned to the United Kingdom at the end of 1956.

In 1958 the battalion went to Germany for a three-year tour and in early 1902 embarked for Kenya. The Mau Mau troubles had been resolved already, but the Gordons had to mount internal security operations in Zanzibar and Swaziland, as well as quell a mutiny of a battalion of the Kenya Rifles.

After a period spent in Edinburgh the 1st Gordons were sent to Borneo during the last year of Confrontation with Indonesia. After jungle training the battalion base camp was set up at Kalabaken on the river of the same name. The companies were dispersed to various parts of the battalion area and carried out a programme of active patrolling. In October the Gordons moved to Sarawak and were responsible for a length of the border with Indonesia. Soon after the hostilities ceased, the battalion returned to the United Kingdom.

The last twenty years have been spent by the 1st Battalion, Gordon Highlanders, chiefly in the United Kingdom and with the British Army of the Rhine. Like all regular battalions, the Gordons have served in Northern Ireland on internal security duties on a number of occasions.

Withdrawal from Empire. The 1st Gordons cordon a town in Zanzibar, 1962. IWM

CHAPTER 11

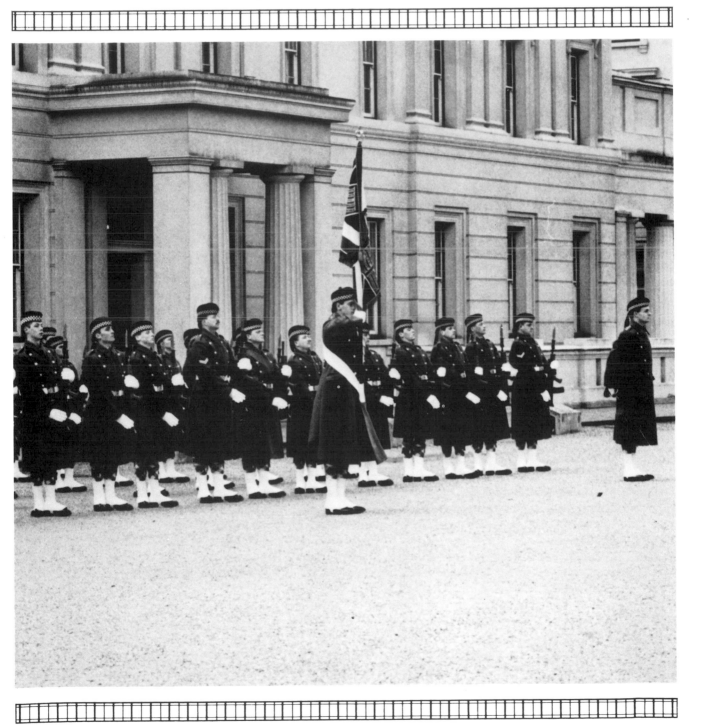

THE ARGYLL AND SUTHERLAND HIGHLANDERS

(Princess Louise's)

The Argyll and Sutherland Highlanders were formed in 1881 from the 91st (Princess Louise's) Argyllshire Highlanders and the 93rd (Sutherland Highlanders) Regiment of Foot. The royal title, borne by the 91st since 1872, commemorates the marriage of the Marquis of Lorne, heir to the Duke of Argyll, to Queen Victoria's daughter Princess Louise, who became the regiment's Colonel-in-Chief.

91ST (ARGYLLSHIRE) HIGHLANDERS
1794–1881

The 91st Highlanders were raised by Duncan Campbell of Lochnell in 1794 on behalf of the Duke of Argyll and the regiment was recruited up to establishment within the space of three months. The officers were predominantly from Argyllshire – seventeen were named Campbell – but the ranks were made up of many non-highlanders owing to the shortage of military manpower in Scotland. A high proportion, however, had had previous military service and the regiment assembled for the first time on 26 May 1794, being initially numbered the 98th (Argyllshire) Highlanders. They wore the kilt of government tartan.

A year later the regiment embarked for service in South Africa and reached the Cape in September. Operations against the Dutch had already started, and after disembarkation the British advanced on Cape Town as far as the pass of Muysenberg. The 98th Highlanders' companies were variously grouped during the action at Wynberg, and the British forced the enemy to abandon their position without difficulty. Two days later the Dutch garrison surrendered Cape Castle, and the regiment remained in various camps in the vicinity of Cape Town. A large force of Dutch ships with reinforcements arrived in 1796, but they surrendered to the Royal Navy before landing. This was the only excitement which enlivened the years of garrison duty until 1802, when the colony was temporarily returned to the Dutch under the terms of the Treaty of Amiens.

The regiment, renumbered the 91st from 1798, returned to England in 1803. In the following year a 2nd Battalion was raised, but in 1809 the 91st lost its highland status and dress. The 1st Battalion spent a brief period in Germany in 1807 before moving to Ireland, and in 1808 it embarked for Lisbon to join Sir Arthur Wellesley's army.

On 17 August the 91st was part of a force which attacked the French at Rolica, and drove them from a strong position. Five days later the French attacked the British at Vimeiro but the 91st, on the extreme left of the line, were not heavily involved in the battle. The French withdrew from the battlefield and shortly afterwards evacuated Portugal. Later in the year, however, the 91st joined Sir John Moore's part of the army which, threatened with annihiliation, was forced to retreat northwards to Corunna. The regiment had the hard task of covering the retreat and were frequently attacked by the French. Few members of the regiment fell out during the march, which continued until 11 January 1809. When the army reached Corunna, the 91st was held in reserve in the centre, but was then moved to the British right in order to turn the enemy's line. It faced a strong attack by enemy cavalry but forced them to retire. During the night the remaining British troops embarked and sailed for England.

In August 1809 the battalion re-embarked for the continent, this time to take part in the ill-fated Walcheren expedition. The 91st remained in occupation with the expeditionary force until the end of December. Like other battalions, it suffered numerous casualties from fever before the evacuation.

The 1st Battalion remained in England until September 1812, when it moved to Portugal to join Wellington's army, but did not take part in any operations until the spring of 1813. The battalion joined in the march which first occupied Burgos and then advanced on Vitoria. During that battle in June, the 91st was part of a covering force and was not much involved in the fighting. In July the French attacked the British positions at Sorauren and the division in which the 91st served arrived in time to turn the enemy's flank. During the hand-to-hand fighting the enemy were forced to withdraw partially: two days later the British attacked the French positions and quickly routed them.

The 91st remained in the area until November, when it took part in the crossing of the Nivelle. In a surprise attack the battalion assisted in the capture of a bridge and the establishment of a bridgehead over the river. This action forced the French to withdraw to the Nive. The crossing of this river was conducted in two places, and the 91st again took part in the assault river crossing. It was, however, in reserve during the subsequent fighting as the French tried desperately to defeat the troops holding a bridgehead. In February 1814 the 91st took part in the

Previous page:
The 1st Battalion, Argyll and Sutherland Highlanders parade with the Queen's Colour at Wellington Barracks, before mounting guard at Buckingham Palace in March 1988. RHQ

advance and attack on the French positions in front of Orthez. There was a successful assault on the lower part of the ridge held by the French front line, and the battalion was then used in an attack on the French left, forcing them to withdraw. Orthez was then abandoned and the British crossed the River Adour, the last major obstacle on the march to Toulouse.

During the battle for Toulouse on 10 April, the 91st were with the Highland Brigade, and supported the attack against some redoubts on a ridge containing enemy artillery. The 91st joined the 42nd in defending one of the captured redoubts and, despite determined counter-attacks, the enemy were repulsed. The French army were forced to withdraw from the remaining defences, and Toulouse was occupied by the British and allied troops. The abdication of Napoleon brought the campaign to an end.

The 2nd Battalion of the 91st Regiment had been part of an expedition to Germany in the summer of 1813, but returned later in the year without taking part in any fighting. In December it re-embarked for the Continent, and in March 1814 took part in the attack on Bergen-op-Zoom. The French troops garrisoning the fortress outnumbered the attacking force and, despite capturing part of the ramparts, the British were forced to withdraw. In September the battalion returned to England and was disbanded in 1815.

The 91st Regiment had returned to Britain in June 1814 and was serving in Ireland when, in April 1815,

91st Highlanders, 1795. A private in uniform worn during service in South Africa.

it re-embarked for the Continent. It was sent first to Oudenarde to cover the approaches to Brussels where the main part of Wellington's army was garrisoned. On 16 June the outposts of the 4th Division, in which the 91st served, were attacked by the French advance guards. Two days later the 91st were employed to cover the Genappe road, a short distance from the battlefield of Waterloo, but during the battle the regiment was not greatly involved in the fighting. After the battle, as the British army advanced into France, the 91st mounted a successful attack on the fortified town of Camron, which had refused to surrender.

* * * * *

The regiment remained in occupation in France until December 1818 and, after a period in Ireland, embarked for the West Indies. There it remained until 1831, being stationed in Jamaica and the Bahamas. Even in peacetime the West Indies was a very unhealthy station and the regiment suffered a steady rate of deaths from disease.

The next overseas posting for the 91st was on the island of St Helena, where Napoleon Bonaparte had spent his last years and was buried. In 1840 the Emperor's body was removed and, escorted by a detachment of the regiment, was placed on board ship to be returned to France. In the meantime other companies forming a 'reserve' battalion had moved to South Africa, and served in detachments at various stations in the Cape colony. There the regiment's task was to protect the settlers both from native tribesmen and Dutch farmers in the Cape and Orange River Colonies, who from time to time caused trouble.

In 1846 war broke out between the Europeans and Kaffirs, the action being mainly in the eastern Cape. The regiment spent many months fighting against the native tribes, whose guerrilla tactics were hard to defeat. Eventually the Kaffirs were cleared from the areas inhabited by the settlers. Although the war ended formally in 1847, the reserve 91st continued to be engaged in operations against the Kaffirs until the battalion left in 1855. Forty-one members of a draft were lost on their way to join the battalion when the troopship *Birkenhead* sank in 1852.

In the meantime the 91st had been serving in Ireland and England. Only a small proportion of its rank and file were Scotsmen during this period, although the regiment retained its Argyllshire name. In 1854 it embarked for Greece where it remained throughout the Crimean War, and afterwards as occupation troops on various Greek islands. In 1858 the regiment was sent to India where it took part in some minor operations against remaining bands of mutineers. The following year the 91st was stationed at Kamptee and moved to Jubbulpore in 1863. A year later, due to the efforts of various officers, the title 91st (Argyllshire) Highlanders was restored to the regiment, and tartan trews were adopted. In 1868 the regiment returned to Great Britain.

The next ten years were spent by the 91st Highlanders in England, Scotland and Ireland. Then in 1879 they were sent as a reinforcement to South Africa to join Lord Chelmsford's army. Cetewayo, the King of the Zulus, had defeated the British and native troops at Isandhlwana in January. The 91st Highlanders marched inland with one of the columns and formed a defensive camp at Ginginhlovo. There the column was attacked by some 10,000 Zulus, but they were quickly driven off. The column then continued to march to relieve other British troops besieged at Eshowe. After the battle of Ulundi in July, in which the 91st was not present, Zulu power was effectively broken. The regiment moved to Cape Town and remained there until 1883, additionally providing detachments on the islands of St Helena and Mauritius, during which time the 91st Highlanders had been amalagamated with the 93rd Highlanders.

93RD SUTHERLAND HIGHLANDERS

1799–1881

The Earl of Sutherland and his family had been active in raising troops for royal service during the latter part of the 18th century, and in 1799 his daughter, who inherited the title, agreed that a regular regiment should be raised under family auspices. Major-General William Wemyss, a cousin, formed the new regiment during the year, adopting a method of conscription by parish quota in the parts of Sutherland which were family territory. Many of those enlisted had served in the Sutherland fencible regiments, the third and last of which had been lately disbanded, and there was apparently little discontent amongst the tenantry for this somewhat high-handed feudal levy. The regiment was thus embodied at Inverness in August 1800 and was numbered the 93rd Highlanders. They wore the kilt of Sutherland tartan, which was slightly lighter than the government or universal pattern, and the pleats were arranged to show the green rather than the blue of the sett.

After a period of service in the Channel Islands, the 93rd Highlanders returned to Scotland in the autumn of 1802 expecting to be disbanded, but renewed hostilities against France determined their retention. Three years later, after serving in various parts of Ireland, the 93rd embarked for the recapture of Cape Town with an expeditionary force, which also included the 71st and 72nd Highlanders in the Highland Brigade under General Ronald Ferguson. After landing, the expedition commander General David Baird ordered an attack on the Dutch colonial force drawn up outside Cape Town. The charge of the highlanders on the left and Beresford's brigade on the right, caused the Dutch to retreat in panic. Cape Town was quickly occupied and the colony transferred back to the British Crown. The 93rd remained in South Africa until 1814.

The 2nd Battalion of the 93rd was formed in 1813. In the following year it served in Newfoundland but only remained in being for two years before disbandment. In 1814 the 1st Battalion was also sent to North America, as part of an expeditionary force whose mission was the capture of New Orleans. Soon after arriving the regiment faced a strong but unsuccessful enemy attack on the British camp. Later, on 28 December, the army was drawn up for battle and was fired on for some five hours by the enemy from behind their barricades, but neither side launched an attack.

Similar deployments were made on 1 and 8 January, and on the latter date the British attempted to storm the enemy positions. The 93rd Highlanders advanced in column towards the enemy centre and 524 men fell, 'holding their ground because they had received no order to withdraw'. According to an American eye-witness: 'Man after man of magnificent highlanders were mown down by the murderous artillery and rifle fire. They moved forward in perfect order, giving three cheers as they advanced.' Another battalion, however, had failed to bring up fascines and scaling ladders, and the American fortifications could not be surmounted. The British then abandoned the attempt, and a few weeks later a peace treaty was concluded.

* * * * *

The 93rd then returned to Great Britain and was stationed in various parts of Ireland until 1824. There followed ten years' service in the West Indies which were uneventful apart from the steady number of deaths each year from disease. In 1838 the 93rd Highlanders left Ireland for Canada where a rebellion had broken out near Montreal. The regiment was involved in maintaining a presence in a number of places and, apart from one skirmish against some American sympathisers in which a detachment took part, the rebellion quickly subsided. The regiment remained in Canada until 1848.

In February 1854 the 93rd Highlanders embarked at Plymouth for garrison service in the Mediterranean, but they were soon required to join the rest of the army to fight in the Crimea, reaching Scutari in

Previous page:
Gen Prinsloo surrenders his command; members of the 1st Bn, Queen's Own Cameron Highlanders look on. July 1900. Watercolour by W. Skeoch Cumming. RHQ

Top left:
The KOSB fought in the Tirah campaign of 1897. Here they capture the heights of Maidan. RHQ

Top right:
A watercolour of the 3rd Carabiniers at Honnechy, 9 Oct 1918. The cavalry had few opportunities for mounted action like this on the Western Front. Watercolour by Lionel Edwards. RHQ

Far left:
A watercolour by R. Simkin of the Royal Scots (The Lothian Regt) in 1913. The officer in full dress on the right wears trews of Hunting Stuart tartan, a distinction granted to the regiment six years earlier. RHQ

Left:
The Royal Scots Fusiliers defend the canal at Jemappes on 23 Aug 1914. Oil painting by Gilbert Holiday. RHQ

Above:
A jovial 'Snaffles' picture of the Argyll and Sutherland Highlanders, c1920. Matthew E. Taylor Collection

Top right:
The pipes and drums of the Seaforth Highlanders lead a parade along Princes Street, Edinburgh in the 1930s. From a watercolour by Conrad Leigh. Valentines

Right:
'The Greys Patrol' a period-piece painting, c1930 by R. Butterworth after G. A. Fothergill.

Top left:
The 2nd Argyll and Sutherland Highlanders hold the Causeway on 31 Jan 1942 during the final withdrawal to Singapore Island. Painting by Peter Archer. RHQ

Top right:
Col George Rusk DSO, MC who commanded the 2nd Black Watch at Tobruk, and to whom this book is in a sense dedicated. Painted by Mollie Guion. RHQ

Left:
HRH The Duke of Gloucester inspects the Scots Guards on Horse Guards Parade in 1962 as Col of the Regt. Oil painting by Raoul Millais. RHQ

Above:
In the grounds of the Holyroodhouse the Royal Scots parade for HM The Queen, and HRH The Princess Anne, Col-in-Chief, on the occasion of the 350th anniversary of the raising of the regiment in 1633. Watercolour by Joan Wanklyn. RHQ

Below:
The 1st Bn Scots Guards march past their Col-in-Chief during the ceremony of Trooping the Colour, 1987. RHQ

May. The Highland Brigade was formed in due course, the 93rd being joined by the 42nd and 79th. The whole force reached the Crimea in September, and on 19 September began the march to Sevastopol. The following day the line of the River Alma was reached, the heights above it being held in considerable strength by the Russians. The river banks were then occupied by the Light Division, and the Highland Brigade with the 93rd in the centre passed through. The Highlanders were subjected to very heavy rifle and artillery fire as they ascended the ridge. After some delay, they reached the summit.

'and then for the first time got a close look at the Russians, who were in column. We at once opened fire, the men firing by files as they advanced. On getting nearer, the front company of the Russian regiment opposite to us, a very large one, brought down their bayonets, and I thought were about to charge us; but on our giving a cheer, they at once faced about and retired.'

The 93rd then charged the enemy who abandoned their positions after a fierce fight.

The march to Sevastopol continued and on the way the port of Balaclava was occupied. The 93rd Highlanders remained there in order to assist the unloading of ships and to defend the town. On 25 October the enemy approached in very great strength from the north-east, and the 93rd Highlanders were hurriedly ordered to take up a position a mile north of Balaclava to hold a small ridge. They were fired on by artillery and then a body of Russian Cavalry, numbering some 400, appeared and charged the highlanders' position. They opened fire at 600 yards, but the momentum of the charge was scarcely checked until the cavalry were at a distance of 200 yards, when their ranks began to break up in confusion in face of the rifle volley of a 'thin red line' of highlanders. 'I did not think it worthwhile,' said Sir Colin Campbell, the brigade commander who was present, 'to form them even four deep,' – a front two deep proving sufficient to repel the Russian cavalry. They then wheeled west into the valley, and were defeated by the British cavalry of the Union Brigade. A Russian officer later admitted that the horses could not face the highlanders' deadly fire, and nearly every man and horse had been wounded.

The 93rd remained in the vicinity of Balaclava throughout the winter, and in May they joined in the expedition to Kerch, a port from which the Russians were re-supplying the whole of their army in the

Gen Sir John Ewart, KCB served with the 93rd Highlanders during the Crimean War, led the storming of the Secundrabagh at Lucknow, and lost an arm at Cawnpore. He was a Lt-Col with the 78th Highlanders and later became the Col of the Argyll and Sutherland Highlanders. RHQ

Crimea. It was surprisingly easily captured, and the highlanders remained in the town for a month before re-embarking. They rejoined the Highland Brigade entrenched in front of Sevastopol and, during the first assault on the fortress, were held in reserve. On the evening of 8 September the four Highland regiments formed up ready to attack at dawn, but during the night the Russians blew up part of the town before completely evacuating it. The regiment remained in the Crimea until peace came in March 1856.

* * * * *

The 93rd Highlanders embarked in June 1857 for South Africa, but they were diverted to India where the mutiny of the Bengal Army had already begun. On their arrival the 93rd Highlanders were ordered to garrison Futtepore, close to where a large force of mutineers were operating. One company fought an engagement against the rebels at Kudjwa, in which the Highlanders charged the village and captured some guns. The 93rd suffered a high number of casualties, but a party of the wounded awaiting treatment succeeded in repelling some of the mutineers who had crept back into the village. In October the regiment marched to Cawnpore and was involved in skirmishes at Buntera and Bunnee. In November preparations were made for the second relief of Lucknow – the first attempt in September having only succeeded in breaking through and re-inforcing the Residency.

Sir Colin Campbell's column of 4,500 troops advanced on Lucknow, and the enemy outposts in the Dilkoosha Palace and Martinière College were seized on 14 November. Two days later the 93rd led the main party along the western bank of the Goomtee River and, fighting past the enclosures of a village, reached the Secundrabagh. Eventually a small breach was made in the wall, and men of the 93rd, led by Lt-Col Ewart and accompanied by loyal Sikh soldiers, forced their way in. The order had been given to

'"Advance", upon which the whole of the British line rose with a cheer towards the building. It was not a cheer, but a concentrated yell of rage and ferocity that made the echoes ring again . . . Pipe Major John MacLeod with seven pipers struck up the Highland Charge.'

There followed desperate hand-to-hand fighting lasting several hours, with the most terrible slaughter. Meanwhile a detachment of two companies of the regiment captured two enemy guns and the barracks. The next main objective was the Shah Nujjif. This seemed impregnable and the Highlanders were fired on incessantly by the sepoys from the loop-holed walls. Advancing during the darkness, the 93rd eventually found a small gap that allowed one man at a time to enter with difficulty. The gap was widened and the 93rd rushed in, with pipers playing, seized the gates and within minutes of the Shah Nujjif was occupied. One officer and five soldiers of the regiment were awarded the Victoria Cross for gallantry in that day's fighting. The following day the Residency was reached and those inside were conducted to safety. But the town itself was still held by upwards of 60,000 mutineers, so Campbell withdrew his column.

Cawnpore, re-captured in July after the massacre of the European inhabitants, was being threatened by a force of 25,000 mutineers, and Campbell's column marched rapidly to relieve it. A bridge of boats was seized by the British, but for a full week the enemy kept up determined rifle and artillery fire on their positions. On 6 December, 4 Brigade under Brigadier the Hon Adrian Hope, which included the 93rd and 42nd Highlanders, attacked. They occupied a sepoy camp with ease and the mutineers were forced to retreat under the weight of advancing highlanders, led by the redoubtable Sir Colin himself. He was subsequently reproved by the Queen for 'exposing himself too much', but that had been his habit since the Peninsular campaigns. The enemy were pursued, but they continued to inflict casualties as they retreated. At Serai Ghat they were prevented from crossing the Ganges, and were forced to disperse.

During January the 93rd Highlanders were involved in the seizing of the Kali Nadi Bridge, and two punitive expeditions. In early March they returned with Sir Colin Campbell to Lucknow, and began to lay seige to it. This time Campbell's force had been increased to 30,000 and the Dilkoosha Palace was again quickly occupied. During the river crossing and preparation of defences and battery positions, the enemy maintained strong fire from the Martinière College. On 9 March the 93rd and 42nd Highlanders, together with the 90th Perthshire Light Infantry, attacked and captured the college. Two days later the 93rd Highlanders, supported by the 42nd and a native regiment, stormed the Begum's palace. For several hours desperate close-quarter combat took place in the narrow streets and enclosures, but the surviving mutineers eventually fled from the palace. The adjutant Lt William McBean was awarded the VC for personally killing eleven mutineers during the fighting for the breach.

During the next week other troops systematically cleared the enemy from the city, but the 93rd were only involved in a few skirmishes.

The 93rd Highlanders then took part in the Rohilcund campaign. On 16 April they formed up to attack Fort Rooyah with the 42nd and 79th Highlanders, but the enemy escaped during the night. Later in the month the regiment was present at the battle of Bareilly, capturing some outlying villages, and a detachment fought with other troops for possession of the city itself. After the city was captured the regiment remained there until October. During the subsequent Oude campaign the 93rd took part in the action at Mittowlie.

When the Mutiny ended the 93rd Highlanders remained in India for several years, and from 1861 were stationed at Peshawar on the North-West Frontier. In 1863 there were incursions across the frontier by Pathan tribesmen, and a punitive expedition, under General Neville Chamberlain, was mounted in the Ambeyla region. The 93rd Highlanders joined this campaign at the end of the year but, apart from extensive marches and guard duties, they were not much in action.

In 1867 the regiment moved to Central India, where it remained until the return to Scotland three years later. The years 1870 to 1873 were spent in Edinburgh, followed by three years in England and three at the Curragh camp near Dublin. The last two years before amalgamation with the 91st Highlanders were spent as garrison troops in Gibraltar.

THE ARGYLL AND SUTHERLAND HIGHLANDERS

1881–1913

After amalgamation the 2nd Battalion remained at home duty for ten years, serving in England and at the Curragh in Ireland. Meanwhile the 1st Battalion moved from Cape Town in 1883 to Natal and thence to Zululand, where their presence assisted in preventing renewed trouble with the tribes. The Argylls were then sent to serve in Ceylon for three years, followed by four years in Hong Kong before returning to the United Kingdom.

The 2nd Argylls, serving in India, joined the Tochi Valley expedition in 1897, the purpose of which was a show of force to impresss the Waziris who had attacked a small group of British officers and their native guards. The expedition lasted for six months and although there were no major actions, living and marching in the extreme heat was most exhausting. After the successful completion of the expedition the 2nd Battalion remained at garrison duty in various Indian stations for the next ten years, before fulfilling a three-year tour in South Africa.

The 1st Battalion was mobilised for service in South Africa in October 1899 and reached Cape Town the following month. Joining Lord Methuen's force on the Modder River, the Argylls were first in action in an attempt to capture a bridge. After wading through the river, the Argylls were pinned down by extremely accurate enemy fire in the open and had to lie all day in the scorching heat. During the night the Boers silently withdrew.

In early December, as part of the Highland Brigade, the 1st Argylls took part in the dawn attack on Magersfontein Hill. Due to inadequate reconnaissance of the enemy's position, which was at the base rather than the top of the hill, the brigade was caught by a devastating fire during the approach. There was much confusion and contradictory orders, as well as attempts by many of the Highlanders to find virtually non-existent cover from which to return fire.

'Then it was that I witnessed one of the bravest deeds I ever saw,' wrote C/Sgt McInnes, 'for suddenly there broke forth the strains of "The Campbells are Coming", and there was Jimmy MacKay, the corporal piper of the 91st, standing up fearlessly playing the regimental tune, facing the storm of bullets in a valiant attempt to stop the retirement becoming a riot. The pipers of the various regiments broke out playing almost immediately after, and there can be no doubt that this altered the aspect of the fight considerably.'

This painting by W. Small shows a corporal of the 2nd Bn, Argyll and Sutherland Highlanders in marching order, 1890. The new Lee-Metford rifle is depicted. It was sighted to 1,800 yds and its magazine held 8 rounds of .303 ammunition. Matthew E. Taylor

The 2nd Argylls halt on the march in the Tochi Valley, India 1897. RHQ

But the Argylls lay in the open for several hours under enemy fire, before being withdrawn with the remnants of the Highland Brigade.

The Argylls were in action in February at Koodoosberg and at Paardeberg, where the brigade assisted in cutting off Cronje's force which led to his surrender. Later in 1900 the battalion joined Sir Ian Hamilton's column in pursuit of Botha, and during 1901 formed part of Colonel Benson's column, which made many forced marches over hundreds of miles. A year after the peace treaty the 1st Argylls returned to England, where they remained until 1909, when they left for a tour of duty in Malta.

A sketch by W. B. Wollen shows Cpl MacKay, 'the intrepid piper', rallying the 1st Argylls caught by the fire of the Boers at Magersfontein Hill, Dec 1899. Such individual acts of bravery, and there were many, mitigated in the public imagination the shortcomings of reconnaissance and planning in this disastrous battle. NAM

Argylls on the march near Poona, India attempt to keep relatively dry as they ford a river, c1904. RHQ

Mounted infantry company of the 2nd Argylls in India, 1904. Experience of the Boer War proved the value of mounted infantry tactics in wide open country, dominated by the rifle. RHQ

THE ARGYLL AND SUTHERLAND HIGHLANDERS

1914–1938

On the outbreak of the First World War the 1st Battalion, Argyll and Sutherland Highlanders, were serving in India, while the 2nd Battalion was at Fort George, Inverness. Mobilised on 4 August, the battalion was sent to France with the BEF and joined 19 Brigade on the extreme left of the line at Quievrechan. On 23 August the withdrawal from Mons began, and the following day the Argylls were in action for the first time, losing two killed and thirteen wounded and missing.

During the battle of Le Cateau on 26 August, the Argylls were called forward in support of other battalions and were subjected to concentrated machine-gun and artillery fire. In attempting to move to better positions overlooking the town, C Company was wiped out, and half of B Company, in support of the Suffolks, were overwhelmed and captured.

'The Suffolks and Argylls opened rapid fire to their front', reads the Official History, 'with terrific effect. Two officers of the highlanders in particular bringing down man after man, and counting their scores aloud as if in a competition. The Germans kept sounding the British "Cease Fire", and gesticulating as if to persuade the men to surrender . . . At length a rush of the enemy from the rear bore down all resistance . . . The Suffolks and their highland comrades . . . had for nine hours been under an incessant bombardment, which had pitted the whole ground with craters, and they had fought to the very last . . .'

The withdrawal continued and the remaining Argylls were involved in various encounters with the enemy until reaching final positions on the River Marne. During the battle of the Marne, the 2nd Argylls acted as flank protection to the 4th Division, and carried out various supporting tasks during the battle of the Aisne.

Moving to the new part of the front in October, the Argylls fought in a number of fast-moving engagements near Armentières during the last week of the month, and on 30 October a platoon of the battalion captured an outpost, killing 56 and capturing 94 prisoners. The battalion remained in this part of the front until May 1915.

The first Territorial battalion of the regiment from Stirlingshire, the 7th Argylls, reached France

During the spring 1915, a sergeant of the 2nd Argylls mans a machine gun fixed up for the anti-aircraft role in Bois de Grenier sector, south of Armentières. IWM

in December joining 4th Division, and at the same time the 1st Argylls reached France from India, as part of 81 Brigade in the 27th Division. The 9th (Dunbartonshire) Battalion arrived in February 1915.

At the start of the second battle of Ypres the 1st Argylls held trenches forward of Sanctuary Wood, with the 9th Argylls in support, but the Germans only shelled the area; their main attacks were elsewhere. Nevertheless it was necessary to withdraw the line half-a-mile to the edge of Sanctuary Wood in early May. The Germans then attacked the Argylls' sector on 8 May, and on reports that they had penetrated the neighbouring division two companies of the 1st Argylls were sent to hold Railway Wood. By the time the 1st Argylls were relieved they had been under fire for thirty-six days and had suffered 488 casualties. The 7th Argylls suffered over 500 casualties in an attack with the Warwicks at Ploegsteert, but the remnants of the battalion remained in action for a week. They returned to the line several times, but were amalgamated temporarily with the 9th Argylls who had also suffered numerous casualties.

A group of cheerful jocks of the 2nd Argylls cook a meal in the front line, Bois de Grenier sector, 1915. IWM

The 6th and 8th Battalions, territorials from Renfrew and Argyllshire, arrived in May with the 51st Highland Division. They manned the line at Festubert and Béthune during the summer. The first 'new' battalion, the 10th Argylls, also reached France with the 9th Scottish Division, with the 11th and 12th Argylls following during the summer.

During the battle of Loos the 2nd Argylls took part in the initial attack on 25 September. Advancing the 80 yards to the German front line the first wave, comprising B and D Companies, was severely cut up by the German machine gunners and only two platoons reached the objective. They could not be supported, however, and only eleven of them managed to return. The 10th Argylls also fought at Loos, and both they and the 6th suffered from German mining activities during the autumn.

* * * * *

The 5th Argylls, the Renfrewshire Battalion of the Territorial Force, joined 157 Brigade in the Lowland Division and landed at Cape Helles, Gallipoli, in July 1915. After a few days manning the front-line trenches, they took part in the assault on Achi Baba. After occupying two enemy trenches they were caught in the open searching for a non-existent third line. They withdrew to the second line, and suffered a large number of casualties while holding against Turkish counter-attacks over the next day-and-a-half.

The 5th Argylls served in and out of the trenches for the next five months, and took part in various raids in the area of Krithia Nullah in December, which provoked Turkish retaliation against the Argylls and HLI. In the meantime the withdrawal from the Peninsula began and the Argylls were amongst the last troops to leave the Cape Helles area for Egypt in January 1916.

The 5th Battalion spent several months in various positions defending the Suez Canal from possible Turkish attack. When the canal defences were extended eastwards into the Sinai desert, the Turks launched an attack on Romani and the Argylls were involved in pursuit of the retreating enemy. During the first battle of Gaza their brigade held positions on the high ground at In Seirat, and in the second battle were heavily bombarded on Lees Hill, but remained in various positions near the two features during the summer.

In the third battle for Gaza the Argylls assisted in clearing enemy troops on two features, Wadi Hesa and Sausage Ridge, and took part in a brilliant night attack against the Turkish positions at Kumman, charging up a hill and ejecting the enemy with the bayonet. The Argylls' last major operation in Palestine in December was the night crossing of the River Auja, north of Jerusalem, when the enemy were taken by complete surprise. In early 1918 the 5th Argylls left the Middle East for France.

* * * * *

The 1st Argylls meanwhile had left the Western Front and reached Salonika in December 1915, and were to remain there until the end of the war. Unlike other theatres there was comparatively little fighting. The Argylls first manned trenches known as the 'Birdcage' between two lakes some fifteen miles east of the town of Salonika, but in August 1916 they moved to the area of the River Struma and set up new defensive positions along the river.

The first set-piece attack for the battalion was at the end of September 1916. Their brigade attacked two Bulgarian-held villages at Bala and Zir, and the Argylls were in the second phase after Bala had been captured. But Zir was strongly held and it took all day before a composite force of Royal Scots and Cameronians, with covering fire from the Argylls in Bala, were able to storm the village. Three counter-attacks by the enemy during the night were repulsed before they gave up the attempt to re-occupy the two villages.

Jocks of the 1st Argylls at bayonet practice at Struma, Bulgarian Front, 1917. Two British divisions served in this theatre during the war. RHQ

1st Argylls prepare to march through Constantinople after the Armistice, 1918. RHQ

A wounded sergeant of the Argylls at 'Clapham Junction' between Sanctuary and Polygon Woods, Ypres salient, 26 Sept 1917. The 2nd, 7th, 8th and 10th Argylls all fought at Third Ypres, while the 6th undertook pioneer tasks. IWM

The 1st Argylls remained on the river line during the autumn and winter of 1916, suffering many casualties from malaria until the cold weather set in. The Bulgarians had been joined by Turkish troops, but during 1917 there were minor adjustments of the line and only sporadic fighting. The 12th (Service) Battalion also served in the same theatre and spent most of the time on the Macedonia sector.

In early 1918 the 1st Argylls went into reserve before moving to the sector west of the River Vardar in July, where they conducted active patrolling and raiding. Malaria caused many more casualties and the battalion strength fell below 300 at this time. Major offensives took place to the west and north in September but did not involve the Argylls, although they were fully occupied during the advance from 21 September when the Bulgarians started to evacuate the front. Hostilities against Bulgaria ended on 30 September and after a period as occupation troops in Sofia and Constantinople, the 1st Argylls were reduced to cadre strength and returned to Scotland in May 1919.

* * * * *

During the winter of 1915, the 2nd Battalion moved to trenches at Festubert and in the early part of the year were involved in tunnelling activities, although they were themselves mined in January 1916.

In February the 9th Argylls became a base battalion, whose task was to train drafts, and in June the 6th became pioneers: in the same month the 14th (Service) Battalion arrived in France. At the same time the 51st Highland Division took over the whole of the corp's frontage to allow the preparation for the new offensive to be conducted, and the 6th and 8th Argylls were ordered to discard their kilts and bonnets and don khaki trousers and caps to conceal their identity from the enemy.

On 1 July 1916 the Somme offensive began. On 14 July the 10th Argylls took part in a surprise dawn attack at Longueval and ejected the Germans from the front line. Fighting took place all day and into the following night, and casualties were high. A few days later the 10th relieved some South African troops in Delville Wood. The Argylls' casualties were over 400.

On 15 July the 2nd Argylls carried out an attack with their brigade on positions in the area of Bazentin and High Wood, but so intense was the fire from the wood that they were unable to reach it. The 7th also fought in the same area, and the 6th (Pioneer) Battalion spent many weeks in wiring, constructing strong points, and extending trench lines.

On 18 August, however, the 2nd Argylls attacked the wood again, but they were shelled in error while

During the final British advance, men of the 5th Argylls cross the River Lys, 18 Oct 1918, on a captured German pontoon. IWM

waiting for the attack by British guns, and then the mines and gas proved ineffective. Only B Company managed to penetrate the enemy's line, and the survivors remained in occupation for six hours until their ammunition ran out.

The 6th Argylls were called upon to fight in an infantry role in the autumn and launched a successful attack at Morval. The 10th Argylls returned to the front at Flers, and on 28 October A and B Companies of the 2nd Battalion managed to capture a ridge near Transloy in the same sector, which had been successfully defended by the Germans against three previous attacks. The 7th and 8th Argylls fought at Beaumont Hamel, the 51st Highland Division's major contribution to the fighting. On 14/15 November the division captured over 2,000 prisoners and a large quantity of equipment.

On the first day of the battle of Arras, 9 April 1917, the 8th Argylls captured the second and third lines of enemy trenches at Roclincourt, in conjunction with the 5th Seaforth. The 10th Battalion also took two trench systems. Pte W. G. Taylor (later Sgt) was shot through both thighs during the attack but,

'he remained in no-man's-land for five days in a shell-hole, 250 yards in front of our lines. Instead of returning he remained there with his Lewis gun, which he eventually brought out with him, picking up targets and collecting ammunition and food from casualties, and it was not until the fifth night when his strength was nearly exhausted that he crawled into our lines, having gained much useful information as to the enemy's dispositions. He was awarded the DCM.'

On the 23 April A and B Companies of the 2nd Argylls were in the first wave of an attack on part of the Hindenburg Line at Fontaine les Croisilles. A Company successfully took their objective, having crossed 1,200 yards, but in mid-morning the enemy successfully counter-attacked and forced back the battalions to the left and right of the Argylls.

'Although attacked in front and rear they held their position killing numbers of the enemy, Captain Henderson (the Company Commander) leading a bayonet charge upon a large body ... taking prisoners in front and being attacked from behind ... the relieving battalion found that the survivors of A Company and of one platoon of B Company ... had held out, although isolated, and had made themselves so unpleasant to the enemy, who had surrounded them, that they had fled early in the morning, abandoning much equipment and many wounded.'

Captain Henderson was awarded a posthumous VC.

In the following month D Company of the 2nd Argylls, although only 65 strong, captured and held a stretch of the Hindenburg Line, taking over 100

Germans prisoners. During the intense fighting for the chemical works at Roeux, the 7th, 8th and 10th Battalions were all heavily involved. The 7th suffered over 500 casualties and only one officer was unscathed. The 8th Argylls were so pressed during one German counter-attack that the CO, Lt-Col Robin Campbell, formed a storming party from battalion headquarters, and in ejecting the enemy, personally shot six Germans with a rifle. This enabled the 6th Seaforth to recapture the works.

In September the 2nd Argylls fought in the third battle of Ypres. A and C Companies advanced and carried the line forward with the 1st Middlesex along the southern edge of Polygon Wood. Thereupon the Germans counter-attacked by night and isolated the two companies, who nevertheless held their positions until relieved by the 5th Cameronians and 4th Suffolks. The 2nd Argylls remained in the sector for the rest of the winter, taking up the responsibility in November for occupying Passchendaele village, after its capture by the Canadians.

The 10th Argylls took part in the fighting at Passchendaele in October and made some important gains there. The 8th Argyll had also fought at Ypres, and they and the 7th both took part in the first phase of the battle of Cambrai, where dramatic gains were made by the infantry exploiting the initial success of the Tank Corps' shock action. The 6th Argylls, still in the pioneer role, were active in the Ypres sector during the autumn before moving to the Italian front for four months.

The 8th Argylls were the most heavily involved in the German spring offensive which began on 21 March 1918. C Company fought for a full twenty-four hours whilst surrounded by the enemy, before they were finally overwhelmed. The 2nd Argylls were held in reserve in various places and, on 17 April, B Company was attacked while holding positions at the Meteren Windmill, but the Germans were repulsed successfully. On 8 May they were again attacked after a heavy gas bombardment. The Germans were initially successful and the battalion had to form a flank position to prevent penetration. During the evening two battalions of Cameronians counter-attacked and relieved the situation.

The 2nd Argylls remained in this sector until August and the 6th Argylls were recalled from the Italian front for work in the area of Armentières. The 14th Battalion, which had served in various parts of the Western Front since June 1916, was reduced to a

Old and New Colour Parties of the 1st Bn Argyll and Sutherland Highlanders after the Presentation of New Colours in Cairo, April 1926. The CO (centre) is Lt-Col G. W. Muir, whose son was to win the VC serving with the Argylls in Korea. RHQ

The 3rd Argyll and Sutherland Highlanders (Special Reserve) provide a Guard of Honour for their Sovereign, HM King George V, at Holyroodhouse in the 1930s. They are wearing full dress, which was soon to be discontinued. RHQ

cadre and 500 of its men drafted to reinforce other battalions: it later re-formed in July 1918. The 11th Battalion became a training cadre in June and subsequently a reinforcement battalion.

The 5th Argylls had reached France from the Middle East in April 1918 and went with the 34th Division to reinforce the French on the Marne in June. They took part in the defence of Beugneux Ridge near Senlis and, during an assault on 'Hill 158' the CO, Lt-Col Barlow, was killed while personally leading the battalion. In July the 7th and 8th Argylls also moved to the French sector with the 51st Highland Division. The 7th took part in the fighting near Nanteuil and Montagne de Bligny and the 8th were in action at Buzancy.

On their return to the Ypres sector the 5th Argylls captured their objectives during the advance on Kemmel Hill and Wytschaete Ridge. During the allied advance the 2nd Battalion launched an attack on 21 September, with its division, on German trenches at Villers Guislain. The Argylls held the positions for a time but they had to be retaken a day later, when more than 100 Germans were captured. On 23 September a platoon of A Company was surrounded and attacked strongly: after fighting for an hour it was wiped out. Then on 29 September A and C Companies were ordered to recapture Villers Guislain, but in the counter-attack they were cut off. Pressure elsewhere, however, ensured a German withdrawal.

The 6th Argylls rejoined the 51st Highland Division in October in the infantry role. At the end of the month they crossed the River Selle, and having taken an objective at Famars, were counter-attacked and almost surrounded. Lt Bisset led the battalion in a bayonet charge and forced the enemy to retire: he was awarded the VC for this exploit. During the final weeks of the war, the Argylls' battalions all advanced considerable distances in the fast-moving fighting.

* * * * *

The 1st Argylls spent some years in India after the war, and then moved to Egypt. They were sent to Sudan for a time during the mutiny of the Egyptian army and in 1930 they returned to Scotland. The 2nd Argylls had in the meantime been stationed in Scotland and then in Ireland during the last period of British rule. From 1927 they served in the West Indies, Hong Kong and Shanghai, before moving to India. Early in 1935 the 1st Argylls embarked for duty in Palestine during the Arab rebellion, remaining there until 1940 where they were frequently involved in operations against the terrorists.

THE ARGYLL AND SUTHERLAND HIGHLANDERS

1939 to the present

The 7th and 8th Argylls went with the 51st Highland Division to France in February 1940, and in April moved to the Saar region. By 13 May the invading Germans had reached the division's forward positions near the Maginot Line but initially did not attack. The Argylls were ordered to abandon these positions on 20/21 May, and were moved westwards to new positions on the Somme near Abbeville. There they remained holding extensive frontages, while the Germans advanced and encircled the main part of the BEF at Dunkirk.

By 4 June the Germans had crossed the river at Abbeville. Both Argyll battalions made contact with enemy patrols and were subjected to heavy artillery fire. Because the companies and platoons were holding widely dispersed positions. The situation developed into a series of battles, and the battalion headquarters were isolated. Despite British artillery fire the German armour and infantry quickly penetrated the front in a number of places, and by 6 June the situation for the 7th Argylls became desperate. Attempts by The Black Watch and acompanying armour to relieve them failed.

A Company, commanded by Lt Fisher, became isolated and fought off frequent enemy attacks during the evening and night. During the daytime on 6 June large enemy formations passed along their flank. The company, already depleted, caused significant casualties on the enemy but provoked further attacks on the company positions. Finally the enemy succeeded in overwhelming them by sheer weight of numbers, and the German commander personally congratulated the captured Highlanders for their bravery in fighting against impossible odds. Other companies fought similar actions and D Company remained the only viable company, so came under command of the 8th Argylls. A few members of the battalion escaped from France, but the casualties were 23 officers and 500 other ranks, killed, wounded, missing or taken prisoner.

Battle-weary jocks of the 7th Argylls during a lull in the fighting near Abbeville, France, early June 1940. Of the battalion, over 500 men were killed, wounded or taken prisoner while fighting with the 51st Highland Division, but the remainder escaped to England with two companies of the 8th Argylls. IWM

Meanwhile C and D Companies of the 8th Argylls, after holding the area of the Château of Belloy for three days, were similarly overwhelmed. A and B Companies, however, were withdrawn westward to the village of Meneslies, and then across the River Bresle in a night move on the 7 June. They were fortunate in not being encircled, as were the remnants of the 51st Highland Division in St Valéry-en-Caux, and escaped to Le Havre where they embarked for Southampton.

Two other battalions of the regiment fought in France during 1940. The 6th Battalion, which had spent the inter-war years amalgamated with the 5th, was sent there in January as a medium machine-gun battalion. It spent four months guarding various positions on the Franco-Belgian border. When the Germans invaded the 6th Argylls were moved to man detachments for refugee control to towns south-west of Brussels. On 15 May they concentrated in the Forêt de Soignes near the capital, but during the withdrawal the platoons were detached to give machine-gun support to other battalions, and they took part in the delaying battle which ended at Dunkirk. Over 400 casualties were lost but 270 officers and men escaped to re-form in the UK. In 1941 they became the 93rd Anti-Tank Regiment, RA (Argyll and Sutherland Highlanders) on changing role.

The 9th Argylls had been converted to artillery in 1939, and formed the 54th Light Anti-Aircraft Regiment, RA. (58th Lt AA Regiment, RA had also been formed by the regiment.) In late September 54th Regiment reached France to join the BEF and were deployed in support of various formations, armed with a mixture of guns, including Bofors. When the Germans invaded Belgium in May, the regiment was moved forward and detachments were in action against air attacks for the next fortnight. On 28 May the regiment was ordered to defend the beach at Dunkirk. Three days later, with ammunition mainly expended, the regiment embarked for England: except for one battery which fought on until late June, and then embarked from west coast ports.

* * * * *

In September 1940 the 1st Argylls were moved from Palestine as part of 16 Infantry Brigade in the 4th Indian Division to meet the Italian threat on the Egyptian/Libyan border. During the first attack on the Italian defences, the Argylls were in divisional reserve. Then on 10 September they passed through the first objectives to secure the coast road to the south-west of Sidi Barrani. The battle lasted several hours during a sandstorm, and the Italians held a series of positions in the sand hills. After a number of co-ordinated company attacks, the battalion succeeded in its task, but suffered over 150 casualties. Sidi Barrani was captured by the troops, and the Italians withdrew westwards.

The Argylls were not used in further operations in the desert, but in May 1941 were sent to assist in the defence of Crete. The Germans had already started to send in parachute troops, and the Argylls fought numerous engagements as they advanced through the mountains to Heraklion, which they reached on 25 May. Due to the successful German landings and seizure of the western part of the island, it was decided to evacuate Crete and the Argylls embarked on 30 May. During the sea voyage to Alexandria the ships were attacked from the air. The total casualties during the battle for Crete were nearly half the battalion.

In July 1941 the 1st Argylls were sent to Asmara in Eritrea to garrison the town and various other stations. Although the Italian army had surrendered in May, there were still isolated enemy forces holding out in the interior. In November the Argylls were ordered to capture Venticinque on the road between Asmara and Gondar, near Lake Tana. This task was accomplished, and after the fall of Gondar, Ambazzo, the last Italian outpost, was occupied jointly by the Argylls and King's African Rifles. The battalion then spent the next five months in Khartoum.

* * * * *

The 2nd Argylls had spent the early part of the war on Singapore Island and in training for jungle warfare on the Malayan peninsula with 12 Indian Brigade. After the Japs invaded Malaya in early December 1941 the Argylls were ordered to move northwards by train and road transport to the area of Kroh, some 350 miles north of Singapore. By the time they reached Kroh the Japanese had encircled the town and the Argylls took up positions to defend nearby Baling, with C Company detached to Grik guarding the main road south supported by one solitary armoured car, and a 3in mortar.

The battalion's orders were to delay the enemy 'subject to not becoming committed', and the first contact with enemy patrols was during the night of 15 December. After a withdrawal to conform to the other battalions, the Argylls' first battle was at Titi-Karangan three days later, and centred on the road leading through a narrow strip of rubber trees and thick jungle. The Japs, on hitting the road ambush position, attempted to deploy through the jungle in an outflanking movement. The whole area, however, was set up by the Argylls as an area ambush and they inflicted heavy casualties on the Japs. In order to prevent encirclement, the Argylls then prepared to attack through the jungle and destroy the enemy's leading troops, but orders came through to the CO, Lt-Col Stewart, to withdraw while continuing to delay the enemy's advance. In the battle some 200 Japs were killed for only 11 Argyll casualties.

Between 19 and 21 December the Argylls with-

The 2nd Argylls exercise in earnest with their armoured cars on Singapore Island, 13 Nov 1941. Soon afterwards they faced the Japanese invasion on the mainland: after a bravely-fought campaign, the survivors were taken captive when Singapore fell. IWM

drew southwards along the road and the fighting intensified. As rearguard battalion they mounted numerous blocking positions during the next two weeks, and fought several major battles. The companies were severely depleted and on 8 January the remaining members of the battalion, reduced to separate groups, were gathered together under Capt Slessor, comprising three other officers, ninety soldiers and two armoured cars. They were ordered to withdraw to Singapore.

On reorganising the battalion, with extra drafts and reinforcements, numbered some 250 all ranks, two 3in mortars and a total of six armoured cars. A further 200 Royal Marines, who had escaped the sinking of the two battleships *HMS Prince of Wales* and *HMS Repulse*, joined and four companies were thus formed for the composite battalion, which was nicknamed the 'Plymouth Argylls'. The Argylls' next task was the protection of a bridgehead on the withdrawal route north of the Causeway under command of 22 Australian Brigade. All the remaining members of 3rd Corps, comprising British and Imperial troops, successfully withdrew across the Causeway on the night of 31 January–1 February, leaving only the Argylls on the mainland. At 7.30am on 1 February the Argylls were ordered to follow across the Causeway before the demolitions were blown. In the words of Eric Linklater: 'Now their pipers played their own regiment out of Malaya. The morning sun was aleady hot when the air was broken by "A Hundred Pipers" and "Hielan Laddie", and the remaining highlanders, with steady bearing and their heads held high, marched from a lost campaign into a doomed island.'

For the next week there was a lull with only artillery fire and air attacks, but on 8 February the Japanese landed on the north-west of the island. The Argylls were moved to the western part and prepared to defend a line with other battalions: but further landings to the north across the Causeway were made on 9 February. The battalion succeeded in causing a delay but, over a period of three days' intensive fighting, casualties mounted up, leaving about 50 men still able to fight when the surrender was ordered. They were taken captive and remained in internment for the duration of the war.

The 1st Argylls spent the summer months of 1942 in Egypt and moved forward to Ruweisat Ridge near El Alamein in August to man part of the defence line with 161 Infantry Brigade. During the battle the battalion was held in reserve and took no part in the fighting.

The 7th Argylls reached Egypt with the 51st Highland Division in August 1942 to join the Eighth Army. During the first hour of the battle of El Alamein, on the night of 23 October, the battalion seized its first and second objectives. In the early hours of the morning B Company suffered a large number of casualties, but the battalion pressed on to capture the third objective line nicknamed 'Greenock'. Fortunately no enemy counter-attack occurred during 24 October, but heavy artillery fire fell on the Argylls' positions. On the evening of the following day the battalion advanced again and forced the enemy to abandon several positions. The Argylls continued to fight and hold the territory gained until relieved on 30 October.

On the night of 3 November the 7th Argylls were ordered to attack a hill near Tel El Aqqaqir but, on reaching it, the enemy were discovered to have hurriedly left what had been a divisional headquarters. Casualties so far had been 275 killed and wounded.

The break-out from Alamein occurred shortly after this event, and the Argylls advanced rapidly with the rest of the Eighth Army towards and past Tobruk. The Argylls' next contact with the enemy was in mid-January near Beurat, and they were then involved in the brigade attack on a feature nicknamed 'Edinburgh Castle' at Corradini. A few days later Tripoli was occupied.

In the meantime the 8th Argylls had reached Algeria in November 1942 with the First Army and moved into Tunisia. Their first engagement was on 19 November when two platoons carried out a surprise night attack. Advancing eastwards, the Argylls met increasing enemy resistance and there was a major battalion battle for Green Hill and Bald Hill when A Company was nearly overwhelmed by a German counter-attack.

During December the 8th Argylls manned several positions, and conducted active patrolling before moving to reinforce 1 Guards Brigade at Medjez-el-Bab. The battalion was constantly in action during a period of particularly bad weather, which lasted through to February 1943. In early March the Argylls were again in action during the battle of Hunts' Gap near Beja, and their task was to capture various objectives on a feature overlooking the gap. The fighting was very fierce but eventually they succeeded.

In April the First Army made progress through the mountains and approached Tunis. On 23 April the 8th Argylls fought a major battle to recapture a feature known as Longstop Hill. They advanced in box formation with Y and R Companies leading and B and X behind, supported by artillery and armour. They passed through a field of corn in full view of the enemy and suffered severe casualties as they climbed the concave slope, but did not lose formation. The Argylls, supported by the North Irish Horse and East Surreys, then fought their way to the summit and destroyed and captured a large number of enemy. The route lay open to Tunis, which was captured ten days later.

The 93rd Regiment, RA (formerly 6th Argylls) had also reached Tunisia with the First Army in December 1942. Equipped with four different types of gun, the batteries and troops were attached to various formations for anti-tank support. In mid-February J Troop stemmed an ememy armoured thrust at Thala, in the desert 300 miles south-west of Tunis. Positions closer to Tunis at Bou Arada and Argoub were defended by troops of Q, S and T Batteries against further armoured attacks. 93rd Regiment continued in action throughout April and until the German surrender in May.

Meanwhile the 7th Argylls had been fighting to the east, also heading for Tunis. In early March 1943 they had reached a position near Medenine, which was rapidly made into a strong blocking position on a route where the Germans were expected to attempt a breakthrough. On 6 March contact was made with enemy infantry, and during the day a large force advanced under a heavy artillery bombardment, and supported by armour. Intense fighting lasted until 9 March and the Argylls and other battalions succeeded in stopping the enemy.

On 20 March the 7th Argylls took part in the assault on the Mareth Line, an attack which lasted until 23 March. After a brief lull, the Germans withdrew and the advance continued. The Argylls' final battle in North Africa was on 5 April at Wadi Akarit, when an assault was launched at dawn and good progress was made through an enemy minefield. Three companies seized their objectives, but suffered high casualties. Three German counter-attacks were mounted and there was heavy fighting as the enemy penetrated close to the Argylls' positions. The operation was, however, very successful and hundreds of enemy were captured, together with a large quantity of equipment. The CO, Lt-Col Lorne Campbell, was awarded the VC for this action – he had already received the DSO at St Valéry and a bar at Alamein.

* * * * *

Preparations for the invasion of Sicily then began in which the 1st, 7th and 8th Argylls took part. The 1st Argylls had been trained in Egypt as 'No 33 Beach Brick', their responsibilities being to hold an area of the beach-head and assist in the re-supply and support of the forward troops. It was a somewhat frustrating, if necessary, task and the Argylls supported the 5th Division on the right of the invasion force during the landing on 10 July 1943. On 28 July the 1st Argylls were ordered to join 154 Brigade in the 51st Highland Division as a fighting battalion. They held positions north of Syracuse for several days before being reformed as the Beach Brick for the invasion of the Italian mainland. This accomplished, they returned to Mena in Egypt in October.

The 7th Argylls also landed on Sicily on 10 July, south of Pachino, and captured 50 Italians in their first engagement. They met no opposition for the next few days as the enemy withdrew northwards, but the fighting intensified as the Argylls reached the Plain of Catania. The battalion was given the task of capturing Gerbini, where the enemy had successfully delayed the 1st and 7th Black Watch. There was much close-quarter fighting throughout the night and the Germans sent in a number of counter-attacks with infantry and tanks. A Company were surrounded during one attack and, as their ammunition was almost expended, had to surrender. Later on 21 July the battalion withdrew its forward positions as it had suffered severe casualties, but the Germans themselves withdrew soon afterwards. Reinforced, the 7th Argylls fought in two further engagements before the enemy finally evacuated the island. The battalion remained in occupation until November, when it returned to the UK.

The 8th Argylls did not reach Sicily until late July, and their first battle was for the town of Centuripe north-west of Catania on 1 August. The capture of the village was an impossible task and was only accomplished the following night in a brigade attack. The 8th Argylls had suffered 10 officers and over 100 soldier casualties in the battle. The Germans evacuated Sicily soon afterwards, and the 8th Argylls prepared for the invasion of Italy.

The 8th Argylls reached Taranto on 25 September under the command of Lt-Col Scott Elliot, and were then moved by ship along the Adriatic coast some 70 miles to Termoli ten days later.

The battalion moved inland from the town but almost immediately met strong resistance from well-hidden German positions in the dark. A fierce battle lasted during the night and into the following day, with armour on both sides fighting furiously. As enemy troops built up Termoli was itself threatened and enemy artillery was brought down on the Argylls' positions, causing numerous casualties. After many hours of fighting, the Germans gave up the attempt to recapture Termoli and withdrew northwards.

The battalion remained on the eastern part of the allied front for the next four months. It took part in the night assault over the River Trigno in late October, and good progress was made northwards towards the River Sangro. On reaching it there was a pause of several days while patrol activities were conducted along the river line. Other forays were mounted, but it took a full-scale divisional attack to seize the river line and its defences. Due to the weather conditions in the depth of winter, the front remained static for several weeks, and in mid-February the 8th Argylls moved across Italy to assist the allied operations against Monte Cassino and the route to Rome.

During the battle for Cassino much of the town was taken, but the enemy still held the monastery with the utmost resolution. On 26 March 1944 the 8th Argylls had been given positions to guard west and north of the town, including Cassino Castle, which were very close to the enemy. The Germans conducted active patrolling and mounted local attacks against these positions over several days, and artillery fire was frequently directed on the Argylls. There they remained for nearly a month. Monte Cassino fell to the Allies in mid-May, and thereafter swift progress was made. The 8th Argylls were in action again on 1 June, mounting a battalion attack on four features surrounding the town of Alatri.

Earlier in December 1943, the 93rd Regiment, RA (formerly 6th Argylls) reached Naples by sea, and for a time was stationed on the east coast of Italy before being moved to the battle zone on the Sangro River. The regiment remained in this sector of the front, working with troops of an Indian Division, until August 1944. The advance to the Gothic Line during the summer of 1944 gave the batteries further periods of activity under various commands. They provided anti-tank support in a fast-moving battle for Ravenna, which gave scope for effective use of the 17-pounder self-propelled gun with which the regiment was equipped. After a period of mainly defensive action during the winter of 1944/5, the 93rd Regiment was withdrawn from the theatre and spent the rest of the war in Egypt, Palestine and Syria.

In February 1944 the 1st Argylls had returned to Italy with the 8th Indian Division and manned part of the then static front facing the Gustav Line near Arielli. The Argylls remained in the same locality for several weeks, carrying out patrols, and training with armoured troops. In May they were moved westwards to the vicinity of Monte Cassino, and there on 11 May took part in a brigade attack on the St Angelo 'horseshoe' ridge to the south of the town. The Argylls faced particular difficulty in crossing the Rapido River in the dark, having lost some of the assault boats, and on landing were in view of enemy positions. Three of the companies were subjected to incessant fire throughout the day and were unable to move. Attempts to get tanks across the river to support the Argylls failed, and for thirty-six hours they remained under enemy fire, making use of the irrigation ditches for cover.

After Cassino the 1st Battalion continued to fight

in operations during the next two months. At the end of July they reached Empoli, carrying out a particularly successful surprise raid on the Germans holding the railway station area. In late August the battalion passed over the Arno and advanced toward the Gothic Line during September. Meanwhile the 8th Argylls had fought a major engagement near Lake Trasimeno in June, and in July they were withdrawn from the line and embarked at Taranto for Egypt. But owing to unexpected German resistance, they returned to Italy in September. During the tortuous advance during October north of Florence, the 8th Argylls were frequently in action, but at the end of the month the line in their sector quietened down.

In early October the 1st Argylls fought for possession of Monte Cavallara. Two of the mountain's peaks were quickly occupied by A and C Companies, but the enemy held 'point 744' and a nearby reserve position. A Company then assaulted point 744 and cleared it after a close-quarter fight, but were immediately fired on from the Germany reserve position. B Company, commanded by Capt D. G. Wood, was sent forward to join A Company for a quick attack and, despite being shelled, charged forward and took the enemy position. Again there was hand-to-hand fighting and two German counter-attacks were launched against the Argylls. During the night one of the platoons withdrew but the other, reduced to Lt L. A. Smith and two other wounded Argylls, occupied the feature until the morning, by which time the Germans had withdrawn from the area.

The 1st Battalion continued to fight in numerous engagements during November and December, and there followed a period of rest and retraining. Their last major battle began on 9 April 1945 during the River Senio offensive. In a well-rehearsed and carefully planned assault, the Eighth Army crossed the river during the dark and seized the northern shore without difficulty. During the next week the battalion advanced north-west towards Ferrara, and by 21 April had reached the outskirts of the town, which the Argylls then occupied.

The 8th Argylls were involved also in operations on the River Senio during March 1945 and, under the temporary command of Major Henry Leask, took part in a major battle to capture bridges over the river. Supported by tanks and artillery the Argylls seized their objectives and swept through a number of enemy posts, enabling other troops to advance rapidly in pursuit of the enemy. Further fighting continued for twelve days and they suffered more than 100 casualties. Hostilities in the Italian theatre ended on 2 May and the 8th Argylls went to Austria as occupation troops until the end of 1946.

* * * * *

During the invasion of Normandy in 1944, the 7th Argylls landed with the 51st Highland Division on 11 June and, three days later, took over the defence of bridges on the River Orne, remaining there for several weeks under long-range artillery fire and sporadic attack. In early July the battalion was involved in supporting the fighting near Colombelles on the outskirts of Caen.

The 2nd Battalion, which had been reconstituted from the 15th Battalion in 1942, reached Normandy in late June with the 15th Scottish Division. Its first operation on 26 June was the capture of bridges at Gavrus on the River Odon, in a brigade attack. The Germans however held the area in great strength, and the Argylls' phase of the attack was delayed owing to other battalions being unable to secure the start-line at Cheux, some four miles north. The following day the Argylls were able to advance and make a bold dash for the bridges in their carriers, making use of the cover of woods and seizing intermediate positions. Adjoining battalions, which had met stiffer resistance, were unable to move up, and the river line was not fully established before the enemy launched their counter-attack on 29 June. For the next two days the enemy continually attacked the area in a determined attempt to dislodge the division, using armour as well as infantry, supported by heavy artillery fire. Later in the month the 2nd Argylls moved to the Caumont area, and on 30 July they took part in the divisional attack with the 3rd Scots Guards equipped with tanks on the high wooded ground three miles to the south of the town. It was a brilliantly executed attack through three enemy battalion positions and a defended minefield, and with minimum casualties.

The Argylls remained in occupation of the Les Loges area for three days. A week later they advanced southwards during the battle for Estry. Passing through the Gordons and HLI, they fought their way towards an important crossroad at La Cavarie, and succeeded in reaching to within a mile of it. Elsewhere the steady build-up of pressure against the Germans enabled the allied armoured divisions eventually to break through the salient.

During these operations the 91st Anti-Tank Regiment RA (the redesignated 5th Argylls) were in support of the 15th Scottish Division. The Regiment continued to fight numerous actions across North-West Europe, until in December 1944 it was absorbed into the 63rd Anti-Tank Regiment, the former Oxfordshire Hussars.

In the meantime the 7th Argylls took part in the break-out from the Caen sector during the night of 7 August, and seized their first objective at Crasmesnil. Successfully holding positions against the enemy's counter-attacks, the Argylls continued to advance on 10 August and attacked the wooded area near St Sylvain during the night. The line then

The re-constituted 2nd Argylls go into action with armoured support between Hills 112 and 113, near the River Odon in Normandy, 15 July 1944. IWM

remained in position until 16 August when the final breakthrough was accomplished. After that time both battalions of the regiment advanced towards the River Seine. The 51st Highland Division then advanced along the coast and liberated amongst other towns, St Valéry-en-Caux, where the original 51st Highland Division had been captured in 1940.

Meanwhile the 2nd Argylls crossed the Seine and Somme and rapidly advanced towards the Escaut Canal, taking up positions on the Gheel bridgehead on 17 September, where they faced a major counter-attack. On 22 September the 2nd Argylls moved forward to the Eindhoven ara, and took part in an operation on the Best-Tilburg road. They assisted in the successful capture of Tilburg a month later, and remained in this area of Holland during October and November.

Another element of the regiment took part in the campaign in the Low Countries. 54 Lt A A Regiment R A (formerly 9th Argylls) had crossed the Channel on 28 August and moved across France to take up anti-aircraft defence of the port of Antwerp, recently captured by the Allies. Later batteries were moved to defend Ostend, Boulogne, and Kloosterzande on the Scheldt Estuary, remaining in Belgium until the end of the war.

The 7th Argylls had also reached the same part of Holland as the 2nd, and in late October were heavily involved in various operations to seize crossings over the numerous canals in the area, and on 1 November occupied s' Hertogenbosch, before advancing to assist in clearing all German troops west of the Maas. At the end of November the 7th Argylls were withdrawn northwards to take up fixed positions in the area of Nijmegen. The 2nd Argylls were further to the south, guarding positions near the River Maas, and remained there until early February 1945.

The 51st Highland Division were called forward to assist the Americans facing the Ardennes offensive in early January 1945. During a period of ten days, the 7th Argylls took part in a number of operations in the snow, first to contain enemy probing attacks, and then to advance to recapture territory lost earlier to the Germans. On the successful outcome of the counter-offensive, the 7th Argylls returned with the division to the Maas sector, ready to take part in the attack across the Dutch-German border.

Both battalions took part in this operation, code-

The 2nd Argylls march forward for the attack on Tilburg, Oct 1944. The canals in this part of Holland were used to great effect to delay the allied advance.
IWM

named 'Veritable', which began on 8 February. The 2nd Argylls advanced with the 15th Scottish Division to the north of the Reichswald Forest, while the 7th Argylls passed through the southern part of the forest with armoured support against light opposition. After Goch had been captured, they assisted in occupying it while under fire from enemy artillery. Meanwhile the 2nd Battalion moved forward of the town and took part in the operations to seize the area of Bucholt. By the end of the month both battalions were preparing for the Rhine crossing.

The 7th Argylls landed on the east bank of the Rhine in the first wave on the night of 23 March and quickly captured their objectives. Progress was rapid but neighbouring battalions met fierce opposition, and the Argylls' next attack on Bienen had to be postponed. When they did attack the village it proved impossible to take, and the battalion suffered high casualties: eventually two battalions of Canadians were needed to eject the Germans and occupy the village. Thereafter the advance speeded up.

The 2nd Argylls met much more opposition on landing in the early hours of 24 March on the east bank of the Rhine. They spent many hours in seizing Hübsch, and were then divided into two parts before advancing eastwards, having to mount several deliberate attacks. They spent until the end of the month in clearing wooded areas and resiting enemy counter-attacks.

During the final advance across Germany the 7th Argylls met little opposition, and passed through Bremen and Bremervorde to the area of the Elbe north of Hamburg, where they had reached when the German surrender was announced. The 2nd Argylls, moving further south, passed quickly through Osnabrück, Hanover and Celle. But progress was slowed down as they reached the Elbe south of Hamburg, where the Germans put up a greater resistance. Uelzen was heavily defended by artillery troops, and it took the Argylls and other battalions four days to eject them. The battalion's final operation was an assault crossing of the Elbe at Artlenburg on the night of 29 April. The crossing itself went well but the Argylls, assembling in a quarry after landing, were caught by German artillery and suffered some 50 casualties. They were also subjected to enemy jet aircraft attacks once they had occupied their objectives. The area remained dangerous for several more days, as enemy ground troops were still active until the final surrender came.

In these two photographs the 1st Argylls mount guard at a road block and check passers-by in Jerusalem, 1947. British soldiers were often targets for both Jewish and Arab terrorists during the dangerous period before the British withdrawal. RHQ

The 2nd Argylls remained in Germany until 1947 and in that year the regiment was reduced to a single battalion: twenty members of the old 2nd Battalion who had survived captivity under the Japanese joined the 1st Battalion. The 1st Argylls moved to Palestine before returning to England, and then embarked for Hong Kong in 1949.

The first Argylls left Hong Kong in August 1950 as part of 27 Brigade for active service with the UN Force in the Korean War. Deployed to the Naktong River Line, they were involved from the start in patrolling against the enemy whose positions were a mile across the river.

After a few weeks the Argylls took part in the UN advance, and on 22 September launched their first battalion attack against a feature called Hill 282. At dawn the following day B Company seized another objective in what the CO called 'a proper Highland charge'. The fighting continued for some time and the Argylls suffered a number of casualties in the enemy's counter-attack and shellfire. Then a tragedy occurred: three USAF Mustangs attacked the Argyll's hill in error with napalm, killing 17 and wounding 76. It was fortunate that the enemy did not take advantage of the situation. The Argylls reinforced the position and under Major Kenneth Muir, the second-in-command, held the hill until ordered to withdraw. Mortally wounded in this action, Major Muir was awarded a posthumous VC.

The battalion then joined the Commonwealth Brigade and came under command of the 1st US Cavalry Divison, and in mid-October the division advanced north of the 38th Parallel. On 17 October the Argylls fought a brisk battle near Sariwan, cleared a road ambush, and fought another fierce engagement in the town itself where all was confusion. The advance continued till the end of October, by which time the UN Force had almost reached the Yalu River.

The Argylls formed part of the Line at Pakchong in early November but later in the month the UN Force was withdrawn some twenty miles, and then south of the 38th Parallel in December – nearly 200 miles in all. The first three months of 1951 were uneventful, but on 4 April the Argylls mounted a successful two-company attack on the Chinese 'volunteers' on a hill outside the border. The Argylls were relieved in the middle of the month and returned to Hong Kong.

The battalion had tours of duty in the United Kingdom and Berlin, and a brief visit to Port Said in 1956 after the Suez invasion. They also served in Cyprus and Borneo, and then in 1967 were sent to Aden during the last year of British presence before

B Coy, tracker team, Singapore 1964. RHQ

independence. There, under the command of Lt-Col Colin Mitchell, they carried out a politically bold and wholly successful operation, the re-entry into Crater, a part of Aden town which had been under the effective control of the terrorists. The Pipe Major Kenneth Robson sounded the regimental charge 'Monymusk' as the battalion marched into the town, and within hours the Argylls had re-established control with maximum efficiency and minimum bloodshed. Maintaining the peace and assisting in the prevention of chaos during the final withdrawal from Aden cost the Argylls 5 dead and 25 wounded.

After returning to the United Kingdom the regiment was warned of its impending disbandment as the junior regiment of the Highland Brigade. There was an immediate public campaign mounted for the reversal of this decision, and eventually the Argyll and Sutherland Highlanders were reduced in 1971 to one regular company, appropriately named 'Balaklava' Company. Due to a change in government, however, the size of the Army was increased and the 1st Battalion was restored in the following year to full strength.

In the 1970s and 80s the battalion has served in the UK, Northern Ireland, BAOR and in a number of overseas stations.

1st Argyll's mortar position at a base camp in Sarawak, 1964, and on patrol. IWM

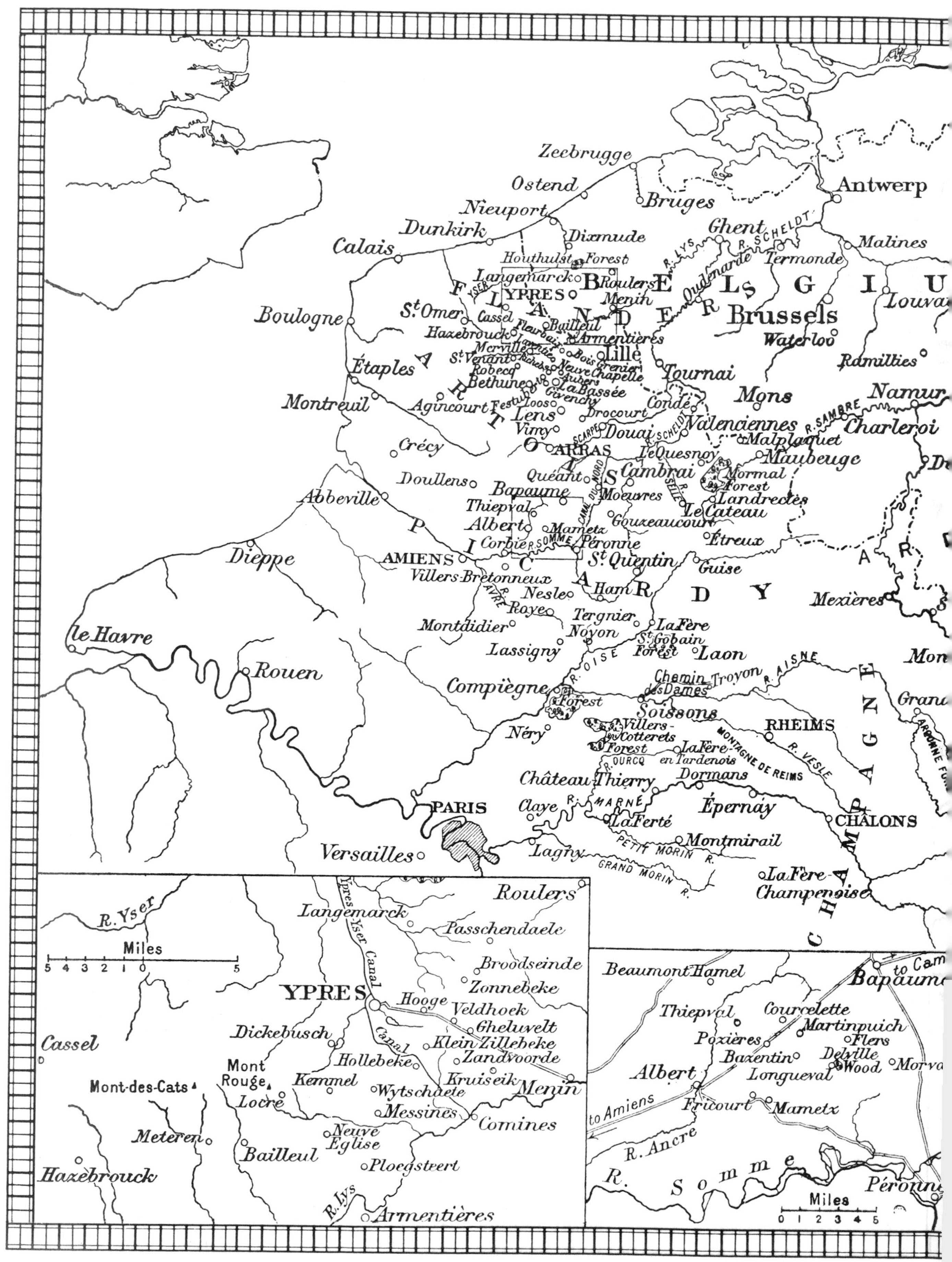

Zeebrugge
Ostend
Antwerp
Bruges
Nieuport
Dunkirk
Dixmude
Ghent
Calais
Malines
Houthulst Forest
Termonde
Langemarck
Roulers
YPRES
Menith
FLANDERS
BELGIUM
Boulogne
St. Omer
Cassel
Brussels
Hazebrouck
Bailleul
Armentières
Waterloo
Lille
Ramillies
Étaples
Tournai
Montreuil
Agincourt
Lens
Mons
Namur
Condé
Vimy
Douai
Valenciennes
R. SAMBRE
Charleroi
Crécy
ARRAS
Malplaquet
Maubeuge
Doullens
Cambrai
Mormal Forest
Abbeville
Bapaume
Landrecies
Thiepval
Le Cateau
Albert
Mametz
Étreux
Dieppe
AMIENS
Péronne
St. Quentin
Guise
Villers-Bretonneux
PICARDY
Nesle
Ham
Mezières
Montdidier
Tergnier
La Fère
le Havre
Noyon
Lassigny
Laon
Rouen
R. OISE
R. AISNE
Chemin des Dames
Troyon
Compiègne
Soissons
RHEIMS
Néry
Villers-Cotterets Forest
La Fère en Tardenois
MONTAGNE DE REIMS
R. VESLE
Château Thierry
Dormans
PARIS
Claye
R. MARNE
Épernay
La Ferté
CHALONS
CHAMPAGNE
Versailles
Lagny
Montmirail
PETIT MORIN R.
GRAND MORIN R.
La Fère-Champenoise
Roulers
R. Yser
Langemarck
Passchendaele
Miles
5 4 3 2 1 0 5
Broodseinde
Zonnebeke
YPRES
Ypres Yser Canal
Hooge
Veldhoek
Gheluvelt
Dickebusch
Klein Zillebeke
Cassel
Hollebeke
Zandvoorde
Mont Rouge
Kemmel
Kruiseik
Menin
Mont-des-Cats
Locre
Wytschaete
Messines
Comines
Meteren
Neuve Eglise
Bailleul
Ploegsteert
Hazebrouck
R. Lys
Armentières
Beaumont Hamel
Bapaume
to Cambrai
Thiepval
Courcelette
Martinpuich
Pozières
Flers
Bazentin
Delville Wood
Albert
Longueval
to Amiens
Fricourt
Mametz
R. Ancre
R. Somme
Péronne
Miles
0 1 2 3 4 5

THE WESTERN FRONT 1914–18

Miles
10 0 10 20 30 40 50

Wesel
R. RHINE
Cologne
Visé
Aix-la-Chapelle
Coblence
Mainz
LUXEMBURG
MOSELLE
Trèves
R. SARRE
ERDUN
Metz
LORRAINE
St Mihiel
Nancy
Grand Couronné
Toul
Strasbourg
R. MEURTHE
R. MEUSE
Mts
VOSGES
Épinal
ALSACE
Mulhausen
Belfort
R. SAÔNE
Basel
SWITZER

A patrol of the Royal Scots charging magazines prior to a raid, 12 July 1918. IWM

APPENDIX

COMMONWEALTH AND OVERSEAS SCOTTISH REGIMENTS

A large number of 'Scottish' regiments have been formed during the past century in the dominions and overseas territories. Most were non-regular. The history of these regiments is highly complicated and a specialist subject in itself. The wartime service of many of them has been well recorded.

The list of regiments below is not exhaustive and additionally a number of companies have existed for a time in South Africa, Canada, Malaya, Singapore, Southern Rhodesia, Calcutta, Bombay, Hong Kong, Rangoon and Shanghai – usually as a constituent company of a regiment of British expatriates. They have not been listed, nor have some other regiments which wore tartan but did not bear a Scottish title.

Affiliations with Scottish regiments in Britain have applied and still apply in many instances. Some of these links are very strong indeed, the overseas regiment being considered part of the home-based regiment.

CANADA

During the First World War Canada provided numerous battalions of the Canadian Expeditionary Force, some of which, in addition to a battalion number, had Scottish titles and wore tartan. Some had indeed been in existence for many years, the earliest being several corps of Glengarry Highlanders, who trace direct descent from the Glengarry Fencibles raised in 1794 in Scotland. Others served only during the war, such as the jocularly-named 236th Battalion, New Brunswick Kilties. The following list shows regiments which existed at various times and with various regimental or battalion numbers. Some remain in being as Militia regiments.

The Lincoln Scots
The Black Watch (Royal Highland Regiment) of Canada – variously named, including 5th Regiment, Royal Scots Fusiliers and Royal Scots of Canada
The Perth Regiment
The Highland Light Infantry of Canada
The Lorne Scots (Peel, Dufferin and Halton Regt)
The Stormont, Dundas and Glengarry Highlanders
The New Brunswick Scottish
The Pictou Highlanders
The North Nova Scotia Highlanders
The Cape Breton Highlanders
The Cameron Highlanders of Ottowa
The Essex Scottish
The 48th Highlanders of Canada
The Argyll and Sutherland Highlanders of Canada (Princess Louise's)
The Lake Superior Scottish
The Queen's Own Cameron Highlanders of Canada
The Calgary Highlanders
The Seaforth Highlanders of Canada
The Canadian Scottish Regiment (Princess Mary's) – unofficially Gordon Highlanders of Canada
The Toronto Scottish Regiment
Canadian Scottish Borderers
The Argyll Light Infantry
The Lanark and Renfrew Scottish
The Newfoundland Highlanders
The Prince Edward Island Highlanders
Edmonton Highlanders
Western Scots
Lethbridge Highlanders
Overseas Highland Battalion
Queen's University Highlanders
Cumberland Highlanders
13th Scottish Light Dragoons

AUSTRALIA

5th Battalion (Victorian Scottish Regiment)
16th Battalion (The Cameron Highlanders of Western Australia)
27th Battalion (South Australian Scottish Regt)
30th Battalion (The New South Wales Scottish Regiment)
41st Battalion (Byron Regiment)
61st Battalion (Queensland Cameron Highlanders)

NEW ZEALAND

The New Zealand Scottish Regiment

SOUTH AFRICA

The First City
The Duke of Connaught and Strathearn's Own Cape Town Highlanders
The South African Scottish – formed from South African Scottish Regiments for active service in the First World War
The Transvaal Scottish
The Pretoria Highlanders
The Kimberley Scottish
Witwatersrand Rifles – affiliated to The Cameronians (Scottish Rifles)

BIBLIOGRAPHY

GENERAL

Adams, Frank: *The Clans, Septs and Regiments of the Scottish Highlands*, Eighth edition, revised by Sir Thomas Innes of Learney (Johnson & Bacon, Edinburgh 1970)

Ascoli, D. N: *A Companion to the British Army 1660–1983* (Harraps, London 1983)

Blake, George: *Mountain and Flood. The History of the 52nd Lowland Division 1939–1946* (Jackson & Son, Glasgow 1950)

Bewsher, Maj F. W: *The History of the 51st (Highland) Division 1914–1918* (William Blackwood, Edinburgh 1921)

Brander, Michael: *The Highlanders and their Regiments* (Seeley Service & Co Ltd, London 1971)

Ewing, J: *History of the 9th (Scottish) Division 1914–1919* (John Murray, London 1921)

Frederick, J. B. M: *Lineage Book of the British Army, Mounted Corps and Infantry* (Hope Farm Press, New York 1969)

Laffin, John: *Scotland the Brave. The Story of the Scottish Soldier* (Cassell, London 1963)

Mackay-Scobie, Maj I. H: *The Scottish Regiments of the British Army* (Oliver and Boyd, Edinburgh 1943)

Martin, Lt-Gen H. G: *The Fifteenth Scottish Division 1939–1945* (William Blackwood, Edinburgh 1948)

Maxwell, Sir Herbert, Bart: *The Lowland Scots Regiments* (James MacLehose & Sons, Glasgow 1918)

Money Barnes, Maj R: *The Uniforms and History of the Scottish Regiments: Britain, Canada, Australia, New Zealand, South Africa, 1625 to the Present Day* (Seeley Service, London 1956)

Murray, A. K: *History of the Scottish Regiments of the British Army* (Thomas Murray & Sons, Glasgow 1862)

Salmond, J. B: *The History of the 51st Highland Division 1939–1945* (William Blackwood, Edinburgh 1923)

Stewart, Col David of Garth: *Sketches of the Character, Manners and Present state of the Highlanders of Scotland, with details of the Military service of the Highland Regiments* (Constable & Co, Edinburgh 1822)

Stewart, Lt-Col J. and Buchan, John: *The Fifteenth (Scottish) Division 1914–1919* (William Blackwood, Edinburgh 1926)

Thompson, R. R: *The Fifty-Second (Lowland) Division 1914–1918* (MacLehose Jackson, Glasgow 1923)

Westlake, Ray: *The Territorial Battalions. A Pictorial History 1859–1986* (Spellmount, Tunbridge Wells 1986)

Wood, Stephen: *The Scottish Soldiers* (Archive Publications, Manchester 1987)

CHAPTER 2

Almack, Edward: *The History of the Second Dragoons (Royal Scots Greys)* (Alexander Moring, London 1908)

Blacklock, Michael: *The Royal Scots Greys* (Leo Cooper, London 1969)

Carver, Lt-Col R. M. P: *Second to None: The Royal Scots Greys 1919–1945* (The Regiment, London 1928)

CHAPTER 3

Erskine, David: *The Scots Guards 1919–1945 (Wm Clowes & Sons, London 1956)*

Goodinge, Anthony: *The Scots Guards* (Leo Cooper, London 1969)

Loraine Petre, F. and others: *The Scots Guards in the Great War 1914–1918* (John Murray, London 1925)

Maurice, Maj-Gen Sir F: *The History of the Scots Guards from the Creation of the Regiment to the Eve of the Great War* (Chatto & Windus, London 1934)

CHAPTER 4

Brander, A. M: *The Royal Scots* (Leo Cooper, London 1976)

Ewing, Maj John: *The Royal Scots 1914–1919* 2 vols (Oliver & Boyd, Edinburgh 1925)

Muir, A: *The First of Foot* (The Regiment, Edinburgh 1961)

Weaver, Lawrence: *The Story of the Royal Scots (The Lothian Regiment)* (Country Life, London 1915)

CHAPTER 5

Buchan, John: *The History of the Royal Scots Fusiliers 1678–1918* (Thomas Nelson, London 1925)

Groves, Lt-Col Percy: *A History of the 21st Royal Scots Fusiliers 1678–1895* (W. & A. K. Johnston, Edinburgh 1895)

Hildyard, Lt Henry J. T: *Historical Record of the 71st Regiment, Highland Light Infantry, 1777–1876* (Harrison & Son, London 1876)

Historical Record of the 74th Highlanders (James MacVeigh, London 1887)

Kemp, Col J. C: *The History of the Royal Scots Fusiliers 1915–1959* (The Regiment, Glasgow 1963)

Oatts, Lt-Col L. B: *Proud Heritage. The Story of the Highland Light Infantry* Vols 1 & 2 (Thomas Nelson, London 1952–59) Vols 3 & 4 (House of Grant, Glasgow 1961–63)

Oatts, L. B: *The Highland Light Infantry* (Leo Cooper, London 1969)

CHAPTER 6

Gillon, Capt Stair: *The KOSB in the Great War* (Thomas Nelson, London 1930)

Gunning, Capt Hugh: *Borderers in Battle* (The Regiment, Berwick-upon-Tweed 1948)

Higgins, Capt R. T. (Ed): *The Records of the King's Own Scottish Borderers* (Chapman Hall, London 1873)

Woollcombe, R: *All the Blue Bonnets* (Arms & Armour Press, London 1980)

CHAPTER 7

Barclay, Brig C. N: *The History of the Cameronians (Scottish Rifles), Vol III 1933–1946* (Sifton Praed, London 1949)

Baynes, J: *The History of the Cameronians, (Scottish Rifles) Vol IV, 1948–1968* (Cassell, London 1971)

Carter, Thomas (Ed): *Historical Records of the Twenty-Sixth or Cameronian Regiment* (Byfield Stanford & Co, London 1867)

Delavoye, A. M: *Records of the 90th Regiment (Perthshire Light Infantry) 1795–1880* (Richardson & Co, London 1880)

Johnson, S. F. H: *The History of the Cameronians (Scottish Rifles), Vol I 1689–1910* (Gale & Polden, Aldershot 1957)

Story, Col H. H: *The History of the Cameronians (Scottish Rifles) Vol II 1910–1933* (The Regiment, Hamilton 1961)

CHAPTER 8

Fergusson, Bernard: *The Black Watch and the King's Enemies* (Collins, London 1950)

Forbes, Archibald: *The Black Watch: The Record of an Historic Regiment* (Cassell, London 1896)

Howard, Philip: *The Black Watch* (Hamish Hamilton, London 1968)
Linklater, Eric and Andro: *The Black Watch* (Barrie & Jenkins, London 1977)
Wauchope, A. G: *A Short History of The Black Watch (Royal Highlanders) 1725–1907* (William Blackwood & Sons, Edinburgh 1908)
Wauchope, A. G. (Ed): *A History of The Black Watch (Royal Highlanders) in the Great War 1914–1918*, 2 Vols (Medici Society, London 1925-26)

CHAPTER 9

Borthwick, Alastair, *Sans Peur, History of the 5th Seaforth Highlanders in World War II*, (Eneas MacKay, Stirling 1946)
Davidson, Maj H. and Mackenzie, Maj Colin: *History and Services of the 78th Highlanders (Ross-shire Buffs)*, 2 Vols (W. & A. K. Johnston, Edinburgh 1901)
Fairrie, Lt-Col A. A: *Cuidich'n Righ: A History of the Queen's Own Highlanders* (The Regiment, Inverness 1983)
Historical Records of the 72nd Highlanders, 1777–1866 (William Blackwood & Sons, Edinburgh 1886)
Historical Records of the Queen's Own Cameron Highlanders, Vols I to VII (Blackwood & Sons, Edinburgh 1909–1961)
Jameson, Capt Robert: *Historical Records of the Seventy-Ninth Regiment of Foot, or Cameron Highlanders* (William Blackwood & Sons, Edinburgh 1863)
Mackenzie, Capt T. A. and others: *Historical Records of the 79th Queen's Own Cameron Highlanders* (Hamilton Adams, London 1887)
Macveigh, James: *The Historical Records of the 78th Highlanders or Ross-shire Buffs, 1793–1887)* (Maxwell & Son, Dumfries 1887)
Sym, Col John (Ed): *Seaforth Highlanders* (Gale & Polden, Aldershot 1962)

CHAPTER 10

Greenhill-Gardyne, Lt-Col C. G: *The Life of a Regiment: The History of the Gordon Highlanders, Vol 1 1794–1816, Vol 2 1816–1898* (David Douglas, Edinburgh 1901–1903)
Greenhill-Gardyne, Lt-Col A. D: *The Life of a Regiment: The History of the Gordon Highlanders, Vol 3 1898–1914* (The Medici Society, London 1939)
Falls, Cyril: *The Life of a Regiment: The Gordon Highlanders in the First World War, 1914–1919, Vol 4* (University Press, Aberdeen 1958)
Miles, Wilfrid: *The Life of a Regiment: The Gordon Highlanders, Vol 5 1919–1945* (University Press, Aberdeen 1961)
Sinclair-Stevenson, Christopher: *The Life of a Regiment: The History of the Gordon Highlanders, Vol 6 1945–1974* (Leo Cooper, London 1968)
Thompson, Revd P. D: *The Gordon Highlanders* (W. & W. Lindsay, Aberdeen 1933)

CHAPTER 11

Anderson, Brig R. C. B: *History of the Argyll and Sutherland Highlanders, 1st Battalion, 1909–1939* (Constable, Edinburgh 1954)
Anderson, Brig. R. C. B: *History of the Argyll and Sutherland Highlanders, 1st Battalion, 1939–1954* (Constable, Edinburgh 1956)
Barker, Lt-Col F. R. P: *History of the Argyll and Sutherland Highlanders, 9th Battalion, 54 Light AA Regiment 1939–45* (Thomas Nelson, London 1950)
Burgoyne, R. H: *Historical Records of the 93rd Sutherland Highlanders* (Richard Bentley, London 1883)
Cameron, Capt I. C: *History of the Argyll and Sutherland Highlanders, 7th Battalion, From El Alamein to Germany* (Thomas Nelson, London 1946)
Cavendish, Brig A. E. J: *An Reisimeid Chataich. The 93rd Sutherland Highlanders 1799–1927* (Published privately, 1928)
Dunn-Pattison, R. A: *The History of the 91st Argyllshire Highlanders* (William Blackwood & Sons, Edinburgh 1910)
Flower, Maj Desmond: *History of the Argyll and Sutherland Highlanders, 5th Battalion, 91st Anti-Tank Regiment, 1939–45* (Thomas Nelson, London 1950)
Graham, Lt-Col, F. C. C: *History of the Argyll and Sutherland Highlanders, 1st Battalion 1939–45* (Thomas Nelson, London 1949)
Goff, G. L: *Historical Records of the 91st Argyllshire Highlanders* (Richard Bentley, London 1891)
Groves, Lt-Col Percy: *History of the 91st Princess Louise's Argyllshire Highlanders* (W. & E. K. Johnston, Edinburgh 1894)
Groves, Lt-Col Percy: *History of the 93rd Sutherland Highlanders* (W. & E. K. Johnston, Edinburgh 1895)
Malcolm, Lt-Col G. I. of Poltalloch: *The Argyllshire Highlanders 1860–1960* (Halberd Press, Glasgow 1960)
Malcolm, Lt-Col G. I. of Poltalloch: *The Argyll's in Korea* Thomas Nelson, London 1952)
Malcolm, Lt-Col A. D: *History of the Argyll and Sutherland Highlanders 1939–1947, 8th Battalion* (Thomas Nelson, London 1949)
McElwee, Maj W. L: *History of the Argyll and Sutherland Highlanders, 2nd Battalion (Re-constituted) 1944–45* (Thomas Nelson, London 1949)
Morrison, A. D: *7th Battalion The Argyll and Sutherland Highlanders, The Great War 1914–1919* (The Regiment, Stirling)
Pratt, Paul (Ed): *History of the Argyll and Sutherland Highlanders, 6th Battalion, 93rd Anti-Tank Regiment RA, (A&SH)* (Thomas Nelson, London 1949)
Sotheby, Lt-Col H. G: *The 10th Battalion, Argyll and Sutherland Highlanders, 1914–1919* (John Murray, London 1931)
Stewart, Brig I. Mac A: *History of the Argyll and Sutherland Highlanders, 2nd Battalion (The Thin Red Line). Malayan Campaign 1941–42* (Thomas Nelson, London 1947)
Sutherland, Douglas: *The Argyll and Sutherland Highlanders* (Leo Cooper, London 1969)

D Coy, 1st Gordons provide a 'tactical guard' for the Governor of Cyprus, Gen Sir John Harding, Mar 1956, during the Eoka campaign. Cpl Richardson leads with Sgt Tollan and 2nd Lt A. J. Henderson on the right.
A. J. Henderson Esq

INDEX

The bold figures refer to the colour pages